Fodor's 2013

NEW ORLEANS

Fodor's Travel Publications   New York, Toronto, London, Sydney, Auckland
www.fodors.com

FODOR'S NEW ORLEANS 2013

Writers: Beth D'Addono, Susan Langenhennig, Ian McNulty, Robert D. Peyton, Todd A. Price, Troy Thibodeaux

Editor: Caroline Trefler

Production Editor: Carolyn Roth
Maps & Illustrations: David Lindroth and Mark Stroud, *cartographers;* Rebecca Baer, *map editor;* William Wu, *information graphics*
Design: Fabrizio La Rocca, *creative director;* Tina Malaney, Chie Ushio, Jessica Ramirez, *designers;* Melanie Marin, *associate director of photography;* Jennifer Romains, *photo research*
Cover Photo: (Street musician, French Quarter): dbimages/Alamy
Production Manager: Angela L. McLean

ISBN 978–0–307–92933–4

ISSN 0743–9385

SPECIAL SALES

This book is available at special discounts for bulk purchases for sales promotions or premiums. Special editions, including personalized covers, excerpts of existing books, and corporate imprints, can be created in large quantities for special needs. For more information, write to Special Markets/Premium Sales, 1745 Broadway, MD 3-1, New York, NY 10019, or e-mail specialmarkets@randomhouse.com.

AN IMPORTANT TIP & AN INVITATION

Although all prices, opening times, and other details in this book are based on information supplied to us at press time, changes occur all the time in the travel world, and Fodor's cannot accept responsibility for facts that become outdated or for inadvertent errors or omissions. So **always confirm information when it matters,** especially if you're making a detour to visit a specific place. Your experiences—positive and negative—matter to us. If we have missed or misstated something, **please write to us.** Share your opinion instantly through our online feedback center at fodors.com/contact-us.

PRINTED IN COLOMBIA

10 9 8 7 6 5 4 3 2 1

CONTENTS

ABOUT
THIS GUIDE

Fodor's Ratings

Everything in this guide is worth doing—we don't cover what isn't—but exceptional sights, hotels, and restaurants are recognized with additional accolades. Fodor's Choice ★ indicates our top recommendations; ★ highlights places we deem highly recommended; and **Best Bets** call attention to notable hotels and restaurants in various categories. Care to nominate a new place? Visit Fodors.com/contact-us.

Trip Costs

We list prices wherever possible to help you budget well. Hotel and restaurant price categories from $ to $$$$ are noted alongside each recommendation. For hotels, we include the lowest cost of a standard double room in high season. For restaurants, we cite the average price of a main course at dinner or, if dinner isn't served, at lunch. For attractions, we always list adult admission fees; discounts are usually available for children, students, and senior citizens.

Hotels

Our local writers vet every hotel to recommend the best overnights in each price category, from budget to expensive. Unless otherwise specified, you can expect private bath, phone, and TV in your room. For expanded hotel reviews, facilities, and deals visit Fodors.com.

TripAdvisor ◎◎

Our expert hotel picks are reinforced by high ratings on TripAdvisor. Look for representative quotes in this guide, and the latest TripAdvisor ratings and feedback at Fodors.com.

Restaurants

Unless we state otherwise, restaurants are open for lunch and dinner daily. We mention dress code only when there's a specific

Ratings		Hotels &
★	Fodor's Choice	**Restaurants**
★	Highly recommended	Hotel
☾	Family-friendly	Number of rooms
Listings		Meal plans
✉	Address	✗ Restaurant
✉	Branch address	Reservations
☎	Telephone	Dress code
🖷	Fax	No credit cards
⊕	Website	$ Price
✎	E-mail	**Other**
🖾	Admission fee	⇨ See also
☉	Open/closed times	☞ Take note
Ⓜ	Subway	Golf facilities
⊹	Directions or Map coordinates	

requirement and reservations only when they're essential or not accepted. To make restaurant reservations, visit Fodors.com.

Credit Cards

The hotels and restaurants in this guide typically accept credit cards. If not, we'll say so.

Experience
New Orleans

NEW ORLEANS TODAY

New Orleans is the ultimate urban illustration of the Japanese concept *wabi-sabi*, which translates literally to "perfect-imperfect," but which suggests that, like a sidewalk buckled with cracks where an oak tree root grew up beneath the concrete, or an old plaster wall with bricks showing through, sometimes things are even more special when they are just a little bit broken. New Orleans is perfect in its sheer persistence; this comeback city's age, incredible heritage and history, and unwavering determination to live on and let the good times roll are what makes it so endearing, and so easy to return to again and again.

Today's New Orleans

...is like no other place in America. It sounds like a tourist brochure cliché, but it's true: New Orleans feels like a place out of step with the rest of the country. Some of that is due to geography: this port city has seen an influx of many, many cultures over the course of its history. It welcomes diversity and tolerates lifestyles that deviate from the norm—a big reason artists and other creative types have long put down roots here. And the fact that the city lies mostly below sea level lends it a certain degree of fatalism and probably, if unconsciously, informs the New Orleans live-for-today attitude.

...is proud of its traditions. Red beans and rice on Monday, St. Joseph's altars, jazz funerals, a Christmas visit to Mr. Bingle in City Park—this is a destination steeped in tradition, one that guards its unique customs. Take Mardi Gras, for example: some of the parading organizations, known as krewes, have been around for more than 150 years, building elaborate floats annually and parading through the streets in masks. The Mardi Gras Indian tradition, likewise, is shrouded in secrecy and ritual: "tribes" of mostly African American revelers spend months constructing fanciful, Native American–influenced costumes in tribute to actual tribes that once helped escaped slaves find freedom.

...is one giant movie set. Or that's how it seems these days, with multiple film projects going on at any given moment. The scenic backdrop is one reason for all the activity; generous tax credits and a growing local film industry are the other drivers behind what civic boosters have dubbed "Hollywood South." In 2011 and 2012 the police drama *21 Jump Street*, a new season of HBO's *Treme*, and *Hours*,

WHAT WE'RE TALKING ABOUT

It's easier than ever to get a room in New Orleans, thanks to a spate of new hotel openings in the French Quarter and beyond, including the Hotel Modern on Lee Circle, and the Saint on Canal Street. In addition, the vast New Orleans Hyatt Regency has reopened, after a

$275 million renovation, right across from the newly renamed Mercedes-Benz Superdome.

It may not be named Desire, but the newest part of the famed New Orleans streetcar line is now in operation. The $45 million project connects

Amtrak's Union Station with Canal Street and the Canal Street streetcar route, giving train passengers access to the French Quarter and CBD and passing right in front of the Mercedes Benz Superdome and the New Orleans Arena. Streetcars once crisscrossed the Big

a Hurricane Katrina suspense drama starring Paul Walker were among the many films and TV shows in production.

...is still recovering. Seven years after Katrina hit the city, the areas where tourists tend to wander—downtown, the riverfront, the French Quarter, Faubourg Marigny, the Warehouse District, and the Garden District/Uptown—all show little outward sign of the storm's devastating floods. But predominantly residential areas like East New Orleans, Lakeview, and the Ninth Ward are still struggling to recover. 2010 Census figures (the latest available) indicated that the city's population was still only 70% of what it had been before the storm.

...is shaping up? Mayor Mitch Landrieu, son of legendary former mayor Moon Landrieu, is working hard to get city government back on track after his 2010 election. The success of grassroots recovery programs is a bright contrast to any lingering skepticism locals feel about projects with government involvement from earlier administrations and elected officials. Locally led projects continue to gain ground, including the Ninth Ward's George Washington Carver High School sports program, Brad Pitt's Make

it Right housing-renewal program, the New Orleans Hope and Heritage Project (which aims to preserve the past and safeguard the future), and Tipitina's Foundation for musicians.

...is on the verge of ____. Fill in the blank; your guess is as good as anybody's. New Orleans has survived an insane amount of fires, floods, epidemics, and scandals since its founding in 1718, and there are many encouraging signs—new buildings, streetcar lines, restorations, festivals—that even Hurricane Katrina couldn't keep this amazing city down. But, questions remain: will the repaired levees hold up against the mighty Mississippi or another (God forbid) big storm? Will New Orleans manage to move past its propensity to political scandals, crime, and all the ills of urban poverty? Despite the many fortune-tellers plying their trade on Jackson Square, no one knows for sure what the future holds for the Crescent City.

Easy, but there numbers have dwindled to three operating lines: the St. Charles Avenue Line, the Riverfront Line, and the Canal Street Line, of which this is an extension. There is a plan to expand the track eastward into the Tremé, Marigny, and the Bywater neighborhoods, subject to funding.

Forget hair of the dog, Nola is increasingly the spot for Downward Facing Dog as the city's yoga scene continues to grow. Named one of the "10 Fantastically Yoga-Friendly Towns" by Yoga Journal, New Orleans yoga studios have grown from a paltry six pre-Katrina to currently more than 25, in neighborhoods from the Lower

Garden District to Uptown and the CBD. Visitors can even find their chi within view of the St. Louis Cathedral at Yoga at the Cabildo on Jackson Square, Tuesday and Thursday mornings at 7:30 and Saturdays at 8:30. At just $12 for an hour's practice, you'll still be able to afford a Bloody Mary when you're done. Gotta love New Orleans.

WHAT'S WHERE

Numbers refer to chapters.

2 The French Quarter. The geographic and cultural heart of the city since the early 1700s, the Quarter is a vibrant commercial and residential hodgepodge of wrought-iron balconies, beckoning court-yards, antiques shops—and, of course, tawdry Bourbon Street honky-tonk. Elsewhere in the Quarter, you'll find fine dining and fabulous local music.

3 Faubourg Marigny, Bywa-ter, and Tremé. The Faubourg Marigny is home to lovingly restored Creole cottages and famous Frenchman Street, which is lined with an assort-ment of music clubs, restau-rants, and funky bars. Grittier Bywater, despite gentrification, retains its working-class cre-dentials while accommodating a burgeoning arts scene and an influx of hipster profession-als. Tremé, the cradle of jazz and second-line parades, fell into decline when much of it was razed to make room for a freeway and other public "improvements," but the HBO series has helped put it back on the map.

4 CBD and Warehouse Dis-trict. The city's trendy urban area is undergoing a serious building boom; it's also where most of the newer hotels are clustered, near Canal Street or the sprawling Morial

Convention Center. There also are museums, fine restaurants, and a bustling casino; Julia Street hosts the city's most adventurous art galleries.

5 The Garden District. Stunning early-19th-century mansions make this a great neighborhood for walking, fol-lowed by an afternoon brows-ing the shops and cafés along ever-evolving Magazine Street. Take the streetcar for a gan-der at the massive and stately St. Charles Avenue homes.

6 Uptown and Carrollton-Riverbend. Audubon Park and the campuses of Tulane and Loyola universities anchor oak-shaded Uptown; hop on the St. Charles streetcar to survey it in period style. You'll find boutiques, eateries, and pubs at the uptown end of Magazine Street, on Maple Street between Broadway and Carrollton, and in the Riverbend.

7 Mid-City and Bayou St. John. Expansive City Park is Mid-City's playground and encompasses the New Orleans Museum of Art and the adjacent (and free) Besthoff Sculpture Garden. A stroll or a kayak along Bayou St. John and a visit to Pitot House on its banks round out a day in this residential neighborhood.

Lake Pontchartrain

W Esplanade Ave.

Metairie

Veterans Memorial Blvd

10

Metairie Rd

Airline Dr

61

Earhart Expy

Jefferson

Earhart Blvd

Fontainebleau Dr

S Claiborne Ave.

Dakin St.

Saint Charles Ave

S Carrollton Ave.

Bridge City

Tulane University

Carrollton

Loyola University

Saint Charles Ave.

Calhoun St

Riverside

Audubon Park

Exposition Blvd

Uptown

6

Audubon Zoo

Westwego

NEW ORLEANS PLANNER

Getting There

By air: Most major and a few regional airlines serve **Louis Armstrong International Airport** (📞 504/464–0831), 15 miles east of downtown New Orleans. A taxi from the airport to the French Quarter costs a flat rate of $33 for two people; for more than two passengers the fixed rate is $14 per person. Shared-ride shuttles to hotels are available for about $20 per person. If you're traveling light and have a lot of extra time, you can take Jefferson Transit's airport bus, which runs between the main terminal entrance and the Central Business District (CBD). Fare is $2.

By car: Interstate 10 is the major thoroughfare into and out of New Orleans and can be used to reach downtown from the airport. Lanes can get backed up during morning and evening rush hours; plan accordingly.

By train: Three Amtrak lines serve New Orleans: the *City of New Orleans* from Chicago; the *Sunset Limited* service between New Orleans and Los Angeles; and the *Crescent*, which connects New Orleans and New York by way of Atlanta. For tickets and schedules, call 📞 800/872–7245 or visit ⊕ www.amtrak.com.

Getting Around

On public transportation: Streetcars are a great way to see the city. The St. Charles line runs from Canal Street to the intersection of Claiborne and Carrollton avenues; along the way it passes the Garden District, Audubon Park, and Tulane and Loyola universities. The Riverfront line skirts the French Quarter along the Mississippi, from Esplanade Avenue to the Ernest N. Morial Convention Center. Some Canal line streetcars make a straight shot from the Quarter to the cemeteries at City Park Avenue; others take a spur at Carrollton Avenue that goes to City Park and the New Orleans Museum of Art.

At present, **bus** travel in New Orleans isn't extremely efficient (although the Regional Transit Authority has pledged to update its aging fleet), but a few lines are of use. The Magazine bus runs the length of shopping mecca Magazine Street, from Canal and Camp streets to the Audubon Zoo entrance at the far edge of Audubon Park. The Esplanade bus serves City Park, and drops Jazz Fest passengers off a few blocks from the Fair Grounds.

Fares for streetcars and buses are $1.25 ($1.50 for express lines); unlimited-ride passes are available for one day ($3; available on bus and streetcar); unlimited 3-day and 31-day passes ($9 and $55) are available at some hotels and grocery stores, and at Walgreens. For route maps, timetables, and more information, visit ⊕ www.norta.com.

By car: If you don't plan to drive outside the city limits, you probably won't need a car—you'll save money traveling by streetcar, cab, and on foot. If you do decide to drive, keep in mind that some streets are in ragged condition, traffic lights routinely malfunction, and parking in the Quarter is tight (and parking regulations vigorously enforced).

By taxi: Taxis are often the most convenient way to move around, and drivers are used to short trips, so don't hesitate to grab a cab if you're leery about walking back to your hotel at night. Most locals will recommend United Cabs, Yellow Checker, and Veterans. Don't get into an unlicensed, unmarked "gypsy" cab. Rates are $2 per mile or 20¢ for every 40 seconds of waiting, plus a base of $3.50; each additional passenger is $1.

Safety

Much of the post-Katrina media coverage has focused on New Orleans's escalating crime rate. Sadly, this isn't just sensationalism—gangs operate in the city's underpopulated neighborhoods, there's a growing homelessness problem, the murder rate is among the highest in the nation, and armed robberies occur all too frequently. These grim statistics should not dissuade you from visiting, but you need to exercise caution if you venture outside the well-touristed areas—especially at night.

The French Quarter is generally safe, but pay attention to your surroundings and your possessions (especially expensive cameras and dangling shoulder bags). Use special caution in the areas near Rampart Street and below St. Philip Street at night, and be alert on all quiet Quarter side streets.

The CBD and Warehouse District are safe, but take a cab at night if there aren't many other pedestrians around.

Be alert and exercise caution walking around in the Bywater or the lower part of Faubourg Marigny at night, and take a cab when traveling between spread-out destinations. Avoid Garden District side streets after dark.

All that said, the New Orleans Police Department does take pains to keep violent crime out of the tourist zones, with many uniformed and plainclothes police stationed throughout the Quarter and at special events.

Helpful Websites

⊕ *www.fodors.com:* Log on to the Travel Talk Forums to get advice from New Orleanians and travelers who have recently visited the Crescent City.

⊕ *www.neworleanscvb.com:* Head here for up-to-date information from the New Orleans Convention and Visitors Bureau.

⊕ *www.nola.com:* Find out what's happening from the city's newspaper, the *New Orleans Times-Picayune.*

⊕ *www.neworleans.com:* This site has often-updated special events and entertainment info.

⊕ *www.offbeat.com:* The website for the monthly magazine *Offbeat* has extensive club and live-music listings, along with features covering the local music scene.

When to Go

May through September are hot and humid—double-100 days (100°F and nearly 100% humidity) aren't uncommon. Just mustering the energy to raise a mint julep to your lips can cause exhaustion. These long, hot summers may explain why things are less hurried down here. But if you visit during sticky July and August, you'll find lower hotel prices and plenty of tables at the top restaurants.

June through November bring heavy rains and occasional hurricanes. Although winters are mild compared with those in northern climes, the high humidity can put a chill in the air December through February. Nevertheless, the holiday season is a great time to visit, with few conventions in town, a beautifully bedecked French Quarter, and "Papa Noel" discounted rates at many hotels.

Perhaps the best time to visit the city is early spring. Days are pleasant, except for seasonal cloudbursts, and nights are cool. The azaleas are in full bloom, the apricot scent of sweet olive trees wafts through the evening air, and the city bustles from one outdoor festival to the next.

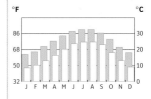

NEW ORLEANS
TOP EXPERIENCES

Food

The city of New Orleans has long been a cultural melting pot, and that goes for her cooking pots as well. There's a stunning variety of homegrown cuisines and styles here—everything from traditional Creole to fresh-caught seafood, from slow-cooked soul food to upscale urban fusions, from gorgeous French-style five-course meals to corner-store po' boys. For the upscale connoisseurs, this is a city where chefs come to make a name for themselves. Internationally recognized stars like John Besh, Paul Prudhomme, and Emeril Lagasse are joined by inventive culinary masterminds such as Susan Spicer (Bayona), Donald Link (Herbsaint) and Scott Boswell (Stella!). This is also a place that places a high premium on simple pleasures, and it's the unsung cooks and chefs of the corner shops, pubs, late-night grills, and even taco stands that deliver some of the best eats.

Cocktails

New Orleans is home to several of the world's oldest and most popular cocktails, dating back to the turn of the 19th century, so it's no surprise that an old guard of traditional New Orleans bartenders have kept the sacred flame alight, honing their skills on homegrown classics like the Sazerac, the Ramos gin fizz, or the ever-popular Hurricane. A new generation of innovative mixologists is, however, combining their prowess with some of the most venerable cocktail traditions and settings, bringing new recipes, fresh ingredients, hand-squeezed juices, and homemade syrups, mixers, and reductions. Hot spots like Cure, Bar Tonique, and Twelve Mile Limit lead the cocktail renaissance. The popular Tales of the Cocktail festival in July celebrates all things shaken and stirred.

Music

Music is so organic to New Orleans that it's almost like humidity—hanging in the air, drifting down the street, working its way in between the clapboards on the sides of houses and clubs. When you follow those strains a little more closely though, you'll realize that every style of music, every band, and every musician has a unique energy that pours into the city, from the stride piano blues of Jon Cleary to the high-energy brass jams of the world-renowned Rebirth Brass Band. Old-school kings of rhythm and blues like Walter Wolfman Washington or Little Freddie King still keep people half their age (and less) dancing into the wee hours of the night. Meanwhile, young hipsters in the New Orleans Cottonmouth Kings play swing jazz standards that are old enough to be their grandparents' age (and then some).

Festivals

To many people, a festival is an event that arrives once a year, spans a few days, and then fades to nice memories. In New Orleans, however, the term "festival" has transcended any single event and has become a lifestyle, a state of mind, and possibly even an obsession. Regardless of the time of year you might be visiting, there's likely something happening—from the large-scale, musical mega-events like Jazz Fest (jazz and heritage), Essence Fest (hip-hop and R&B), and the Voodoo Experience (rock and electronic) to the funky neighborhood celebrations like Boogaloo on the Bayou or Festivus. Legendary figures like Louis Armstrong and Tennessee Williams have events thrown in their honor. So pack your sunscreen and a hat, slip into some dancing shoes, and get ready to plunge into the festival state of mind.

NEW ORLEANS TOP ATTRACTIONS

Bourbon Street

(A) Crude and crass, New Orleans's most famous entertainment strip isn't to everyone's taste, but you have to see it at least once—preferably under the nighttime neon lights. Tawdry strip clubs and souvenir shops scream for attention, but take a closer look: you'll find local jazz musicians showing off their chops, elegant restaurants, and faded bars where luminaries like Mark Twain and Tennessee Williams imbibed.

Jackson Square

(B) Flanked by St. Louis Cathedral, the antebellum Pontalba apartment buildings, and the Mississippi River, postcard-pretty Jackson Square has been the hub of New Orleans life since the city's colonial start. Artists, musicians, and fortune-tellers congregate on the plaza surrounding the square, but the manicured park itself is a peaceful oasis in the midst of the French Quarter bustle.

Garden District

(C) A field day for architecture buffs and gardeners, the leafy Garden District is a remarkably intact collection of 19th-century Greek Revival mansions and raised cottages, many built by wealthy merchants during New Orleans's cotton heyday. Cap a visit here with lunch at Commander's Palace and browsing the shops and cafés on Magazine Street.

St. Charles Avenue Streetcar

(D) Three streetcar lines converge on Canal Street, but this one packs the most bang for the buck-and-a-quarter. Following a route in use since a steam train first plied the avenue in 1835, the old-school streetcars clatter through the CBD, then roll along the oak-shaded median past some of the city's most exclusive addresses. Stops include Audubon Park, the Garden District, and the Riverbend shopping district.

Audubon Park

(E) Picturesque Audubon Park, across from the campuses of Tulane and Loyola universities and on the St. Charles Avenue streetcar line, is an uptown oasis featuring waterfowl-filled lagoons, oak trees draped in Spanish moss, and wide-open green spaces. The park also includes the world-class Audubon Zoo, the Audubon Park Golf Course, Audubon Stables, and Audubon Tennis Courts, and has great views of the Mississippi River.

French Market

(F) French trappers, seafood vendors, and more than a few rowdy sailors traipsed through these open-air stalls once upon a time. Today the place more resembles a bazaar, and alongside vegetable stalls and charcuteries selling alligator-on-a-stick, crawfish, and Cajun sausages you'll find stands packed with jewelry, bags, cheap sunglasses, and antiques. The quality of the merchandise varies (it's a great place to pick up Mardi Gras beads and hot sauces), but the scene is a lot of fun— especially on weekends and whenever live music takes over the market.

City Park

(G) Accessible by the Canal Street streetcar line, City Park offers 1,300 acres of recreational and cultural opportunities in the heart of New Orleans's Mid-City. The park is home to the New Orleans Museum of Art and the adjacent, first-rate Besthoff Sculpture Garden. The New Orleans Botanical Gardens, the Carousel Gardens Amusement Park, Storyland, and the miniature train that tours the park are other big draws. There's a walking track around the lake near the museum, where you'll find a genuine Venetian gondola for hire. The Spanish mission–style Old Casino Building houses the Parkview Café for a light bite, a cool drink, or an ice-cream treat on a hot day.

NEW ORLEANS FINE ARTS

For a relatively small city, New Orleans has a remarkably active and varied performing-arts community. *Below we highlight our Fodor's Choices for the arts—the best of the best in several genres. For more listings, visit the New Orleans Arts section of ⊕ www.fodors.com.*

Classical Music

Philharmonic orchestral and chamber groups thrived in New Orleans during the 19th century. As jazz achieved society status during the 20th century, classical music took a backseat; however, many professional and amateur players ensure the scene stays active.

Louisiana Philharmonic Orchestra. The always good, sometimes excellent LPO has returned to the beautifully renovated Mahalia Jackson Theater for the Performing Arts and continues to perform at Tulane and Loyola university auditoriums and at local churches. There's also a concert series in parks around town during the spring months. ⊠ *1010 Common St., Suite 2120, CBD* ☎ *504/523–6530* ⊕ *www.lpomusic.com.*

Film

Generous state tax breaks and scenic architecture have made New Orleans a popular place to film movies, which has given the Big Easy another nickname: "Hollywood South."

Zeitgeist Multidisciplinary Arts Center. Working with volunteer staff and a shoestring budget, Zeitgeist founder and filmmaker Rene Broussard has almost single-handedly preserved the spirit of independent film in New Orleans with this funky and eclectic art space. Live performance art is also featured. ⊠ *1618 Oretha Castle Haley Blvd., Uptown* ☎ *504/827–5858* ⊕ *www.zeitgeistinc.net.*

Opera

New Orleans has long had a love affair with opera. The first grand opera in North America was staged here, and in the mid-19th century New Orleans had three full-time opera companies. Through the 20th century the city continued to produce famous singers, including Norman Treigle, Phyllis Treigle, Ruth Falcon, and Jeanne-Michelle Charbonnet.

New Orleans Opera Association. Returning to the Mahalia Jackson Theater for the Performing Arts and the Placido Domingo Stage, the October-through-April opera season generally showcases three operas, as well as a small handful of special events. Opera on Tap is an innovative series bringing performances to area pubs. ☎ *504/529–3000* ⊕ *www. neworleansopera.org.*

Theater

New Orleans has a diverse theater scene, from touring Broadway productions at the Mahalia Jackson Theatre to original works performed by local companies.

Southern Repertory Theater. This well-established theater company specializes in original and first-rate contemporary theater productions. They stage premieres by regional and international playwrights and are the city's only year round professional theater. ⊠ *Canal Place, 3rd level, 365 Canal St., French Quarter* ☎ *504/522–6545* ⊕ *www.southernrep.com.*

NEW ORLEANS SPORTS: SAINTS AND STINGERS

1

For a city that loves to play, New Orleans was never considered much of a professional sports town. Season after season of disappointing scores had even earned the New Orleans NFL team the pitiful nickname, "The Aints." But things changed in the last few years, when two of the city's pro teams went the distance. The victories represented comeback—not just for the teams, but for the entire city.

New Orleans Saints

The Saints went marching in to victory in Miami in 2010 when they became Super Bowl champions for the first time. The win meant more than just a football championship, though. Throughout the entire winning season—which opened with 13 wins in a row—New Orleans was abuzz and united with Saints spirit like never before. The New Orleans Saints Super Bowl XLIV victory parade, which fell just a week before Mardi Gras, drew 800,000 people. It was the largest parade crowd some locals claim they've ever seen, which is truly impressive for America's party city.

Today, despite an ethics scandal that has rocked the NFL, Saints fever continues unabated. Fans are as enthusiastic as ever, and celebrate in Champions Square, just outside the rechristened Mercedes-Benz Superdome, a hot spot for pre- and post-game partying. Whether you're at the Dome or watching the Saints on TV, keep an eye out for some of the Saints' most famous fans: Halo Saint, who wears a gold Transformer-esque getup; Da Pope, dressed as the pontiff himself; Whistle Monsta, in black-and-gold face paint, Saints uniform, and a giant gold whistle atop his helmet; and Voodoo Man, sporting a tux jacket, top hat, and ghostly face paint.

Where they play: Mercedes-Benz Superdome (⊠ *Sugar Bowl Dr., CBD*)

Season: August–January

How to buy tickets: With a wish and a prayer, or at least your fingers crossed. Individual tickets are technically not for sale—the Saints have been sold out on season tickets alone since 2006. Your best bet is the **NFL Ticket Exchange** (⊕ *www. nfl.com*).

Famous players, past and present: Drew Brees, Rickey Jackson, Archie Manning

Past highlights: Won Super Bowl XLIV in 2010; made playoffs in 2011.

New Orleans Hornets

Still relatively new to New Orleans are the Hornets, who relocated to the Crescent City in 2002. Hurricane Katrina sent the team to Oklahoma City in 2005–07, but the Hornets returned to New Orleans for the 2007–08 season. Local interest and attendance swelled that spring, and the team made the NBA playoffs that season and the next. After a less successful 2009–10 season, the team made it back to the playoffs in spring 2011. While a championship still eludes the Hornets, enthusiasm for the team continues

Where they play: New Orleans Arena (⊠ *1501 Girod St., CBD*)

Season: October–April

How to buy tickets: Ticket office (☎ *504/525–HOOP* ⊕ *www.nba.com/ hornets*)

Past highlights: Making the NBA playoffs in 2008, 2009, and 2011.

LOCAL FOR A DAY

Tired of time-share hawkers and tap dancers? Want to spend some time enjoying New Orleans the way locals do? Step one: get out of the Quarter.

Get Some Exercise

Go for a jog along the **St. Charles Avenue streetcar tracks.** You'll have plenty of company anywhere between Jackson Avenue and the university area—just follow the well-worn trails along the wide median (to really pass for a local, refer to it as the "neutral ground"). Keep an eye out for streetcars as well as vehicles crossing the tracks. If that sounds too risky, hit the paths in **City Park,** or rent a bicycle and head for **Audubon Park,** where you can get on a paved jogging and bike trail that runs along the Mississippi River levee well into Jefferson Parish.

Find a Market

The **Crescent City Farmers Market** sets up at the corner of Girod and Magazine streets in the CBD on Saturday mornings; on Tuesday from 9 am to 1 pm, it's held Uptown at Tulane Square, on Leake Avenue at Broadway. While you may not want to lug a bag of broccoli back to your hotel, there's always some good prepared food for sale (and a guest-chef-created weekly Green Plate Special), local chefs foraging for ingredients, and an entertaining bunch of vendors. If you happen to be around the first Saturday of the month (except July and August) head to the Freret Market uptown, a food, art, and flea fest where the merchandise is high quality and the crowd never less than colorful.

Queue Up for Breakfast

Locals have their favorite brunch spots, where on weekends you'll find lines of hungry customers stretching onto the sidewalk. Both **Surrey's Café and Juice Bar** (⊠ *1418 Magazine St., Garden District* ☎ *504/524–3828* and ⊠ *4807 Magazine St., Uptown* ☎ *504/895-5757*) for huevos rancheros and exotic fresh juice, and **Slim Goodies Diner** (⊠ *3322 Magazine St., Uptown* ☎ *504/891–3447*) for sweet-potato pancakes, are open weekdays, when there's less chance of a wait. Thanks to word-of-mouth advertising, **Elizabeth's** (⊠ *601 Gallier St., Bywater* ☎ *504/944–9272*) gets its share of tourists, but the Saturday and Sunday brunch crowd still mostly consists of neighborhood denizens.

Hang Out by the River

Locals love Riverview Drive—better known as **The Fly**—the riverside stretch of Audubon Park behind the zoo, even if they have no idea how it got its nickname (probably from a butterfly-shape building that used to stand here). There is a Little League baseball complex (where spectators can sip Abita beer sold at the snack bar) and a football-soccer field, but most people are content to spread out on a blanket, have a picnic or barbecue, and watch the ships go by on the Mississippi. The nearby **dog park,** on the levee just upriver from the park, is another popular gathering spot, especially in late afternoon.

Shop Local

Whether it's at the incredibly diverse array of boutiques on the "six miles of style" that make up **Magazine Street** or at the stately antiques dealerships in the **French Quarter,** locals prefer to spend their money at businesses owned and staffed by New Orleanians. If you love the city, shop, eat, and sip locally instead of spending money at malls or national chain restaurants and bars. Look for the lime-green-and-blue "Stay Local!" logo stickers on store windows.

NEW ORLEANS WITH KIDS

New Orleans is a grown-up town in a lot of ways, but there are lots of activities to keep the kids interested, too. See the full listings in the neighborhood exploring chapters for contact info.

Get Out and Play

Audubon Park. This beautiful Uptown park is the perfect place to let the kids run free for a couple of hours. They can explore the lagoon complex, where they'll find ducks and an impressive (sometimes squawky) assortment of migratory birds nesting on Bird Island. Several play structures throughout the park—the biggest is at the downtown, lakeside corner of the park near St. Charles Avenue—provide a place for kids to swing, slide, and climb. And a walk around the 1.8-mile paved jogging path is an ever-popular family pastime. (*Uptown*)

City Park. There's plenty to do here for the younger set, including two free playgrounds: one with swings near the Peristyle, and a playground for older kids, just off Marconi Drive, that has more challenging things to clamber on. Storyland, a fairy-tale theme park, is open on weekends year-round, and features a number of sculptures created by Blaine Kern Studios, the maker of Mardi Gras floats. Adjacent Carousel Gardens Amusement Park has low-impact rides, a miniature train that tours the park, and a beautiful 100-year-old carousel as a centerpiece. (*Mid-City*)

Animals Everywhere!

Aquarium of the Americas. Loads of exotic sea creatures, a penguin exhibit, and an interactive area where kids can get their hands wet make the aquarium a favorite family destination. There's a fun museum shop and an IMAX theater next door. (*The French Quarter: Riverfront*)

Audubon Insectarium. This amazing attraction features insects for everyone—from a beautiful exhibit on butterflies to gross-out fun with the bug chef. (*The French Quarter: Riverfront*)

Audubon Zoo. A well-designed showcase with animals from all over the world, the zoo also has a hands-on area for kids—where young volunteers show off real live zoo residents—and a petting zoo with docile goats, among other beasties. (*Uptown*)

Kiddie Culture

Louisiana Children's Museum. The Warehouse District museum tries to sneak in a little education while giving kids a place to romp, role-play, and dabble in the arts. (*Warehouse District*)

For Kids of All Ages

Blaine Kern's Mardi Gras World at Kern Studios. The city's most famous float-building family offers tours of their company's vast studio, where kids can try on costumes and watch the artists at work. (*Warehouse District*)

Streetcars. You can't leave New Orleans without taking the kids for a ride in a streetcar, which you can also use to get to several of the sites listed here, including City Park (on the Canal Street line) and Audubon Park (St. Charles Avenue). (*See the "Riding the Streetcar" feature in the Uptown and Carrollton-Riverbend chapter.*)

FREE AND ALMOST FREE

Free Museums and Galleries

Buy a **Power Pass** (three days, $124.99 per person ⊕ *www.visiticket.com*) to save a significant amount on the admittance fees to the city's leading museums and attractions. It costs nothing, however, to browse the **Warehouse District galleries** on and around Julia Street, where you'll find works by established and up-and-coming artists. Make a detour through the lobby and mezzanine of the **Renaissance Arts Hotel** (⊠ *700 Tchoupitoulas St.*), which has an impressive collection on display.

The Sydney and Walda Besthoff Sculpture Garden in City Park, next to the New Orleans Museum of Art, is free and has major work by important 20th-century artists, including Henry Moore, Jacques Lipchitz, Barbara Hepworth, and Seymour Lipton, dramatically set among lagoons and moss-laden oak trees.

Uptown, on the Tulane University campus, the **Newcomb Art Gallery** hosts shows featuring work by internationally known artists—photographer Diane Arbus and master silversmith William Spratling are two examples—as well as themed exhibitions and work by Newcomb's art school alumni.

Free Music

Outdoor festivals like the **Satchmo Summer Fest** and **French Quarter Festival** are great places to hear live music for free. Street bands also serenade visitors daily in the French Quarter—although if you linger, you'll be asked to toss a few bucks into the hat.

Drop by the **Jean Lafitte National Historic Park's French Quarter visitor center** (⊠ *419 Decatur St.* ☎ *504/589–3882*) to get a schedule of upcoming shows; the park hosts concerts by Louisiana musicians in the courtyard.

The **New Orleans Jazz National Historical Park** (⊠ *916 N. Peters St.* ☎ *504/589–4806*) sponsors live performances and lectures Tuesday to Saturday at its French Market office. The performers—who are almost invariably good—cover the jazz spectrum, from traditional brass band music to modern jazz.

If you're in town on a Wednesday from early April to late June or from mid-September to October, check out the free **Wednesday at the Square** and **Harvest the Music** concert series at Lafayette Square in the CBD, across from Gallier Hall. At both festivals around 5 pm, a horde of downtown workers and fest-loving residents converge on the square to hear good local bands, dance, and socialize. There's plenty of food and drink available for purchase.

Free Ride

The **Canal–Algiers ferry** offers some of the best views of the city, and there's no charge if you're not in a car. It's a fun thing to do with kids, and a great way to get a sense of the Mississippi River's magnitude. The pedestrian entrance is on the plaza at the foot of Canal Street, across from Harrah's Casino; it docks on the West Bank at Algiers Point, a quaint historic neighborhood that makes for a good daytime stroll. At night, though, stay onboard for the return trip.

A ride on one of the **streetcars** is a fun, cheap way to see the city. For just $1.25, you can take a ride Uptown, to the Riverfront, or to City Park, with stops at various attractions along the way. All three lines pick up on Canal Street. Open the window, sit back, and enjoy the sights.

OFFBEAT NEW ORLEANS

Cemeteries

The old cemeteries in and around New Orleans, where tombs have to be built above the boggy ground to keep the remains of loved ones from drifting away, are fascinating places to visit. Those near the French Quarter (**St. Louis No. 2** and **St. Roch,** for example) are best visited on a tour or with a group. Lake Lawn Metairie Cemetery (⊠ *5100 Pontchartrain Blvd.* ☎ *504/486–6331*), on the other hand, is safe to visit on your own: the office even has audio guides to help motorists find their way around the stately cemetery, the final resting place of luminaries like Al Hirt, Louis Prima, and Civil War general P.G.T. Beauregard. Guided tours are available by appointment. One note: because it's a busy cemetery, officials prefer that people visit between 8:30 and 10:30 am or after 3:30 pm, when there's less chance of disrupting a funeral in progress.

Sno-balls

Back in the days before air-conditioning New Orleanians developed the sno-ball as a way to cope with stifling summers: it's a ball of shaved ice served in a cup or Chinese take-out container, topped with anything from simple syrup to condensed milk. A New Orleans inventor designed the patented SnoWizard ice-shaving machine to produce the finest shaved ice imaginable, so a sno-ball in New Orleans is different (many would say better) than others. **Hansen's Sno-Blitz Sweet Shop** (⊠ *4801 Tchoupitoulas St., Uptown* ☎ *504/891–9788* ☼ *May–Aug.*) has been dishing them out since 1939; another stalwart is **Plum Street Snoball** (⊠ *1300 Burdette St., Carrollton-River-bend* ☎ *504/866–7996* ☼ *Mar.–Oct.*).

Weird Museums

Home to a small but interesting collection of art and artifacts related to voodoo history and practice in the city, the **New Orleans Historic Voodoo Museum** (⊠ *724 Dumaine St.* ☎ *504/680–0128*) offers insight into a spiritual tradition that persists to this day. If you're not squeamish about toying with the black arts, there are handcrafted voodoo dolls and gris-gris (magic talisman) bags sold in the small shop. *(See the French Quarter listings.)*

Louis Dufilho, America's first licensed pharmacist, operated an apothecary, La Pharmacie Francaise, in a 1823 town home. Today it holds the **New Orleans Pharmacy Museum** (⊠ *514 Chartres St.* ☎ *504/565–8027*), a collection of ancient medicine bottles, a huge leech jar, eyeglasses, and some truly unsettling surgical instruments. *(See the French Quarter listings.)*

Tiny Abita Springs, north of Lake Pontchartrain, is notable for three things: artesian spring water, Abita beer, and an oddball institution known as the **Abita Mystery House** (⊠ *22275 Hwy. 36, at Grover St., Abita Springs* ☎ *985/892–2624* ⊕ *www.abitamysteryhouse.com*). Artist John Preble's strange vision is an obsessive collection of found objects (combs, old musical instruments, paint-by-number art, and taxidermy experiments gone awry) set in a series of ramshackle buildings, including one covered in broken tiles. Combine a trip to here with a tour of the Abita Brewery (⊕ *www.abita.com*)—tours are Wednesday, Thursday, and Friday 2–3 pm, or Saturday at 11, noon, 1 pm, and 2 pm; or lunch at the Abita Brew Pub (⊕ *www.abitabrewpub.com*). For more information see the New Orleans Side Trips on *www.fodors.com*.

GREAT ITINERARIES

NEW ORLEANS HIGHLIGHTS

Including a trip to plantation country

Day 1: The French Quarter

Start by getting to know the city's most famous neighborhood. Sure, it's a cliché, but the café au lait and beignets at **Café du Monde** are a good place to begin, followed by a stroll around **Jackson Square** and **St. Louis Cathedral.** Cross the seawall and take in the views of the Mississippi River from **Woldenberg Riverfront Park.** Wander along North Peters Street to the shops and market stalls in the **French Market,** followed by a stroll around the mostly residential **Lower Quarter** and **Faubourg Marigny.** After lunch, explore the antiques stores and art galleries on **Royal and Chartres streets,** winding it all up with a cocktail in a shady courtyard; try **Napoleon House,** an atmospheric bar and café that makes a mean Pimm's Cup, or the French Quarter mainstay **Pat O'Brien's.** Save **Bourbon Street** for after dinner at one of the Quarter's esteemed restaurants; like anything that's lived hard and been around as long, it's much more attractive in low light.

Day 2: The Garden District and Uptown

The **St. Charles Avenue streetcar** rumbles past some of the South's most prized real estate; take a seat in one of the antique wooden seats and admire the scenery on the way to leafy **Audubon Park.** In the park you can follow the paved footpath to the **Audubon Zoo,** keeping an eye out for the zoo's white tigers, a pair of albino brothers named Rex and Zulu, after two of the city's most famous carnival krewes. Board an inbound **Magazine Street** bus near the zoo entrance and take it a couple of blocks past Louisiana Avenue, where a number

of restaurants, some with sidewalk tables, are clustered. Continue on Magazine to Washington Avenue and head left through the **Garden District.** Prytania Street, just past **Lafayette Cemetery No. 1** (Anne Rice fans, take note), is a good axis from which you can explore the neighborhood's elegant side streets. Catch a downtown-bound streetcar on St. Charles, or wrap up the afternoon shopping and dining on Magazine Street.

Day 3: Art, History, and Culture

Dedicate one day to a deeper exploration of the city's cultural attractions. Art lovers shouldn't miss the **Warehouse District,** where a pair of fine museums—the **Ogden Museum of Southern Art** and the **Contemporary Arts Center**—anchor a vibrant strip of contemporary art galleries, most of which feature local artists. History buffs will want to check out the **National World War II Museum,** also in the Warehouse District, and the **Historical New Orleans Collection** in the French Quarter, which hosts changing exhibits in a beautifully restored town home. New Orleans music aficionados can browse the bins at the **Louisiana Music Factory,** which has a wide selection of CDs—and occasional in-store performances—by Louisiana musicians.

Day 4: Remembering Katrina

It may strike some as macabre, but touring neighborhoods that were devastated by Hurricane Katrina and its subsequent floods has become a ritual for many visitors, not unlike the hordes that have made Lower Manhattan's Ground Zero a pilgrimage site. You can opt for a guided bus tour, which takes you to **Lakeview** and the infamous **17th Street Canal levee breach;** some companies also travel to the **Ninth Ward** and **Chalmette.** ⇨ *If you have your own transportation, follow a drive*

1

through Hurricane Katrina's aftermath in our Remembering Katrina feature at the end of this chapter. After a somber tour of Katrina's devastation, a good antidote is to look to the many signs of renewal and rebirth. **City Park,** which sustained extensive wind and flood damage, reopened its stately botanical gardens; nearby stands the venerable **New Orleans Museum of Art** and the adjacent **Sydney and Walda Besthoff Sculpture Garden.** Wrap the day up with dinner and live music downtown at one of the clubs on **Frenchmen Street,** in the Faubourg Marigny neighborhood, where the city's inexhaustible party spirit is in evidence.

Day 5: Head Out of Town

Consider a day trip out of town to visit one of the region's elegant **plantation homes,** explore **Cajun Country,** or take a guided **swamp tour.** Some tour companies offer a combination of these destinations, with lunch included. Many of the antebellum mansions between New Orleans and Baton Rouge have been painstakingly restored and filled with period furniture; nature lovers will want to set aside time to explore the grounds and lush flower gardens. Swamp tours may sound hokey, but they're actually a good way to see south Louisiana's cypress-studded wetlands (and get up close and personal with the alligators and other critters that live there). Continue the nautical theme in the evening with a ride to **Algiers Point** aboard the Canal Street Ferry for lovely sunset views of the New Orleans skyline.

TIPS

If you're venturing out in your own vehicle, be aware that street conditions, which weren't great to begin with, are still in disrepair in some places. Others are undergoing massive repaving, so prepare to be patient with construction-zone traffic patterns.

Summers in New Orleans arrive early and stick around longer than most people would like. If visiting in the hot months, stay hydrated, limit your midday outdoor activities, and be prepared for sudden, sometimes torrential downpours.

Bring a sweater or light jacket with you: air-conditioning in restaurants and other destinations can be aggressive.

New Orleanians are friendly, but odd requests from people on the street who offer to tell you where you got your shoes ("You got them on your feet," followed by demanding that you pay for this information) and other overtures from chatty, rather dubious-looking types should be ignored (feel free to pretend you don't speak English). Trust your intuition; if something doesn't feel right, don't worry about coming across as mean, just continue along your way.

Before you book your trip, visit ⊕ *www.neworleansonline.com,* click travel tools, and download coupons for lodging, dining, attractions, tour, and shopping discounts—this site is owned by the New Orleans Tourism Marketing Corporation and is a great source for event information. The site ⊕ *www.neworleanscvb.com* also has a selection of downloadable coupons.

A GOOD GARDEN DISTRICT WALK

As New Orleans expanded upriver from Canal Street in the 19th century, wealthy newcomers built their majestic homes in the Garden District, one of the most beautiful neighborhoods in the country. Today the area is home to politicians, fifth-generation New Orleanians, and celebrities, including local favorite John Goodman. A walk through the Garden District, just a 20-minute streetcar ride from the French Quarter, provides a unique look at life in New Orleans, past and present.

Start out at **the Rink**, a small shopping complex at the Washington Avenue and Prytania Street intersection, one block from the streetcar stop. Walk a block east on Prytania (the main artery of the district) to the corner of Fourth Street to see **Colonel Short's Villa**, known for its ornate cornstalk fence, which supposedly was built for his wife who was homesick for Kentucky. Towards Third Street, the **Briggs-Staub House** is one of the few Gothic Revival houses in the city. No expense was spared in the construction of the **Lonsdale House** across the street, which functioned as a Catholic chapel for more than 70 years. The **Maddox House**, next door, is an example of the five-bay Greek Revival expansion. Across Prytania at the corner of Second is the **Women's Guild of the New Orleans Opera Association House**, with its distinctive octagonal turret; it now functions as a catering hall for weddings and other social events. At First and Prytania streets is the regal **Bradish-Johnson House**, now a private girls' school, and the relatively modest raised **Toby-Westfeldt House**, an example of a Creole colonial home.

Turn right and walk down First Street. Built in 1869, **Morris House** on the corner of Coliseum and **Carroll House** next door, where the classic *Toys In the Attic* was filmed, are decorated with "iron lace,"

exemplifying the era's romantic, Italianate style. Across Chestnut Street, **Brevard House**, also known as Rosegate for the ornate cast-iron gate that extends the length of the block, was the home of author Anne Rice from 1989 to 2004. One block farther on the right is the **Payne House**, where Confederate president Jefferson Davis died.

Walk back up First Street, toward Coliseum. The street takes you past some of the most beautiful and historic homes in the South. The **Italianate Mansion** at First and Coliseum streets was the former home of rock singer Trent Reznor. Actor John Goodman now lives there. Across the street from each other at Coliseum and Third streets are the white-columned **Robinson House**, thought to be the first house in New Orleans with indoor plumbing, and the intricate iron-balconied **Musson House**, built by Edgar Degas's maternal uncle. The white-columned **Nolan House**, at 2707 Coliseum, is where Benjamin Button was raised in the film *The Curious Case of Benjamin Button*. Next door, one of New Orleans's most famous restaurants, **Commander's Palace**, is a great place to stop off for lunch, and across Washington Avenue is the white-walled **Lafayette Cemetery No. 1**, arguably the most beautiful cemetery in the city.

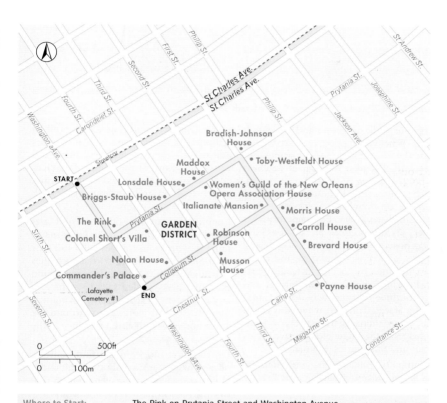

Where to Start:	The Rink on Prytania Street and Washington Avenue
Distance:	1 mile
Timing:	45 minutes (without stops inside)
Where to Stop:	Women's Guild of the New Orleans Opera Association House for interior tours on Monday; Lafayette Cemetery No. 1, open to visitors from Monday through Saturday
Best Time to Go:	Mornings, especially in spring and fall; Monday for the Women's Guild tours
Worst Time to Go:	Midday, especially in summer; Sunday when the cemetery is closed
Good in the Hood:	Stein's Deli, Tracey's Irish Channel Bar, Coquette bistro and wine bar, Commander's Palace

A GOOD GALLERY WALK IN THE WAREHOUSE DISTRICT

Julia Street in the Warehouse District is the epicenter of New Orleans's contemporary art scene, and for art enthusiasts, a day on (and just off of) Julia is a requirement. The street is lined with galleries, specialty shops, and modern apartment buildings, with the greatest concentration stretching from South Peters Street to Carrollton Avenue.

Start your walk on Camp and St. Joseph streets. Whet your appetite for art-buying inside the airy, contemporary, stone-and-glass-walled **Ogden Museum of Southern Art** (✉ 925 Camp St. ☎ 504/539–9600), which houses the largest collection of Southern art anywhere. Across the street, the multidisciplinary **Contemporary Arts Center** (✉ 900 Camp St. ☎ 504/528–3805) hosts performances, concerts, and lectures, and runs stimulating and eclectic exhibitions by local and foreign artists. Pop in if there's an exhibition, and then continue on your way down Camp to Julia Street. Turn left when you get to Julia, where there are five gallery and studio spaces in the single block between this corner and St. Charles Avenue.

At Camp and Julia streets, you'll find the **Jean Bragg Gallery of Southern Art** (✉ 600 Julia St. ☎ 504/895–7375), located in the first of the Thirteen Sisters addresses that make up the historic Julia Street Row. Jean Bragg shows a mix of contemporary and historical paintings depicting Louisiana scenery and life, works by the famed Mississippi artist Walter Anderson, and pottery and crafts from the renowned Newcomb College.

As you head toward the river on Julia Street, detour up Magazine Street toward the French Quarter for a visit to **New Orleans Artworks at New Orleans Glassworks and Printmaking Studio** (✉ 727 Magazine St. ☎ 504/529–7279). Watch free, live, artist demonstrations from a front-row seat or shop the vibrant gallery full of sculptures and glassware in exotic shapes and hues—your purchase will fund education programs at this nonprofit gallery and school. Once outside the studio again, return to Julia and continue your walk toward the Mississippi.

Longtime champion of the visual arts scene in New Orleans, **Arthur Roger** maintains a world-class gallery (✉ 432-434 Julia St. ☎ 504/522–1999) that occupies two adjacent Julia Street addresses behind gleaming glass-walled facades. The gallery is a leader in representing prominent local artists and works from around the globe and is an influential presence in the national art scene.

On the next block, you'll find contemporary work with a political edge and a public conscience at **Jonathan Ferrara Gallery** (✉ 400a Julia St. ☎ 504/522–5471). Directly next door, the lofty whitewashed brick-and-glass space inside **Søren Christensen** (✉ 400 Julia St. ☎ 504/569–9501) provides a gorgeous backdrop for equally gorgeous and always excellent exhibitions, largely of contemporary painting, but sometimes of photography and sculpture.

Keep heading toward the river to **Le Mieux Galleries** (✉ 332 Julia St. ☎ 504/522–5988), where Gulf South artists are the stars; drawings, paintings, photography, and sculpture from throughout the region are showcased here.

1

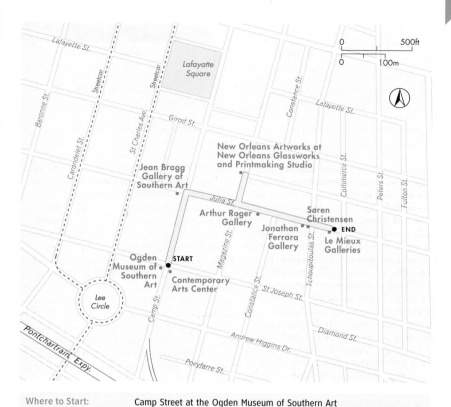

Where to Start:	Camp Street at the Ogden Museum of Southern Art
Distance:	About a half mile
Timing:	Several hours to all day, depending on how much time you have and how much you want to see
Where to Stop:	Julia and Commerce streets
Best Time to Go:	First Saturday of every month, when Art Walks are hosted by Warehouse District galleries from 6 to 9 pm. Two Saturdays not to be missed if you happen to be in town are Jammin' on Julia in April and Whitney White Linen Night in August, wildly popular, all-out art block parties enjoyed by enthusiastic crowds.
Worst Time to Go:	Sunday, when nearly all galleries are closed
Good in the Hood:	Award-winning chefs Donald Link and Stephen Stryjewski showcase charcuterie and Southern cuisine at Cochon (✉ 930 Tchoupitoulas St. ☎ 504/588–2123). Next door, Butcher (✉ 930 Tchoupitoulas St. ☎ 504/588–7675) is a more casual deli offering sandwiches and small plates (with smaller prices to match).

BEST FESTS AND PARADES

New Year's Eve
Join the crowd on the Mississippi River near Jax Brewery for fireworks, live music, and the annual countdown to midnight (marked by "Baby Bacchus" dropping from the top of the brewery).

Mardi Gras, February or March
The biggest event in the city's busy festival calendar has been around for well over a century, and for a celebration of frivolity, people here take Carnival very seriously. There are almost daily parades—even one for dogs (the Krewe of Barkus)—in the two weeks leading up to Fat Tuesday, when pretty much the entire city takes the day off, gets in costume, and hits the streets (⇨ *See our Mardi Gras feature in Chapter 2*). ⊕ *www.mardigrasneworleans.com*.

St. Patrick's Day, March
A couple of big parades roll on the weekend closest to March 17: one starts at Molly's in the Market and winds through the French Quarter; the other, in Uptown, goes down Magazine Street. On St. Paddy's Day, the streets around Parasol's Restaurant & Bar, in the Irish Channel neighborhood, turn into one big, green block party. Two days later (March 19) the town celebrates St. Joseph's Day with home-cooked food and goodie bags filled with cookies and lucky fava beans. Check the *Times-Picayune* classified ads for announcements of altars that you can visit, and be prepared to make a small contribution to cover costs—$5 a person or so.

Tennessee Williams/New Orleans Literary Festival, March
This annual tribute to the *Streetcar Named Desire* playwright, who spent much of his career in New Orleans, draws well-known and aspiring writers, lecturers, and a handful of Williams's acquaintances. It closes with contestants reenacting Stanley Kowalski's big "Stella-a-a!" moment. ☎ *504/581–1144* ⊕ *www.tennesseewilliams.net*.

Easter, March or April
Three fun parades hit the streets of the French Quarter on Easter Sunday: one led by local entertainer Chris Owens, another dedicated to the late socialite Germaine Wells, and a gay parade that takes the festive bonnet tradition to a whole new level.

French Quarter Festival, April
A lot of locals consider this the best festival. With stages set up throughout the Quarter and on the river at Woldenberg Park, the focus is on local entertainment—and, of course, food. ☎ *504/522–5730* ⊕ *www.fqfi.org*.

New Orleans Jazz & Heritage Festival, April–May
Top-notch local and international talent take to several stages the last weekend of April and first weekend of May. The repertoire covers much more than jazz, with big-name rock and pop stars in the mix, and there are dozens of lectures, quality arts and crafts, and awesome food to boot. Next to Mardi Gras, Jazz Fest is the city's biggest draw; book your hotel as far in advance as possible (⇨ *See our Jazz Fest feature in Chapter 10*). ☎ *504/410–4100* ⊕ *www.nojazzfest.com*.

New Orleans Wine & Food Experience, May
Winemakers and oenophiles from all over the world converge for five days of seminars, tastings, and fine food. The Royal Street Stroll, when shops and galleries host pourings and chefs set up tables on the street, is especially lively. ☎ *504/529–9463* ⊕ *www.nowfe.com*.

Essence Music Festival, July

Held around Independence Day, this three-day festival draws top names in R&B, pop, and hip-hop to the Mercedes-Benz Superdome. The event also includes talks by prominent African American figures and empowerment seminars. ⊕ *www.essence.com/essence/emf.*

Tales of the Cocktail, late July

Every summer, heralded mixologists, distillers, writers, chefs, and cocktail connoisseurs converge in the city that gave birth to the Sazerac and the Ramos gin fizz—among other libations—for several days of cocktail competitions, seminars, tastings, pairing dinners, and many more spirited events. ⊕ *www.talesofthecocktail.com.*

Satchmo SummerFest, August

This weekend-long tribute to the late, great Louis Armstrong honors Satchmo in the French Quarter, with jazz performances staged throughout the streets, seminars and discussions with Louis Armstrong scholars, a Satchmo Club Strut down Frenchman Street, and the Louis Armstrong Birthday Party. ⊕ *www.fqfi.org/satchmosummerfest.*

Southern Decadence, early September

On Labor Day weekend hundreds of drag-queens-for-a-day parade through the Quarter. What began as a small party among friends has evolved into one of the South's biggest gay celebrations. The parade rolls (and as the day wears on, staggers) on Sunday, but Decadence parties and events start Thursday evening.

Art for Art's Sake, early October

Art lovers and people-watchers pack the Warehouse District and Magazine Street galleries for this annual Saturday-evening kickoff to the arts season. What's on the walls usually plays second fiddle to the party scene, which spills out into the streets.

Voodoo Experience, October

Part music festival, part giant interactive art exhibition, Voodoo Experience is an evolving festival held every Halloween weekend; it attracts eclectic young masses with its mix of edgy national acts, local bands, and art installations in various media. ⊕ *www.thevoodooexperience.com.*

Celebration in the Oaks, late November–early January

City Park's majestic oaks, Botanical Gardens, Carousel Garden, and Storyland amusement park are awash in holiday lights and decorations during this popular weeks-long event. There are food and rides, a miniature train decked out for Christmas, and entertainment by local school groups. ☎ *504/482-4888* ⊕ *www.neworleanscitypark.com.*

A New Orleans Christmas, December

The lighting of Canal Street kicks off this monthlong celebration. Royal Street shops and historic homes don holiday decorations, restaurants feature special *reveillon* menus, and thousands of carolers gather in Jackson Square for a candlelit sing-along. Around Christmas, bonfires are lit on the levee at various points along the Mississippi, from below New Orleans up into Cajun Country. Legend says the bonfires were lighted by the early settlers to help Papa Noel (the Cajun Santa Claus) find his way up the river. Steamboat tour companies offer special cruises for the occasion.

GET OUTTA TOWN

Cajun Country

The land that gave the world one of its great cuisines—and a refuge for French-Canadian exiles in the 18th century—is worth at least one overnight. **Lafayette**, with its attractive downtown and plentiful accommodations, makes a good hub for exploring the region. The Cajun kitsch can be a bit much at times, but there are some outstanding restaurants and museums, including the **Paul and Lulu Hilliard University Art Museum** and **Acadian Village**, a re-creation of an early-19th-century Acadian settlement. Venture south to picturesque **Abbeville**, where restaurants serve up some mean oysters on the half shell, or to **New Iberia** and nearby **Avery Island**, home of the famous Tabasco hot sauce and a gorgeous 250-acre garden. **Breaux Bridge**, site of the annual Crawfish Festival, has antiques shops and some excellent Cajun restaurants, including **Café des Amis** and **Mulate's**, both known for their dance parties. **St. Martinville**, south of Breaux Bridge, is an attractive small town and home of the **Evangeline Oak**, immortalized in Longfellow's classic poem "Evangeline."

To the north lie **Grand Coteau**, a quaint, historic village set on a natural bluff, and **Opelousas**, a hotbed of zydeco music; nearby **Plaisance** hosts the annual **Southwest Louisiana Zydeco Music festival** each Labor Day weekend. A bit farther afield, the normally quiet town of **Mamou** goes bonkers on Fat Tuesday, when the traditional **Courir de Mardi Gras** takes to the streets; Saturday mornings, little **Fred's Lounge** gets packed to the gills with locals and more than a few tourists two-stepping and waltzing to live Cajun music.

Plantation Country

For *Gone with the Wind* fans, the stretch of the Mississippi north of New Orleans is the ultimate Southern experience. Tour buses ply the highway on both sides of the river, but with a car and a map, it's easy to explore on your own. Fortunes were made here in the 18th and 19th centuries—on the backs of the slaves that worked these plantations—and vestiges of the Old South's wealthy heyday remain in the region's lavish homes, many lovingly restored and open to the public. Highlights include **Oak Alley**, with its procession of ancient oak trees that flank the entrance; **Houmas House**, notable for its architecture, gardens, and fine Latil's Landing restaurant; and **Nottoway**, the largest extant plantation house. Several homes offer accommodations and dining for those who want to linger.

Many of the small towns that dot Plantation Country are fun to explore, but **St. Francisville**, about 25 miles north of Baton Rouge, deserves special mention. The historic town center is a well-preserved collection of antebellum homes and buildings, and the river landing there is one of the few places in south Louisiana where the Mississippi isn't hemmed in by levees. A cluster of fine plantation homes are nearby, including **Rosedown Plantation and Gardens** and the attractive **Oakley House at Audubon State Historic Site**, where John James Audubon taught drawing to the plantation owner's daughter while executing some of the works in his Birds of America series. **Baton Rouge** itself is worth a visit to see the **Old State Capitol** (and the new one, where Governor Huey P. Long met his untimely end) and its lively downtown.

REMEMBERING KATRINA

For nearly 300 years, New Orleans captured the imaginations of people around the world with its unique heritage and lifestyle—a rich tapestry of food, music, pageantry, and irreverent, laissez-faire culture. On August 29, 2005, however, New Orleans captured the attention of the world in a different way: as the site of one of the country's worst natural and manmade disasters and, for a few terrifying days, as a pit of human suffering.

New Orleans is the first major American city to be nearly drained of its population, and even today, more than seven years later, the city has recovered only about two thirds of its former population. Some neighborhoods still show signs of devastation, and while businesses and residents have trickled back into the heavily damaged areas, many are still waiting for a number of factors to kick in—insurance settlements, rebuilding of infrastructure, and direction from city officials—before they return.

That being said, much of New Orleans has been restored and rejuvenated, and visitors are finding that the city retains its sense of joy and hospitality. For many people, however, it's important to see firsthand the places that millions of people came to know through news reports and images—neighborhoods like the Lower Ninth Ward, where a torrent of water tossed houses and cars, and the 17th Street Canal, where brackish Lake Pontchartrain poured through a collapsed floodwall and inundated much of the city.

The following pages include a recap of the disaster, a self-guided driving tour of damaged neighborhoods, and information on organizations making a profound impact on the rebuilding of the city.

Above, post-Katrina devastation

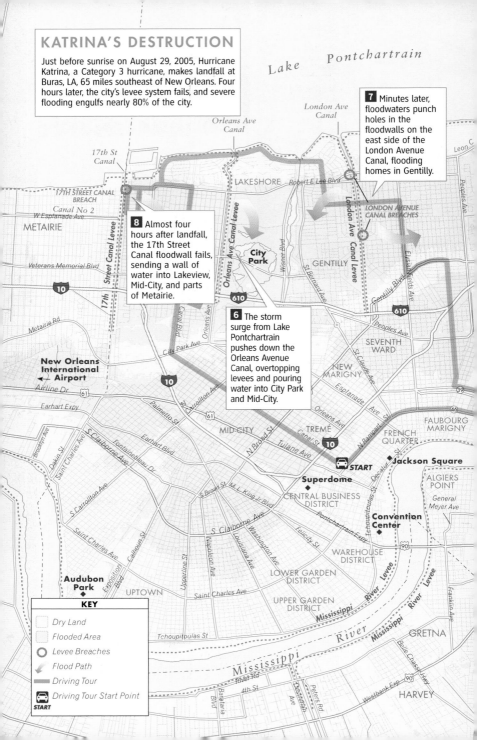

KATRINA'S DESTRUCTION

Just before sunrise on August 29, 2005, Hurricane Katrina, a Category 3 hurricane, makes landfall at Buras, LA, 65 miles southeast of New Orleans. Four hours later, the city's levee system fails, and severe flooding engulfs nearly 80% of the city.

7 Minutes later, floodwaters punch holes in the floodwalls on the east side of the London Avenue Canal, flooding homes in Gentilly.

8 Almost four hours after landfall, the 17th Street Canal floodwall fails, sending a wall of water into Lakeview, Mid-City, and parts of Metairie.

6 The storm surge from Lake Pontchartrain pushes down the Orleans Avenue Canal, overtopping levees and pouring water into City Park and Mid-City.

KEY

- Dry Land
- Flooded Area
- ○ Levee Breaches
- ◤ Flood Path
- ▬ Driving Tour
- 🚗 Driving Tour Start Point
- START

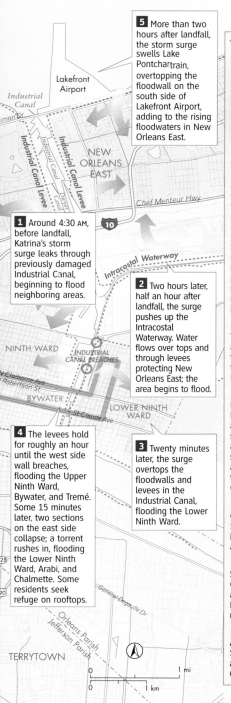

5 More than two hours after landfall, the storm surge swells Lake Pontchartrain, overtopping the floodwall on the south side of Lakefront Airport, adding to the rising floodwaters in New Orleans East.

1 Around 4:30 AM, before landfall, Katrina's storm surge leaks through previously damaged Industrial Canal, beginning to flood neighboring areas.

2 Two hours later, half an hour after landfall, the surge pushes up the Intracostal Waterway. Water flows over tops and through levees protecting New Orleans East; the area begins to flood.

4 The levees hold for roughly an hour until the west side wall breaches, flooding the Upper Ninth Ward, Bywater, and Tremé. Some 15 minutes later, two sections on the east side collapse; a torrent rushes in, flooding the Lower Ninth Ward, Arabi, and Chalmette. Some residents seek refuge on rooftops.

3 Twenty minutes later, the surge overtops the floodwalls and levees in the Industrial Canal, flooding the Lower Ninth Ward.

THE DAYS THAT FOLLOWED

August 30
The breach at the 17th Street Canal gets larger; Lakeview floodwaters rise to nine feet. Many people climb onto roofs to escape. Crowds build at the Superdome, seeking refuge. Rescuers in helicopters and boats pick up hundreds of stranded people, and reports of looting begin to emerge.

August 31
The first buses arrive at the Superdome to take refugees to the Astrodome in Houston.

September 1
National Guard arrives. Looting, carjacking, and other violence spreads. Crowds at the Superdome swell to 25,000, with another 20,000 at the New Orleans Convention Center.

September 2
Congress approves $10.5 billion for immediate rescue and relief efforts.

September 4
Superdome and Convention Center are fully evacuated. Nearly 45,000 refugees.

September 8
An additional $52 billion in aid approved by Congress.

September 17
Business owners are allowed back into Algiers, French Quarter, the CBD, and Uptown.

September 23
A storm surge from Hurricane Rita overtops an Industrial Canal levee, reflooding the Lower Ninth Ward; surge also tops the London Avenue Canal, reflooding Gentilly.

September 26
After suspending re-entry due to Hurricane Rita, the city allows residents to return.

February 18, 2006
The first official Mardi Gras parade (in Orleans Parish), Pontchartrain, rolls.

February 28
Amid controversey, thousands turn out to celebrate Mardi Gras.

April 28
First day of New Orleans Jazz and Heritage Festival.

May 20
C. Ray Nagin is re-elected Mayor of New Orleans.

June 24
Approximately 20,000 attend American Library Association meeting, the largest conference in the city post-Katrina.

Hurricane Katrina was the third-strongest landfalling U.S. hurricane ever recorded.

Nearly 80% of the city was flooded.

Almost 200,000 homes, 71%, were damaged by flooding.

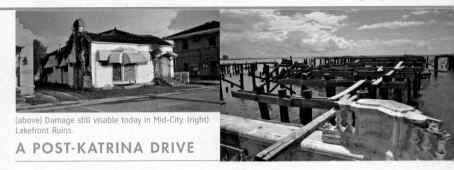

(above) Damage still visable today in Mid-City. (right) Lakefront Ruins.

A POST-KATRINA DRIVE

If you haven't visited New Orleans recently, you'll be surprised at the development in neighborhoods like the Central Business District and Mid-City. New hotels and attractions, and special events continue to draw tourists and fuel the city's rebirth. To try to understand the scope of Hurricane Katrina's damage, you need to visit the neighborhoods it affected. This tour will give you a glimpse of the destruction and the challenges the city faces as it continues rebuilding. Use appropriate caution, as crime is a problem in some neighborhoods, and, above all, be respectful and mindful of people's property and privacy.

TO MID-CITY AND 17TH ST. CANAL

Start at the intersection of Canal and North Rampart streets. Driving on Canal, away from the Mississippi River, alongside the streetcar tracks, you'll pass under the **Interstate 10** elevated freeway at **North Claiborne Avenue** and into Mid-City. You'll see a handful of buildings that are still boarded up, some bearing the ominous stain of the flood line. It's hard to imagine now, but you would have needed a boat to travel this route after the storm. Drive for about 3 miles and you'll reach **City Park Avenue** and a pair of historic cemeteries. Take a right, then a quick left onto **Canal Boulevard.** Past Interstate 610,

you'll enter the **Lakeview neighborhood**, inundated with up to 9 feet of water when floodwalls on the 17th Street Canal collapsed.

At about 5.5 miles, turn left on **Robert E. Lee Boulevard** and follow this road as it crosses **West End Boulevard.** Six blocks past West End, you'll come to **Bellair Drive**, just before the bridge over the 17th Street Canal. Turn left. After one block, you'll reach the spot where the floodwall break occurred. A historic marker memorializes the spot. There are massive public works in progress, including the new floodgates and a temporary canal pumping station, on the site of a former fishing community.

ACROSS THE LAKEFRONT AND THROUGH GENTILLY

Drive five more blocks, through a stand of oak trees, and turn left. Take another left on **Fleur de Lis Drive**, a wide boulevard, and then turn right back onto **Robert E. Lee.** Drive four blocks, and then turn left at the second traffic signal, between a bank and shopping center, and enter the **West End.** Past a row of apartments and restaurants, **Lake Pontchartrain** comes into view (mile 8).

Drive along **Lakeshore Drive** (Robert E. Lee Boulevard can be used as an alternate). You'll notice new construction along the lakefront, and

New Orleans (Orleans parish) population: 462,270 (August 2005), 295,450 (December 2007), 344,000 (December 2010).

There are now more restaurants open in the New Orleans metropolitan area than there were before the storm.

Almost all New Orleans major hotels have reopened; 37,100 of 38,000 rooms are now available.

(above and right) Lower Ninth Ward, damage

especially at each of the many waterways and inlets that lead from the lake into the center of the city. You are outside of the protective levees at this point (you'll see them on your right).

When the road crosses back over the levee and **Bayou St. John**, you'll take a right at the traffic circle, turning onto **Paris Avenue**. After Paris Avenue crosses **Robert E. Lee**, the damage becomes apparent, although there are signs of ongoing construction and rebuilding. Eight blocks past Robert E. Lee, you'll turn left onto **Fillmore Avenue**. Once on Fillmore, you'll cross the **London Avenue Canal**, which was topped by storm surge and responsible for destroying much of the surrounding neighborhood. At 12.6 miles, turn right on **Elysian Fields Avenue**. Drive 1 mile, and turn left onto **Gentilly Boulevard** (a shady ridge that stayed mostly above water). At mile 14, turn right on **Franklin Avenue**.

The street passes under a freeway and through a hard-hit section of the **Seventh Ward** before arriving at **North Claiborne Avenue**.

TO THE LOWER NINTH WARD

Cross North Claiborne, then turn left onto **North Robertson**. This street takes you into the **Upper Ninth Ward** and, in about 1.5 miles, over the **Industrial Canal**. To the left is the Lower Ninth Ward. Just past the bridge, turn left onto **Tennessee Street** (note the **Katrina memorial** at the intersection of North Robertson and Tennessee). To your left, you'll see the **levee wall**—this is the site of the levee breach that destroyed the neighborhood. There was no harder hit area anywhere in the city, which is evident by the remaining number of empty lots—houses and their occupants were wiped right off their foundations. Go seven blocks to **North Tonti**, turn right, then drive

one block and take a right again on **Reynes**. Most of the houses and debris have been cleared, so there are few reminders that this was once a densely populated neighborhood; the sleek, modern houses sponsored by the Make it Right Foundation have become interesting new landmarks. Cross **North Claiborne** and, five blocks later, take a right on **St. Claude Avenue**, where you will cross another drawbridge.

St. Claude Avenue proceeds through the Upper Ninth Ward back toward the French Quarter. To your right is where the water line began, and nearly everything behind it was inundated. Just past Elysian Fields Avenue, St. Claude, an emerging arts district, curves to the left and merges with **North Rampart Street** before arriving at Esplanade Avenue and the French Quarter's edge; it's less than a mile on North Rampart to your Canal Street starting point.

REBUILDING NEW ORLEANS

The immediate aftermath of Hurricane Katrina is over, but the hard work of rebuilding a city continues. Some remarkable organizations stepped up to that challenge, and many others were formed in direct response. These are a few of the players that continue to inspire hope around the city and the region. For a full list of voluntourism opportunities, go to *www.neworleanscvb. com/travel-professionals/toolkit/voluntourism/*.

Habitat for Humanity

BUILD NOW
Helping hard-hit New Orleanians navigate the maze of claims, licenses, permits, and zoning laws, the Build Now Foundation has put dozens of families and individuals back into homes on their original lots. The organization constructs elevated site-built homes in flood-damaged neighborhoods; find the homes in neighborhoods including the Lower Ninth Ward, Lakeview, Gentilly, and Chalmette. ⊕ *www.buildnownola.com*

COMMON GROUND RELIEF
Combining recovery efforts with environmental awareness and grassroots activism, Common Ground Relief has organized some 25,000 volunteers. They have gutted more than 3,000 homes, founded an independent health clinic and women's shelter, created a free legal clinic, and cofounded the Lower Ninth Ward Urban Farming Coalition. They also run a wetlands restoration program and a job training program. ⊕ *www.commongroundrelief.org*

HABITAT FOR HUMANITY
Utilizing an incredible array of volunteer forces and partnerships with AmeriCorps, Habitat for Humanity has rebuilt hundreds of homes in New Orleans, including one of the most prominent and beloved post-Katrina projects, the Musician's Village. Located on Roman Street in the Upper Ninth Ward, the site has provided home and shelter for dozens of returning musicians and is now home to

the new Ellis Marsalis Center for Music, dedicated to the education, development, and preservation of New Orleans unique musical heritage. ⊕ *www.habitatnola.org*

MAKE IT RIGHT
With Brad Pitt as one of its founders, the Make it Right Foundation altered the landscape of post-Katrina Lower Ninth Ward, from one of despair to one of hope—not to mention wonder. The futuristic designs of the affordable, environmentally friendly houses makes each home more than a living unit—they're works of art. ⊕ *www. makeitrightnola.org*

REBUILDING TOGETHER NEW ORLEANS (RTNO)
Along with parent organization the Preservation Resource Center of New Orleans, RTNO has been a champion of efforts to rebuild New Orleans in a way that is sensitive to its past and heritage. One of the great New Orleans landmarks they helped restore was the historic Doullut Steamboat Houses, a pair of architectural and aesthetic wonders, built next to the river in the Holy Cross neighborhood. ⊕ *www.rtno.org*

Rebuilding Together

The French Quarter

WORD OF MOUTH

"We had fun wandering the streets of the French Quarter, seeing St. Louis Cathedral, Jackson Square, the French Market . . . there were a few parades that we caught a glimpse of and sometimes we stopped to sit on the sidewalk to watch/listen to street performers. There's never a dull moment."

—globetrotterxyz

GETTING ORIENTED

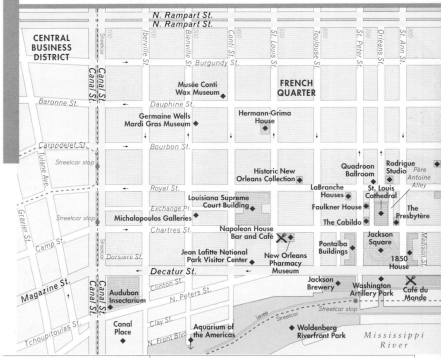

GETTING AROUND

French Quarter streets are laid out in a **grid pattern**. Locals describe locations based on proximity to the river or the lake and to uptown or downtown. Thus, "it's on the downtown, lakeside corner" indicates that a destination is on the northeast corner. Locals also refer to the **number block** that a site is on (as in "the 500 block of Royal Street"). Numbers across the top of the map are applicable to all streets parallel to North Rampart Street. Streets perpendicular to North Rampart start at 500 at Decatur Street and progress north in increments of 100.

MAKING THE MOST OF YOUR TIME

Many visitors never leave the French Quarter, which is the center of New Orleans. Daytime offers history buffs, antiques lovers, shoppers, and foodies a feast of delights; street performers around **Jackson Square** are always going; and the Quarter lights up with fine and casual dining, live music, and the world-infamous **Bourbon Street** debauchery at night. It is a destination you can enjoy 24 hours a day.

SAFETY

Exercise the same caution here that you would in any major city. The French Quarter close to the river is busy day and night, and there is safety in numbers. Farther from the river and closer to Rampart Street, crowds thin, and opportunities for theft grow slightly higher. It's advisable to use extra caution at the outer edges of the French Quarter.

TOP REASONS TO GO

Queue up for beignets. Anytime is the right time for sugary beignets and café au lait from Café du Monde, an institution.

Take in Jackson Square. Mule-drawn carriage tours, artists selling their wares, and quirky street performers and musicians converge against the iconic St. Louis Cathedral backdrop.

Go treasure hunting. The French Market and the random stores and warehouses that surround it are great for finding souvenirs and antiquing.

Drink up. From rowdy Bourbon Street to fancy hotel bars, you'll never go thirsty. Savor your cocktail in a beautiful courtyard, or ask for a "go-cup."

Gallery hop on Royal Street. Antiques and art for big-budget shoppers abound on this classy thoroughfare.

Groove to live music. The French Quarter has some of the most famous music venues in the city, including Preservation Hall, the Palm Court Jazz Café, and One-Eyed Jack's.

QUICK BITES

Café du Monde. Open around the clock for late-night treats or a sweet breakfast, Café du Monde has been serving café au lait and beignets (and not much else) for more than a century. If the café is crowded, there's a take-out window around the side. ✉ *800 Decatur St., French Quarter* ☎ *504/525–4544* ⊕ *www.cafedumonde.com.*

Napoleon House Bar and Café. This café is famous for its Pimm's Cup, enjoyed in the lush courtyard or the cool, dark interior. The house was built in 1797 and, according to local lore, was chosen as Napoléon's New World residence in an escape plan hatched for the exiled emperor. ✉ *500 Chartres St., French Quarter* ☎ *504/524–9752* ⊕ *www. napoleonhouse.com.*

Verti Marte Deli. This distinctly New Orleans take on the deli is open 24 hours. Try the All That Jazz po' boy (ham, turkey, shrimp, and two cheeses) or the traditional french fry version. ✉ *1201 Royal St., French Quarter* ☎ *504/525–4767.*

Sightseeing
★★★★★
Dining
★★★★★
Lodging
★★★★★
Shopping
★★★★★
Nightlife
★★★★★

Unlike tourist destinations that locals despise, even New Orleanians love to get lost in the history and romance of the French Quarter, the city's oldest sector. Your feet on ancient pavement along a pretty side street, you'll stand transfixed and marvel at the age and beauty, at the city's power to endure. Keep walking, slowly, and take the time to look up and appreciate the fabled wrought-iron railings of French Quarter balconies or to peer down cobblestone corridors for a glimpse of secret courtyard gardens.

Updated by Troy Thibodeaux

The neighborhood will not run out of ways to entertain you. During the day, the French Quarter offers several different faces to its visitors. The streets running parallel to the river all bear distinct personas: Decatur Street is a strip of tourist shops, hotels, restaurants, and bars uptown from Jackson Square; downtown from the square, it becomes a hangout for hipsters and leather-clad regulars drawn to shadowy bars, vintage clothing resellers, funky antiques emporiums, and novelty shops. Chartres Street remains a relatively calm stretch of inviting shops and eateries. Royal Street is, perhaps aptly, the address of sophisticated antiques shops and many of the Quarter's finest residences. Bourbon Street claims the strip bars, sex shops, extravagant cocktails, and flashy music clubs filmmakers love to feature. Dauphine and Burgundy streets are more residential, with just a few restaurants and bars serving as retreats for locals.

After dark, you'll find fine dining and easygoing eateries aplenty, and music pouring from the doorways of bars as freely as the drinks flowing within them (and out of their doors—plastic "go cups" for your cocktails are standard at the exit of every bar and club, and consuming alcohol on public streets is still legal in New Orleans). On any ordinary evening, a stroll through the French Quarter is a moving concert, where the strains of traditional jazz, blues, classic rock and roll, and electronic dance beats all commingle.

WHEN TO GO

Save Bourbon Street for after dinner at one of the Quarter's esteemed restaurants; like anything that has lived hard and been around a long time, it's much more attractive in low light.

For all its evening-time adult entertainment, the French Quarter by day is quite kid-friendly. Children adore beignets with chocolate milk; watching tankers flying flags from every corner of the world ply the Mississippi's muddy brown waters; walking through the tunnel tank under water of a much clearer hue at the Aquarium of the Americas; munching crunchy treats made out of bugs at the Audubon Insectarium; and savoring the same delicious po' boy sandwiches and fried seafood that their parents love to eat.

> **GET A GO CUP**
>
> Open containers of alcohol are allowed on the streets of New Orleans, as long as they're not in glass containers. So when you're ready to leave, ask your bartender for a "go cup," pour your drink into the plastic cup, and head out, drink in hand.

THE VIEUX CARRÉ

Vieux Carré, French for "Old Square," is technically the entire French Quarter, but you'll notice a divide at Decatur Street to the river, as things start to feel more modern, and chain stores and restaurants pop up. The historic part of the French Quarter is where you can slip down a quiet street, gaze up at a row of balconies, and forget for a moment that you are living in the 21st century. The exquisite and intimate old-world urbanity of the Vieux Carré is what makes New Orleans instantly recognizable on picture postcards, television shows, and film the world over.

TOP ATTRACTIONS

Bourbon Street. Ignore your better judgment and take a stroll down Bourbon Street, past the bars, restaurants, music clubs, and novelty shops that have given this strip its reputation as the playground of the South. The bars of Bourbon Street were among the first businesses of the city to reopen after Katrina; catering to the off-duty relief workers, they provided a different form of relief. Today, the spirit of unbridled revelry here is as big as ever. The noise, raucous crowds, and bawdy sights are not family fare; if you go with children, do so before sundown. Saint Ann Street marks the beginning of a short strip of gay bars, some of which retain links to the long history of gay culture in New Orleans. Although Bourbon is usually well patrolled, it is wise to stay alert to your surroundings. The street is blocked to make a pedestrian mall at night; often the area is shoulder to shoulder, especially during major sports events, on New Year's Eve, and during Mardi Gras. ⊠ *French Quarter*.

The Cabildo. Dating from 1799, this Spanish colonial–style building is named for the Spanish council—or *cabildo*—that met there. The transfer of Louisiana to the United States was made in 1803 in the front room on the second floor overlooking the square. This historic transaction was reenacted in the same room for the 200th anniversary of the purchase in 2003. The Cabildo later served as the city hall and then the Supreme Court.

Three floors of multicultural exhibits recount Louisiana history—from the colonial period through Reconstruction—with countless artifacts, including the death mask of Napoléon Bonaparte. In 1988 the building

2

suffered terrible damage from a four-alarm fire. Most of the historic pieces inside were saved, but the top floor (which had been added in the 1840s), the roof, and the cupola had to be replaced. The Cabildo is almost a twin to the **Presbytère** on the other side of the cathedral. ■TIP➜ **Both sites—as well as the Old U.S. Mint and the 1850 House—are part of the Louisiana State Museum system. Buy tickets to two or more state museums and receive a 20% discount.** ⊠ *Jackson Sq., 701 Chartres St.* ☎ *504/568–8975* ⊕ *lsm.crt.state.la.us* ⊠ *$6* ⊙ *Tues.–Sun. 10–4:30 (last entrance 4 pm).*

Hermann-Grima House. One of the largest and best-preserved examples of American architecture in the Quarter, this Georgian-style house has the only restored private stable and the only working 1830s Creole kitchen in the Quarter. American architect William Brand built the house in 1831. The house fortunately sustained only minor damage during Katrina and is open for visits and tours. Cooking demonstrations on the open hearth are held here all day Tuesday and Thursday from October through May. The gift shop sells local crafts and books. ⊠ *820 St. Louis St., French Quarter* ☎ *504/525–5661* ⊕ *www.hgghh. org* ⊠ *$12, combination ticket with Gallier House $20* ⊙ *Mon., Tues., Thurs., and Fri. 10–2, Sat. noon–3; tours on the hr.*

Historic New Orleans Collection. This private archive and exhibit complex, with thousands of historic photos, documents, and books, is one of the finest research centers in the South. It occupies the 19th-century town house of General Kemper Williams and the 1792 Merrieult House. Changing exhibits focus on aspects of local history. Architecture, history, and house tours are offered several times daily. A museum shop sells books, prints, and gifts. ⊠ *533 Royal St., French Quarter* ☎ *504/523–4662* ⊕ *www.hnoc.org* ⊠ *Tour of houses or archive galleries $5* ⊙ *Tues.–Sat. 9:30–4:30 (museum and research library), Sun. 10:30–4:30 (museum only). Tours at 10, 11, 2, and 3.*

♻ Fodor's Choice ★

Jackson Square. Surrounded by historic buildings and plenty of the city's atmospheric street life, the heart of the French Quarter is this beautifully landscaped park. Among the notable buildings around the square are **St. Louis Cathedral** and **Faulkner House.** Two Spanish colonial–style buildings, the **Cabildo** and the **Presbytère,** flank the cathedral. The handsome rows of brick apartments on each side of the square are the **Pontalba Buildings.** The park is landscaped in a sun pattern, with walkways set like rays streaming out from the center, a popular garden design in the royal court of King Louis XIV, the Sun King. In the daytime, dozens of artists hang their paintings on the park fence and set up outdoor studios where they work on canvases or offer to draw portraits of passersby. These artists are easy to engage in conversation and are knowledgeable about many aspects of the Quarter and New Orleans. Musicians, mimes, tarot-card readers, and magicians perform on the flagstone pedestrian mall surrounding the square, many of them day and night.

Originally called the Place d'Armes, the square was founded in 1718 as a military parade ground. It was also the site of public executions carried out in various styles, including burning at the stake, beheading,

A statue of General Andrew Jackson presides over his namesake park, Jackson Square.

breaking on the wheel, and hanging. A **statue of Andrew Jackson,** victorious leader of the Battle of New Orleans in the War of 1812, commands the center of the square; the park was renamed for him in the 1850s. The words carved in the base on the cathedral side of the statue—"The Union must and shall be preserved"—are a lasting reminder of the Federal troops who occupied New Orleans during the Civil War and who inscribed them. ⊠ *French Quarter* ☽ *Park daily 8 am–dusk; flagstone paths on park's periphery open 24 hrs.*

LaBranche Houses. This complex of lovely town houses, built in the 1830s by Widow LaBranche, fills the half block between Pirate's Alley and Royal and St. Peter streets behind the Cabildo. The house on the corner of Royal and St. Peter streets, with its elaborate, rounded cast-iron balconies, is among the most frequently photographed residences in the French Quarter. ⊠ *700 Royal St., French Quarter.*

Fodor's Choice ★ **The Presbytère.** One of twin Spanish colonial–style buildings flanking St. Louis Cathedral, this one, on the right, was designed to house the priests of the cathedral; instead, it served as a courthouse under the Spanish and later under the Americans. It is now a museum showcasing a spectacular collection of Mardi Gras memorabilia, and displays highlight both the little-known and popular traditions associated with New Orleans's most famous festival. Opened in October 2010, "Living with Hurricanes: Katrina and Beyond" is a $7.5 million exhibition exploring the history, science, and powerful human drama of one of nature's most destructive forces. The building's cupola, destroyed by a hurricane in 1915, was restored in 2005 to match the one atop its twin, the Cabildo.

2

✉ *751 Chartres St., on Jackson Sq., French Quarter* ☎ *504/568–6964* ⊕ *lsm.crt.state.la.us* ✉ *$6* ⊘ *Tues.–Sun. 10-4:30 (last entrance at 4).*

St. Louis Cathedral. The oldest active cathedral in the United States, this iconic church and basilica at the heart of the Old City is named for the 13th-century French king who led two crusades. The current building, which replaced two structures destroyed by fire, dates from 1794 (although it was remodeled and enlarged in 1851). The austere interior is brightened by murals covering the ceiling and stained-glass windows along the first floor. Pope John Paul II held a prayer service for clergy here during his New Orleans visit in 1987; to honor the occasion, the pedestrian mall in front of the cathedral was renamed Place Jean Paul Deux. Of special interest is his portrait in a Jackson Square setting, which hangs on the cathedral inner side wall. Pick up a brochure ($1) for a self-guided tour; books about the cathedral are available in the gift shop. Docents often give free tours.

■ TIP → Nearly every evening in December brings a free concert at the cathedral, in addition to the free concert series throughout the year.

The statue of the Sacred Heart of Jesus dominates St. Anthony's Garden, which extends behind cathedral-basilica to Royal Street. The garden is also the site of a monument to 30 members of a French ship who died in a yellow-fever epidemic in 1857. The garden has been redesigned by famed French landscape architect Louis Benech, who also redesigned the Tuileries gardens in Paris, and impressively restored in 2011. ✉ *615 Père Antoine Alley, French Quarter* ☎ *504/525–9585* ⊕ *www.stlouiscathedral.org* ✉ *Free* ⊘ *Dailiy 7–5.*

WORTH NOTING

Beauregard-Keyes House. This stately 19th-century mansion with period furnishings was the temporary home of Confederate general P.G.T. Beauregard. The house and grounds had severely deteriorated by the 1940s, when the well-known novelist Frances Parkinson Keyes moved in and helped restore it. Her studio at the back of the large courtyard remains intact, complete with family photos, original manuscripts, and her doll, fan, and teapot collections. Keyes wrote 40 novels in this studio, all in longhand, among them local favorite, *Dinner at Antoine's.* The house suffered some roof damage during Katrina, resulting in water stains along the dining room ceiling. Undaunted, the staff has reopened the site and continues its normal tour schedule. If you do not have time to tour the house, take a peek through the gates at the beautiful walled garden at the corner of Chartres and Ursulines streets. Landscaped in the same sun pattern as Jackson Square, the garden is in bloom throughout the year. ✉ *1113 Chartres St., French Quarter* ☎ *504/523–7257* ⊕ *www.bkhouse.org* ✉ *$10* ⊘ *Mon.–Sat. 10–3, tours on the hr.*

1850 House. This well-preserved town house and courtyard provide rare public access beyond the storefronts and into the interior of the exclusive **Pontalba Buildings.** The rooms are furnished in the style of the mid-19th century, when the buildings were built as upscale residences and retail space. Notice the ornate ironwork on the balconies of the apartments: the original owner, Baroness Micaela Pontalba, popularized cast (or molded) iron with these buildings, and it eventually replaced

Micaela Pontalba

Every life has its little dramas, but how many of us can claim a life dramatic enough to inspire an opera? The Baroness Micaela Almonester de Pontalba is in that rarefied number, albeit posthumously. In 2003, on the 200th anniversary of the Louisiana Purchase, the New Orleans Opera Association commissioned an opera based on Pontalba and the mark she left on New Orleans—a legacy you can easily see even now in the Pontalba Buildings, the elegant brick apartments lining Jackson Square.

Micaela Almonester was of Spanish stock, the daughter of the wealthy entrepreneur and developer Don Andres Almonester, who was instrumental in the creation of the Cabildo and Presbytère on Jackson Square. Don Almonester died while Micaela was still young, but not before passing on to his daughter a passion for building and urban design. The rest of her life became a tale of the impact a single will can have upon an urban environment, as well as a tragedy-torn drama of international scope.

At the time of the Louisiana Purchase, in 1803, New Orleans was in cultural upheaval. Following a period under Spanish rule during the late 18th century, the French had reacquired the colony—and merrily sold it to the Americans. The often-complex blending of French and Spanish society was further complicated by the anticipated imposition of American laws and mores, so foreign to the population of New Orleans. Micaela Almonester was right in the middle of the confusion: daughter of Spanish gentry, she fell in love and married a Frenchman, who took her to Paris with his family to avoid coming under American rule in New Orleans.

The Pontalbas' marriage was particularly unhappy, and Micaela's relationship to her in-laws was poisoned by mistrust over family property. Control of her New Orleans inheritance became part of an increasingly bitter feud that included separation from her husband and, at its dramatic pinnacle, her attempted murder by her father-in-law. After the old baron inflicted four gunshot wounds on his daughter-in-law, he committed suicide, believing he had protected his son and his property. But Micaela, now Baroness de Pontalba following the old baron's death, survived her wounds. Within two years, she had recovered enough to conceive the plan for the buildings that bear her name, but a long series of delays, including a bitter divorce, halted the project. Micaela finally returned to New Orleans in the 1840s, in order to direct construction of the elegant apartment buildings that would complete the square her father had been so instrumental in developing during the previous century. The Pontalba Buildings, designed by James Gallier in the French style favored by Micaela, were dedicated in 1851 to great fanfare. Each building (one along each side of Jackson Square) contained 16 grand and lavishly detailed apartments.

Following the dedication of the buildings, Pontalba returned to France. She had been living in Paris for nearly 50 years by now, her children had grown up there, and it had become her home. Yet the pilgrimage she had made to New Orleans, in order to complete a dream in the name of her father's memory, hints that her heart had never really left her childhood home.

2

much of the old handwrought ironwork in the French Quarter. The initials for her families, *A* and *P*—Almonester and Pontalba—are worked into the design. A gift shop and bookstore run by Friends of the Cabildo is downstairs. The Friends of the Cabildo offer an informative two-hour walking tour of the French Quarter ($15; 10 and 1:30) from this location that includes admission to the house tour. ✉ *523 St. Ann St., on Jackson Sq., French Quarter* ☎ *504/524–9118* 💲 *$3* ⊙ *Tues.–Sun. 10–4:30.*

Faulkner House. The young novelist William Faulkner lived and wrote his first book, *Soldiers' Pay,* here in the 1920s. He later returned to his native Oxford, Mississippi, where his explorations of Southern consciousness earned him the Nobel Prize for literature. The house is not open for tours, but the ground-floor apartment Faulkner inhabited is now a bookstore, **Faulkner House Books** (⇨ *Shopping, French Quarter*) specializing in local and Southern writers. ✉ *624 Pirate's Alley, French Quarter* ☎ *504/524–2940* ⊕ *www.faulknerhouse.net* ⊙ *Daily 10–5:30.*

Gallier House. Famous New Orleans architect James Gallier designed this as his family home in 1857. Today it contains an excellent collection of early Victorian furnishings. The tour includes the house, servants' quarters, and a gift shop. ✉ *1132 Royal St., French Quarter* ☎ *504/525–5661* ⊕ *www.hgghh.org* 💲 *$12, combination ticket with Hermann-Grima House $20* ⊙ *Tours Mon., Thurs., and Fri. 10, 11, noon, and 2, Sat. noon, 1, 2, and 3.*

Gauche House. One of the most distinctive houses in the French Quarter, this mansion and its service buildings date from 1856. The cherub design of the effusive ironwork is the only one of its kind. It was once the estate of businessman John Gauche and is still privately owned. This house is not open to the public. ✉ *704 Esplanade Ave., French Quarter.*

Germaine Wells Mardi Gras Museum. During a 31-year period (1937–68), Germaine Cazenave Wells, daughter of Arnaud's restaurant founder Arnaud Cazenave, was queen of Carnival balls a record 22 times for 17 different krewes, or organizations. Many of her ball gowns, in addition to costumes worn by other family members, are on display in this dim, quirky, one-room museum above Arnaud's restaurant. ✉ *Arnaud's restaurant, 813 Bienville St., 2nd fl. (enter through restaurant), French Quarter* ☎ *504/523–5433* ⊕ *www.arnaudsrestaurant.com/mardi-gras-museum* 💲 *Free* ⊙ *Daily during restaurant hrs.*

Haunted House. Locals agree that this is the most haunted house in a generally haunted neighborhood. Most blame the spooks on Madame Lalaurie, a wealthy but ill-fated socialite who lost both parents as a

---

PIRATE'S ALLEY

Pirate's Alley takes its name, in part, from the popular myth that Jean Lafitte met here with General Andrew Jackson before the Battle of New Orleans. During this meeting, Lafitte supposedly made his offer to double-cross the British. The legend apparently has no historical foundation, but its romance was so appealing that the name of the alley (originally Orleans Alley) was officially changed. It's a picturesque way to get from Jackson Square to the shops and galleries of Royal Street.

Continued on page 59

IT'S MARDI GRAS TIME IN NEW ORLEANS!

by Todd Price

Odds are, most of what you know about Mardi Gras is wrong. The bare breasts of Bourbon Street have nothing to do with the real experience—a party steeped in tradition that New Orleanians throw (and pay for) themselves. They generously invite the rest of the world to join in the fun, so hold on to your fairy wings, your tutus, and your beads; things are about to get crazy!

Mardi Gras (French for "Fat Tuesday") is actually the final day of Carnival, a Christian holiday season that begins on the Twelfth Night of Christmas (January 6) and comes crashing to a halt on Ash Wednesday, the first day of Lent. The elite celebrate with private balls, while the rest of the city takes to the streets for weeks of parades and mischief. Don't be shy—after a few moments of astonished gaping, and maybe some Hurricane cocktails, you too will be bebopping to the marching bands, yelling for throws, and draped in garlands of beads.

On Mardi Gras day, New Orleanians don costumes and masks, drink Bloody Marys for breakfast and roam the streets until dark. It's an official city holiday, with just about everyone but the police and bartenders taking the day off. Two of Carnival's most important parades, Zulu and Rex, roll that day before noon, smaller walking crews meander through the side streets, tribes of Mardi Gras Indians emerge in Tremé, and silent bands of skeletons mysteriously appear. For one day, an entire city becomes a surreal, flamboyant party.

(top) Masked revelers get in the Mardi Gras spirit

MARDI GRAS HISTORY

"The Carnival at New Orleans," a wood engraving drawn by John Durkin and published in *Harper's Weekly*, March 1885.

On February 24, 1857, a group of men dressed like demons paraded through the streets of New Orleans in a torch-lighted cavalcade. They called themselves the **Mistick Krewe of Comus**, after the Greek god of revelry. It was the start of modern Mardi Gras.

Based on European traditions, these men formed a secret society and sent 3,000 invitations to a ball held at New Orleans's Gaiety Theater. Many years later, when a 1991 City Council ordinance—later ruled unconstitutional—required all krewes to reveal their members to obtain a parade permit, Comus stopped parading. Its annual ball, however, remains one of the city's most exclusive.

Through the years, other groups of men organized Carnival krewes, each with its own character. In 1872, 40 businessmen founded the School of Design, whose ruler would be dubbed **Rex**. The krewe still parades on Mardi Gras morning and holds its lavish ball Mardi Gras night. Rex and his queen are considered the monarchs of the entire Carnival celebration, and their identities are kept secret until Lundi Gras morning, when their pictures claim the front page of the *Times-Picayune* newspaper.

For many decades, these "old-line" crews were strictly segregated, so other parts of society started their own clubs. The **Zulu Social Aid and Pleasure Club** was organized in 1909 by working-class black men, and they started parading in 1915. Zulu was one of the first krewes to integrate, and today members spanning the racial and economic spectrums parade down St. Charles Avenue on Mardi Gras day, preceding Rex.

Parade standards changed in 1969, when a group of businessmen founded the **Krewe of Bacchus,** named after the god of wine. The sassy group stunned the city with a stupendous show featuring lavish floats that dwarfed the old-line parades. The king was Danny Kaye, not a homegrown humanitarian, as was custom, but a famous entertainer. And you didn't have to be socially prominent—or white—to join the after-party, which they called a rendezvous, not a ball.

The arrival of Bacchus ushered in an era of new krewes with open memberships, including satiric krewes such as **Tucks** and **Muses**, that put on many of today's most popular parades.

PEOPLE STILL TALK ABOUT...

1972: Major parades rolled one last time through the French Quarter's narrow streets.

2000: The 19th century Krewe of Proteus returned after a seven-year hiatus.

2006: Despite the 2005 devastation of Katrina, New Orleanians insisted on holding a smaller (but no less enthusiastic) Mardi Gras.

2010: Saints quarterback Drew Brees reigned as king of Bacchus, tossing Nerf footballs to the crowds a week after winning the Super Bowl.

EXPERIENCE MARDI GRAS

Don't forget your costume! Mardi Gras spectators are often the wackiest.

Carnival parades begin in earnest two weekends before Mardi Gras day, with krewes rolling day and night on the final weekend. Almost all krewes each year select **a different theme**, ranging from the whimsical to hard-edged satire. Off-color jokes and political incorrectness are part and parcel of the subversiveness that characterizes Carnival. Throws will sometimes reflect a parade's theme, which is one reason why locals dive for the cups, doubloons, and other plastic trinkets. The floats and high school marching bands make up the bulk of the parades, with the odd walking club, dance troupe, or convertible car tossed into the mix.

Night parades also have the **flambeaux,** torch-bearing dancers who historically lighted the way for the parades. These days they provide little more than nostalgia and some fancy stepping to the bands, but they still earn tips for their efforts.

There are no day parades Monday, but **Lundi Gras,** literally "Fat Monday,"

has become a major event downtown by the riverfront. Rex and the Zulu King each arrive by boat to greet their subjects and each other. Zulu also hosts free concerts throughout the day. On Mardi Gras day, nearly every corner of New Orleans sees something marvelous, including walking clubs that follow unannounced routes and Mardi Gras Indians who wage mock battles to prove who's the prettiest. Mardi Gras and the Carnival season end with the arrival of Ash Wednesday.

FOR EARLY BIRDS

While most revelers arrive in New Orleans the Friday before Mardi Gras, many major parades actually start earlier in the week. They follow the traditional route down St. Charles Avenue to Canal Street. Note: times might change

Wednesday: Ancient Druids, 6:30 pm

Thursday: Babylon, 5:45 pm; Chaos, 6:30 pm; Muses, 6:30 pm

MARDI GRAS PARADE SCHEDULE

KREWES (EST.)	Rolls	Participants	Claim to fame	Watch for	Prize throws
Hermes (1937)	Friday 6 pm	Local businessmen	Oldest continuous night parade	Large line-up of marching bands	Lighted medallion beads
Le Krewe d'Etat (1996)	Friday 6:30 pm	Sardonic lawyers and well-heeled elites	Led by a dictator instead of a king	The Dictator's "Banana Wagon" pulled by mules	"D'Etat Gazette" with drawings of every float
Morpheus (2000)	Friday 7 pm	Lovers of traditional parades	Youngest parading krewe in New Orleans	Old-school floats and generous throws	Plush moons
Iris (1917)	Saturday 11 am	Upper crust ladies	Oldest all-female krewe	Flirtatious ladies throwing silk flowers	Ceramic beads
Tucks (1969)	Saturday 12 pm	Exuberant and irreverent young men and women	Took name from defunct Friar Tucks bar	Tongue-in-cheek themes	Plastic plungers and stuffed Friar Tucks dolls
Endymion (1966)	Saturday 4:15 pm	Partiers from around the country	Largest Mardi Gras parade; follows a unique route through Mid-City	Massive, spectacular floats and celebrity riders	Plush Endymion mascots
Okeanos (1949)	Sunday 11 am	Civic-minded business leaders	Queen selected by lottery	Trailer carrying a traditional jazz band	Frisbees
Mid-City (1934)	Sunday 11:45 am	Men from Mid-City	First krewe to have "animated" floats	Floats decorated in colored tinfoil	Bags of potato chips
Thoth (1947)	Sunday 12 pm	Guys with a charitable bent	Unique route passes retirement homes and Children's Hospital	Lavishing throws on children	Thoth baseballs
Bacchus (1968)	Sunday 5:15 pm	Devotees of the god of wine	First "superkrewe"	The Bacchagator and King Kong floats	Wine colored "king" doubloons
Proteus (1882)	Monday 5:15 pm	Members of the city's oldest families	Second-oldest krewe	Beautiful floats built on 19th century wagons	Plush seahorses
Orpheus (1993)	Monday 6 pm	Musicians and music lovers of any gender	Founded by singer Harry Connick Jr.	Latest parade technology, including confetti blowers	Stuffed Leviathan with flashing eyes
Zulu (1916)	Tuesday 8 am	Predominantly African American	Oldest African American Mardi Gras parade	Riders in blackface	Hand-painted coconuts
Rex (1872)	Tuesday 10 am	The most elite men in New Orleans society	King of Carnival	Crossing St. Charles to toast Rex mansion	Traditional Rex beads

WHERE TO WATCH THE PARADES

French Quarter side streets offer some degree of refuge while still sustaining a high party pitch.

Canal Street on the edge of the French Quarter is party animal central; mostly tourists.

The corner of **Napoleon and St. Charles** avenues is a crowded but exciting place to watch.

FRENCH QUARTER

CENTRAL BUSINESS DISTRICT

Lee Circle

WAREHOUSE DISTRICT

LOWER GARDEN DISTRICT

UPTOWN

Columns Hotel

UPPER GARDEN DISTRICT

St. Charles Ave

Magazine St

Tchoupitoulas St

Great acoustics under the 610 overpass before **Lee Circle** make this a favorite spot for brass bands.

The **Columns Hotel** front porch provides a good vantage point for those who don't need to catch more beads. It charges a fee for access to its bar and bathrooms.

Energetic (sometimes rowdy) revelers camp out in front of bars between **Jackson Avenue and Lee Circle.**

Most big parades begin Uptown, either at Jefferson Avenue and Magazine Street or Napoleon Avenue and Magazine, turn down St. Charles Avenue toward Canal Street, then follow

Canal to their finish. Although it's chaotic all along the route, Uptown is more family friendly; as you head downtown you'll encounter fewer locals and families and more lewd acts. By Mardi Gras weekend it is difficult to walk down Bourbon Street, where drinking, exchanging

beads, and exhibitionism are popular activities. Unlike in Uptown, where parades are the focal point, downtown the parades seem merely a blip on the screen of general frenzy.

KREWES START HERE

●	Thoth
●	Le Krewe d'Etat
	Mid-City
	Morpheus
	Okeanos
○	Bacchus
	Hermes
	Iris
	Orpheus
	Proteus
	Tucks
●	Rex
●	Zulu

MARDI GRAS TRADITIONS

Indian

Royalty

Dancer

New Orleans's many Carnival traditions often collide on Mardi Gras. Here are some of the characters you're bound to meet.

Mardi Gras Royalty. Each krewe selects monarchs to preside over its parade and ball. In old-line krewes, members choose the king, who is often a prominent local philanthropist and businessman. Super krewes like Bacchus and Endymion pick celebrity kings or grand marshals. Some krewes elect a queen; others have a more elaborate process. To become the reigning woman of the Twelfth Night Revelers, a debutante must find a golden bean in a faux king cake.

Mardi Gras Indians. The African American Mardi Gras Indians began their rituals in the late 19th century in response to being excluded from white Mardi Gras festivities. On Fat Tuesday morning—dressed in intricately beaded and feathered "suits" that often take all year to create—the tribes chant songs and square off in mock battles to decide whose Big Chief is the prettiest. You'll find the Uptown tribes across St. Charles Avenue from the Garden District between Jackson and Washington avenues. Downtown tribes generally meander through Tremé on Ursulines Street.

Dancers. First it was troupes of suburban middle-school girls—dressed a tad too provocatively for their age—that entertained between parade floats. Later, grown women thought this looked fun and created groups like the Pussyfooters and Camel Toe Lady Steppers. Despite the risqué names, many members are lawyers, professors, and other professionals; all members practice choreographed routines for months. In 2010, the 610 Stompers, the first all-male troupe, took to the streets in tight blue gym shorts and red satin jackets. Their motto was "Ordinary Men, Extraordinary Moves."

MARDI GRAS SAFETY

■ Use common sense; don't bring excess cash, valuables, or tempting jewelry.

■ Establish a meeting spot where your family or group will convene at preset times throughout the day.

■ Do not throw anything at the floats or bands, a ticketable and truly hazardous act.

■ You will probably get away with flashing in the French Quarter, but elsewhere you might get ticketed.

■ Be aware that cell phone photos and videos shot on Bourbon Street can wind up on the Internet; think twice before you flash for beads.

■ Each year accidents occur when children (or adults) venture too near the wheels of floats. If you have kids with you, pick a spot some way back from the parade.

MARDI GRAS YEAR-ROUND

A sculptor working on a float at Blaine Kern's Mardi Gras World.

BACKSTREET CULTURAL MUSEUM
This small museum in Tremé chronicles New Orleans's street culture, including the Mardi Gras Indians. Elaborate costumes are on display.

BLAINE KERN'S MARDI GRAS WORLD
Tour the workshop of one of the most prominent Carnival float builders. Floats from previous parades are on display in the warehouse.

GERMAINE WELLS MARDI GRAS MUSEUM
This free Mardi Gras museum is full of photos, masks, and more than two dozen mid-20th-century ball gowns, most worn by Germaine Wells, daughter of the restaurant's founder and queen of more than twenty-two Mardi Gras balls.

PRESBYTERE
Part of the Louisiana State Museum, this historic building on Jackson Square hosts a permanent Mardi Gras exhibit on the second floor.

MARDI GRAS LINGO

King cake: An oval cake decorated with purple, green, and gold sugar and glaze, eaten from January 6—"Twelfth Night"—until Mardi Gras. A plastic baby is hidden inside, and by tradition whoever gets it must buy the next cake.

Krewe: A term used by Carnival organizations to describe themselves, as in Krewe of Iris.

Lundi Gras: French for "Fat Monday," the day before Mardi Gras.

Mardi Gras: "Fat Tuesday" in French; the day before Ash Wednesday and the culmination of the festivities surrounding Carnival season.

Purple, green, and gold: The traditional colors of Mardi Gras (purple represents justice, green faith, and gold power), chosen by the first Rex in 1872.

Throw: Anything tossed off a float, such as beads, plastic cups, doubloons (fake metal coins), or stuffed animals.

"Throw me somethin', mister": Phrase shouted at float riders to get their attention so they will throw you beads.

MARDI GRAS RESOURCES

■ **Arthur Hardy's Mardi Gras Guide** (⊕ www.mardi-grasguide.com).

■ **MardiGras.com** (The *Times-Picayune*) (⊕ www.mardigras.com).

■ **New Orleans Convention and Visitors Bureau** (⊕ www.neworleanscvb.com).

MARDI GRAS DATES

2013 February 12

2014 March 4

2015 February 17

2016 February 9

child, then two husbands before finding a third and moving with him into this mansion on Royal Street. Madame Lalaurie fell out with society when a fire in her attic exposed atrocious treatment of her slaves: according to newspaper reports, well-intentioned neighbors who rushed into the house found seven mutilated slaves in one of the apartments. Madame Lalaurie fled town that night, but occupants of the house have told of hauntings ever since. One tour guide claims that when clients faint from the heat it is always by this house, and that cameras often mysteriously refuse to function when pointed at the house, which is not open to the public. ⊠ *1140 Royal St., French Quarter.*

> ### TALK OF THE TOWN
>
> Although it's just two blocks away from Bourbon Street in the French Quarter, Burgundy Street is not pronounced like the wine (New Orleanians say "bur-GUN-dee" instead). And if you trot out your high school French to ask for directions to Chartres Street, a bemused local will probably ask if you mean "CHAW-tuhs." Farther uptown, the streets named for the muses offer more challenges: Calliope ("CAL-ee-ope") and Melpomene ("MELL-pa-meen").

Jean Lafitte National Park Visitor Center. This center has free visual and sound exhibits on the customs of various communities throughout the state, as well as information-rich daily riverfront tours called "history strolls." The one-hour daily tour leaves at 9:30 am; tickets are handed out one per person (you must be present to get a ticket), beginning at 9 am, for that day's tour only. Arrive at least 15 minutes before tour time to be sure of a spot. The office also supervises and provides information on Jean Lafitte National Park Barataria Unit, a nature preserve (complete with alligators) across the river from New Orleans, and the Chalmette Battlefield, where the Battle of New Orleans was fought in the War of 1812. Each year in January, near the anniversary of the battle, a reenactment is staged at the Chalmette site. You'll need a car to visit the preserve or the battlefield. ⊠ *419 Decatur St., French Quarter* ☎ *504/589–2636* ⊕ *www.nps.gov/jela* ☼ *Daily 9–5.*

Lafitte's Blacksmith Shop. The striking anvil no longer sounds in this ancient building, the oldest bar in the Quarter. You'll hear only the clinking of glasses at this well-loved bar that's a favorite for locals and tourists from all walks of life. Legend has it that the pirate Jean Lafitte and his cronies operated a blacksmith shop here as a front for their vast illicit trade in contraband. The building, dating from 1772 and thus a rare survivor of the 18th-century French Quarter fires, is interesting as one of the few surviving examples of soft bricks reinforced with timber, a construction form used by early settlers. A fresh application of exterior plaster protects the soft brick and brightens a facade that long stood weather-beaten. Despite the addition of a few flat-screen TVs, a drink here just after sundown, when the place is lit only by candles, lets you slip back in time for an hour or so. ⊠ *941 Bourbon St., French Quarter* ☎ *504/593–9761* ⊕ *www.lafittesblacksmithshop.com.*

Latrobe House. Architect Henry Latrobe designed this modest house with Arsene Latour in 1814. Its smooth lines and porticoes started a passion for Greek Revival architecture in Louisiana, evidenced later in many plantation houses upriver as well as in a significant number of buildings in New Orleans. This house, believed to be the earliest example of Greek Revival in the city, is not open to the public. ✉ *721 Governor Nicholls St., French Quarter.*

Louisiana Supreme Court Building. The imposing Victorian building that takes up the whole block of Royal Street between St. Louis and Conti streets is the Old New Orleans Court, erected in 1908. Later it became the office of the Wildlife and Fisheries agency. After years of vacancy and neglect, this magnificent edifice was restored and reopened in 2004 and is now the elegant home of the Louisiana Supreme Court. ✉ *400 Royal St., French Quarter.*

Michalopoulos Galleries. One of New Orleans's most beloved artists, James Michalopoulos exhibits his expressionistic visions of New Orleans architecture in this small gallery. Michalopoulos's palette-knife technique of applying thick waves of paint invariably brings van Gogh to mind—but his vision of New Orleans, where no line is truly straight and every building appears to have a soul, is uniquely his own. His work has become a prized adornment of many a New Orleanian's walls. Michalopoulos was commissioned to create the official poster of the New Orleans Jazz and Heritage Festival in 1998, 2001, 2003, 2006, and 2009, bringing a new perspective to some of New Orleans's greatest musicians: Mahalia Jackson, Louis Armstrong, Dr. John, and Fats Domino. ✉ *617 Bienville St., French Quarter* ☎ *504/558–0505* ⊕ *www.michalopoulos.com* ☉ *Mon.–Sat. 10–6, Sun. 11–6.*

☾ **Musée Conti Wax Museum.** The history of New Orleans and Louisiana unfolds in colorful vignettes in this kitschy but fun museum. Local legends are captured life-size at seminal moments: Madame Lalaurie discovered torturing her slaves; Napoléon in his bathtub, arguing with his brothers over the Louisiana Purchase; Marie Laveau selling gris-gris to downtown customers; the Duke and Duchess of Windsor attending a Mardi Gras ball. Written and audio explanations supplement the visual scenes. A miniature Mardi Gras parade fills one corridor. The museum is an enjoyable way to acquaint yourself and your children with New Orleans history, although the history depicted here tends toward the sensational and the occasionally unsubstantiated. ✉ *917 Conti St., French Quarter* ☎ *504/525–2605 or 800/233–5405* ⊕ *www. neworleanswaxmuseum.com* ⊡ *$7* ☉ *Mon., Fri., Sat. 10–4.*

New Orleans Historic Voodoo Museum. A large collection of artifacts and information on voodoo as it was—and still is—practiced in New Orleans is here in a two-room, rather homegrown museum. Items on display include portraits by and of voodoo legends, African artifacts believed to have influenced the development of the religion, and lots of gris-gris (bundles with magical ingredients). The gift shop sells customized gris-gris, potions, and handcrafted voodoo dolls. ✉ *724 Dumaine St., French Quarter* ☎ *504/680–0128* ⊕ *www.voodoomuseum.com* ⊡ *$7* ☉ *Daily 10–6.*

New Orleans Jazz National Historical Park. In 1987, the U.S. Congress declared jazz a "national American Treasure," and in the following

2

years, the New Orleans Jazz National Historical Park was created to preserve and display that treasure. The park offers free performances and educational events in three locations around the French Quarter: the Vistor Center, Perseverance Hall in **Louis Armstrong Park**, and the newly renovated third floor of the **Old U.S. Mint**. Four of the park's rangers are also working musicians, including local favorite Bruce "Sunpie" Barnes; don't miss the chance to catch their lively and informative demonstrations exploring the full range of Louisiana's musical heritage. Saturday mornings at 11, kids can sit in and jam with master musicians at Perseverance Hall. Call for event times and locations. ⊠ *Visitor Center, 916 N. Peters St., French Quarter* ☎ *504/589–4841* ⊕ *www. nps.gov/jazz* ☜ *Free* ☉ *Visitor Center Tues.–Sun. 9–5; Old U.S. Mint Tues.–Sun. 10–4; Perseverance Hall in Louis Armstrong Park, Sat. 9–5.*

New Orleans Pharmacy Museum. This building was the apothecary shop and residence of Louis J. Dufilho, America's first licensed pharmacist with his own shop, in the 1820s. His botanical and herbal gardens are still cultivated in the courtyard. To tour the musty shop is to step back into 19th-century medicine. Even the window display, with its enormous leech jar and other antiquated paraphernalia, is fascinating. Watch for free 19th-century seasonal health tips posted in the front window. ⊠ *514 Chartres St., French Quarter* ☎ *504/565–8027* ⊕ *www. pharmacymuseum.org* ☜ *$5* ☉ *Tues.–Thurs. 10–2, Fri. and Sat. 10–5.*

Old Ursuline Convent. The Ursulines were the first of many orders of religious women who came to New Orleans and founded schools, orphanages, and asylums and ministered to the needs of the poor. Their original convent was built in 1734 and is now the oldest French-colonial building in the Mississippi Valley, having survived the disastrous 18th-century fires that destroyed the rest of the Quarter. **St. Mary's Church,** adjoining the convent, was added in 1845. The original tract of land for a convent, school, and gardens covered several French Quarter blocks. Now an archive for the archdiocese, the convent was used by the Ursulines for 90 years. The Ursuline Academy, the convent's girls' school founded in 1727, is now Uptown on State Street, where the newer convent and chapel were built. The academy is the oldest girls' school in the country. The Old Ursuline Convent is open to the public for self-guided tours Monday through Saturday. ⊠ *1100 Chartres St., French Quarter* ☎ *504/529–2651* ☜ *$5* ☉ *Mon.–Sat. 10–4.*

Pontalba Buildings. Baroness Micaela Pontalba built these twin sets of town houses, one on each side of Jackson Square, in the late 1840s; they are known for their ornate cast-iron balcony railings. Baroness Pontalba's father was Don Almonester, who sponsored the rebuilding of St. Louis Cathedral in 1788. The strong-willed Miss Almonester also helped fund the landscaping of the square and the erection of the Andrew Jackson statue in its center. The Pontalba Buildings are publicly owned; the side to the right of the cathedral, on St. Ann Street, is owned by the state, and the other side, on St. Peter Street, by the city. On the state-owned side is the **1850 House,** and at 540-B St. Peter Street on the city-owned side is a plaque marking this apartment as that of Sherwood Anderson, writer and mentor to William Faulkner. ⊠ *French Quarter.*

Quadroon Ballroom. In the early 1800s, the wooden-rail balcony extending over Orleans Street was linked to a ballroom where free women of color met their French suitors. The quadroons (technically, people whose racial makeup was one-quarter African) who met here were young, unmarried women of legendary beauty. A gentleman would select a favorite beauty and, with her mother's approval, buy her a house and support her as his mistress. The sons of these unions, which were generally maintained in addition to legal marriages with French women, were often sent to France to be educated. This practice, known as *plaçage*, was unique to New Orleans at the time. The Quadroon Ballroom later became part of a convent and school for the Sisters of the Holy Family, a religious order founded in New Orleans in 1842 by the daughter of a quadroon to educate and care for African-American women. The ballroom itself is not open to visitors, but a view of the balcony from across the street is enough to set the historical stage. ⊠ *Bourbon Orleans Hotel, 717 Orleans St., 2nd fl., French Quarter.*

Rodrigue Studio. Cajun artist George Rodrigue began his career as a painter with moody yet stirring portraits of rural Cajun life, but he gained popular renown in 1984 when he started painting blue dogs, inspired by the spirit of his deceased pet, Tiffany. Since then, the blue dog has found thousands of manifestations in various settings in the cult artist's paintings. Of late, Rodrigue has ventured a few new non-blue-dog works, which, after nearly two decades of singular focus, seems like a radical move. Rodrigue's principal gallery, a single room rather eerily lined almost entirely with paintings of the blue dog (and her evil red twin), sits directly behind St. Louis Cathedral. ⊠ *730 Royal St., French Quarter* ☎ *504/581–4244* ⊕ *www.georgerodrigue.com* ☉ *Daily 10–6.*

THE RIVERFRONT

Development along Decatur Street can make this strip feel like a commercial corridor, but some of the best of old New Orleans is still here, picturesque as ever and just as classic: the mighty Mississippi River, Café du Monde, and the French Market. You'll find the best of the new—Audubon's Insectarium and Aquarium of the Americas—here as well.

Gaze across the Mississippi River from the French Quarter, and you'll get a sense of the geography of the city and of how it all began: as a port city that would open the gateway for goods to make their way from the old world into the new America and out in reverse. Turn around, and take in a city skyline that, too, combines the old and the new—where cathedral spire and stately European-style apartment residence nod and bow like good neighbors to modern, spindly bridge and stalwart hotel-and-condo high-rise.

TOP ATTRACTIONS

Fodor's Choice ★

Aquarium of the Americas. Power failures during Katrina resulted in the major loss of the aquarium's collection of more than 7,000 aquatic creatures. In a dramatic gesture of solidarity, aquariums around the country joined together with the Aquarium of the Americas in an effort to repopulate its stock. The museum, now fully reopened, has four major exhibit areas—the Amazon Rain Forest, the Caribbean Reef, the Mississippi River, and the Gulf Coast—all of which have fish and animals native to that environment. A special treat is the Seahorse Gallery, which showcases seemingly endless varieties of these beautiful creatures. The aquarium's spectacular design allows you to feel part of the watery worlds by providing close-up encounters with the inhabitants. A gift shop and café are on the premises.

Woldenberg Riverfront Park, which surrounds the aquarium, is a tranquil spot with a view of the Mississippi. ■TIP➔ **You can combine tickets for the aquarium and Audubon Insectarium** ($33), the aquarium and the **Entergy IMAX Theater** ($28), or all three ($40), but the best deal is the "Audubon Experience": aquarium, IMAX, Insectarium, and **Audubon Zoo** for $35 (tickets are good for 45 days). ✉ *1 Canal St., French Quarter* ☎ *504/581–4629 or 800/774–7394* ⊕ *www.auduboninstitute.org* 🎟 *$21* ☉ *Tues.–Sun. 10–5.*

> **DON'T BET ON IT!**
>
> At some point during your visit to the French Quarter, you are bound to come across someone on the street who will offer you the following wager: "I bet you [insert dollar amount] I know where you got them shoes." It's a con, of course, and an old one at that. The answer is "You got them on your feet in New Orleans, Louisiana."

🐛 **Audubon Insectarium.** Shrink down to ant size and experience "Life Underground," explore the world's insect myth and lore, venture into a Louisiana swamp, and marvel at the hundreds of delicate denizens in the Japanese butterfly garden. Then tour the termite galleries and other sections devoted to the havoc insects wreak so you can sample Cajun-fried crickets and other insect cuisine without a twinge of guilt. All this and more awaits you at the Audubon Insectarium, a $25 million facility that opened in the historic Customs House in 2008. ✉ *423 Canal St., French Quarter* ☎ *800/774–7394* ⊕ *auduboninstitute.org* 🎟 *$16; combined with Aquarium of the Americas $33* ☉ *Tues.–Sun. 10–5.*

French Market. The sounds, colors, and smells here are alluring: street performers, ships' horns on the river, pralines, muffulettas, sugarcane, and Creole tomatoes. Originally a Native American trading post, later a bustling open-air market under the French and Spanish, the French Market historically began at Café du Monde and stretched along Decatur and North Peters streets all the way to the downtown edge of the Quarter. Today the market's graceful arcades have been mostly enclosed and filled with shops and eateries, and the fresh market has been pushed several blocks downriver, under sheds built in 1936 as part of a Works Progress Administration project. This area of the French Market, which begins at Ursulines Street and contains a large **flea market** as well as a farmers' market area and its own praline and food stands, was slated for major renovation even before Katrina tore away its awnings and the 2005 hurricane season devastated the farming communities that provided its produce. Renovations were completed in late 2009, and today, the French Market is a great place to shop for cheap souvenirs, sunglasses, or beads; it's also home to an expanded farmers' market.

DID YOU KNOW?

In the French Quarter, you're never too far from a Lucky Dog, one of New Orleans's most prized before-, during-, or after-drinking snacks. Shaped like a hot dog, the vending carts were immortalized by John Kennedy Toole in *A Confederacy of Dunces*, his Pulitzer prize–winning novel set in New Orleans.

Latrobe Park, a small recreational area at the uptown end of the French Market, honors Benjamin Latrobe, designer of the city's first waterworks. A modern fountain evoking a waterworks marks the spot where Latrobe's steam-powered pumps once stood. Sunken seating, fountains, and greenery make this a lovely place to relax with a drink from one of the nearby kiosks. ⊠ *Decatur St., French Quarter* ⊙ *Shops daily 9–6:30; farmers' market and flea market daily 8–6:30 (hrs may vary depending on season and weather).*

Mississippi River. When facing the river, you see to the right the **Crescent City Connection,** a twin-span bridge between downtown New Orleans and the Westbank, and a ferry that crosses the river every 30 minutes. The river flows to the left downstream for another 100 miles until it merges with the Gulf of Mexico. Directly across the river are the ferry landing and a ship-repair dry dock in a neighborhood called **Algiers Point.** Downriver from the French Quarter, the city is working on grand plans for redeveloping the river adjacent to the Faubourg Marigny and Bywater into riverfront parks and public areas. For now, **Woldenberg Riverfront Park** and **Spanish Plaza** are prime territory for watching everyday life on the Mississippi: steamboats carrying tour groups, tugboats pushing enormous barges, and oceangoing ships.

BORDERLAND

In New Orleans, street medians are known as "neutral grounds." Why? The term evolved in the days following the Louisiana Purchase, when the Europeans and Creoles who inhabited the French Quarter did little to welcome American immigrants into their neighborhood. Americans instead settled outside the city center and established what are now the CBD/Warehouse and Garden districts. Canal Street became the first "neutral ground" in the clash of cultures.

Woldenberg Riverfront Park. This stretch of green from Canal Street to Esplanade Avenue overlooks the Mississippi River as it curves around New Orleans, which inspired the Crescent City moniker. The wooden promenade section in front of Jackson Square is called **Moon Walk,** named for Mayor Moon Landrieu (father of current mayor Mitch Landrieu), under whose administration in the 1970s the riverfront beyond the flood wall was first opened to public view. Today, the French Quarter Festival main stages are located here every April. It's a great place for a rest (or a muffuletta sandwich or café au lait and beignet picnic) after touring the Quarter, and you'll often be serenaded by musicians and amused by street performers. The park is also home to art pieces including the modest **Holocaust Memorial,** with its spiral walkway clad in Jerusalem stone. At the center of the spiral are nine sculptural panels by Jewish artist Yaacov Agam. A statue of local businessman Malcolm Woldenberg, the park's benefactor, is located near *Ocean Song,* local artist John T. Scott's large kinetic sculpture whose wind-powered movements are intended to evoke the patterns of New Orleans music. ⊠ *French Quarter.*

WORTH NOTING

Canal Place. The stores of this upscale shopping and office complex were significantly damaged by looting following Katrina but with the reopening of Saks Fifth Avenue in 2006, the return of the city's signature downtown shopping complex was complete. The **Theatres at Canal Place** offers an upscale moviegoing experience that includes reserved seating and cocktails. ✉ *333 Canal St., French Quarter* ☎ *504/522–9200* ✆ *Mon.– Sat. 10–7, Sun. noon–6.*

Canal Street. At 170 feet wide, Canal Street is the widest main street in the United States and one of the liveliest—particularly during Carnival parades. It was once scheduled to be made into a canal linking the Mississippi River to Lake Pontchartrain; plans changed, but the name remains. In the early 1800s, after the Louisiana Purchase, the French Creoles residing in the French Quarter segregated themselves from the Americans who settled upriver from Canal Street. The communities had separate governments and police systems, and what is now Canal Street—and, most specifically, the central median running down Canal Street—was neutral ground between them. Today, animosities between these two groups are history, but the term "neutral ground" has survived as the name for all medians in the city.

Some of the grand buildings that once lined Canal Street remain, many of them former department stores and businesses now serving as hotels or restaurants. The former home of Maison Blanche (921 Canal St.), once the most elegant of the downtown department stores, is now a **Ritz-Carlton** hotel. One building still serving its original purpose is **Adler's** (722 Canal Street), the city's most elite jewelry and gift store. For the most part, these buildings are faithfully restored, so you can still appreciate the grandeur that once reigned along this fabled strip. ✉ *French Quarter.*

Jackson Brewery. More commonly known as Jax Brewery, this former brew house was remodeled in the 1980s and is now home to a three-section shopping-and-entertainment complex. Outside are multilevel terraces facing the river, and inside are shops, a small museum preserving the history of the brewery, a food court, casual restaurants, and a dance club. ✉ *600 Decatur St., French Quarter* ☎ *504/566–7245* ⊕ *www.jacksonbrewery.com* ✆ *Daily 10–7.*

Old U.S. Mint. Minting began in 1838 in this ambitious Ionic structure, a project of President Andrew Jackson. The New Orleans mint was to

CHESS CHAMPIONS

Frances Parkinson Keyes's historical novel *The Chess Players* is based on the life of Paul Morphy, a New Orleanian considered one of the greatest modern chess masters. The Beauregard-Keyes House was originally built for Morphy's grandfather, and the present location of Brennan's restaurant was once Morphy's residence. If you're interested in challenging a living chess master, stop by Jude Acers' sidewalk table outside the Gazebo Café on Decatur Street. The two-time world-record holder for simultaneous games, Acers is at his table most days and takes on all challengers for a small fee.

provide currency for the South and the West, which it did until Louisiana seceded from the Union in 1861. Both the short-lived Republic of Louisiana and the Confederacy minted coins here. When Confederate supplies ran out, the building served as a barracks, then a prison, for Confederate soldiers; the production of U.S. coins recommenced only in 1879. It stopped again, for good, in 1909. After years of neglect, the federal government handed the Old Mint over to Louisiana in 1966; the state now uses the quarters to exhibit collections of the Louisiana State Museum. At

> ### WHISTLING 'DIXIE'
>
> One popular theory for the origin of the term "Dixie" points back to Citizens Bank of New Orleans, which issued bilingual $10 bank notes bearing the French word "dix" (meaning "ten") on the reverse. The notes thus became known as "dixies," and the term eventually became synonymous with Louisiana, and then with the entire South. Historians are still debating this etymology—but it's a good story nonetheless.

the Barracks Street entrance, notice the one remaining sample of the mint's old walls—it'll give you an idea of the building's deterioration before its restoration. The principal exhibit here is the **New Orleans Jazz Collection,** a brief but evocative tour through the history of traditional New Orleans jazz. The collection has been closed since Katrina, but work continues toward a grand reopening. In the meantime, the second floor houses smaller exhibits on the history of jazz that include some of the hightlights of the collection, such as Louis Armstrong's first cornet. The third floor of the building is now a performance space for the Jazz National Historic Park, offering free performances throughout the week. Check in with the helpful Park Ranger office on the first floor for performance details.

The **Louisiana Historical Center,** which holds the French and Spanish Louisiana archives, is open free to researchers by appointment. At the foot of Esplanade Avenue, notice the memorial to the French rebels against early Spanish rule, the first instance of a New World rebellion against a European power. The rebel leaders were executed on this spot and give nearby Frenchmen Street its name. ⊠ *400 Esplanade Ave., French Quarter* ☎ *504/568–6993* ▣ *Free* ☉ *Tues.–Sun. 10–5.*

Washington Artillery Park. This raised concrete area on the river side of Decatur Street, directly across from Jackson Square, is a great spot to photograph the square and the barges and paddle wheelers on the Mississippi. The cannon mounted in the center and pointing toward the river is a model 1861 Parrot Rifle used in the Civil War. This monument honors the local 141st Field Artillery of the Louisiana National Guard that saw action from the Civil War through World War II. Marble tablets at the base give the history of the group, represented today by the Washington Artillery Association. ⊠ *Decatur St. between St. Peter and St. Ann Sts., French Quarter.*

3

Faubourg Marigny, Bywater, and Tremé

WORD OF MOUTH

"Just the other side of the French Quarter is the Faubourg Marigny district, a secret with locals for quite some time. Lots of smaller historic places to stay, great eats, and local music."

—lilsusiesunshine

GETTING ORIENTED

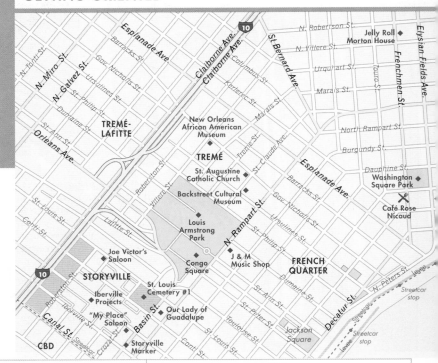

SAFETY

Use common sense when exploring these neighborhoods, especially at night. The Marigny is the safest of the three to explore during daylight hours, and Frenchmen Street is a safe, crowded, nightlife hotspot. Outside of Frenchmen Street, it's best to drive or cab at night. Bywater is mostly safe, but it's next to some rough neighborhoods; it's advisable to travel by car, especially if you're going into the Lower Ninth Ward. The part of Tremé closest to Canal Street is home to the Iberville Projects, an area you'll generally want to steer clear of. Use caution throughout Tremé.

GETTING HERE AND AROUND

The Marigny and Tremé border the French Quarter to the east and north, and are within easy walking distance. The **bus** and **streetcar** will also land you in or around these neighborhoods. Renting bicycles in the French Quarter and the Marigny is a great way to see the area. **Bicycle Michael's** (☎ 504/945–9505 ⊕ www.bicyclemichaels.com) has rentals starting at $25 for a half day; Bob at **Big Easy Bike Tours** (☎ 504/377–0973 ⊕ www.bigeasybiketours.com) gives popular guided tours, starting at $49 for a three-hour excursion.

Bywater is a little farther out, past the Marigny to the east. It makes most sense to drive or take the bus or a cab. The **No. 5 Marigny/Bywater bus** runs along the south edge (riverside) of the French Quarter, out to the far edge of Bywater. The **No. 88 St. Claude/Jackson Barracks bus** runs along the north edge (lakeside) of the French Quarter all the way into the Lower Ninth Ward. The ride from the French Quarter takes about 15 minutes.

TOP REASONS TO GO

Explore Frenchmen Street. This bustling strip of bars, clubs, restaurants, cafés, and shops is the heart of the Marigny. At night, this is *the* place to hear live music and watch eccentric street artists.

Experience the birthplace of jazz. Tremé is fertile ground for New Orleans musical traditions. Visit the site of Congo Square, where jazz was born (now in Louis Armstrong Park), or drop by the Backstreet Cultural Museum.

Discover the Bywater arts scene. This neighborhood is an enclave of artists, musicians, and creative outliers, and you'll see it in everything from the decorated cars and funky boutiques to the intricate street art that adorns the sides of warehouses and buildings.

Enjoy the Marigny architecture. In 1974 the entire Marigny neighborhood was added to the National Register of Historic Places, and 25 years later was awarded the distinguished "Great Places in America" designation by the American Planning Association.

MAKING THE MOST OF YOUR TIME

The Marigny and Tremé are easy to visit from the French Quarter. At night, Frenchmen Street is *the* place for live music. In Bywater, spend some time exploring galleries, parks, cafés, and vintage stores. At night, off-the-beaten-path bars, restaurants, and music clubs light up.

QUICK BITES

Café Rose Nicaud. The sidewalk tables are for people-watching at this café serving coffee and tea, sandwiches, salads, pastries, and hot breakfast. ⊠ *632 Frenchmen St., Faubourg Marigny* ☎ *504/949–3300* ☉ *Daily 7–6.*

Schiro's Café and Julie's Little India Kitchen. A combination café, bar, restaurant, grocery store, Laundromat, and five-bedroom guesthouse, Schiro's is a funky and beloved all-purpose neighborhood hangout. ⊠ *2483 Royal St., Faubourg Marigny* ☎ *504/944–6666* ☉ *Weekdays 11–9:30, Sat. 9 am–9:30 pm, Sun. 9–3.*

Sightseeing
★★

Dining
★★

Lodging
★

Shopping
★★

Nightlife
★★★★

From Tremé's musical history, to the edgy alternative-arts scene in Bywater, to the bohemian comingling of the two in the Marigny, these three neighborhoods may look like only sleepy rows of houses crowded up against pothole-riddled streets, but they continue to be the driving engines for much of the most innovative and energetic creative work in New Orleans. Thanks to a remarkable mixture of old New Orleans families and newly transplanted musicians and artists, a terrific mixture of historic legacy and new energy thrives here.

Updated
by Troy
Thibodeaux

With that said, it's important to remember that these are still largely working-class neighborhoods. That's part of the magic and authenticity of these areas (and one reason that artists and musicians flock here), but it also means that you'll likely encounter some rougher stretches of inner-city neighborhoods mixed in with the 19th-century homes that hearken back to a long and rich history.

The Marigny, with its famous Creole cottages, is one of the earliest neighborhoods in the city, formed in 1805 when the young Bernard Xavier Philippe de Marigny de Mandeville embarked on what is now practically an American pastime—creating subdivisions. Marigny's other famous contribution to American culture is the introduction of the dice game craps. He apparently had more enthusiasm for the game than luck in it and was eventually forced to sell his plantation off in small plots, creating what was at first a French-speaking suburb, but soon overflowed with Caribbean, German, and Irish immigrants. By the early-20th-century Spanish and Italian immigrants were flocking into this downtown neighborhood as well.

Tremé, meanwhile, is steeped in black history. Built and populated largely by free people of color, the neighborhood is home to Congo Square (now Louis Armstrong Park), which was a gathering place for slaves. French and Spanish colonial tradition often allowed for slaves to have Sundays off, and Congo Square is where they gathered to play music, dance, and set up a marketplace. This remarkable yet troubling setting is the birthplace of jazz. The Tomb of the Unknown Slave, with its rusty chains and shackles dangling from a large metal cross, sits on the grounds of nearby St. Augustine Catholic Church and is a haunting reminder of that violent legacy.

Bywater, similar to the Marigny, was formed from subdivided plantation land and populated largely by Caribbean Creoles and French colonialists during the Haitian revolution. Now crisscrossed with train tracks and bordered by an industrial canal and the Mississippi River with its waterfront docks and warehouses, the neighborhood has a more industrial vibe than many other parts of the city.

Next door to Bywater, just across the Industrial Canal bridge, is the Lower Ninth Ward, which was the most devastated of all New Orleans neighborhoods during Hurricane Katrina and the levee failures. Signs of the storm remain all across the city, but nowhere more so than in this area, still blighted with empty lots, boarded-up houses, and broken roads.

In the wake of such hardships, however, these neighborhoods have emerged as interlinked vibrant communities and cultural touchstones. Filled with New Orleans treasures—architectural, historical, musical, and artistic—this area is now the heart of a renewed creative energy, evident in everything from the rebuilding of houses along the canal's floodwall to the live music flowing out the doors of neighborhood clubs. From the splendor of Mardi Gras Indians dancing in the streets of Tremé to the ripples of heat rising off sand-cast glass sculptures at Studio Inferno in Bywater, this is perhaps one of the most distinctive strings of neighborhoods you'll find anywhere in the nation.

FAUBOURG MARIGNY

The Faubourg Marigny (pronounced FOE-berg MAR-ah-Nee, and mostly just referred to as "The Marigny") is made up of two distinct sections. The Marigny Triangle is the trendy area, with the Frenchmen Street commercial district on the border of the French Quarter. Maze-like streets here are lined with beautiful cottages, Creole plantation homes, and charming guesthouses. You'll have no problem finding great restaurants, bars, music clubs, and hip shops.

On the other side of Elysian Fields Avenue, the Marigny Rectangle begins. With architectural styles ranging from classic Creole cottage to Victorian mansion, the streets are more peaceful and the residents more bohemian—what the French Quarter used to be like 20 years ago. On the far end of this neighborhood, along Franklin Avenue, you'll find another cluster of terrific spots like Mimi's, Feelings Café, and the remarkable institution that is Schiro's Café and Julie's Little India Kitchen (⇨ *See Quick Bites*).

TOP ATTRACTIONS

Fodor's Choice ★ **Frenchmen Street.** The street's three-block stretch closest to the French Quarter is where it's at, complete with cafés, bars, and music clubs. While the true magic happens come nightfall—when live music spills from the doorways of clubs and crowds gather for street performers—it is still a great daytime destination. ⊠ *Frenchmen St. between Decatur and Dauphine Sts., Faubourg Marigny.*

New Orleans Healing Center. This new community center sets an ambitious goal for itself: "To provide a holistic, safe, sustainable center that heals, fulfills, and empowers the individual and the community, and to become a model for urban, community healing around the world." To that end, this innovative collaboration (not to mention the innovative construction of the center) includes more than a dozen of New Orleans' most progressive (and intriguing) organizations. Visitors can check out everything from the Wild Lotus Yoga Studio to the Crossroads Art Bazaar, from the Café Istanbul Performance Hall to the Island of Salvation Botanica, which is the famous voodoo shop run by the internationally renowned priestess Sallie Ann Glassman. This is a great place to explore and touch base with the spiritual side of New Orleans. ⊠ *2372 St. Claude Ave., Faubourg Marigny* ⊕ *www.neworleanshealingcenter.org.*

WORTH NOTING

American Aquatic Gardens. A commercial nursery and boutique gift shop, this small but wonderfully relaxing garden invites walks past grasses, reeds, flowers, and sculptures. Trees and fences that once shadowed some of the displays were lost during Katrina, but the sound of water still surrounds visitors, and the grounds remain a tranquil retreat from the city for gardening enthusiasts and backyard snoozers alike. ⊠ *621 Elysian Fields, Faubourg Marigny* ☎ *504/944–0410* ⊕ *www. americanaquaticgardens.com* ⊙ *Daily 9–4.*

OFF THE BEATEN PATH **Jelly Roll Morton House.** Jazz enthusiasts will want to follow Frenchmen Street beyond the borders of the Marigny to pay homage to Jelly Roll Morton at the pianist and composer's modest former home, now a private residence with nary a plaque to suggest its import. Morton was a Creole of color (free African-American of mixed race), a clear distinction from darker blacks in those days; Morton himself always explained his roots as French. Though rather affluent when Morton lived here, the neighborhood has since declined—plan to take a car or taxi here. ⊠ *1443 Frenchmen St., Seventh Ward.*

New Orleans Center for Creative Arts (*NOCCA*). Many of New Orleans's most talented musicians, artists, and writers have passed through this high school arts program on their way to fame, including Harry Connick Jr., the Marsalis brothers, Donald Harrison, and Terence Blanchard. More than just a beautiful campus built along the Marigny's industrial riverfront area, NOCCA hosts a year-round schedule of celebrated performances, showings, and events open to the public. ⊠ *2800 Chartres St., Faubourg Marigny* ☎ *504/940–2787* ⊕ *www.nocca.com.*

Venusian Gardens and Art Gallery. This former 19th-century historic church building now serves as Eric Ehlenberger's otherworldly art studio, gallery, and event space, displaying his luminous sculptures and

CAFÉ CULTURE

Frenchmen Street, and the Marigny in general, is full of outdoor bars and cafés that make perfect perches for watching the eclectic street life. Café Rose Nicaud (pictured) is named for the free woman of color who was the originator of the New Orleans coffee stands.

dioramas. Take a stroll beneath a sea of glowing jellyfish or bask in a neon-lit landscape. ✉ *2601 Chartres St., Faubourg Marigny* ☎ *504/943–7446* ⊕ *www.venusian gardens.com* ⊗ *Weekdays 10–4; appointments preferred.*

Washington Square Park. This park provides a large green space in which to play Frisbee or catch some sun. During the recovery period following the storm, relief groups created a campground here, offering free food and music. The far side of the park borders Elysian Fields, named for Paris's Champs-Élysées. Though it never achieved the grandeur of its French counterpart, Elysian Fields is a major thoroughfare. Small-scale festivals or events sometimes take place in Washington Square, which is the only city public space with a French-style double alley of oaks. ✉ *Bordered by Royal, Dauphine, and Frenchmen Sts. and Elysian Fields, Faubourg Marigny.*

> ## HUBIG'S PIES
>
> Local culinary delights almost unknown outside the city are the fried fruit turnovers made by Hubig's Pies on Dauphine Street in the Marigny. Simon Hubig founded the bakery in Fort Worth, Texas, and the New Orleans plant was just one member of the chain. Forced by the Depression to close the other locations, Hubig held on to the New Orleans plant alone and brought on the current proprietors as partners. The pies are available in corner groceries around town.

BYWATER

Bywater, a crumbling yet beautiful old neighborhood east of the train tracks at Press Street, is a haven to those musicians and artists who find the Marigny too expensive and crowded. The Mississippi River runs the length of its boundary, and the bars and coffee shops scattered around the neighborhood combine elements of its working-class roots and more recent hipster influx for a lively and distinctly local experience. Although you won't find the head-swiveling density of sights here that you will in the French Quarter, a tour through Bywater gives you a feel for New Orleans as it lives day to day, in a colorful, overgrown, slightly sleepy cityscape reminiscent of island communities and tinged with a sense of perpetual decay.

TOP ATTRACTIONS

Alternative Art Spaces. Bywater is home to dozens of alternative art spaces, many of which have banded together under the loose umbrella of the St. Claude Arts District (SCAD). From old candle factories to people's living rooms, this burgeoning scene—centered around St. Claude Avenue and nearby streets—is producing some of the most intriguing and innovative work in the city, with several major artists and arts organizations involved. In addition to gallery space, several independent theater spaces have sprung up as well, offering venues for live performances, magic and burlesque shows, fringe theater, and more. The second Saturday of each month is opening night when galleries and venues host new shows and parties. ✉ *Bywater* ⊕ *www.scadnola.com.*

An artist works on a Mardi Gras mural that's right at home in the colorful Marigny neighborhood.

WORTH NOTING

Christopher Porché-West Galerie. Legendary independent photographer Christopher Porché-West operates out of this working studio and exhibit space. The atmosphere depends on the current focus and vigor of Porché-West's activities; sometimes it is more work-oriented, sometimes more formally set up for exhibits of his work or of other artists. The gallery occupies an old pharmacy storefront, and it is open whenever the artist happens to be in, or by appointment (he's almost always nearby). ⊠ *3201 Burgundy St., Bywater* ☎ *504/947–3880.*

Dr. Bob. This small compound of artists' and furniture-makers' studios includes the headquarters of Dr. Bob, beloved local folk artist whose easily recognizable work can be found hanging all across New Orleans. "Be Nice or Leave," "Shalom, Ya'll," and "Shut Up and Fish" are just a few of his popular themes. Dr. Bob's shop is chock-full of original furniture, colorful signs, and unidentifiable objects of artistic fancy. Prices start at $30 for a small "Be Nice" and most pieces are in the $200–$500 range. The sign outside advertises the open hours: "By chance or appointment." ⊠ *3027 Chartres St., Bywater* ☎ *504/945–2225.*

Mercury Injection Studio Arts. Glassworks, mirrors, sculptures, and paintings fill this tiny studio of artist Michael Cain. Michael is usually around, even outside normal operating hours. So don't be discouraged if the doors are closed; knock, and if he's in, you're in for a show as he blows his fanciful pieces into existence. Visits by appointment are also available. ⊠ *727 Louisa St., Bywater* ☎ *504/301–9942 or 504/723–6397* ⊙ *Daily 10–3 or by appointment.*

CLOSE UP

The Lower Ninth Ward

The Lower Ninth Ward has long been a cultural touchstone for New Orleans, generating some of the most venerable artists and colorful traditions in the city. In the wake of post-Katrina flooding, the neighborhood became a touchstone for the whole nation, and indeed the world, as a symbol of tragedy. No neighborhood endured as much destruction or suffering as this low-lying residential stretch that fell victim to the failed levees.

Nowadays, the neighborhood is a very changed place. Signs of the deluge persist—empty lots where houses were literally swept off their foundations, boarded-up buildings with overgrown weeds and an eerie quiet—but signs of life and renewed vigor show, too. A slow but steady rebuilding effort by hard-hit locals joined by aid organizations and volunteers is reclaiming the landscape one lot at a time. Traditional New Orleans shotgun-style homes are now joined by sleek, raised, modern houses, compliments of the Brad Pitt–led efforts of Project Pink and the Make it Right Foundation. In addition, groups like Habitat for Humanity and Global Green have embarked on innovative and environmentally sustainable rebuilding projects in and around this neighborhood, such as the New Orleans Musicians Village and the Holy Cross Project.

One of the most fascinating and heart-warming locations in the neighborhood, however, has to be the **House of Dance and Feathers** (✉ *1317 Tupelo St.* ☎ *504/957-2678*). This tiny backyard museum is a labor of love for community character Ronald Lewis, a retired streetcar conductor. Formed almost by accident (after his wife threw his extensive collection

of Mardi Gras Indian and second-line paraphernalia out of the house and into the yard), this small glass-paneled building is a treasure trove of Mardi Gras Indian lore and local legend. Intricately beaded panels from Indian costumes, huge fans and plumes of feathers dangling from the rafters, and photographs cover almost every available inch of wall space.

Lewis, who, among many other things, can list "president of the Big Nine Social and Pleasure Club" and "former Council Chief of the Choctaw Hunters" on his résumé, is a qualified and dedicated historian whose vision and work have become a rallying point for a hardscrabble neighborhood.

The Lower Ninth Ward is not the safest area of New Orleans, and we advise you to visit during the day in a car or with a tour. One safe and informative way to learn about Hurricane Katrina's effect on the city, including the Lower Ninth Ward, is to sign up for a bus tour offered by **Grayline Tours** (☎ *504/569-1401 or 800/535-7786*). For those visitors interested in contributing to the ongoing recovery of the neighborhood and city, the Louisiana Serve Commission's website (⊕ *www.volunteerlouisiana. gov*) has a section about opportunities to volunteer while on vacation called "Voluntourism" that can link you up with numerous opportunities.

A unique Creole cottage in Tremé, across the street from the Backstreet Cultural Museum.

Studio Inferno Glassworks. Famous for their New Orleans–themed glasswork, flaming hearts, and innovative designs, artists at this working studio give demonstrations of glass casting in a spacious red warehouse in the heart of Bywater. You can also see the artists at local festivals and events, including Jazz Fest, where they have been a popular feature for years. The gallery–gift shop is a wonderland of vivid color and design. ✉ *3000 Royal St., Bywater* ☎ *504/945–1878* ⏰ *Mon.–Sat. 10–4.*

TREMÉ

Just across Rampart Street from the French Quarter, you'll find the Tremé neighborhood (pronounced truh-MAY), one of the oldest and most significant neighborhoods in the city, and perhaps even in the country. The sleepy rows of cottages, churches, and corner stores belie the raucous historical and musical legacy of this area. This is the birthplace of jazz after all, not to mention the site of the old Congo Square gathering place for African and Caribbean slaves, and the location of the fabled Storyville red-light district. Through its many incarnations, it has always remained true to its heritage as one of the oldest African American neighborhoods in the nation. Now the focus of a popular HBO television series (which you might encounter filming in the neighborhood), Tremé continues to be one of the great driving forces in the musical culture of New Orleans.

TOP ATTRACTIONS

★ **Backstreet Cultural Museum.** Since 1999 when the Backstreet Cultural Museum opened its doors, it has become a focal point of Mardi Gras Indian, parade, and second-line culture in the city. Local photographer

The Tremé Brass Band marches in the Day of the Dead second-line parade, on Claiborne Avenue.

and self-made historian Sylvester Francis is an enthusiastic guide through this rich collection of Mardi Gras Indian costumes and other musical artifacts tied to the street traditions of New Orleans, and the museum hosts traveling and featured exhibits in addition to its permanent collection. Sylvester is also an excellent source for current musical goings-on in Tremé and throughout town. ⊠ *1116 St. Claude St., Tremé* ☎ *504/522–4806* ⊕ *www.backstreetmuseum.org* ✉ *$8* ☉ *Tues.– Fri. 10–5, Sat. 10–4.*

New Orleans African American Museum. Set in a historic villa surrounded by a lovely small park and gardens, this terrific museum is a prime example of the West Indies–style, French colonial architecture that used to fill much of the French Quarter. The house was built in 1829 by Simon Meilleur, a prosperous brick maker: the main house was constructed with Meilleur's bricks, and the brick patio behind it bears imprints identifying the original manufacturer. A year-round calendar of events and exhibits spotlight African and African diaspora art and artists. Museum-sponsored bus and walking tours of historic Tremé are a great way to see and learn about this neighborhood. ⊠ *1418 Governor Nicholls St., Tremé* ☎ *504/566–1136* ⊕ *www.noaam.org* ✉ *$7* ☉ *Wed.–Sat. 11–4 and by appointment.*

St. Louis Cemetery No. 1. Just one block from the French Quarter, St. Louis Cemetery No. 1 is the oldest and most famous of New Orleans's cities of the dead. Its stately rows of crypts are home to many of the city's most legendary figures, including Homer Plessy of the *Plessy vs. Ferguson* 1896 U.S. Supreme Court decision establishing the separate but equal "Jim Crow" laws, and voodoo queen Marie Laveau, whose

CLOSE UP

HBO's Treme

The Tremé neighborhood has always held a special place in the hearts of musicians and musical historians for its role in the development of jazz and other African American musical traditions, but it wasn't until more recently that the neighborhood captured the imagination of a much wider audience, thanks to the HBO series *Treme*. In the wake of Hurricane Katrina and the levee failures that inundated New Orleans, the award-winning team of David Simon and Eric Overmyer (*The Wire*) decided to turn their lens on the Crescent City. They found the ornate and deeply rooted traditions of working class Tremé to be the perfect focal point for the larger story of recovery and perseverance in New Orleans. With its third season set to air in fall 2013, *Treme* is widely regarded as one of the best and most accurate representations of New Orleans ever captured on film—which is no small feat for anyone trying to render the intricacies of the social, cultural, musical, political, and socioeconomic dynamics of this city.

"The aesthetic has an anthropological quality," says Henry Griffin, a New Orleans writer, filmmaker, and professor who plays a character in the series based loosely on himself. "They're trying to re-create an exact period of history: the years right after the storm."

To that end, the producers employ a small army of local writers, fact-checkers, and historians to help ensure the script and scene work are as accurate and realistic as possible. The casting team uses locals whenever possible, and the location scouts and set producers go to remarkable lengths to ensure the authenticity of sets, props, and costumes. "What really sets

it apart," Griffin says, "is that other shows or films about New Orleans are always made for a bigger audience first, and then later the directors might consider what locals think of it. *Treme*, on the other hand, is made for New Orleans first, and then developed for the wider audience."

The show has cast a spotlight on many of New Orleans's underground spots. Suddenly, crowds of music lovers swell on Tuesday nights to catch Kermit Ruffins performing at **Bullets Sports Bar** (⌂ *2441 AP Tureaud* ☎ *504/948–4003*)—a bar that has long been a staple of Tremé nightlife. Local institutions like Bywater nightclub **Vaughn's** (⌂ *4229 Dauphine St.* ☎ *504/947–5562*), the Mid-City café **Angelo Brocato's** (⌂ *214 N. Carrollton Ave.* ☎ *504/486–1465*), and the French Quarter restaurant **Bayona** (⌂ *430 Dauphine St.* ☎ *504/525–4455*) have also been featured.

Many locals consider Sunday nights, when new episodes air, "*Treme* night." **The R Bar** (⌂ *1431 Royal St.* ☎ *504/948–7499*), in the Marigny, hosts a popular party with its oversized film screen over the bar. Residents also scan Craigslist.com for opportunities to work as extras on the show.

Treme has proved to be a galvanizing creative force in the city of New Orleans, bringing people together to celebrate their own world and traditions. More than that, it's a recognition, a rendering, and a celebration of the perseverance and unique temperament of this city and its denizens in the face of an unprecedented national tragedy—and that has a healing quality all its own.

grave is still a choice destination among the spiritual, the superstitious, and the curious. The Basin Street location of this cemetery is near a downtown housing project, so visitors are advised to exercise great caution when exploring this site. The safest way to visit is to join one of the many group tours that come through each day. The nonprofit group **Save Our Cemeteries** (☏ *504/525–3377*) gives guided tours Friday, Saturday, and Sunday, leaving from the Basin Street Station Visitors Center each morning at 10 am. ✉ *499 Basin St., bounded by Basin, Conti, Tremé, and St. Louis Sts., Tremé* ⊗ *Mon.–Sat. 9–3, Sun. 9–noon.*

WORTH NOTING

J&M Music Shop. A plaque on this 1835 building marks it as the former site of the recording studio that

JAZZ FUNERALS AND SECOND LINES

If you're lucky, you'll get swept up in a jazz street parade during your New Orleans visit. The parades themselves are often referred to as "second lines," a term that originated in the city's jazz funerals. Traditionally, a brass band accompanies a New Orleans funeral procession to the grave site, playing dirges along the way. On the return from the grave, however, the music becomes upbeat, celebrating the departed's passage to heaven. Behind the family, friends, and recognized mourners, a second group often gathers, taking part in the free entertainment and dancing—hence, the "second line."

launched the rock-and-roll careers of such greats as Fats Domino, Jerry Lee Lewis, Little Richard, and Ray Charles. Although the patrons of the laundromat that now resides in this space probably don't pay it much heed, this is one of the most significant musical landmarks in New Orleans. Owned by Cosimo Matassa, the studio operated from 1945 to 1955. ✉ *840 N. Rampart St., Tremé.*

Louis Armstrong Park. There's a certain sad irony to this park. On the one hand, it's a joy to behold, with its huge, lighted gateway entrance and its meandering pathways through 32 acres of grassy knolls, lagoons, and historic landmarks. Elizabeth Catlett's famous statue of Louis Armstrong is joined by other artistic landmarks, such as the bust of Sidney Bechet, and it now houses the New Orleans Jazz National Historical Park. On the other hand, it's often nearly deserted, and as it's bordered by some rough stretches of neighborhood, it's extremely inadvisable to visit after dark. This is unfortunate because the park has the historical significance and the potential to be a wonderful cultural focal point for New Orleans.

To the left inside the park is **Congo Square,** marked by an inlaid-stone space, where slaves in the 18th and early 19th centuries gathered on Sunday, the only time they were permitted to play their music openly. The weekly meetings held here have been immortalized in the travelogues of visitors, leaving invaluable insight into the earliest stages of free musical practices by Africans in America and African Americans. Neighborhood musicians still congregate here at times for percussion jams, and it is difficult not to think of the musical spirit of ancestors hovering over them. Marie Laveau, the greatly feared and respected voodoo queen of antebellum New Orleans, had her home a block away on St. Ann Street and is reported to have held voodoo rituals here regularly.

Behind Congo Square is a large gray building, the **Morris F.X. Jeff Municipal Auditorium;** to the right, behind the auditorium, is the newly renovated **Mahalia Jackson Center for the Performing Arts,** which is home to the New Orleans Opera, the New Orleans Ballet, and hosts an excellent year-round calendar of events—everything from readings to rock concerts. The St. Philip Street side of the park houses the **Jazz National Historical Park,** anchored by **Perseverance Hall,** the oldest Masonic temple in the state. ⚠ Armstrong Park is patrolled by a security detail, but be very careful when wandering, and do not visit after dark. ⊠ *N. Rampart St. between St. Philip and St. Peter Sts., Tremé* ⊗ *Auditorium and performing arts center open by event; check local newspapers for listings.*

Our Lady of Guadalupe, International Shrine of St. Jude (*Old Mortuary Chapel*). Constructed in 1826 to house funerals for victims of the city's yellow-fever epidemics, this chapel is the oldest church building in New Orleans. It was a house of worship for the city's Italian immigrant population in the late 19th and early 20th centuries. In 1935, parishioners began a devotion to St. Jude Thaddeus, patron saint of lost causes. Today, the church serves as the International Shrine of St. Jude, and the faithful make offerings and prayers at St. Jude's statue, which is set in a nook to the left of the altar. In the rear of the chapel, to the right of the entrance, stands the statue of St. Expedite, the only such statue in a North American church, whose devotees claim he is the saint to petition for quick fixes for problems or cures against procrastination. An old (apocryphal) story holds that the nuns of the parish received a crate from Rome containing the statue—no identifying information for the saint it depicts. The word "expedite" was stamped on the shipping crate, so the sisters promptly erected the statue to St. Expedite. ⊠ *411 N. Rampart St., Tremé* ☎ *504/525–1551* ⊕ *www.judeshrine.com.*

St. Augustine Catholic Church. Ursuline nuns donated the land for this church in 1841. Upon its completion in 1842, St. Augustine's became an integrated place of worship; slaves were relegated to the side pews, but free blacks claimed just as much right to center pews as whites did. The architect, J.N.B. de Pouilly, attended the École des Beaux-Arts in Paris and was known for his idiosyncratic style, which borrowed freely from a variety of traditions and resisted classification. Some of the ornamentation in his original drawings was eliminated when money ran out, but effusive pink-and-gold paint inside brightens the austere structure. The church grounds now also house the Tomb of the Unknown Slave, a monument dedicated in 2004 to the slaves buried in unmarked graves in the church grounds and surrounding areas. Following Hurricane Katrina, the Archdiocese of New Orleans planned to close seven churches in the city, including St. Augustine. Public outcry, the church's historical significance, and parishioners' dedication saved the parish, and its 10 am Sunday gospel-jazz services continue. ⊠ *1210 Governor Nicholls St., Tremé* ☎ *504/525–5934* ⊕ *staugustinecatholicchurch-neworleans.org.*

Storyville. The busy red-light district that lasted from 1897 to 1917 has been destroyed, and in its place stands the Iberville Projects, one of New Orleans's infamous public-housing projects. Storyville spawned splendid Victorian homes that served as brothels and provided a venue for the raw sounds of ragtime and early jazz; an extremely young Louis Armstrong cut his teeth in some of the clubs here. The world's first electrically lighted saloon, Tom Anderson's House of Diamonds, was at the corner of Basin and Bienville streets, and the whole area has been the subject of many novels, songs, and films. In 1917, after several incidents involving naval officers, the government ordered the district shut down. Some buildings were razed almost overnight; the housing project was built in the 1930s. Only three structures from the Storyville area remain, the former sites of three saloons: **Lulu White's Saloon** (*237 Basin St.*), **Joe Victor's Saloon** (*St. Louis and Villere sts.*), and **"My Place" Saloon** (*1214 Bienville St.*). Currently, a historical marker on the "neutral ground" (median) of Basin Street is the only visible connection to Alderman Sidney Story's experiment in legalized prostitution. ⊠ *Basin St. next to St. Louis Cemetery No. 1, Tremé.*

CBD and Warehouse District

WORD OF MOUTH

"We went (to Mardi Gras World) last time and found it really interesting to see the workshop where some of the floats are built and to see floats and figures from past Mardi Gras."

—november_moon

GETTING ORIENTED

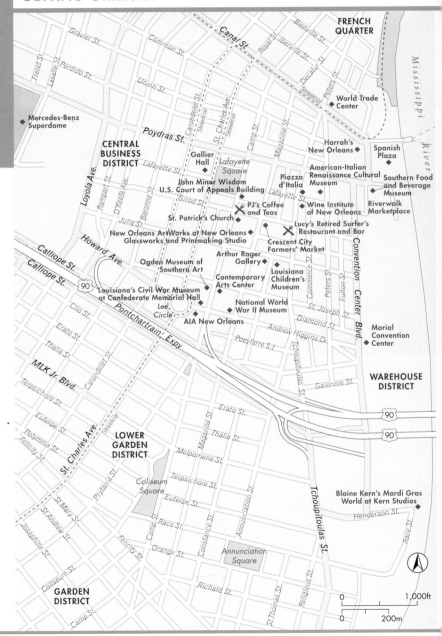

FRENCH QUARTER

Gravier St.
Common St.
Canal St.
Bienville St.
Iberville St.
Royal St.
Decatur St.
Peters St.

Mississippi River

Frenet St.
LaSalle St.
Perdido St.
Union St.

World Trade Center

Mercedes-Benz Superdome

Poydras St.
Carondelet St.
St. Charles Ave.
Camp St.
Magazine St.

Harrah's New Orleans
Spanish Plaza

CENTRAL BUSINESS DISTRICT
Lafayette St.
Gallier Hall
Lafayette Square

American-Italian Renaissance Cultural Museum
Southern Food and Beverage Museum

Loyola Ave.
Rampart St.
O'Keefe Ave.
Baronne St.

John Minor Wisdom U.S. Court of Appeals Building
Girod St.
Lafayette St.
Piazza d'Italia

Riverwalk Marketplace

PJ's Coffee and Teas
Wine Institute of New Orleans

Julia St.
St. Patrick's Church
New Orleans ArtWorks at New Orleans Glassworks and Printmaking Studio

Lucy's Retired Surfer's Restaurant and Bar

Crescent City Farmers' Market

Howard Ave.
Calliope St.
Calliope St.
90

Arthur Roger Gallery
Ogden Museum of Southern Art
Contemporary Arts Center
Louisiana Children's Museum

Commerce St.
Peters St.
Fulton St.
Convention Center Blvd.

Louisiana's Civil War Museum at Confederate Memorial Hall
Lee Circle
National World War II Museum
St. Joseph St.
Morial Convention Center

Pontchartrain Expy.
AIA New Orleans
Diamond St.
Andrew Higgins Dr.
Poeyfarre St.

Clio St.
Erato St.
Thalia St.
MLK Jr. Blvd.
Terpsichore St.
Gaiennie St.

WAREHOUSE DISTRICT

Euterpe St.
Polymnia St.
Felicity St.
St. Charles Ave.

Erato St.
Thalia St.
Magazine St.

90
90

LOWER GARDEN DISTRICT
Melpomene St.

Coliseum Square
Terpsichore St.
Euterpe St.

Blaine Kern's Mardi Gras World at Kern Studios
Henderson St.

St. Mary St.
St. Andrew St.
Josephine St.
Prytania St.
Camp St.
Race St.
Constance St.
Annunciation St.
Orange St.

Annunciation Square

Tchoupitoulas St.
Religious St.
St. Thomas St.
Race St.

GARDEN DISTRICT
Coliseum St.
Camp St.
Richard St.

0   1,000ft
0   200m

GETTING HERE AND AROUND

The CBD and Warehouse District together comprise a fairly small area and can easily be traveled on foot; the close proximity of the Warehouse District's museums and galleries makes for easy walking and gallery hopping. The CBD is adjacent to the French Quarter, just across Canal Street. To travel to or from Uptown or the Garden District, you can take a cab, drive, or take the **streetcar**—use any stop from Canal Street to Lee Circle. If you have an extra 20 minutes, walking is also feasible.

Parking lots abound, and plenty of **street parking** is available for reasonable fees, payable by cash or card at the green parking ticket machines stationed on each block on both sides of the street. Pay attention to the end time on your ticket—local police are known for their skill in catching parking violations.

MAKING THE MOST OF YOUR TIME

Arts- and culture-loving travelers can easily spend the better part of a day to a full day between the **museums and galleries** here. Prospective art buyers should check with desired galleries for days of operation, and plan their visit around that. The area is also a great **nightlife destination,** with cutting-edge restaurants, music clubs, galleries, and Harrah's New Orleans, open 24 hours a day, 7 days a week. Plan to spend at least half a day and one night here.

SAFETY

While the CBD and the Warehouse District have a safer feel than some parts of the French Quarter and other areas downtown, parts of the CBD can be more deserted at night than highly trafficked tourist areas. Staying close to the river and to the pulse of Warehouse District nightlife is the safest bet after the sun goes down. By day, these areas are bustling with commerce during the week and tourism every day.

TOP REASONS TO GO

Gallery crawl through the Warehouse District. Browse the bevy of art galleries that line Julia Street and its surround.

Feast on cutting-edge dining. Sample some of the finest in Louisiana contemporary cuisine from chefs who are quickly becoming household names.

Get cultured. Revisit a defining chapter of our nation's history at the National World War II Museum, or discover a new favorite artist in the airy, urban oasis of the Ogden Museum of Southern Art.

Experience carnival season year-round. At Blaine Kern's Mardi Gras World at Kern Studios, see floats from years past, watch video footage, and stock up on souvenirs.

QUICK BITES

Lucy's Retired Surfers Restaurant and Bar. The brightly decorated bar and dining room provide a nice spot for a margarita, a cup of coffee, or a Southwestern-style snack. ⊠ *701 Tchoupitoulas St., Warehouse District* ☎ *504/523–8995* ⊕ *www.lucysretiredsurfers.com.*

PJ's Coffee and Teas. This local chain serves delicious, cold-brewed iced coffee and a small selection of pastries and sandwiches. ⊠ *644 Camp St., CBD* ☎ *504/529–3658* ⊕ *www.pjscoffee.com.*

4

Sightseeing
★★★★
Dining
★★★★
Lodging
★★★★
Shopping
★★
Nightlife
★★

Catchy flags hung in the Warehouse District bear a repeating pattern of encouraging slogans these days. "Welcome to your blank canvas." "Raise your own bar." "Get caught in our brainstorms." These banners reflect the ongoing growth of new and established businesses and cultural sites in this neighborhood, which is a particularly ripe atmosphere for art, design, and entertainment. No longer just bland commercial and urban residential neighborhoods, the CBD (Central Business District) and Warehouse District (also, appropriately, known as the Arts District) now comprise a vibrant, vital sector of downtown New Orleans.

Updated
by Troy
Thibodeaux

Maybe it's that the Warehouse District does truly feel like a blank canvas—the landscape is one of solid, old, brick-and-stucco walls that, though aging, somehow feel fresh and make one think of starting anew. (To wit, some artists have even used them as literal canvases for mural work—local favorite Michalopolous, famous for his impressionistic images of New Orleans houses, painted a creamy-yellow classic home on the side of a building at the corner of Commerce and Girod; there's also a soothing mural of rural life at the site of the weekly Farmer's Market.) Maybe it's the expanses of blue sky here, where the buildings feel a bit more spread out than in the French Quarter, or the spirit of creativity that pervades a neighborhood chock-full of art museums and galleries. Perhaps it's the more modern, sleek feel of the CBD in close proximity—or the bevy of contemporary restaurants and bars popping up or gaining renown here. Whatever the "it" factor is, this neighborhood has got plenty, and it's inspiring a new host of entrepreneurs, creative types, and their patrons to flock to the Warehouse District and the CBD. Confidence in the area is reflected in the fact that the American Institute of Architects opened AIA New Orleans here in November

A ride on the streetcar is a great way to tour New Orleans in period style.

2010, Louisiana's only design center and one of only seven AIA Centers in the United States.

By day, the CBD hums with commerce and productivity, and the Warehouse District hosts visitors to the New Orleans Morial Convention Center and to this neighborhood's many museums and art galleries. You'll find the National World War II Museum, the Ogden Museum of Southern Art, the Contemporary Arts Center, the Louisiana Children's Museum, and Louisiana's Civil War Museum at Confederate Memorial Hall—all within a three-square-block radius. Art lovers will appreciate the concentration of upscale contemporary-art galleries and artist studios in the Warehouse District and can even try their hand at glassmaking and printmaking. Discerning palates with a taste for culture and cuisine are sated, feet itching to dance are scratched, and throats craving custom libations can be slaked in this up-and-coming cosmopolitan playground.

By night, you'll find hip, successful restaurants, bustling live-music venues old and new, and numerous neighborhood and hotel bars ranging from the most casual to the very chic. All of these places are patronized by scores of young professionals and graduate students, who mix with tourists and longtime residents who know what's up.

CENTRAL BUSINESS DISTRICT

The CBD covers the ground between Canal and Poydras streets, with some spillover into the Warehouse District's official territory. The neighborhood includes many iconic commerce buildings, including the

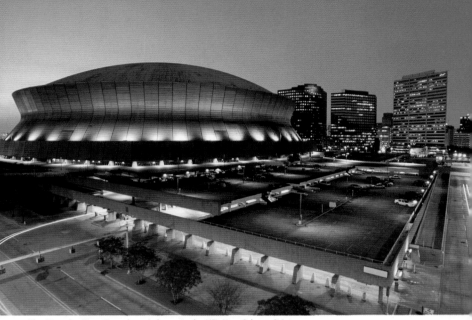

The Mercedes-Benz Superdome is home to the NFL New Orleans Saints.

Louisiana Superdome, the World Trade Center, the convention center, and Harrah's Casino. There are also beautiful old government and office buildings, particularly around central Lafayette Square. Canal Street is the CBD's main artery and the official dividing line between the business district and the French Quarter; street names change from American to French as they cross Canal into the Quarter. Served by the streetcar, the palm tree–lined Canal Street is regaining some of its former elegance, particularly as it nears the river.

TOP ATTRACTIONS

Harrah's New Orleans. The only land-based casino in the New Orleans area, Harrah's contains 115,000 square feet of gaming space divided into five areas, each with a New Orleans theme: Jazz Court, Court of Good Fortune, Smugglers Court, Mardi Gras Court, and Court of the Mansion. There are also 100 table games, 2,100-plus slots, and live entertainment at Masquerade, which includes an ice bar, lounge, video tower and dancing show. Check the website for seasonal productions, including music, theater, and comedy. Dining and libation choices include the extensive Harrah's buffet, Cafés on Canal food court, Besh Steak House, Bamboo Court, Gordon Biersch, Grand Isle, and Ruth's Chris Steak House. The last three are part of Harrah's newly developed Fulton Street Mall, a pedestrian promenade that attracts casual strollers, club goers, and diners. ⊠ *8 Canal St., CBD* ☎ *504/533–6000 or 800/427–7247* ⊕ *www.harrahs.com* ☉ *Daily 24 hrs.*

Mercedes-Benz Superdome. Home to the NFL's New Orleans Saints, the Mercedes-Benz Superdome (until 2011 the Louisiana Superdome) has been the site of many Sugar Bowls, several NCAA Final Four basketball tournaments, the BCS champion-ship game, a record nine Super Bowls (with the 10th happening in 2013), and the 1998 Republican National Convention. The Super-dome was badly damaged during Hurricane Katrina and in its after-math, when it served as a refuge of last resort for evacuees. The sta-dium underwent extensive renova-tions in the year that followed, and reopened for football in Septem-ber 2006, when the Saints beat the Atlanta Falcons, at the time setting a record for the largest television audience in ESPN history.

Built in 1975, the Superdome currently seats up to 71,000 people, has a 166,000-square-foot main arena, and a roof that covers almost 10 acres at a height of 27 stories. Since the Saints' Super Bowl victory in 2010, the Superdome has been covered in gold siding and given a brand-new outdoor festival space appropriately named Champions Square. Exte-rior LED lighting added in 2011 gives the arena an eye-catching, ever-changing facade. Enhancements to the "Dome" in 2011 added 3,100 new seats, enhanced sight lines, additional premium club lounges, and expansions of the Plaza Concourse and Champions Square.

The bronze statue on the Poydras Street side of the Superdome is the Vietnam Veterans Memorial. Across from it is a large abstract sculpture called the *Krewe of Poydras*. The sculptor, Ida Kohlmeyer, meant to evoke the frivolity and zany spirit of Mardi Gras. A couple of blocks down Poydras Street from the Superdome is the Bloch Cancer Survivors Monument, a block-long walkway of whimsical columns, figures, and a triumphal arch in the median of Loyola Avenue. The **New Orleans Arena,** behind the Superdome, is home to the NBA New Orleans Hor-nets, whose 2011 play-off season sparked the popular citywide "I'm In" campaign. The streets around the Superdome and Arena are usu-ally busy during business hours, but at night and on weekends, except during a game, this area should not be explored alone. ⊠ *1 Sugar Bowl Dr., CBD* ☎ *504/587–3663* ⊕ *www.superdome.com.*

WORTH NOTING

Gallier Hall. This Greek Revival building, modeled on the Erectheum of Athens, was built in 1845 by architect James Gallier Sr. It served as City Hall in the mid-20th century. Today it hosts special events and is the mayor's official perch during Mardi Gras parades; the kings and queens of many parades stop here to be toasted by the mayor and dig-nitaries. The grand rooms inside the hall are adorned with portraits and decorative details ordered by Gallier from Paris. ⊠ *545 St. Charles Ave. (entrance on side at 705 Lafayette St.), CBD* ☎ *504/658–3627* ⊙ *Weekdays 8–4; visits by appointment.*

John Minor Wisdom United States Court of Appeals Building. New York archi-tect James Gamble Rogers was summoned to design this three-story granite structure as a post office and court building in 1909. By the 1960s the post office had moved to larger digs, and McDonough No. 35 High School found refuge here after Hurricane Betsy in 1965. Today the Renaissance Revival building houses the Fifth Circuit Court of Appeals in an elaborately paneled and ornamented series of courtrooms. The dark, cool corridors of the ground floor have an arcaded, bronzed ceiling. As you enter the building and pass security, turn left and continue around the corner to find the library, where you can pick up information on the courthouse. Outside, a repeating sculpture of four women stands atop each corner of the building: the four ladies represent History, Agriculture, Industry, and the Arts. The building is named for Judge John Minor Wisdom, the New Orleans native who was instrumental in dismantling the segregation laws of the South. Judge Wisdom received the Presidential Medal of Freedom in 1993. ⊠ *600 Camp St., CBD* ☏ *504/310–7777* ⊙ *Weekdays 8–5.*

Lafayette Square. Planned in 1788 as a public place for Faubourg St. Marie, the city's first suburb, Lafayette Square occupies one city block in the midst of the Federal Complex and Gallier Hall. The leafy square shaded by oak, magnolia, and maple trees, and landscaped with hydrangeas and azaleas, offers a shady spot to sit. Statues include Benjamin Franklin, Henry Clay, and New Orleans education activist John McDonough, along with more contemporary sculptures such as Tara Conley's intriguing and whimsical bronze *Bunny* and Aria de Capo's colorful concrete-and-steel, *Alice in Wonderland*–invoking *Flowers for Theresa.* Recently, the Square has been experiencing a renaissance brought about in large part by two Wednesday night concert series: the Young Leadership Council's Wednesday at the Square, held in late spring and early summer, and Second Harvest Food Bank's Harvest the Music in the fall. ⊠ *Between Camp St., St. Charles Ave., N. Maestri and S. Maestri Sts., CBD.*

Riverwalk Marketplace. This three-block-long shopping center contains several retail chains, local specialty shops, and a food court. Plaques along the river walkway relate bits of the Mississippi River's history and folklore. Nearby at the Poydras Street streetcar stop is a 200-foot-long mural in tropical motifs that was a gift to the city by Mexican artist Julio Quintanilla. Various cruise ships leave from the Julia Street Wharf slightly upriver; you can often see them from the front of the Riverwalk. ⊠ *1 Poydras St., CBD* ☏ *504/522–1555* ⊕ *www.riverwalkmarketplace. com* ⊙ *Mon.–Sat. 10–7, Sun. noon–6.*

Southern Food and Beverage Museum. This small museum in the Riverwalk Marketplace educates visitors on a variety of subjects surrounding two favorite Southern pastimes: eating and drinking. Learn about the fishers and farmers, the chefs and inventors, and the widely varying cultures that all contribute to this region's tradition of cocktails and cuisine. Complete with a food gift shop and a tasting room with chef demonstrations. The museum is planning to relocate in spring of 2013; call ahead for update. ⊠ *Riverwalk Marketplace 1 Poydras St., CBD* ☏ *504/569–0405* ⊕ *www.southernfood.org* ⊠ *$10.*

Spanish Plaza. For a terrific view of the river and a place to relax, go behind the **World Trade Center** at 2 Canal Street to Spanish Plaza, a large, sunken space with beautiful inlaid tiles and a fountain. The plaza was a gift from Spain in the mid-1970s; here you can hear occasional live music and purchase tickets for riverboat cruises in the offices that face the river. ■TIP→ If you happen to be in town on the Monday before Mardi Gras (Lundi Gras), you can watch Rex, the King of Carnival, arrive here from across the river to take symbolic control of the city for a day. ✉ *Poydras St. at river, CBD.*

WAREHOUSE DISTRICT

Bordered by the river, St. Charles Avenue, Poydras Street, and the Pontchartrain Expressway, and filled with former factories and cotton warehouses, the Warehouse District began its renaissance when the city hosted the World's Fair here in 1984. Structures that housed the international pavilions during the fair now make up the New Orleans Morial Convention Center and a number of hotels, restaurants, bars, and music clubs.

New Orleanians will always remain sensitive to the plight of the many citizens who suffered in the days following Hurricane Katrina as they sought refuge in and around the battered convention center. However, in the year following the hurricane, the center underwent an extensive renovation, and the surrounding neighborhood has since regained its former charm and vibrancy. Today, the Warehouse District is one of the trendiest residential and arts-and-nightlife areas of the city, dotted with modern renovations of historic buildings, upscale loft residences, excellent eateries, and a number of bars and music venues. Julia Street, the main thoroughfare, is headquarters for the city's gallery district.

TOP ATTRACTIONS

Fodor's Choice ★

Blaine Kern's Mardi Gras World at Kern Studios. If you're not here for the real thing, Mardi Gras World is a fun (and family-friendly) backstage look at the history and artistry of Carnival. Mardi Gras World's entertainment complex moved from Algiers Point to join Blaine Kern Studios and private-event venues on the east bank of New Orleans in 2009. The massive 400,000-square-foot complex, just upriver from the New Orleans Convention Center, has an enhanced guided tour through a maze of video presentations, decorative sculptures, and favorite megafloats from Mardi Gras parades such as Bacchus, Rex, and Endymion. Visitors enter through a plantation alley that is part Cajun swamp-shack village, part antebellum Disneyworld (Kern was a friend of, and inspired by, Walt Disney). Admission includes king cake and coffee. Hour-long tours begin on the half hour. ✉ *1380 Port of New Orleans Pl., Warehouse District* ☎ *504/361–7821 or 800/362–8213* ⊕ *www.mardigrasworld.com* ✆ *$19.95* ⊙ *Daily 9:30–4:30.*

Contemporary Arts Center. Founded in 1976, the center endured long, hard years of economic and cultural stagnation to finally emerge as a keystone to the now vibrant Warehouse District arts scene. Today the center hosts cutting-edge exhibits, featuring both local artists and the work of national and international talent. Two theaters present jazz productions, films, dance, plays, lectures, and experimental and conventional concerts, including a New Orleans music series. Hours vary during concerts, performances, lectures, and special events; call or check the website for details. ⊠ *900 Camp St., Warehouse District* ☎ *504/528–3805, 504/528–3800 theater box office* ⊕ *www.cacno.org* ⊠ *Gallery admission $5* ⊗ *Thurs.–Sun. 11–4.*

★ **Julia Street.** Contemporary-art dealers have adopted this strip in the Warehouse District as their own. The street is lined with galleries, specialty shops, and modern apartment buildings, with the greatest concentration stretching from South Peters Street to St. Charles Avenue. The first Saturday evening of each month gallery owners throw open their doors to show off new exhibits, to the accompaniment of wine, music, and general merriment. White Linen Night in August and Art for Art's Sake in October also find the galleries welcoming visitors with artist receptions and live entertainment. ⊠ *Warehouse District.*

☾ **Louisiana Children's Museum.** An invaluable resource for anyone traveling with kids, this top-notch museum is 30,000 square feet of hands-on educational fun. Favorite activities include a mini grocery store (with both carts and registers manned by visitors), a role-play café, Mr. Rogers' Neighborhood, and a giant bubble station. A welcoming environment is provided for children with disabilities: most exhibits are accessible, and some are aimed directly at increasing children's awareness of disabilities. Art teachers lead classes daily; theatrical storytelling takes place every morning and afternoon; and special activities such as jewelry making, face painting, and scavenger hunts are held each week. An indoor playground is reserved for toddlers ages three and under, and Toddler Time activities are held at 10 am on Tuesday and Thursday. There's also a mini fitness center with a kid-size stationary bicycle and rock-climbing wall. ⊠ *420 Julia St., Warehouse District* ☎ *504/523–1357* ⊕ *www.lcm.org* ⊠ *$8* ⊗ *Tues.–Sat. 9:30–4:30, Sun. noon–4:30 (last ticket sold at 4).*

Fodor's Choice ★ **National World War II Museum.** The brainchild of historian and writer Dr. Stephen Ambrose, who taught for many years at the University of New Orleans until his death in 2002, this moving, well-executed examination of World War II covers far more ground than simply D-Day. The seminal moments are re-created through propaganda posters and radio clips from the period; nearly 4,000 oral histories of the military personnel involved; a number of short documentary films (including an especially emotional film on the Holocaust featuring interviews with survivors); and collections of weapons, personal items, and other artifacts from the war. The exhibits occupy a series of galleries spread through the interior of a huge warehouse space. One spotlighted exhibit, in a large, open portion of the warehouse near the entrance, is a replica of the Higgins boat troop landing craft, which were manufactured in New Orleans. In 2009 the museum unveiled the first phase of its $300 million expansion, which will eventually quadruple the size of the facility. Across the street from the current facility, there's a 4-D theater experience produced by Tom Hanks and a canteen featuring the food of celebrity-chef John Besh. This is the first of six new pavilions proposed for the expanded campus, due to be completed in 2015. ■ TIP→ A large exhibition space entitled The United States Freedom Pavilion: The Boeing

4

Center, honoring all service branches and including a restored Boeing B-17 and an immersive submarine experience, is slated to open in 2013. Check the website for updates on the expansion and a list of current movies, lectures, events, and programs. ✉ *945 Magazine St.(main entrance on Andrew Higgins Dr.), Warehouse District* ☎ *504/528–1944* ⊕ *www. nationalww2museum.org* 🖅 *$19; combination ticket with 4-D presentation $24* ⊙ *Daily 9–5.*

☾ **Ogden Museum of Southern Art.** Art by Southerners, art made in the South,

Fodor's Choice   art about the South, artistic explorations into Southern themes, and
★   more fill this Smithsonian affiliate's elegant building. More than 1,200 works collected by local developer Roger Ogden since the 1960s are on permanent display, along with pieces from Washington, D.C., and 15 Southern states spanning the 18th–21st centuries, plus featured exhibits. A central stair hall filters natural light through the series of galleries, and a rooftop patio affords lovely views of the surrounding area. The gift shop sells logo items, crafts by local artists, and books and movies celebrating the South. Thursday nights (6–8 pm) come alive with "Ogden After Hours," featuring live music, artist interviews, refreshments, children's activities, and special gallery exhibits. ✉ *925 Camp St., Warehouse District* ☎ *504/539–9600* ⊕ *www.ogdenmuseum.org* 🖅 *$10* ⊙ *Wed.–Mon. 10–5, additional hrs Thurs. 6–8 pm.*

WORTH NOTING

AIA New Orleans Center for Design. In 2010, the American Institute of Architects opened the doors of AIA New Orleans, Louisiana's only design center of its kind, and one of only seven AIA design centers in the United States. This storefront faces out on historic Lee Circle and inspires with its mix of old and new; aging brick and plaster combine with a gleaming glass facade and exposed interior ductwork in a space that feels contemporary yet firmly grounded in New Orleans history. Regular exhibitions of current and locally relevant work are free and open to the public during business hours; check their website for after-hours events and lectures. ✉ *1000 St. Charles Ave., Warehouse District* ☎ *504/525–8320* ⊕ *www.aianeworleans.org* 🖅 *Free* ⊙ *Weekdays 9:30–5:30.*

American-Italian Renaissance Cultural Center. Italian–New Orleans customs are explained and artifacts exhibited in this small, thoughtful museum, which also has wine tastings and other events. The center will be undergoing a $2.5 million renovation starting in 2012, so check the website and call for information on coming exhibits.

Note that the Modern **Piazza d'Italia** by architect Charles Moore is a secret oasis behind the American-Italian Renaissance Cultural Center, tucked in the center of the block bounded by Tchoupitoulas, St. Peter, Lafayette, and Poydras streets. Its postmodern style is reminiscent of a Roman ruin. The park is a gathering place for the large Italian community on St. Joseph's Day and Columbus Day. ✉ *537 S. Peters St., Warehouse District* ☎ *504/522–7294* ⊕ *www.americanitalianculturalcenter. com* 🖅 *$8* ⊙ *Tues.–Fri. 10–4.*

Arthur Roger Gallery. A highlight of Julia Street, this gallery showcases quality contemporary art, including work by local and regional artists.

✉ *432–434 Julia St., Warehouse District* ☎ *504/522–1999* ⊕ *www. arthurrogergallery.com* ⊗ *Tues.–Sat. 10–5.*

Crescent City Farmer's Market. This year-round market offers an array of locally grown produce, fresh baked goods, cut flowers, wild-caught Louisiana seafood, fresh dairy, farm-raised meat, and handcrafted meals from regional vendors, along with entertainment by local musicians and cooking demonstrations. The first Saturday every month is especially kid-friendly—it's when the Marketeers Club convenes for activities and lessons like healthy pizza cooking and old-fashioned butter churning. ✉ *700 Magazine St., Warehouse District* ☎ *504/861–4488* ⊕ *www. crescentcityfarmersmarket.org* ⊗ *Sat. 8 am–noon.*

Lee Circle. At the northern edge of the Warehouse District, an 1884 bronze statue of Civil War general Robert E. Lee stands high above the city on a white marble column in a traffic circle. New Orleanians say it's because you can never turn your back on a Yankee. Developments over the past several years have greatly improved the area immediately around the circle, which now includes the **Contemporary Arts Center,** the **Ogden Museum of Southern Art,** the **National World War II Museum,** and **Louisiana's Civil War Museum at Confederate Memorial Hall.** ✉ *Warehouse District.*

Louisiana's Civil War Museum at Confederate Memorial Hall. This ponderous stone building at Lee Circle was built in 1891 to house a collection of artifacts from the Civil War, making it the oldest museum in the state. The displays include uniforms, flags, and soldiers' personal effects, which thankfully survived Hurricane Katrina intact. ✉ *929 Camp St., Warehouse District* ☎ *504/523–4522* ⊕ *www.confederatemuseum.com* ▣ *$7* ⊗ *Wed.–Sat. 10–4.*

ⓒ **New Orleans ArtWorks at New Orleans Glassworks and Printmaking Studio.** See daily free demonstrations of all stages of glassmaking and design, printmaking, and silver alchemy in this 25,000-square-foot warehouse space. Special "make and take" exhibits for youngsters are popular, as are a variety of group and individual classes. Email or call in advance to make reservations for hands-on instruction in the studio. A shop and gallery up front display and sell the finished products. ✉ *727 Magazine St., Warehouse District* ☎ *504/529–7279* ⊕ *www. neworleansglassworks.com* ⊗ *Daily 10–5.*

Wine Institute of New Orleans. This hybrid institute known by the acronym w.i.n.o. is part wine school, part high-tech wine-tasting experience. A state-of-the-art Italian wine-serving system dispenses wine by the ounce so patrons can design their own flights and taste many more wines than at traditional tastings. Educate your palette with their selection of 120 wines, or sip a refreshing beer—both pair just as well with charcuterie, artisanal cheese, and other small plates. w.i.n.o. also offers a weekly wine-tasting class on Tuesday evenings. Classes fill up quickly, so plan ahead. ✉ *610 Tchoupitoulas St., Warehouse District* ☎ *504/324–8000* ⊕ *www.winoschool.com* ⊗ *Mon.–Thurs. 11–10, Fri. and Sat. noon–midnight, Sun. 2–10.*

The Garden District

WORD OF MOUTH

"The Garden District is better if you're more interested in a little more R & R than being close to the activity of the French Quarter. We love the area and have never felt unsafe. It's got more old-world charm, beautiful part of the city, and very easy to get to/from the Quarter on streetcar or taxi."

—dfr4848

GETTING ORIENTED

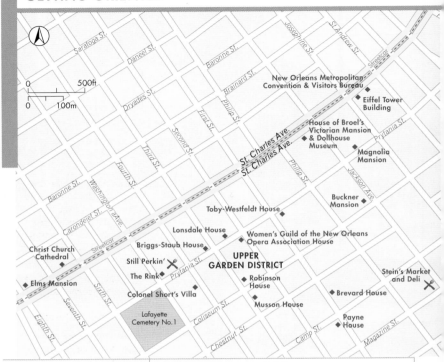

QUICK BITES

Stein's Market and Deli. Grab a sandwich at this traditional Jewish and Italian deli with an impressive beer selection. Daily specials include a Philly cheese steak with pickled peppers. ⊠ *2207 Magazine St., Lower Garden District* ☎ *504/527–0771* ⊕ *www.steinsdeli.net.*

Still Perkin'. This popular independent café offers coffees, teas, muffins, scones, and tarts made by local bakeries. ⊠ *2727 Prytania St., Upper Garden District* ☎ *504/899–0335* ⊕ *www.neworleanscoffeeshop.com.*

GETTING HERE AND AROUND

The Garden District is easily accessible by car, streetcar, and city bus, or on foot from the CBD or Uptown. It's easy and free to park your car on any side street, but you have to pay to park along busier stretches of Magazine Street and Prytania Street.

The **streetcar** runs every 20 or 30 minutes (more frequently during rush hour), 24 hours a day, and makes several stops along St. Charles Avenue. You may have to wait longer than 30 minutes for the trolley to arrive at night, but it's generally a safe, if leisurely, mode of transportation. It takes about 20 minutes on the streetcar to get to Jackson Avenue in the Lower Garden District from Canal Street. The **No. 11 bus** runs up Magazine Street, making stops at all major intersections every 20 minutes. The ride from Canal Street to Jackson Avenue takes about 10 minutes depending on traffic.

TOP REASONS TO GO

Ogle awesome architecture. View antebellum homes built during New Orleans's most prosperous era by renowned architects, including Henry Howard, Lewis E. Reynolds, William Freret, and Samuel Jamison.

Shop locally. Browse through colorful vintage and antiques shops for one-of-a-kind accessories, costumes, and keepsakes.

Feast on Magazine Street. Pick from a variety of restaurants, from French bistros to those offering Japanese and Mediterranean food.

Check out local art. Peruse fine and funky jewelry and design at the galleries on Magazine Street. Or visit Garden District Gallery, a relative newcomer across from Commander's Palace, featuring gorgeous work by local artists.

Take in some history. View the aboveground tombs at Lafayette Cemetery No. 1, in continual use since 1833 and arguably one of the most beautiful in the city.

MAKING THE MOST OF YOUR TIME

Plan at least half a day to see the Garden District's gorgeous **mansions**, shop 6-mile **Magazine Street**, and visit the beautiful **Lafayette Cemetery No. 1**. Across the street is **Commander's Palace**, an incredibly popular restaurant. **Coliseum Square Park** in the Lower Garden District is beautiful and a great place for R & R if you have extra time.

SAFETY

Safety isn't a major concern in the Garden District, as the neighborhood hires its own security service in addition to what the New Orleans police offer. At night the neighborhood is quiet and the streets are not well lit, so it's always wise to walk with someone, especially in the Lower Garden District. Visitors should avoid the rougher area bordered by Tchoupitoulas and Magazine streets around Jackson Avenue, near the St. Thomas housing projects, as well as Central City on the opposite side of St. Charles Avenue, particularly at night.

Sightseeing
★ ★ ★
Dining
★ ★
Lodging
★ ★
Shopping
★ ★ ★ ★
Nightlife
★

Boasting some of the most beautiful homes in the city, the Garden District has acquired fame for its antebellum mansions and manicured gardens. Residents take great pride in their gorgeous properties, and the neighborhood is in bloom 12 months a year. Although most homes are closed to the public, with the exception of special-event tours, the views from the other side of the intricate cast-iron fences are still impressive. A stroll through the neighborhood is a peaceful break from more touristy areas of New Orleans.

Updated by Troy Thibodeaux

Originally the Livaudais Plantation, the Garden District was laid out in the late 1820s and remained part of the city of Lafayette until incorporated into New Orleans in 1852. The neighborhood attracted "new-moneyed" Americans who, snubbed by the Creole residents of the French Quarter, constructed grand houses with large English-style gardens featuring lush azaleas, magnolias, and camellias. Three architectural styles were favored: the three-bay Greek Revival, center-hall Greek Revival, and raised cottage. Renovations and expansions to these designs through the years allowed owners to host bigger and more ostentatious parties, particularly during the social season between Christmas and Carnival. Today, many of the proud residents represent fourth- or fifth-generation New Orleanians.

The Garden District is divided into two sections by Jackson Avenue. Upriver from Jackson is the wealthy **Upper Garden District,** where the homes are meticulously kept. Below Jackson, the **Lower Garden District** is rougher in areas, and though the homes are often structurally just as beautiful as their counterparts, they have a distinct faded beauty. Coliseum Square, in the center of the neighborhood, is surrounded by especially gorgeous homes with tropical gardens. The Lower Garden District along Magazine Street has been increasingly gentrified over the past few years, with new boutiques and bars catering to a younger crowd. Artists, like local favorite Simon, who paints the colorful store signs that can be spotted throughout the city, have set up shop in this rapidly developing area.

The Garden District is a great neighborhood to stroll (⇨ *See our Garden District Walking Tour in Chapter 1*). Magazine Street, near the southern border of the neighborhood, is an excellent shopping destination with many antiques and novelty shops as well as restaurants and bars. St. Charles Avenue to the north also has several restaurants and bars.

UPPER GARDEN DISTRICT

A morning walk in this unique neighborhood is like stepping back in time. Besides beautiful mansions with wrought-iron fences that wrap around vibrant manicured gardens, the neighborhood has Lafayette Cemetery No. 1, one of the city's oldest and most beautiful cemeteries, and historic Commander's Palace, one of the city's best-known restaurants. Return to present day by visiting the stretch of Magazine Street that runs alongside the Upper Garden District, which boasts an eclectic mix of restaurants and chichi boutiques.

TOP ATTRACTIONS

Brevard House. Though Anne Rice moved out of her elegant Garden District home in 2004, the famous novelist's fans still flock to see the house that inspired the Mayfair Manor in her series *Lives of the Mayfair Witches*. The house is a three-bay Greek Revival, extended over a luxurious side yard and surrounded by a fence of cast-iron rosettes that earned the estate's historical name, Rosegate. ⊠ *1239 1st St., Upper Garden District.*

Elms Mansion. Built in 1869, this home saw the Confederate president Jefferson Davis as a frequent guest. The house, which has been meticulously maintained and furnished with period pieces, is the site of many receptions. Self-guided tours of the interior are free. Group tours are conducted on weekdays by appointment. Highlights include a carved oak staircase and mantelpiece and 24-karat gilt moldings and sconces. ⊠ *3029 St. Charles Ave., Upper Garden District* ☎ *504/895–9200* ✉ *Group tours $6 per person* ☉ *Self-guided tours Tues.–Fri. 10–2; group tours by appointment.*

House of Broel's Victorian Mansion and Dollhouse Museum. Antique furnishings fill this restored antebellum home. The dollhouse collection includes miniatures of Victorian, Tudor, and plantation-style houses. The home also features a wedding store. Walk-ins are welcome, however larger groups should call

TOURS

Historic New Orleans Tours. This excellent guided tour of the Garden District meets twice daily (11 am and 1:45 pm) in front of the Garden District Book Store (2727 Prytania Street) inside the Rink. No reservations are needed, but arrive 15 minutes early. It's also possible to buy tickets online. The tour last about 2 hours and takes you to the former home of Ann Rice as well as beautiful Lafayette Cemetery No. 1. ☎ *504/947–2120* ⊕ *www. tourneworleans.com.*

Gorgeous Creole-style mansions line the streets of the Garden District.

ahead. ⊠ *2220 St. Charles Ave., Upper Garden District* ☎ *504/522-2220 or 800/827-4325* ⊕ *www.houseofbroel.com* ✉ *Mansion and museum tour $10* ⊘ *Weekdays 11–3.*

Fodor's Choice ★ **Lafayette Cemetery No. 1.** Built in 1833, Lafayette Cemetery No. 1 was the first planned cemetery in the city, and remains a testament to the city's history. The cemetery was built during a time when the area was seeing a large influx of Italian, German, Irish, and American immigrants from the North. Many who fought or played a role in the Civil War have plots here, indicated by plaques and headstones that detail the site of their death. Several of the tombs also reflect the toll the yellow-fever epidemic took on the city during the 19th century, which affected mostly children and newcomers to the city; 2,000 yellow-fever victims were buried here in 1852. Movies such as *Interview with the Vampire* and *Easy Rider* have used this walled cemetery for its eerie beauty. Open to the public every day except Sunday, the cemetery is a short walk from the streetcar and a beautiful spot to learn about New Orleans's history. ⊠ *1400 block of Washington Ave., Upper Garden District* ⊘ *Weekdays 7–2:30, Sat. 7–noon; Save Our Cemeteries tours Jan. and Feb., Mon., Wed., Fri., and Sat. at 10:30; Mar.–Dec., Mon.–Sat. at 10:30.*

Lonsdale House. As a 16-year-old immigrant working in the New Orleans shipyards, Henry Lonsdale noticed how many damaged goods were arriving from upriver. Spotting a need for more-protective shipping materials, Lonsdale developed the burlap bag (clued in by his parents, who had picked up a sample in India). He made a fortune in burlap, only to lose it all in the 1837 depression. Lonsdale next turned to coffee importing, an industry that ran into problems during the Civil War: the

Union blocked imports from Brazil, the major supplier of coffee to New Orleans. Lonsdale hit upon the momentous idea of cutting the limited coffee grinds with chicory, a bitter root, and New Orleanians have been drinking the blend ever since. The house, built with his entrepreneurial dollars, displays many fine details, including intricate cast-iron work on the galleries and a marble entrance hall. The statue of Our Mother of Perpetual Help in the ornate gazebo in the

front yard is a remnant of the house's more than 70 years as an active Catholic chapel, which ended with its controversial sale to novelist Anne Rice in 1996. Actor Nicholas Cage purchased the home in 2005 and put it up for sale in 2009 after facing foreclosure on the property, as well as on the Allure Mansion he owned in the French Quarter. ⊠ *2523 Prytania St., Upper Garden District.*

Women's Guild of the New Orleans Opera Association House. This fundamentally Greek Revival house, built in 1865, has a distinctive Italianate octagonal turret, added in the late 19th century. The last private owner, Nettie Seebold, willed the estate to the guild in 1955. Furnished with period pieces, the house underwent extensive renovations in 2008 and is once again being used for receptions and private parties. The house is open for walk-in tours from 10 to noon and 1 to 4 on Mondays. ⊠ *2504 Prytania St., Upper Garden District* ☎ *504/899–1945* 🚪 *$7.*

WORTH NOTING

Briggs-Staub House. The only Gothic Revival house in the district was built in 1849. Garden District Americans shunned the Gothic Revival style as linked to Creole-Catholic tradition, but Londoner Charles Briggs ignored decorum and had James Gallier Sr. design this anomaly, touted as a "Gothic cottage." The interior departed from a strict Gothic breakup of rooms to make it better suited for entertaining. ⊠ *2605 Prytania St., Upper Garden District.*

Buckner Mansion. This 1856 home was built by cotton factor Henry S. Buckner in overt competition with the famous Stanton Hall in Natchez, built by Buckner's former partner. Among the luxurious details are 48 fluted cypress columns and a rare honeysuckle-design cast-iron fence. The triple ballroom was used by debutantes practicing their walks and curtsies. Now privately owned, the house served as the campus of Soulé College from 1923 to 1975. ⊠ *1410 Jackson Ave., Upper Garden District.*

Christ Church Cathedral. This Gothic Revival Episcopal church completed in 1887 has steeply pitched gables, an architectural detail that was a precursor to the New Orleans Victorian style. The cathedral is the oldest non–Roman Catholic church in the Louisiana Purchase: the congregation was established in 1805, and this is the third building erected on the

5

TAKE A PEEK

The Women's Guild of the New Orleans Opera Association House is open for interior tours on Monday. It's one of the only houses in the Garden District open to the public.

same site. Visitors are welcome to walk into the main building when services are not in session. ✉ *2919 St. Charles Ave., Upper Garden District* ⊕ *www.cccnola.org.*

Colonel Short's Villa. Occupied for a brief time by the Union governor Michael Hahn during the Civil War, the house was stylistically influential in the district because the two-story galleries of its dining room wing had railings made of cast iron rather than wood. Its architect, Henry Howard, is known for designing Nottaway—the largest plantation home in America—and other monumental homes. The fence, with a pattern of morning glories intertwining with cornstalks, is the most famous example of cast iron in the Garden District. Legend has it that Colonel Short purchased the fence for his wife,

THE FLAIR TO SCARE

Popular New Orleans–born author Anne Rice used her hometown as the backdrop for dozens of novels, most dealing with the occult. The Garden District's Brevard House, which she occupied until 2004, was the inspiration for the haunted house of her Mayfair witches series. She also enjoyed the macabre beauty of Lafayette Cemetery No. 1; her most famous blood-sucking protagonist rose from its crypts in her best-selling novel *The Vampire Lestat*. Adding a touch of theater to a book signing at Garden District Book Shop, Rice was paraded from Brevard House to the cemetery in an ice-packed coffin.

who was homesick for Kentucky. A similar cornstalk fence appears in the French Quarter at 915 Royal Street. ✉ *1448 Fourth St., Upper Garden District.*

Musson House. This Italianate house was built by impressionist painter Edgar Degas's maternal uncle, Michel Musson—a rare Creole inhabitant of the predominantly American Garden District. Musson had moved to his Esplanade Street residence before Degas made his visit to New Orleans, so it's unlikely the artist ever stayed at this address. A later owner added the famous "lace" iron galleries. ✉ *1331 Third St., Upper Garden District.*

Payne House. Confederate president Jefferson Davis died here on December 6, 1889; a monument out front outlines his political and military careers. Cast iron ornaments the capitals of the Ionic columns, each embossed with the date (1848) and place (New York) of manufacture. ✉ *1134 First St., Upper Garden District.*

The Rink. This small collection of specialty shops was once the location of the South's first roller-skating rink, built in the 1880s. Locals can be found here browsing the **Garden District Book Shop,** which stocks regional, rare, and old books, along with a wide assortment of autographed first editions by local and regional writers. ✉ *Washington Ave. and Prytania St., Upper Garden District.*

Robinson House. Styled after an Italian villa, this home built in the late 1850s is one of the largest in the district. Doric and Corinthian columns support the rounded galleries. It is believed to be the first house in New Orleans with "waterworks," as indoor plumbing was called then. Years

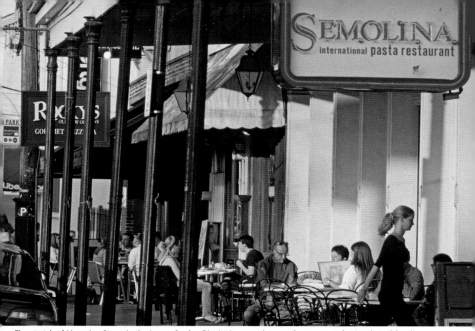

The stretch of Magazine Street in the Lower Garden District is a popular area for young professionals and families.

of extensive renovation based on the original plans culminated with a re-landscaping in 2005. ⊠ *1415 Third St., Upper Garden District.*

Toby-Westfeldt House. Dating from the 1830s, this unpretentious French-Creole–style home sits amid a large, plantation-like garden, surrounded by a copy of the original white-picket fence. Thomas Toby, a Philadelphia businessman, moved to New Orleans and had this house built well above the ground to protect it from flooding. The house is thought to be the oldest in this part of the Garden District. ⊠ *2340 Prytania St., Upper Garden District.*

LOWER GARDEN DISTRICT

The Lower Garden District has a distinct faded beauty that isn't seen in its counterpart. You can see the remnants of a more vibrant past beneath the crumbling facade of the aging mansions. The area's most beautiful homes are clustered around Coliseum Square, full of lush, untamed, tropical gardens that poke out from rusted ironclad fences onto the crumbling sidewalks. Its centerpiece, Coliseum Square Park, has a beautiful fountain and walking trails that wind around looming oak trees. The stretch of Magazine Street here has been revitalized with offbeat shops selling original art, antiques, vintage clothing, and jewelry, catering in particular to a young professional and student crowd. Art galleries sell exotic jewelry and trinkets made by both local artists and artisans worldwide. The neighborhood quiets down a lot at night; however, there are still some good nighttime hangouts, especially if you head toward St. Charles Avenue.

TOP ATTRACTIONS

Coliseum Square Park. Established in the mid-19th century, this lush green park is the centerpiece of the Lower Garden District. With bike and walking trails lining the park as well as a beautiful fountain, the park is a great spot to stop and relax after a walk through the neighborhood. Bordered by Race Street and Melpomene Street, Coliseum Square Park is only two blocks away from the St. Charles streetcar stop. ✉ *1729 Coliseum St., Lower Garden District.*

SPEAK BIG EASY

The "muse streets" that transverse the Lower Garden District are not pronounced like the Greek goddess names you may recall. New Orleanians have their own way of speaking: Calliope isn't "kal-eye-oh-pee;" it's "kal-ee-ope." Melpomene is pronounced "mel-puh-meen," and Terpsichore is "terp-sih-core." Clio is usually "clee-oh," but sometimes completely misread as "C-L 10."

Goodrich-Stanley House. This restored Creole cottage is an excellent example of the modest prototype for much of the far more elaborate architecture of the surrounding Garden District. The scale, derived from the climate-conscious design prevalent in the West Indies, made it easily adaptable to the higher pretensions of the Greek Revival look, as well as the slightly more reserved Colonial Revival. Built in 1837, the house has had one famous occupant: Henry Morton Stanley, renowned explorer of Africa and founder of the Congo Free States who most famously uttered the phrase "Dr. Livingstone, I presume" upon encountering the long-lost Scottish missionary. ✉ *1729 Coliseum St., Lower Garden District.*

WORTH NOTING

Eiffel Tower Building. Thirty years ago, engineers in Paris discovered hairline fractures in the Eiffel Tower supports. To lighten the load, they removed the restaurant on the second platform. New Orleans auto dealer McDonald Stephens bought the restaurant, which was disassembled into 11,000 pieces for shipping. Ever the romantic, Stephens hired New Orleans architect Steven Bingler to build a "jewel box" out of the pieces for his four beloved daughters. Bingler's vision, assembled on St. Charles Avenue in 1986, incorporated scattered pieces from the original restaurant into a contemporary outer structure meant to resemble the Eiffel Tower. The building went through many reincarnations, most unsuccessful, and fell into ruin until the New Orleans Culinary Institute signed a 20-year lease in 2004. It is currently a lounge and restaurant catering to a younger crowd. ✉ *2040 St. Charles Ave., Lower Garden District.*

Magnolia Mansion. This oversize Creole cottage, historically known as the Harris-Maginnis House, is notable for the unusually deep portico stretching over the front garden and the 11 carved Corinthian columns. It has operated as a bed and breakfast since 2002. ✉ *2127 Prytania St., Lower Garden District* ⊕ *www.magnoliamansion.com.*

Uptown and Carrollton-Riverbend

WORD OF MOUTH

"On this beautiful, sunny, 78-degree day, when we walked into the zoo, with all the palm trees, live oak trees, and manicured/landscaped grounds, where everything is lush and green, I immediately began thinking 'This is better than any zoo I've ever seen.'"
— bkluvsNola

GETTING ORIENTED

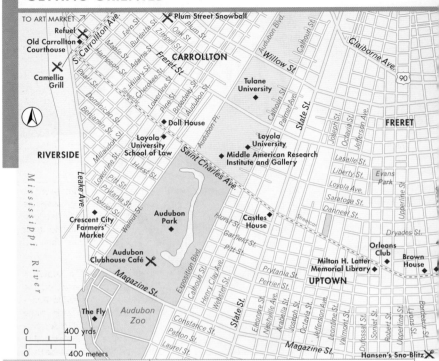

QUICK BITES

Audubon Clubhouse Café. You can eat breakfast or lunch in the airy dining room overlooking the Audubon Park Golf Course, or relax with a drink on the oak-shaded veranda. ⊠ *Golf Club Dr., off Magazine St., Uptown* ☎ *504/212–5285* ⊕ *www.auduboninstitute.org.*

Refuel. Stop for coffee and a snack at this modern café, open for breakfast and lunch. At weekend brunch try the grits, often praised as the best in the city. ⊠ *8124 Hampson St., Riverbend* ☎ *504/872–0187* ⊕ *www.refuelcafe.com* ⊗ *Closed Mon. No dinner.*

GETTING HERE AND AROUND

Uptown and the Carrollton-Riverbend are great walkable neighborhoods. The **St. Charles streetcar** is a somewhat reliable and picturesque mode of transportation running approximately every 20 minutes 24 hours a day, all the way from Canal Street at the edge of the French Quarter to South Claiborne Avenue. It stops at all main intersections across St. Charles Avenue, leaving you within walking distance of Audubon Park and Zoo. Expect the entire ride, from Canal Street to the Carrollton-Riverbend, to take about an hour (considerably more during rush hour or holidays). The **No. 11 bus** runs the length of Magazine Street up to Audubon Park from Canal Street. A bit more reliable, the bus system runs every 20 minutes, making stops at five major intersections. The last bus departs from Audubon Park at 12:40 am on weekdays and at 2:05 am on weekends. The fare is $1.25 for both the streetcar and the bus. Take a taxi when visiting the area late at night as public transit comes less frequently (about every 30 minutes).

6

TOP REASONS TO GO

Ride the streetcar. Take the scenic and leisurely trolley ride from Canal Street to Audubon Park, ogling the stately mansions that stretch along St. Charles Avenue.

Monkey around in Audubon Park and Zoo. Considered one of the best in the nation, Audubon Zoo offers a wide range of interesting exhibits for visitors of all ages. The adjoining park has beautiful walking trails lined with 100-year-old oaks.

Hang with locals at The Fly. This quieter stretch of Audubon Park is known locally as "The Fly." The levee, a walkway along the park, provides some spectacular views of the Mississippi.

Explore Carrollton-Riverbend. This up-and-coming neighborhood has burgeoning business stretches along Oak Street, Maple Street, and South Carrollton Avenue.

Shop 'til you drop. New Orleans's "Magnificent Mile," Magazine Street is the city's premier shopping destination.

MAKING THE MOST OF YOUR TIME

You could easily spend a full day in this neighborhood: a half-day minimum for visiting the **Audubon Zoo** and enjoying the park that surrounds it, and a half day for exploring the retail stretch along **Magazine Street.** If you have extra time, head to **The Fly,** the riverside park on the other side of the zoo where locals like to picnic on weekends.

SAFETY

Most of Uptown and the Carrollton-Riverbend are safe to walk around during the day and evening. However, there are certain pockets where travelers should exercise caution. The area between Magazine Street and the river up to Jefferson Avenue can be dangerous to walk around at night. Also avoid the area close to the river west of Audubon Park and dark side streets when out late at night.

RIDING THE STREETCAR

Take in the beautiful mansions and fun local vibe of Uptown via the St. Charles Avenue streetcar, which runs the length of the avenue, from Canal Street right outside of the French Quarter to the Carrollton-Riverbend. The relaxing ride takes about an hour and costs $1.25 one way.

The St. Charles streetcar line runs through Uptown (above) and the CBD (right page, bottom).

If you're coming from the French Quarter, board at Canal and Carondelet. Jump off at Jackson Avenue (the ride will take 20 minutes) and follow our Garden District Walking Tour (⇨ *See Chapter 1*). Reboard at Louisiana Avenue, which forms the boundary between the Garden District and Uptown. As you approach Louisiana Avenue, the huge white mansion on your left at the intersection was formerly the **Bultman Funeral Home,** where Tennessee Williams staged his play *Suddenly Last Summer*. Note that unless you have an unlimited day pass ($5), you'll need to ask for a 25¢ transfer when you pay—otherwise you'll have to repay the fare (in exact change) each time you board.

STREETCAR HISTORY

In the early 1900s streetcars were the most prominent mode of public transit and ran on many streets. By the early 20th century, New Orleans had almost 200 miles of streetcar lines, and a ride cost just 5¢. In the 1920s, buses started to overtake the old-fashioned system. Today, three lines remain, operating along Canal Street, St. Charles Avenue, and Carrollton Avenue.

The **Columns Hotel,** formerly a mansion, is on the right after Peniston Street. It's a great place to stop off for a cocktail on the grand veranda. Next you'll pass the Gothic-style **Rayne Memorial Methodist Church,** built in 1875, a block past the hotel, on the left. The 1887 Queen Anne–style **Grant House** up the block was designed by popular local architect Thomas Sully with a decorative porch and balcony balustrades.

As you continue, the large avenue at the next stop is Napoleon. The spectacular **Academy of the Sacred Heart,** a private girls' school, is on the right in the next block, past Jena Street. Across the street, the Mediterranean **Smith House** claims one of the most picturesque settings on the avenue. It was built in 1906 for William Smith, president of the New Orleans Cotton Exchange. The oldest house on St. Charles Avenue (circa 1850s) is the **4621 St. Charles House** on the right, before Valence Street. Next door, **Anthemion** is an early example of the Colonial Revival movement. The **Brown House,** on the right before Bordeaux Street, is the largest mansion on St. Charles Avenue.

Several houses in the next block past the Brown House are turn-of-the-20th-century buildings that re-create an antebellum style. On the left, the neighboring **Rosenberg House** and **Stirling House** contrast Colonial and Classical

Revival. The Tudor style of the house on the left, with its steep gables, Gothic arches, and half timbering, was popular when banana magnate Joseph Vaccaro built it in 1910. The **Orleans Club,** on the right at the corner of Robert Street, is an elegant ladies club. The **Milton H. Latter Memorial Library,** a beaux arts mansion that is now a public library, is on the left at Soniat Street. The library is worth a visit as it is one of the few mansions along St. Charles that is open to the public.

Several blocks ahead, the **Benjamin House,** between Octavia and Joseph streets, is a stunning mansion (circa 1912) made of limestone, an expensive and unusual building material for New Orleans. In the next block, past Joseph Street on the right, is the **McCarthy House,** a 1903 Colonial Revival home with ornate columns and flattop doors and windows. The plantation home used in the film *Gone With the Wind* was a set, but it inspired the columned New Orleans **Tara,** built in 1941, coming up on the right side of the avenue at the corner of Arabella.

As you cross Nashville Avenue, the Colonial Revival **Wedding Cake House** is on the right. Its most notable feature is the beveled leaded glass in its front door, one of the most beautiful entryways in the city. As you enter the university district, dominating the next block

6

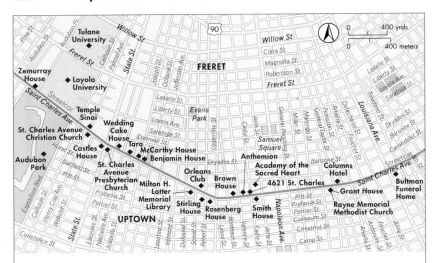

on the left is the neo-Gothic **St. Charles Avenue Presbyterian Church.**

Castles House, on the left after State Street, is a similar Colonial Revival, as is the **St. Charles Avenue Christian Church,** two blocks up on the left. On the right, across from the church, is **Temple Sinai,** the first Reform Jewish congregation in New Orleans. This building dates from 1928; the annex on the corner was built in 1970.

Just beyond Calhoun Street, **Loyola University,** on the right, takes up the block past Temple Sinai. **Tulane University,** founded in 1884, is directly beside Loyola and houses the Newcomb Art Gallery and the Middle American Research Institute and Gallery. Campuses for both universities extend back several blocks off the avenue and are worth a visit. On the left, across the avenue from the two universities is **Audubon Park and Zoo,** Uptown's premier attraction.

Back on the streetcar, the heavy stone archway on the right just after Tulane University is the guarded entrance to **Audubon Place.** The private drive has some of the most elegant mansions in the city. **Zemurray House,** the columned white home facing the archway, was built in 1907 by the president of the United Fruit Company. It is now the official residence of Tulane's president. The **Doll House,** a miniature house in the corner yard on the right at Broadway, is said to be the smallest house in New Orleans to have its own postal address.

At Broadway, to the left, is the **Loyola University School of Law,** an Italianate building that housed the Dominican Sisters and the college they operated for almost a decade until the 1980s. The street continues several more stops past Broadway along St. Charles until it turns at the Riverbend onto Carrollton Avenue, once the entrance to a former resort town.

You'll travel through the Carrollton-Riverbend neighborhood before reaching the end of the line at **Palmer Park.** The park is the setting for an arts market held the last Saturday of every month. Reboard the trolley headed downtown at S. Carrollton Avenue and Claiborne Avenue where the St. Charles Avenue line both begins and ends.

Sightseeing
★★
Dining
★★★
Lodging
★
Shopping
★★★★
Nightlife
★★★

Discover the more residential face of New Orleans in the sprawling Uptown and Carrollton-Riverbend neighborhoods. Just a 30-minute streetcar ride from Canal Street, you'll find blocks of shops on bustling Magazine Street, stunning homes along oak-lined streets, and the first-class Audubon Park and Zoo. Head farther into Uptown and spend a couple of hours walking the length of the levee in the Riverbend for stunning views of the Mississippi.

Updated
by Troy
Thibodeaux

Uptown encompasses the area upriver from Louisiana Avenue between Tchoupitoulas Street and S. Claiborne Avenue, on the west side of the Garden District. The neighborhood has as many sumptuous mansions as its neighbor, as well as Loyola and Tulane universities and the large urban park named for John James Audubon. The area is more family and student populated, versus the old-money feel of the Garden District.

The architecture is incredibly diverse throughout Uptown and the Carrollton-Riverbend, with examples ranging from Colonial Revival to long, single-story family homes known locally as "shotgun" houses. Traveling along the avenue from downtown to uptown provides something of a historical narrative: the city's development unfolded upriver, and the houses grow more modern the farther uptown you go.

Magazine Street, the main artery of Uptown, stretches for miles, with antiques and home-decor shops, boutiques, galleries, restaurants, and cafés. Several other shopping strips have developed throughout the area, most notably on Prytania Street and Freret Street. Casual cafés, bars, and shops abound. Meander along the side streets between St. Charles Avenue and Magazine Street, which are lined with small, brightly painted family homes, decorated with fading Mardi Gras beads year-round. Breathe in the alluring fragrance of the sweet olive trees that grow in abundance throughout the neighborhood.

Farther northwest, Carrollton-Riverbend technically begins where the streetcar curves from St. Charles Avenue onto S. Carrollton Avenue.

Carrollton was once a resort town where New Orleanians could retreat from the hustle and bustle of the French Quarter and relax by the river. Annexed in 1874, the Carrollton-Riverbend is now home to many university students, and still serves as a respite from tourist overload. The retail stretch along Oak Street has become widely known as the setting of the Oak Street Po-Boy Festival. The stretch also has two fixtures of New Orleans nightlife that draw locals and visitors alike: the Maple Leaf for live music and Jacques-Imo's Café for delicious and creative interpretations of local cuisine. Nearby Maple Street is another popular destination for the college crowd, with bustling bars, bookshops, and restaurants stretching the length from Broadway to S. Carrollton Avenue.

> **PERFECT PICNIC**
>
> Spicy seafood to go makes for the perfect New Orleans picnic. For seasonal boiled specialties—crawfish, crabs, shrimp, andouille sausage, corn, potatoes, and garlic—stop by the **Big Fisherman** (⊠ *3301 Magazine St.*) on your way to Audubon Park. Ask if there are fresh crawfish pies available. And don't forget the paper towels at the supermarket next door.

The river winds its way around the southern edge of Uptown around Carrollton, providing a gorgeous setting for picnics and family outings. Walk the stretch of the levee from the Riverbend back downtown along the river and relax at "The Fly," a popular hangout on the other side of Audubon Zoo, where locals enjoy views of the river while setting up picnics or team sports.

UPTOWN

Pristine oak-lined streets, colorful residential homes, and diverse restaurants and shops are what make Uptown such a fun, relaxing neighborhood to explore. Stately mansions line the length of St. Charles Avenue, where you'll find colorful Mardi Gras beads hanging from tree limbs and telephone wires throughout the year. Wander the side streets between St. Charles and Magazine Street and you'll find that smaller shotgun and Victorian-style homes maintain the same old-world charm. In recent years Magazine Street has becoming a bustling shopping strip filled with 6 miles of shops, bars, and restaurants all the way from the CBD up to Audubon Park. Nearby Prytania Street is also home to several restaurants and the iconic Prytania movie theater. Built in 1915, the theater is the oldest running in New Orleans.

TOP ATTRACTIONS

Fodor's Choice ★

Audubon Park. Formerly the plantation of Etienne de Boré, the father of the granulated sugar industry in Louisiana, Audubon Park is a large, lush stretch of green between St. Charles Avenue and Magazine Street, continuing across Magazine Street to the river. Designed by John Charles Olmsted, nephew of Frederick Law Olmsted (who laid out New York City's Central Park), it contains the world-class **Audubon Zoo**; a 1.7-mile track for running, walking, or biking; picnic and play areas; Audubon Park Golf Course; tennis courts; a swimming pool; horse stables; and a river view. Calm lagoons wind through the park, harboring egrets,

Kids love feeding the giraffes at the Audubon Zoo.

catfish, and other indigenous species. The park and zoo were named for the famous ornithologist and painter John James Audubon, who spent many years working in and around New Orleans. ⊠ *6500 Magazine St., Uptown* ☎ *504/581–4629* ⊕ *www.auduboninstitute.org* ✉ *Free.*

Audubon Zoo. Consistently ranked since its redevelopment as one of the top zoos in the nation, the Audubon Zoo presents a wide array of animals in exhibits that mimic their natural habitats. The Louisiana Swamp exhibit re-creates the natural habitat of alligators, including rare white alligators (technically leucistic gators), nutria (large swamp rodents), and catfish; alligator-feeding time is always well attended. New attractions include the "Cool Zoo," a splash park featuring a 28-foot white alligator slide, bubbling fountains, and splash zones set aside for toddlers and young children. Other highlights include the Reptile Encounter, Komodo Dragon exhibit, and white Bengal tigers. Several new attractions are available for additional ticket fees: a zoo train tour that departs every 30 minutes from the swamp exhibit; the children's zoo area; and the Safari Simulator Ride. ⊠ *6500 Magazine St., Uptown* ⊕ *www.auduboninstitute.org* ✉ *$16; combination ticket for zoo, Aquarium of the Americas, and Audubon Insectarium $35* ⊙ *Tues.–Sun. 10–5*

Columns Hotel. Built in 1883 as a private home, the Columns has been the scene of TV ads, movies, and plenty of weddings. The interior scenes of Louis Malle's *Pretty Baby* were filmed here. The Victorian Lounge (once the main dining room) now houses a popular bar, and the grand veranda is perfect for sipping cocktails on warm evenings. The elegant rooms of the first floor are open to the public and look exceptional during the December holidays adorned with wreaths and twinkling lights;

note the stained-glass skylight topping the mahogany stairwell. ✉ *3811 St. Charles Ave., Uptown* ☎ *504/899–9308 or 800/445–9308* ⊕ *www.thecolumns.com.*

Loyola University. The Jesuits built this complex facing the avenue in 1912. Today, it is known for its strong law, communications, and music programs. The modern Gothic-style building on the corner is the **Louis J. Roussel Building,** which houses the music department. The campus extends for two blocks behind the Gothic and Tudor edifice of the **Church of the Holy Name of Jesus.** The fourth floor of the neo-Gothic **library** holds the school's gallery, which is open to the public from Monday to Saturday. ✉ *6363 St. Charles Ave., Uptown* ⊕ *www.loyno.edu.*

> ## STATE (STREET) OF HARMONY
>
> The homes along the first few blocks of State and Palmer streets off St. Charles Avenue are some of Uptown's loveliest and most exclusive. Residents prefer the privacy of living just off the thoroughfare. Here, old-guard socialite families live in harmony alongside limousine liberals. On Palmer, between St. Charles and Loyola avenues, James Carville, Democratic strategist and Tulane professor, lives with Republican strategist (and wife) Mary Matalin in a house they bought in 2008 for $2.2 million. Neighbors joke that the rooms are large enough to absorb the noise of their arguments.

Tulane University. Next to Loyola University on St. Charles Avenue, the university's three original buildings face the avenue: **Tilton Hall** (1902) on the right, **Gibson Hall** (1894) in the middle, and **Dinwiddie Hall** (1924) on the left. The Romanesque style, with its massive stone look and arches, is repeated in the several buildings around a quad behind these. Modern campus buildings extend another three blocks to the rear. Tulane is known for its medical school, law school, and fine main library. The **Sophie H. Newcomb College for Women** was Tulane's coordinate women's college until it was dissolved as part of a post-Katrina renewal plan. The college's memorial institute maintains the **Newcomb College Center for Research on Women,** a women's resource center that brings in speakers, writers, and academics. Also on the Tulane campus is the **Middle American Research Institute.**

The newly renovated **Middle American Research Institute and Gallery** (☎ *504/865–5110,* ⊕ *mari.tulane.edu*), located on the third floor of Tulane's Dinwiddie Hall, includes the world's oldest documented Guatemalan textile collection. Established in 1924, the collection also includes unusual artifacts like poison-dart arrows from Venezuela and shrunken heads from the Brazilian rain forest. The pre-Columbian, Central and South American artifacts are complemented by an associated collection of books on Latin American culture housed in Tulane's main library. The gallery is open to the public, but appointments are recommended. ✉ *6823 St. Charles Ave., Uptown* ⊕ *www.tulane.edu.*

WORTH NOTING

Academy of the Sacred Heart. Unusual aspects of this Colonial Revival building, a Catholic girls' school built in 1900, include wide, wraparound balconies (or galleries) and colonnades facing a large garden. The academy is exceptionally beautiful during the December holidays, when the galleries are decked with wreaths and garlands. ✉ *4521 St. Charles Ave., Uptown.*

Anthemion. The emergence of Colonial Revival architecture in the late 19th century indicated local weariness with the excesses of the Greek Revival craze that had dominated the midcentury. Anthemion is an excellent example of this return to simplicity. Built in 1896 for the druggist Christian Keppler, it served as the headquarters of the Japanese consulate from 1938 to 1941. ✉ *4631 St. Charles Ave., Uptown.*

Brown House. Completed in 1904 for cotton magnate William Perry Brown, the Brown House is one of the largest mansions on St. Charles Avenue. Its solid monumental look, Syrian arches, and steep gables make it a choice example of Romanesque Revival style. ✉ *4717 St. Charles Ave., Uptown.*

Castles House. Local architect Thomas Sully designed this 1895 Colonial Revival house after the Longfellow House in Cambridge, Massachusetts. The interior has often appeared in the pages of design magazines. ✉ *6000 St. Charles Ave., Uptown.*

Milton H. Latter Memorial Library. A former private home now serves as the most elegant public library in New Orleans. Built in 1907 and taking up an entire city block, this Italianate–beaux arts mansion was once the home of silent-screen star Marguerite Clark. It was then purchased by the Latter family and given to the city as a library in 1948 in memory of their son, who was killed in World War II. Sit and leaf through a copy of Walker Percy's *The Moviegoer* or John Kennedy Toole's *Confederacy of Dunces* (two popular novels set in New Orleans), or just relax in a wicker chair in the solarium. This is one of the few mansions on St. Charles Avenue open to the public. Local artisans contributed the murals and carved mantels. ✉ *5120 St. Charles Ave., Uptown* ☎ *504/596–2626* ⊕ *www.neworleanspubliclibrary.org* ☉ *Mon. and Wed. 9–8, Tues. and Thurs. 9–6, Sat. 10–5, Sun. noon–5.*

Orleans Club. This sumptuous mansion was built in 1868 as a wedding gift from Colonel William Lewis Wynn to his daughter. The dormer windows, typical of French Empire style, were added during a remodeling in 1909. The side building, on the uptown side of the main building, is an auditorium added in the 1950s. The house is closed to the public but serves as headquarters to a ladies' social club and hosts many debutante teas and wedding receptions. ✉ *5005 St. Charles Ave., Uptown.*

NICE DIGS

Of all things, a Borders Books store most recently occupied the former Bultman Funeral Home, a colossal mansion with an enclosed garden that was one of the most elegant funeral homes in the South. Now the site is being renovated to house a Fresh Market grocery store. A balcony bears a wrought-iron motif of downward crossed arrows, a symbol of death. Tennessee Williams set his play *Suddenly Last Summer* here in the solarium.

6

CARROLLTON-RIVERBEND

Locals describe the Riverbend area as the curve the St. Charles streetcar makes when it turns onto S. Carrolton Avenue. Much of the area is also referred to as Carrollton. Before becoming part of New Orleans in 1874, the area was a resort town, providing a relaxing getaway with riverfront views. Now the area is mostly composed of smaller one- and two-story family homes, shady oak-lined streets, and plenty of small restaurants and cafés. With the success of local events, such as the annual Oak Street Po-Boy Festival in November (⊕ *www.poboyfest.com*), the retail strip on Oak Street has blossomed with shops, restaurants, and popular bars such as the Maple Leaf, where the Rebirth Brass Band plays every Tuesday night. Nearby Maple Street is a great shopping destination in its own right, attracting the college crowd with an array of sports bars and cafés.

> **QUICK COOL-DOWN**
>
> When the weather heats up in spring and summer, sno-balls are a favorite way to cool down in New Orleans. Locals line up at seasonal stands throughout Uptown for ground ice flavored with everything from chocolate to cherry to bubble-gum syrup. Some perennial favorites are **Hansen's Sno-Bliz** at 4801 Tchoupitoulas, **Plum Street Snowball** at 1300 Burdette, and **SnoWizard Snowball Stand** at 4001 Magazine.

EXPLORING

Arts Market of New Orleans. Spend a morning perusing the craftsmanship of more than 100 artists from all over the region in this open-air market held the last Saturday of each month in beautiful Palmer Park. Vendors include local favorite Dr. Bob, known for the "Be Nice or Leave" signs you'll see all over the city. Musicians, a kids' tent, and food stands round out the event. ⊠ *Palmer Park, corner of S. Carrolton and S. Claiborne, Carrollton-Riverbend* ⊕ *www.artscouncilofneworleans. com* ⊑ *Free* ☉ *Last Sat. of month, 10–4.*

Crescent City Farmers' Market. Rub shoulders with New Orleans's chefs as they rush to pick up fish and meat orders before their restaurants open. Each month a different chef is featured to prepare delicious lunch plates showcasing local and seasonal ingredients. Visitors can indulge in tasty treats like homemade popsicles, juice, and fresh-baked bread, as well as sampling the fresh local produce. ⊠ *Between Leake Ave. and Broadway, Carrollton-Riverbend* ⊕ *www.crescentcityfarmersmarket. org* ⊑ *Free* ☉ *Tues. 9–1.*

The Fly. Spend an afternoon picnicking at this lush green park with spectacular views of the Mississippi, just on the other side of Audubon Zoo. Officially called Audubon Riverside Park, locals call it "The Fly" after a butterfly-shape building that used to be on-site. It's a popular place for picnics and pickup sports. The park is particularly beautiful in the early evening, when you can watch the sunset just past the river. ⊠ *Exposition Blvd., Carrollton-Riverbend.*

Mid-City and Bayou St. John

WORD OF MOUTH

"Go out to City Park and visit Storyland. On the way back stop at Angelo Broccatos for the best Italian ice cream in this hemisphere."

—bkluvsNola

GETTING ORIENTED

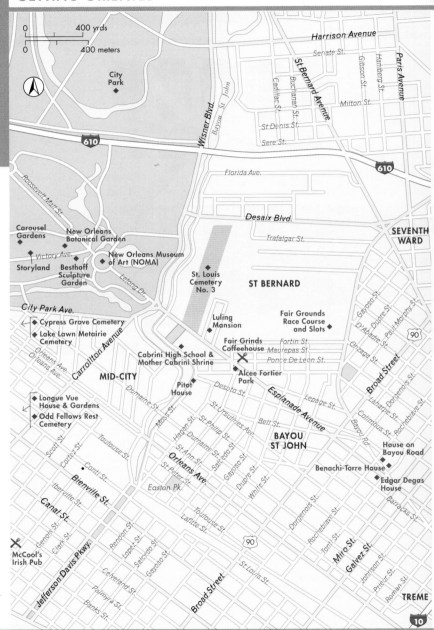

0   400 yrds
0   400 meters

City Park

Harrison Avenue

Senate St.

St Bernard Avenue

Gibson St.

Hamberg St.

Paris Avenue

Cadillac St.

Buchanan St.

Milton St.

Wisner Blvd.

Bayou St. John

St Denis St.

Sere St.

610

610

Florida Ave.

Roosevelt Matt St.

Desaix Blvd.

Trafalgar St.

SEVENTH WARD

Carousel Gardens

New Orleans Botanical Garden

New Orleans Museum of Art (NOMA)

Victory Ave.

Storyland

Besthoff Sculpture Garden

Lelong Dr.

St. Louis Cemetery No. 3

ST BERNARD

City Park Ave.

Cypress Grove Cemetery

Lake Lawn Metairie Cemetery

Carrollton Avenue

Orleans Ave.

Orleans Ave.

Luling Mansion

Fair Grinds Coffeehouse

Fair Grounds Race Course and Slots

Gayoso St.

Dupre St.

Paul Morphy St.

D'Abadie St.

90

Fortin St.

Maurepas St.

Ponce De Leon St.

Onzaga St.

Broad Street

MID-CITY

Dumaine St.

Cabrini High School & Mother Cabrini Shrine

Alcee Fortier Park

Pitot House

Desoto St.

Esplanade Avenue

Lepage St.

Laharpe St.

Dorgenois St.

Rochebiave St.

Longue Vue House & Gardens

Odd Fellows Rest Cemetery

Moss St.

Hagan St.

St Philip St.

St Ursulines Ave.

Bell St.

BAYOU ST JOHN

Bayou Rd.

Columbus St.

House on Bayou Road

Scott St.

Cortez St.

Toulouse St.

Conti St.

Brienville St.

Durmaine St.

St Ann St.

Salcedo St.

Gayoso St.

Dupre St.

White St.

Benachi-Torre House

Edgar Degas House

Orleans Ave.

St Peter St.

Easton Pk.

Iberville St.

Canal St.

Genois St.

Clark St.

Rendon St.

Lopez St.

Salcedo St.

Gayoso St.

Toulouse St.

Lafitte St.

90

Dorgenois St.

Tonti St.

Miro St.

Galvez St.

Barracks St.

Rochebiave St.

McCool's Irish Pub

Jefferson Davis Pkwy.

Cleveland St.

Palmyra St.

Banks St.

Broad Street

St Louis St.

Johnson St.

Prieur St.

Roman St.

TREME

10

GETTING HERE AND AROUND

From downtown there are two easy ways to get into Mid-City: Canal Street or Esplanade Avenue, both of which border the French Quarter. There are two **streetcar** lines that run down Canal Street: one will take you straight down Canal to Metairie Cemetery, and the other will turn down Carrollton Avenue and deposit you in an ideal location right in front of City Park. The **No. 91 Jackson-Esplanade bus,** which you can catch anywhere along Rampart Street along the French Quarter, turns onto Esplanade Avenue and will take you right in front of City Park. The streetcar ride from downtown takes approximately 30 minutes. Allow about 15 minutes for the bus ride down Esplanade.

MAKING THE MOST OF YOUR TIME

City Park and the Mid-City **cemeteries** are generally open during daylight hours, but the **outdoor patios** of Esplanade Avenue restaurants and cafés stay open well into the night. Allow yourself at least half a day, starting in the afternoon, so you can enjoy both activities. **City Park** is one of the largest urban parks in the nation, and you could easily spend an entire vacation exploring its art collections, vintage carousels, botanical gardens, and gondola rides.

SAFETY

Things can change from cute to creepy in the span of a block or so, so exercise good judgment if you go walking off the main thoroughfares. The areas around Bayou St. John and City Park tend to be safe, especially during daylight hours, but areas closer to Broad Street (which runs roughly parallel to the bayou about half a mile south toward the French Quarter) are rougher, and should definitely be avoided on foot at night. Carrollton Avenue is the main thoroughfare through Mid-City (and connects to the Uptown and Carrollton-Riverbend neighborhoods) and is usually well trafficked, but elsewhere in the neighborhood it's advisable to drive at night.

TOP REASONS TO GO

Explore City Park. This gorgeous and sprawling park is home to dozens of attractions, including a museum, sculpture garden, and amusement park.

Take a cemetery tour. Mid-City is home to some of the largest, safest, and best-kept cemeteries in New Orleans.

Stroll along Bayou St. John. The grassy banks offer biking and walking trails and splendid views of some of the most historic and lovely homes and landmarks in the city.

QUICK BITES

Fair Grinds Coffeehouse. Just off Esplanade Avenue, Fair Grinds Coffeehouse is the neighborhood spot for coffee, tea, and small snacks—including vegan treats. ✉ *3133 Ponce de Leon St., Bayou St. John* ☎ *504/913–9072* ⊕ *www. fairgrinds.com.*

Finn McCool's Irish Pub. More than just your average corner bar, Finn McCool's Irish Pub live streams European football games and hosts a popular trivia quiz on Monday nights. The kitchen serves delicious fish-and-chips. ✉ *3701 Banks St., Mid-City* ☎ *504/486–9080* ⊕ *www.finnmccools.com.*

7

MID-CITY'S CEMETERIES

(above and bottom right) St. Louis Cemetery No. 3. (top right) Cypress Grove Cemetery.

Of all Mid-City's charms, one of the most fascinating is the prolific number of cemeteries, and the haunting beauty of these "cities of the dead." A tour de force for the imagination, these graves hold the final resting places of famous musicians, Storyville madams, voodoo practitioners, politicians, and pirates.

The historical development of these aboveground cemeteries emerges from two main points. New Orleans, most of which lies below sea level, has a high water table, which caused (and continues to cause, in some circumstances) buried coffins to pop out of the ground when a heavy rain occurred. Raised graves and vaulted tombs were also an old tradition among the French and Spanish.

Mid-City cemeteries are some of the safest and most-trafficked in the city. **Save Our Cemeteries, Inc.** (☎ *504/525–3377* ⊕ *www.saveourcemeteries.org*) is a great source for historical knowledge, safety info, and tours.

CEMETERY SYMBOLISM

Most vaults or plots are infused with funerary symbolism, revealing a secret language between the living and dead. An anchor stands for hope, the broken column represents life cut short, and the broken flower symbolizes a life terminated. Sculpted ivy is a symbol of enduring friendship. Clasped hands stand for unity and love, even after death. For more, visit ⊕ *www.nolacemeteries.com*.

Cypress Grove Cemetery. This expansive and still-used cemetery was originally founded by the Fireman's Charitable and Benevolent Association in 1840. As the cemetery expanded, other societies and individuals joined the volunteer firemen in building impressive monuments, and leading architects and craftsmen were called upon to design and build tombs commemorating the lives of many of New Orleans's most prominent citizens. Crafted in marble, granite, and cast iron, the tombs here are among the nation's leading examples of memorial architecture. ⊠ *120 City Park Ave., Mid-City* ۞ *Daily 8–5.*

Lake Lawn Metairie Cemetery. The largest cemetery in the metropolitan area, known to locals simply as Metairie Cemetery, is the final resting place of nine Louisiana governors, seven New Orleans mayors, three Confederate generals, and musician Louis Prima. Many of New Orleans's noted families are also interred here in elaborate monuments ranging from Gothic crypts to Romanesque mausoleums to Egyptian pyramids. The arrangement of tombs reflects the cemetery's former life as a horse-racing track, with the tombs arranged around the perimeter and interior. ⊠ *5100 Pontchartrain Blvd., Mid-City* ۞ *Daily 8–5.*

Odd Fellows Rest. The secretive Independent Order of Odd Fellows association founded this cemetery in 1849. Built to house the remains of those pushed to the fringes of 1800s New Orleans society—often African-Americans, immigrants, and victims of yellow fever plagues—the cemetery is famous for its "verbally expressive" tributes. Poetic passages in numerous languages grace the graves and monuments. "In the midst of life, we are in death," one tomb declares. While the 1849 dedication ceremony was lavish—a splendid ceremony and a grand procession parade led by two circus bandwagons, one pulled by 16 horses—the local chapter of the Order of Odd Fellows has long since disappeared, and the cemetery shows signs of neglect and vandalism. ⊠ *5055 Canal St., Mid-City* ۞ *Daily 8–5.*

St. Louis Cemetery No. 3. One block from the entrance to City Park, at the end of Esplanade Avenue, this cemetery, established in 1854, was built on an old leper colony. Governor Galvez exiled the lepers to this area of high ground along Bayou St. John, but during the yellow fever outbreak of 1853 they were removed yet again to make room for the dead. Storyville photographer E. J. Bellocq lies here, and the cemetery is notable for its neat rows of elaborate aboveground crypts, mausoleums, and carved stone angels soaring overhead. ⊠ *3428 Esplanade Ave., Bayou St. John* ۞ *Mon.–Sat. 9–3, Sun. 9–noon.*

Sightseeing
★★
Dining
★
Lodging
★
Shopping
★
Nightlife
★

With its tree-lined streets and avenues, neighborhood gathering places and historic landmarks, the Mid-City and Bayou St. John neighborhoods are decidedly more tranquil than their downtown counterparts. While you may not find "Huge-Ass Beers to Go" or music blaring out of every doorway here, you will find a quieter form of charm in the gardens, galleries, and lagoons of City Park, in the elaborately constructed tombs of the cemeteries, and on the tree-shaded patios and decks of the restaurants and cafés where you can listen to the church bells keep time as you relax with a cold drink.

Updated
by Troy
Thibodeaux

Above the French Quarter and below the lakefront, neither Uptown nor quite downtown, Mid-City is an amorphous yet proud territory embracing everything from massive, lush City Park to gritty storefronts along Carrollton Avenue. Much of this area was low-lying swamp until the late 1800s, and you can still see where the high ground was, such as along the Esplanade Ridge (now Esplanade Avenue) and along the banks of Bayou St. John. These are the stretches with many of the largest and most historic homes, churches, and landmarks, such as the St. Louis Cemetery No. 3. Edgar Degas, the famous French impressionist painter, found refuge in this neighborhood when he lived and painted here, and his home is now a guesthouse and cultural center open to the public.

Another of the neighborhood's most famous landmarks is the Fairgrounds Race Course and Slots, which is an institution among horserace fans worldwide and home of the internationally famous New Orleans Jazz and Heritage Festival, held every spring on the last weekend in April and first weekend in May. Both the festival and horseracing cultures run deep in this neighborhood. The Luling Mansion, for example, with its stately row of hitching posts out front, is often called the "Jockey's Mansion," a reference to its days as a boardinghouse for traveling jockeys, and racetrack paraphernalia turns up regularly as decor in people's yards and homes. The neighborhood plays host to more than a dozen festivals and celebrations a year, from block parties like Boogaloo on the Bayou to grand-scale mega-events like the Voodoo Festival. It's easy to discern which festival is approaching by the bright flags and signs that spring up on people's yards and porches.

Of course, not all of Mid-City is quaint or picturesque. The worn storefronts along Carrollton Avenue speak of a neighborhood made up of tremendous ethnic and economic diversity. You'll be amazed to find great restaurants, cultural landmarks, and restored former plantation homes just blocks away from tough, inner-city blocks.

That being said, one of the neighborhood's simplest, most enduring, and most popular pleasures is a stroll along Bayou St. John. The waterway runs for miles, from Mid-City to the lakefront, and you'll find all sorts of people out enjoying the wide grassy banks—walking, biking, fishing, or just strolling along and admiring the reflection of a sunset in the smooth water.

MID-CITY

Mid-City is primarily a working-class neighborhood, which is evident in many of its iconic cultural landmarks and gathering places, such as great Irish pubs (Finn McCool's), bowling alleys that double as concert halls, and City Park, which hosts sporting events, allows fishing, and provides picnic and cookout spaces. Along Carrollton Avenue, you can find everything from old-school Italian ice-cream parlors to strips of inexpensive Central American restaurants. Recently, the neighborhood has begun to make room for the expansion of the New Orleans medical corridor, a complex of cutting-edge hospitals and medical facilities, which city planners have promised will herald an economic boom for the neighborhood and the region. In the short term, this expansion has fueled some interesting building projects, such as converting the old Falstaff Brewing Company building into modern condominiums and apartments. This is not the best neighborhood for traditional sightseeing, but Mid-City is a residential area brimming with energy and continually rebounding, one block at a time, from the heavy damage that was inflicted upon it by post-Katrina flooding.

TOP ATTRACTIONS

City Park. This 150-year-old, 1,300-acre expanse of moss-draped oaks and gentle lagoons is 2 miles from the French Quarter, but feels like it could be another world. With the largest mature grove of live oaks in the world, including old grove trees that are more than 600 years old, the park offers a certain natural majesty that's difficult to find in urban areas. The art deco benches, fountains, bridges, and ironwork are remnants of a 1930s Works Progress Administration refurbishment and add to the dreamy scenery that visitors enjoy boating and biking through. Highlights include the **New Orleans Museum of Art,** the **Sydney and Walda Besthoff Sculpture Garden,** the **New Orleans Botanical Garden,** the kid-friendly **Carousel Gardens Amusement Park and Storyland,** a

Fodor's Choice
★

City Park is one of the most serene places in all of New Orleans.

golf course, equestrian stable, sports facilities, and picnic areas. Check the park's website for seasonal activities and special events, such as music festivals, the annual Easter egg hunt, and the eye-popping wonderland that is Celebration in the Oaks, around the Christmas holiday. Most of the park's offerings are free, but several of the venues inside City Park charge their own separate admission fees. ⊠ *Bordered by City Park Ave., Robert E. Lee Blvd., Marconi Dr., and Bayou St. John, Mid-City* ☎ *504/482–4888* ⊕ *www.neworleanscitypark.com.*

Carousel Gardens Amusement Park. This small amusement park, open seasonally, has a New Orleans treasure as its centerpiece—a 1906 carousel, one of only 100 antique wooden carousels left in the nation, that is on the National Register of Historic Places. In addition to the cherished "flying horses," the park has rides like the new Musik Express, Rockin' Tug, Coney Tower, Ferris Wheel, Bumper Cars, Monkey Jump, Red Baron miniplane, Scrambler, and Tilt-A-Whirl. The rides here are mostly geared to younger children, not hard-core thrill seekers, but adults and kids both like the miniature train that takes passengers on a gentle sightseeing tour through City Park. ⊠ *Victory Ave., City Park, Mid-City* ☎ *504/482–9432* 🎟 *$3 admission; rides $3 each* ☉ *Mar. 10–May 27, weekends 11–6; Memorial Day through Labor Day, Thurs. 10–6, Fri. 10–10, Sat. 11–10, Sun. 11–6.*

New Orleans Botanical Garden. This garden, opened in 1936 as a Depression-era project of the Works Progress Administration (WPA), is one of the few remaining examples of public garden design from the WPA and art deco period. The garden's collections contain more than 2,000 varieties of plants from all over the world, which are complemented by sites such as the Conservatory of the Two Sisters and the Yakumo Nihon Teien Japanese Garden, and theme gardens containing aquatics, roses, native plants, ornamental trees, and shrubs and perennials. The garden serves as a showcase of three notable talents: New Orleans architect Richard Koch, landscape architect William Wiedorn, and artist Enrique Alférez. Adding a touch of fun, the Historic Train Garden, open on weekends, offers visitors the chance to enjoy baguette-sized cars rolling through a miniature New Orleans village. ⊠ *Victory Ave., City Park, Mid-City* ☎ *504/483–9488* ⊠ *$6* ☉ *Tues.–Sun. 10–4:30.*

Storyland. This whimsical park adjacent to the amusement park has been a favorite romping ground for generations of New Orleans kids. The park's figures and settings are culled from children's literature and created by some of the city's premiere Mardi Gras float builders. With more than 25 larger-than-life storybook exhibits, kids can climb aboard Captain Hook's pirate ship, visit the old lady who lived in a shoe, and journey with Pinocchio into the mouth of a whale. ⊠ *Victory Ave., City Park, Mid-City* ☎ *504/482–9432* ⊕ *neworleanscitypark.com* ⊠ *$3* ☉ *Daily 10–5.*

Fodor's Choice ★ **New Orleans Museum of Art (NOMA)**. Gracing the main entrance to City Park, this traditional fine-arts museum, built in 1911, is considered by many to be the centerpiece of the whole area. Drawing from classic Greek architecture, the gorgeous structure now boasts several modern wings that bring additional light and space to the grand old building. An elegant central staircase carries visitors to the upper floors, and the many formal rooms offer superb gallery exhibits. The jeweled treasures, particularly some of the famous eggs by Peter Carl Fabergé, are a favorite exhibit, along with European and American paintings, sculpture, drawings, prints, and photography. The museum holds one of the largest glass collections in the country and has developed an Art of the Americas collection that includes a range of Latin American and Native American works. Several period-room installations feature 18th- and 19th-century American furniture and decorative arts. The comprehensive Asian art wing includes a good selection of Japanese paintings of the Edo period. African, Oceanic, pre-Columbian, and Louisiana art are also represented. In addition, the museum offers a year-round schedule of traveling and special exhibits, special events, openings, guest lectures, and tours.

Henry Moore's handsome *Reclining Mother and Child* greets visitors at the entrance of the **Sydney and Walda Besthoff Sculpture Garden**. Most of the garden's 60-some sculptures, representing some of the biggest names in modern art, were donated by local pharmacy magnate and avid collector Sydney Besthoff. Meandering trails and bridges over bayou lagoons carry visitors through a fascinating combination of famed traditional sculpture and contemporary works, including major pieces by Jacques Lipchitz, Barbara Hepworth, and Joel Shapiro. The garden is open Wednesday to Sunday 10 to 4:45; admission is free. ⊠ *City Park, 1 Collins Diboll Circle, Mid-City* ☎ *504/658–4100* ⊕ *www.noma.org* ⊠ *$10* ☉ *Tues.–Thurs. and weekends 10–5, Fri. 10–9.*

7

Longue Vue House and Gardens. While technically in the Lakewood neighborhood, this beautiful destination is in easy walking distance of the Mid-City streetcar. Fourteen separate gardens are arranged throughout 8 acres of beautifully maintained property, embellished with fountains, architectural flourishes, and gorgeous pathways. This city estate was fashioned in the 1940s after the great country houses of England, and the villa-style mansion is decorated with its original furnishings of English and American antiques, priceless tapestries, modern art, porcelain, and pottery. Longue Vue is open Tuesday through Saturday, and guests can visit the house by guided tour or explore the gardens at their own leisure. Themed gardens include the formal Spanish court, modeled after a 14th-century Spanish garden, as well as a Discovery Garden, which introduces kids to the intricacies and wonders of horticulture. ✉ *7 Bamboo Rd., Lakewood* ☎ *504/488–5488* ⊕ *www.longuevue.com* 💵 *$10* ⏱ *House and garden Tues.–Sat. 10–4:30, Sun. 1–5; shop Tues.– Sat. 10–5, Sun. 1–5.*

BAYOU ST. JOHN

Just up Esplanade Avenue from the French Quarter, the Bayou St. John neighborhood is known for its beautiful shady lanes, gorgeous homes, and laid-back vibe. Great restaurants, cafés, and corner bars dot the landscape, with sidewalk seating and relaxed patios. It's also home to the New Orleans Fairgrounds Race Course and Slots, one of the nation's premier horse-racing venues and home to the world-famous New Orleans Jazz and Heritage Festival. St. Louis Cemetery No. 3 opens its gates onto Esplanade Avenue, inviting visitors to come explore the intricate rows of aboveground tombs, towering vaults, and statuesque mausoleums. At the end of the avenue, you'll discover Bayou St. John, the scenic waterway that begins in Mid-City, meanders through Faubourg St. John, and ends at the lakefront.

TOP ATTRACTIONS

Bayou St. John. A bayou is a natural inlet, usually a slow moving, narrow waterway that emerges from the swamp at one end and joins a larger body of water at the other. This bayou—the only one remaining in New Orleans—borders City Park on the east and extends about 7 miles from Lake Pontchartrain to just past Orleans Avenue. It is named for John the Baptist, whose nativity (St. John's Eve, June 23), the most important day in the year for voodoo practitioners, was notoriously celebrated on the bayou's banks in the 1800s. The first European settlers in the area, believed to have been trappers, coexisted with Native Americans here beginning in 1704. Today, the Bayou is still a popular destination among New Orleanians, whether for tradition's sake, such as the famed Mardi Gras Indians who gather for their annual celebrations, or simply for a relaxing afternoon of fishing, boating, or picnicking along the grassy banks. Scenic biking and walking trails run alongside the waterway all the way to the lakefront, where you can watch the graceful old homes of picturesque Moss Street morph into the dazzling waterfront mansions of Bancroft Drive. ⊠ *From foot of Jefferson Davis Pkwy. to Lakeshore Dr., Bayou St. John.*

Pitot House. One of the few surviving houses that lined the bayou in the late 1700s, and the only Creole-colonial style country house in the city open to the public, Pitot House is named for James Pitot, who bought the property in 1810 as a country home for his family. In addition to being one of the city's finest merchants, Pitot built one of the first cotton presses in New Orleans, served as the city's mayor from 1804 to 1805, and later as parish court judge. The Pitot House was restored and moved 200 feet to its current location in the 1960s to make way for the expansion of Cabrini High School. It is noteworthy for its stucco-covered brick-between-post construction, an example of which is exposed on the second floor. The house is typical of the West Indies style brought to Louisiana by early colonists, with galleries around the house that protect the interior from both rain and sunshine. There aren't any interior halls to stifle ventilation, and opposing doors encourage a cross breeze. The house is furnished with period antiques from the United States, including special pieces from Louisiana. ⊠ *1440 Moss St., Bayou St. John* ☎ *504/482–0312* ⊕ *www.louisianalandmarks.org* 🖼 *$7* ☉ *Wed.–Sat. 10–3 or by appointment.*

WORTH NOTING

Alcee Fortier Park. This tiny sliver of a park was named for philanthropist Alcee Fortier, who owned much of the surrounding area in the 19th century and founded a public school. A neighborhood favorite, the park is almost completely maintained by the efforts of local volunteers who tend the collection of whimsical sculpture and art, keep up the landscaping, and make sure the concrete tables with chess boards built into them are ready for game time (complete with baskets of chess pieces). It's a focal point of the Bayou St. John neighborhood, surrounded by a concentration of hip restaurants, neighborhood groceries, and boutique shops. ⊠ *Esplanade Ave. and Ponce de Leon Blvd., Bayou St. John.*

Benachi-Torre House. This historic Greek Revival mansion was built in 1859 for the Greek consul in New Orleans and was a significant part of the original expansion of New Orleans into this neighborhood. Directly across from the Degas House, this intersection forms something of a historical hub. The house earned the nickname "Rendezvous des Chasseurs" (meeting place of hunters) during the 19th century when much of this area was still undeveloped swampland. The gorgeous house and gardens are now primarily a private event space and a popular setting for New Orleans weddings. ⊠ *2257 Bayou Rd., at N. Tonti St., Bayou St. John* ☎ *800/308–7040* ⊕ *www.benachihouse.com.*

Cabrini High School and Mother Cabrini Shrine. Mother Frances Cabrini, the first American-citizen saint (she was canonized in 1946), purchased the land between Esplanade Avenue and Bayou St. John near City Park in 1905 and built the Sacred Heart Orphan Asylum here. She stayed in the Pitot House, which was on her property until she gave it to the city during construction of the orphanage. In 1959 the institution was converted to a girls' high school in St. Cabrini's name. Her bedroom has been preserved as it was when she lived here, filled with personal

7

effects and maintained as a shrine. Tours of her room and Sacred Heart Chapel are available by appointment. ✉ *3400 Esplanade Ave., Bayou St. John* ☎ *504/483–8690.*

Edgar Degas House. Impressionist painter Edgar Degas, whose mother and grandmother were born in New Orleans, stayed with his Musson cousins in this house during an 1872 visit to New Orleans, producing more than 70 works while here. Today this is a bed-and-breakfast and historic home, with public tours given by Degas's great grand nieces, a film on Degas's family and their sojourn in New Orleans, special events, lectures, and discussions of the historic neighborhood. Feel free to drop by for a look if you're in the neighborhood, but check the website or call ahead for event dates or to make an appointment for a full tour. ✉ *2306 Esplanade Ave., Bayou St. John* ☎ *504/821–5009* ⊕ *www.degashouse. com* ⊠ *$15* ⊙ *Tours by appointment.*

Fair Grounds Race Course and Slots. The third-oldest racetrack in the country sits just off Esplanade Avenue, among the houses of Bayou St. John. In recent times, the race track has weathered some difficult challenges, first with a fire that destroyed the historic old grandstand in the mid-1990s, and then when Hurricane Katrina dealt the grounds a blow in 2005. The newly renovated facility is modern and comfortable throughout, complete with clubhouse restaurant, grandstand café, and concession-snack bars. A slots facility was added in 2008, and the annual schedule now includes the popular Starlight Racing series, held Friday nights. The grounds are also home to the annual Jazz Fest and Heritage Festival. For the clubhouse, be sure and make reservations and be aware that proper attire is required (collared shirts, closed shoes, no shorts). ✉ *1751 Gentilly Blvd., Bayou St. John* ☎ *504/943–2200 for box and restaurant reservations, 504/944–5515 for general information* ⊕ *www.fairgroundsracecourse.com* ⊠ *Grandstand free, clubhouse $6* ⊙ *Thanksgiving–Mar., check website for days and times.*

House on Bayou Road. This West Indies Creole–style house served as the main house to an indigo plantation. It was built in 1798 by Domingo Fleitas, who was originally from the Canary Islands. Today, it houses a bed-and-breakfast and the **New Orleans Cooking Experience,** a cooking school in residence. Call well in advance to book a cooking class. ✉ *2275 Bayou Rd., Bayou St. John* ☎ *504/945–0992* ⊕ *www. houseonbayouroad.com.*

Luling Mansion. Also called the "Jockey's Mansion," this massive, three-story Italianate mansion is a neighborhood landmark (and now a popular setting for Hollywood film crews). Designed by architect James Gallier Jr., it was built in 1865 for Florence A. Luling. When the Louisiana Jockey Club took over the Creole Race Course (now the Fair Grounds) in 1871, it purchased this nearby mansion. For the next 20-odd years, it served as the racing organization's clubhouse. It is not open to the public. ✉ *1436–1438 Leda St., Bayou St. John.*

Where to Eat

WORD OF MOUTH

"We eventually made our way to the informal destination—Café du Monde. The line was long so we wandered on, looking for an alternative. Then I realized 'Who am I kidding? There IS no alternative to Café du Monde!' We doubled back, took our place in line and enjoyed the sights and sounds of New Orleans."

—starrs

By Todd A. Price

New Orleanians are obsessed with food. Over lunch, they're likely talking about dinner. Ask where to get the best gumbo, and you'll spark a heated debate among city natives. Food unites the city.

Everyone, no matter what neighborhood they're from or what they do for a living, wants a plate of red beans and rice on Monday, has a favorite spot for a roast beef po'boy, and holds strong opinions about the proper flavor for a shaved ice "sno-ball."

The menus of New Orleans's restaurants reflect the many cultures that have contributed to this always-simmering culinary gumbo pot over the last three centuries. It's easy to find French, African, Spanish, German, Italian, and Caribbean influences—and increasingly Asian and Latin American as well. The speckled trout amandine at Antoine's could have been on the menu when the French Creole institution opened in 1840. Across the Mississippi River on the West Bank, Tan Dinh serves fragrant bowls of pho soup that remind New Orleans's large Vietnamese population of the home they left in the 1970s. And at MiLa, husband-and-wife team Slade Rushing and Allison Vines-Rushing apply the cutting-edge culinary techniques they learned in New York City to the dishes they grew up eating in Mississippi and Louisiana.

For years, New Orleans paid little attention to food trends from the East and West coasts. Recently, however, the city has taken more notice of the "latest things." In Orleans Parish, you'll now find gastropubs, gourmet burgers, and numerous small-plate specialists. In a town where people track the crawfish season as closely as the pennant race, no one has to preach the virtues of eating seasonally. New Orleans is still one of the most unique places in America to eat. There's no danger that will change.

NEW ORLEANS DINING PLANNER

RESERVATIONS

Most restaurants in New Orleans accept reservations, and many popular places are booked quickly, especially on weekend nights. Reservations are always a good idea: we mention them only when they're essential or not accepted. Reserving several weeks ahead is not too far in advance for trips during Mardi Gras, French Quarter Fest, Jazz Fest, and other special events.

WHAT TO WEAR

Unless otherwise noted, restaurants listed in this book allow casual dress. Reviews mention dress only when men are required to wear a jacket or tie. In a luxury restaurant or in one of the old-line, conservative Creole places, dress appropriately.

TIPPING

The standard for tipping in New Orleans is no different from that in the rest of the country—at least 15% or 20%. Sales taxes for restaurants are 9.75%, which means that doubling the tax is a widespread practice. Most menus contain a notice when a service charge is automatically added to the bill for large groups.

PRICES

Meals in the city's more upscale restaurants cost about what you'd expect to pay in other U.S. cities. Bargains are found in the more casual restaurants, where a simple lunch or dinner can frequently be had for less than $25. However, even the more expensive restaurants offer fixed-price menus of three or four courses for substantially less than what an à la carte meal costs. Serving sizes are more than generous—some would say unmanageable for the average eater—so many diners order two appetizers rather than a starter and a main course, which can make ordering dessert more practical. Some restaurants offer small- or large-plate options.

Prices in the reviews are the average cost of a main course at dinner or, if dinner is not served, at lunch.

USING THE MAPS

Throughout the chapter, you'll see mapping symbols and coordinates (✛ 3:F2) at the end of each review. Maps are located within the chapter. The first number after the ✛ symbol indicates the map number. Following that is the property's coordinate on the map grid.

Lake Pontchartrain

LAKESHORE

Leon C Simon Dr

Robert E Lee Blvd

Robert E Lee Blvd

LAKE VIEW

City Park

GENTILLY

Chef Menteur Hwy

610

ST BERNARD

Peoples Ave

NORTH BYWATER

City Park Ave

Esplanade Ave

90

10

61

BAYOU ST JOHN

SEVENTH WARD

39

N Claiborne Ave

N Robertson St

MID-CITY
old-school
New Orleans,
both high-end
and low

TREME

FAUBOURG MARIGNY
funky ethnic
and upscale
bar snacks

46

BYWATER
hipster
hangout
with cheap
eats

FRENCH QUARTER
classic Creole to
cutting-edge
contemporary

10

CBD
expense-
account meals,
upscale hotel
restaurants

ALGIERS POINT

General Meyer Ave

428

Tulane University

CARROLLTON

Loyola University

WAREHOUSE DISTRICT
celebrity chefs
and cool spots
for condo
dwellers

90

FRERET

LOWER GARDEN DISTRICT

GRETNA

428

90

UPTOWN
from po'boy
joints to chic
neighborhood
bistros

GARDEN DISTRICT
grand dining
amid historic
mansions

Tchoupitoulas St

Mississippi River

HARVEY

River Rd

4th St

0   1 mi
0   1 km

BEST BETS FOR
NEW ORLEANS DINING

With hundreds of restaurants to choose from, how will you decide where to eat? Fodor's writers and editors have selected their favorite restaurants by price, cuisine, and experience in the Best Bets lists below. In the first column, Fodor's Choice properties represent the "best of the best" in every price category.

Fodor's Choice ★

Acme Oyster and Seafood Restaurant, $, p. 146

August, $$$$, p. 156

Bayona, $$$, p. 146

Boucherie, $, p. 174

Café du Monde, $, p. 147

Central Grocery, $, p. 148

Cochon, $$, p. 165

Cochon Butcher, $, p. 165

Company Burger, $, p. 171

Domenica, $$, p. 157

Emeril's Delmonico, $$$, p. 167

Galatoire's, $$$, p. 148

Herbsaint, $$$, p. 158

Mosca's, $$, p. 177

Patois, $$$, p. 173

Stella!, $$$$, p 154

Sucré, $, p. 170

BEST BY PRICE

$

Acme Oyster and Seafood Restaurant, p. 146

Boucherie, p. 174

Café du Monde, p. 147

Casamento's, p. 171

Cochon Butcher, p. 165

Mahony's Po-Boy Shop, p. 173

Port of Call, p. 154

$$

Cochon, p. 165

Domenica, p. 157

Irene's Cuisine, p. 149

Mosca's, p. 177

Rio Mar, p. 166

$$$

Bayona, p. 146

Emeril's Delmonico, p. 167

Galatoire's, p. 148

Herbsaint, p. 158

Patois, p. 173

$$$$

Antoine's, p. 146

August, p. 156

Broussard's, p. 147

Commander's Palace, p. 167

Stella!, p. 154

BEST BY CUISINE

AMERICAN

Emeril's, $$$, p. 166

Iris, $$, p. 150

ASIAN

Sukho Thai, $$, p. 155

Tan Dinh, $, p. 178

CAJUN

Bon Ton Café, $$$, p. 157

Cochon, $$, p. 165

K-Paul's Louisiana Kitchen, $$$, p. 150

CREOLE

Arnaud's, $$$, p. 146

Brigtsen's, $$$, p. 174

Commander's Palace, $$$$, p. 167

Emeril's Delmonico, $$$, p. 167

Galatoire's, $$$, p. 148

Upperline, $$$, p. 174

ITALIAN

A Mano, $$, p. 156

Domenica, $$, p. 157

Irene's Cuisine, $$, p. 149

Mosca's, $$, p. 177

SEAFOOD

Acme Oyster and Seafood Restaurant, $, p. 146

Casamento's, $, p. 171

GW Fins, $$$, p. 149

BEST BY EXPERIENCE

BRUNCH

Brennan's, $$$, p. 147

Commander's Palace, $$$$, p. 167

Mr. B's Bistro, $$$, p. 151

Palace Café, $$, p. 152

Stanley, $, p. 154

CHILD-FRIENDLY

Acme Oyster and Seafood Restaurant, $, p. 146

Angelo Brocato's, $, p. 175

Crabby Jack's, $, p. 177

Johnny's Po-Boys, $, p. 150

Port of Call, $, p. 154

MOST ROMANTIC

Bayona, $$$, p. 146

Gautreau's, $$$, p. 172

Martinique Bistro, $$, p. 173

Stella!, $$$$, p. 154

8

THE FRENCH QUARTER

In the city's oldest neighborhood, grand restaurants founded before the Civil War can be found around the corner from contemporary, cutting-edge culinary destinations.

(above and bottom right) Classic New Orleans architecture and cuisine at Arnaud's. (top right) An elegant setting at Tujague's.

When you need a place to celebrate a birthday, an anniversary, or just the joy of being alive, head to the historic district of the French Quarter. At Galatoire's, the city's most respected members start lunch with a cocktail and are still carrying on three hours later. At K-Paul's, Paul Prudhomme kicked off the Cajun craze in the 1980s, and the massive plates of blackened fish and crawfish étouffée here still feel like revelations. And on a quiet backstreet, the culinary genius Scott Boswell redefines contemporary cuisine at Stella! on a nightly basis.

While the Quarter, as locals call it, is an essential stop for any visitor, it's also a living neighborhood. The residents can be found grabbing a pastry before work at Croissant d'Or, making a lunch stop at Johnny's Po'boys, or meeting friends for garlicky plates of pasta at Irene's Cuisine.

GODDESS GOURMET

The tiny **Green Goddess** (⊠ *307 Exchange Alley* ☎ *504/301–3347* ✛ *1:D3*) blends the do-it-yourself attitude of a punk rocker with the laid-back affability of a hippy. The truly global dishes, like Korean oyster pancakes or bison meat loaf, might confound even the most ardent foodie, but hip young gourmets keep returning for creative dinners that can feel like performance art.

BAR BITES

Some of the French Quarter's bastions of Creole cuisine are relatively formal, and you'll feel more comfortable in a jacket, or wearing a dress. If you prefer a more casual dress code and attitude, dine in the bar areas of these institutions. **Antoine's** (✉ 713 St. Louis St. ☎ 504/581–4422 ✛ 1:C3) sold its first meal in 1840 and little has changed since then—although one of the front dining rooms was converted into a bar where you can pull up a stool and order a Sazerac. The bar snacks include unusual items like a po' boy version of its original "Oyster Foch" appetizer, with fried oysters, pâté de foie gras, and a thick, meaty classic French sauce made with butter, shallots, and white wine. If the kitchen isn't slammed, they'll make you anything on the regular menu. (See the full review for more info.)

Arnaud's (✉ 813 Bienville St. ☎ 504/523–5433 ✛ 1:D3) has one foot in the past and one in the present. Founded in 1918, it has managed to preserve its history without feeling like an artifact. Chris Hannah, the restaurant's nationally known bartender, takes the same attitude, drawing inspiration equally from the local historical archives and the latest trends. It's worth eating at the bar, which has its own menu, just to pass the night in Hannah's company. Besides, souffléed potatoes might be the world's best accompaniment to a drink. (See the full review for more info.)

At **Tujague's** (✉ 823 Decatur St. ☎ 504/525–8676 ✛ 1:C4) dinner requires committing to a five-course set menu, but at the bar next door, you can order any item, like spicy shrimp in red rémoulade sauce, à la carte. You can also get a po' boy version of the signature boiled beef brisket with horseradish sauce. Trust us, this is a contender for one of the best sandwiches in the city. The wooden stand-up bar is even older than the restaurant. In 1856 it was imported from France, where it had already seen years of use from Parisian drinkers.

COLD COMFORTS

If anyone says they're not bothered by New Orleans's heat, they're lying. Thankfully, suffering through the summer has spurred the city to create cool treats so tempting, you'll want one even on a "frigid" 50°F day. **La Divina Gelateria** (✉ 621 St. Peter St. ☎ 504/302–2692 ✛ 1:C4), hidden behind the cathedral on Pirate's Alley, crafts creative gelato, like a chocolate made with Louisiana's own Abita Turbodog beer, and refreshing sorbets that use local citrus and berries. The New Orleans chain first opened on Magazine Street and now has a location in Uptown at Loyola University. At **Stanley's Service Bar** (✉ 547 St. Ann St. ☎ 504/587–0093 ✛ 1:C4), the take-out annex of Stanley's, you'll find a half-dozen homemade ice creams and sorbets with local flavors like pecan pie and bananas Foster. And don't forget New Orleans's classic hot-weather antidote: an iced café au lait from **Café du Monde** (✉ 800 Decatur St. ☎ 504/525–4544 ✛ 1:C4).

FAUBOURG MARIGNY

The Faubourg Marigny means music, and the area restaurants and bars cater to the club-hopping crowd with small plates and kitchens that stay open well past midnight.

(above) Frenchmen Street is a local favorite for food and entertainment. (bottom right) Singer John Boutté. (top right) Mimi's is a popular spot for late-night snacks.

The carefully preserved and colorfully painted cottages and shotgun houses of the Faubourg Marigny are home to artists, hipsters, and gay couples. Hidden among the residential zones, you'll find cool cafés, interesting ethnic options, and neighborhood hangouts with cheap eats. Travelers who stay at the area's small inns particularly appreciate the many options for breakfast.

Most travelers make a beeline for Frenchmen Street, a three-block stretch of live music clubs known as "Bourbon Street for locals" that begins on Esplanade Avenue at the edge of the French Quarter. Half the bars sell food, including snacks that can be gobbled down in a flash so that you can get back to the dance floor. Given the bohemian population and the large number of foreign visitors, it's no surprise that the Marigny boasts some of New Orleans's most eclectic and challenging food.

CAKE MAN

Steve "Cake Man" Himelfarb began his baking career selling slices of chocolate cake door to door. Now he's settled down at **Cake Café and Bakery** (✉ *2440 Chartres St.* ☎ *504/943–0010* ✛ *3:B5*), which has become a neighborhood fixture for homemade biscuits, challah French toast, and salads and sandwiches at lunch. Although Himelfarb no longer delivers, you can still get a red velvet cupcake to go.

TASTE OF THE CITY

John Boutté
Singer

The New Orleans–born singer John Boutté works a club like it's a concert hall. After New Orleans flooded in 2005, his mournful cover of Annie Lennox's "Why" captured an entire city's pain. More recently, his jaunty "Tremé Song" opens each episode of the acclaimed HBO series *Treme*. Boutté's most recent album is *Stew Called New Orleans*, and most Saturday nights, you can catch him at **d.b.a.** (⌧ *618 Frenchmen St.* ☎ *504/942–3731 ⊹ 1:A5*) playing an early show. Like everyone else in New Orleans, Boutté has strong opinions about where to eat.

Fodor's: Where do you go for New Orleans's best food?
John Boutté: My mom's kitchen. But when I go out to get something to eat in the Marigny, I like the old **Schiro's Cafe** (⌧ *2483 Royal St.* ☎ *504/944–6666 ⊹ 3:B5*).

Fodor's: What else do you like?
JB: **El Gato Negro** (⌧ *81 French Market Pl.* ☎ *504/525–9752 ⊹ 1:B5*). The service is nice. The food is fresh. Prior to the storm, I wasn't a big fan of Latin food. But their fish tacos are incredible. Their chicken mole is incredible. And the carrot and ginger margarita, oh my God, man. Off the hook.

Fodor's: Musicians often need food after a show. What are your late-night favorites?
JB: I try not to eat late at night, but sometimes you can't help yourself. You can go to **Mimi's in the Marigny** (⌧ *2601 Royal St.* ☎ *504/872–9868 ⊹ 3:B5*), and they have good tapas.

Fodor's: In the morning, where do you get breakfast?
JB: For breakfast, there is a cool place in Mid-City called **Huevos** (⌧ *4408 Banks St.* ☎ *504/482–6264 ⊹ 3:B3*). Really good place with nice folks. I'm always into service. If you've got good service, it usually goes along with the good food.

Fodor's: When you're on the road, what do you miss from New Orleans?
JB: What I really miss is something like making a quick, homemade oyster soup. Just chop up some celery, add a little butter, throw in your oysters, a little chicken stock, some heavy cream. That's a really good meal.

LATE-NIGHT FOOD

Take a 10-minute stroll from Frenchmen Street to **Mimi's in the Marigny** (⌧ *2601 Royal St.* ☎ *504/872–9868 ⊹ 3:B5*), a hipster hangout that also turns out classic Spanish tapas, such as empanadas, Serrano ham, and *patatas bravas* until 2 am Sunday–Thursday, and 4 am Friday and Saturday.

Find a lighter take on pub grub at **13 Monaghan** (⌧ *517 Frenchmen St.* ☎ *504/942–1345 ⊹ 1:B5*). At this smoke-free bar, many of the menu items are vegetarian, such as the tofu scramble or the portobello mushroom sandwich. It's open nightly until 3:30 am. **Yuki** (⌧ *525 Frenchmen St.* ☎ *504/943–1122 ⊹ 1:B5*) ups the exotic quotient on Frenchmen Street with traditional Japanese *izakaya*, tapas-like bar snacks that pair perfectly with beer, sake, or *shochu*. You can play it safe with grilled chicken or the oddly familiar deep-fried mashed potatoes. But the adventurous should opt for octopus balls or pork tongue. It's open until midnight Sunday–Thursday, and 2:30 am Friday and Saturday.

8

THE CBD (CENTRAL BUSINESS DISTRICT)

The CBD, or Central Business District, is as much about pleasure as work. Amid the modern high-rises, you'll discover many of New Orleans's most celebrated restaurants.

(above) Domenica brings upscale Italian to the CBD. (bottom right) *Cochon de lait* sandwich at Lüke. (top right) Sample the city's oysters at Drago's.

Taking advantage of company expense accounts, big-name modern restaurants have found a home in the CBD. Rising celebrity-chef John Besh, for example, has three places here: his flagship Restaurant August, the brasserie Lüke, and the rustic Italian venture Domenica inside the restored 1893 Roosevelt Hotel. This area is where you'll find exciting contemporary cuisine that keeps up with the latest national trends in fine dining. Despite the CBD's proximity to the French Quarter, the restaurants largely draw a local crowd and still know how to satisfy local appetites.

The CBD also has a plethora of budget options, especially for lunch when the office workers seek substance before returning to their desks. If you're trying to save money, or just want to avoid the many tourist traps in the French Quarter, it's worth crossing Canal Street to explore the CBD.

RUTH'S CHRIS

The steak chain Ruth's Chris started here, and it still honors those New Orleans roots with items like local-style "barbecue" shrimp (sautéed instead of smoked) and steaks brushed with butter. The original Ruth's Chris location didn't survive Katrina, so locals now head to this snazzy new outlet inside **Harrah's** hotel (✉ *525 Fulton St.* ☎ *504/587–7099* ✛ *2:B5*).

LUNCH LIKE A LOCAL

In New Orleans, the three-martini lunch lives on (although it's more likely to be a three-Sazerac lunch). But, as in most of America, the average office worker wants a quick midday meal that's not too expensive. Sometimes visitors need the same.

The Store (✉ *814 Gravier St.* ☎ *504/322–2446* ✛ *2:A3*) is designed for the office crowd. The menu of mainly sandwiches puts an upscale spin on familiar favorites, like the burger that can be topped with cheddar, Brie, or bleu cheese. Entrée-size salads are also a good bet. There is also a Latin American–theme sibling restaurant next door from the same owners, called La Tienda.

Due to trade through the port, New Orleans has always had a close relationship with the Caribbean. **Liborio's** (✉ *321 Magazine St.* ☎ *504/581–9680* ✛ *2:A4*), which opened in 1969, reflects that history. The lunch crowd here keeps coming back for classics like fried plantains, the shredded beef *ropa vieja*, and Cuban sandwiches with pork and ham. Expect to see lots of lawyers and judges taking a recess from the nearby courthouses.

Li'l Dizzy's (✉ *610 Poydras St.* ☎ *504/212–5656* ✛ *2:B3*) began as a humble café in the Tremé, the neighborhood north of the French Quarter. This second outlet, located in the converted lobby of an old bank, has a loftier vibe but the same Creole soul fare. Try the gumbo, fried chicken, or *trout Baquet*, a fillet topped with a buttery lemon-garlic sauce and a mound of crabmeat. Save room for a slice of bread pudding.

Midday is also a great time to taste the city's most celebrated restaurants at a discount. During the week, many places offer reasonably priced, three-course set lunches for around $20, including **MiLa**, the **Grill Room** inside the Windsor Court Hotel, and John Besh's **August**. At those prices, you can afford to order a few extra cocktails.

AFTERNOON EATS

Travelers aren't always on a regular schedule. The following restaurants stay open all afternoon to satisfy your hunger. At Cafe Adelaide's **Swizzle Stick Bar** (✉ *300 Poydras St.* ☎ *504/595–3305* ✛ *2:B4*) you can fill up on elevated bar snacks, like turtle soup, a burger with an absinthe-spiked barbecue sauce, or "corndogs" made with shrimp and *tasso* (a spicy smoked Cajun pork). The restaurant and bar are run by the same team behind Commander's Palace in the Garden District. Down the block at the Hilton Riverside, **Drago's** (✉ *2 Poydras St.* ☎ *504/584–3911* ✛ *2:B5*) charbroils oysters loaded with butter, herbs, garlic, and Parmesan cheese. The rest of the menu can be hit or miss, but those oysters are legendary for a reason. A few blocks over in the Warehouse District, Donald Link's celebrated restaurant **Herbsaint** (✉ *701 St. Charles St.* ☎ *504/524–4114* ✛ *2:B3*) offers an abbreviated "bistro" menu with salads, sandwiches, and seasonal entrées on weekdays 1:30–5:30 pm.

8

UPTOWN

Stretching from the Garden District to the city's western border, the collection of neighborhoods known as Uptown is the place to break bread with the locals and capture the daily rhythms of the Crescent City.

(above) Diners sample modern Southern fare at Boucherie. (bottom right) Camellia Grill is a favorite with locals. (top right) Enjoy sweet treats at the city's famed bakeries.

Most of Uptown is residential, and the homes range from little brightly colored shotguns to imposing historic mansions. The restaurants also cover the gamut: there are corner po' boy shops and seafood joints, as well as bistros overseen by nationally known chefs. Whether you're looking for a meal that's budget friendly or fancy, you'll be certain to find plenty of delicious options. The boutique-lined strip of Magazine Street runs the entire length of Uptown, and along the way you'll discover everything from bakeries and sno-ball stands to family eateries and nationally known dining destinations. And nearly overnight, Freret Street has blossomed from an abandoned corridor to a collection of high-end pizza, burger, and hot dog restaurants. Exploring this vast zone really requires a car or several taxi trips, and too many visitors don't make the effort. That's too bad, because they're missing out on one of New Orleans's most vibrant areas.

MARKET MEALS

Each Tuesday from 9 am to 1 pm at the **Crescent City Farmers Market** (✉ *200 Broadway St.* ☎ *504/861–4488* ⊕ *www. crescentcityfarmersmarket. org* ✛ *3:D2*), the professionals can show you what to do. Every month a different restaurant, from Commander's Palace to perhaps a neighborhood crepe stand, puts together lunch offerings like Gulf fish tacos or Mississippi shiitake mushroom soup.

BEST OF BREAKFAST

If the cup of coffee at **Slim Goodies** (✉ *3322 Magazine St.* ☎ *504/891–3447* ✛ *3:D4*) doesn't wake you up, then the hipster staff and jukebox packed with vintage rock and R&B is guaranteed to get you moving. The kitchen turns out big plates with funny names, like the Little Goat, with scrambled eggs, bell peppers, pesto, and goat cheese; or the Orleans Slammer, with hash browns, chili, and bacon and eggs.

At **Coulis** (✉ *3625 Prytania St.* ☎ *504/304–4265* ✛ *3:D3*), a quieter crowd of couples from the neighborhood and staff from the nearby hospital queue up for classic breakfast fare upgraded with fine-dining touches. Gruyère is an option in the omelets, fresh salsa accompanies the huevos rancheros, and eggs Benedict is served over a jalapeño corn cake and topped with finely shredded pork "debris."

For another reliable morning option, seek out **Riccobono's Panola Street Cafe** (✉ *7801 Panola St.* ☎ *504/314–1810* ✛ *3:C2*) located blocks from any major street in a tree-lined neighborhood. Although there might be a line out front on the weekends, the kitchen and efficient staff keep the tables turning at a steady clip.

For an old-school alternative, head to **Camellia Grill** (✉ *626 Carrollton Ave.* ☎ *504/309–2679* ✛ *3:C2*), where you almost always have to wait, no matter the day or time. Opened in 1946, this Southern diner is beloved by college students and generations of alumni. Everyone sits at the snaking marble counter, where waiters in white shirts and bow ties generously ladle out wisdom, fist bumps, and oversized plates of eggs, chili omelets, and pecan waffles. But don't linger over that cup of joe too long, or the hungry hordes waiting for your stool might begin shooting you dirty looks. Even Southern hospitality has its limits. In 2010, a second location that almost exactly replicates the original opened in the French Quarter (✉ *540 Chartres St.* ☎ *504/522–1800* ✛ *1:C4*),

SWEET TREATS

For traditional baked goods, stop by **La Boulangerie** (✉ *4600 Magazine St.* ☎ *504/269–3777* ✛ *3:D3*), where you'll be greeted by a French accent and cases of croissants and turnovers. Near Audubon Park, a culinary school–trained pastry chef opened the café **Tartine** (✉ *7217 Perrier St.* ☎ *504/866–4860* ✛ *3:D2*), where you can satisfy your sweet tooth with a flaky éclair or a delicate French-style macaroon. **Maple Street Patisserie** (✉ *7638 Maple St.* ☎ *504/247–7912* ✛ *3:C2*) is run by a Polish-born baker, but he's also a master of New World treats like Cuban pastries filled with guava and cheese, as well as all-American doughnuts. If you want a truly New Orleans sweet, pay a visit to **Tee-Eva's** (✉ *5201 Magazine St.* ☎ *504/899–8350* ✛ *3:D3*), where the gregarious namesake is known for pralines and miniature pecan, cream-cheese pecan, and sweet-potato pies.

8

RESTAURANT REVIEWS

Listed alphabetically within neighborhood.

THE FRENCH QUARTER

$ SEAFOOD 👶 Fodor's Choice ★

🍴 **Acme Oyster and Seafood Restaurant.** A rough-edge classic in every way, this no-nonsense eatery at the entrance to the French Quarter is a prime source for cool and salty raw oysters on the half shell; legendary shrimp, oyster, and roast-beef po' boys; and tender, expertly seasoned red beans and rice. Expect lengthy lines, often a half-block long—trust us, though, it's worth it. Crowds lighten in the late afternoon. [S] *Average main: $12* ✉ *724 Iberville St., French Quarter* ☎ *504/522–5973* 🌐 *www.acmeoyster.com* ✍ *Reservations not accepted* ✥ *1:D3.*

$$$$ CREOLE

🍴 **Antoine's.** If Antoine's wasn't already a culinary deity, Frances Parkinson Keyes made it one with her 1948 novel *Dinner at Antoine's.* Though some people believe Antoine's heyday passed before the turn of the 20th century, others wouldn't leave New Orleans without at least one order of oysters Rockefeller, a dish invented here—baked oysters topped with a parsley-based sauce and bread crumbs. Other notables on the bilingual menu include *pommes de terre soufflées* (fried potato puffs), pompano *en papillote* (baked in parchment paper), and baked Alaska. Tourists generally sit in the front room, but walking through the grand labyrinth is a must. Be prepared for lackluster service. A jacket is preferred, but casually dressed diners can order most of the classic menu at the adjoining Hermes Bar. [S] *Average main: $36* ✉ *713 St. Louis St., French Quarter* ☎ *504/581–4422* 🌐 *www.antoines.com* ✍ *Reservations essential* ⏲ *No dinner Sun.* ✥ *1:C3.*

$$$ CREOLE

🍴 **Arnaud's.** This grande dame of classic Creole restaurants still sparkles. In the main dining room, ornate etched glass reflects light from charming old chandeliers while the late founder, Arnaud Cazenave, gazes from an oil portrait. The adjoining jazz bistro offers the same food but is a more casual and music-filled dining experience. The ambitious menu includes classic dishes as well as more contemporary ones. Always reliable are Shrimp Arnaud (cold shrimp in a superb rémoulade), Oysters Bienville, Petit Filet Lafitte, and praline crepes. Jackets are requested in the main dining room. Check out the Mardi Gras museum upstairs. [S] *Average main: $35* ✉ *813 Bienville St., French Quarter* ☎ *504/523–5433* 🌐 *www.arnauds.com* ✍ *Reservations essential* ⏲ *No lunch Mon.–Sat.* ✥ *1:D3*

$$$ SOUTHWESTERN Fodor's Choice ★

🍴 **Bayona.** "New World" is the label Louisiana native Susan Spicer applies to her cooking style, and resulting delicious dishes include the goat cheese crouton with mushrooms, one of the Bayona's specialties, or the Caribbean pumpkin soup with coconut. A legendary favorite at lunch is the sandwich of smoked duck, cashew peanut butter, and pepper jelly. ■ **TIP→ A three-course small-plates lunch is available on Saturday for $25.** The imaginative dishes on the constantly changing menu are served in an early-19th-century Creole cottage that glows with flower arrangements, elegant photographs, and trompe l'oeil murals suggesting Mediterranean landscapes. Don't skip the sweets, like a maple-semolina cake with golden-raisin compote and pomegranate sauce. [S] *Average* *main: $28 ✉ 430 Dauphine St., French Quarter ☎ 504/525–4455 🌐 www.bayona.com ⏲ Closed Sun. No lunch Mon. and Tues. ✣ 1:C3.*

$$ CREOLE 🍴 **Bourbon House.** On one of the French Quarter's busiest corners is Dickie Brennan's biggest and flashiest restaurant yet (he also owns Palace Café and Dickie Brennan's Steakhouse), and it's a solid hit with seafood aficionados. The raw bar is prime real estate, with its sterling oysters on the half shell, chilled seafood platters, and antique, decorative oyster plates, but the elegant main dining room is more appropriate for digging into the Creole catalog—oysters Bienville, catfish pecan, and redfish on the "half shell" with lump crab meat. Take your frozen bourbon-milk punch in a to-go cup. Why? Because you can. [S] *Average main: $24 ✉ 144 Bourbon St., French Quarter ☎ 504/522–0111 🌐 www.bourbonhouse.com ✣ 1:D3.*

$$$ CREOLE 🍴 **Brennan's.** Lavish breakfasts are what first put Brennan's on the map, and they're still a big draw, from morning to night, on the two floors of luxuriously appointed dining rooms in this gorgeous 1795 building. The best seats include views of the lush courtyard and fountain. Eye-opening cocktails flow freely at breakfast, followed by dishes like poached eggs with hollandaise, creamed spinach, artichoke bottoms, and Canadian bacon; all are listed with suggested wines. Headliners at lunch and dinner include textbook versions of oysters Rockefeller and seafood gumbo, and bananas Foster, which was created here. And talk about consistency: chef Lazone Randolph has been creating culinary delights in Brennan's kitchen for more than 45 years. The wine list is a stunner, both in quantity and quality. [S] *Average main: $35 ✉ 417 Royal St., French Quarter ☎ 504/525–9711 🌐 www.brennansneworleans.com ✍ Reservations essential ✣ 1:C3.*

$$$$ CREOLE 🍴 **Broussard's.** If local restaurants were judged solely by the beauty of their courtyards, Broussard's would certainly be a standout—but the food here is also consistently outstanding. Expect dishes like crab cakes with Creole tomato-olive relish; a hearty corn, shrimp, and sweet-potato bisque; and tender, grilled, pork-fillet medallions with horseradish, molasses, and mustard glaze—you won't forget your meal anytime soon. Fight the good fight for an outdoor table, and ask about the selection of savory sauces to accompany your entrée. [S] *Average main: $40 ✉ 819 Conti St., French Quarter ☎ 504/581–3866 🌐 www.broussards.com ⏲ No lunch ✣ 1:C3.*

$ CAFÉ Fodor's Choice ★ 🍴 **Café du Monde.** No trip to New Orleans is complete without a cup of chicory-laced café au lait and some of the addictive, sugar-dusted beignets at this venerable Creole institution. The tables under the green-and-white-striped awning, with views of Jackson Square, are jammed at every hour with locals and tourists. **TIP→ If there's a line for table service, head around back to the takeout window and get your coffee and beignets to go. You can enjoy them overlooking the river right next door, or in Jackson Square.** The most magical time to go is just before dawn, before the bustle starts, when you can hear the birds in the crepe myrtles across the way. The New Orleans–area satellite locations (Riverwalk Marketplace in the CBD, Lakeside Shopping Center in Metairie, Esplanade Mall in Kenner, Oakwood Mall in Gretna, and Veterans Blvd. in Metairie) lack the character of the original. [S] *Average main: $3 ✉ 800*

Decatur St., French Quarter ☎ 504/525–4544 🌐 www.cafedumonde.com ▭ No credit cards ✥ 1:C4.

$ CAFÉ Fodor's Choice ★ 🐤

🍴 **Central Grocery.** This old-fashioned Italian grocery store makes authentic muffulettas, one of the gastronomic gifts of the city's Italian immigrants. Good enough to challenge the po' boy as the champion local sandwich, a muffuletta is made by filling round loaves of seeded bread with ham, salami, provolone, Emmentaler cheese, and a salad of marinated olives; there is a version without meat for vegetarians. The sandwiches, about 10 inches in diameter, are sold in wholes and halves. ■ **TIP→ The muffulettas are huge! Unless you're starving, you'll do fine with a half.** You can eat at one of the counters or get your muffuletta to go and dine on a bench on Jackson Square or the Moon Walk along the Mississippi riverfront. The Grocery closes at 5 pm. [S] *Average main: $8 ✉ 923 Decatur St., French Quarter ☎ 504/523–1620 ⏲ Closed Sun. and Mon. No dinner. ✥ 1:C4.*

$ CAFÉ

🍴 **Croissant d'Or Patisserie.** Locals and visitors come to this colorful pastry shop for excellent and authentic French croissants, pies, tarts, and custards, as well as an imaginative selection of soups, salads, and sandwiches. You can get your goodies to go, but try to get a table during breakfast hours for great people-watching. It's open 6:30 am to 3 pm. [S] *Average main: $6 ✉ 617 Ursulines St., French Quarter ☎ 504/524–4663 ✍ Reservations not accepted ⏲ Closed Tues. No dinner ✥ 1:B4.*

$$$$ STEAKHOUSE

🍴 **Dickie Brennan's Steakhouse.** "Straightforward steaks with a New Orleans touch" are the words to live by at this clubby shrine to red meat, the creation of a younger member of the Brennan family of restaurateurs. Start with stellar martinis in the dark cherrywood-paneled lounge, then head back to the cavernous dining room to dig into classic cuts of top-quality beef and seafood. The standard beefsteak treatment is light seasoning and a brush of Creole-seasoned butter, but other options include béarnaise, housemade Worcestershire, and pepper-cream bourbon sauce. [S] *Average main: $38 ✉ 716 Iberville St., French Quarter ☎ 504/522–2467 🌐 www.dickiebrennanssteakhouse.com ⏲ No lunch Sat.–Thurs. ✥ 1:D3.*

$$$ CREOLE Fodor's Choice ★

🍴 **Galatoire's.** With many of its recipes dating to 1905, Galatoire's epitomizes the old-style French-Creole bistro. Fried oysters and bacon en brochette are worth every calorie, and the brick-red rémoulade sauce sets a high standard. Other winners include veal chops with optional béarnaise sauce, and seafood-stuffed eggplant. Downstairs in the white-tableclothed, narrow dining room, lit with gleaming brass chandeliers, is where boisterous regulars congregate and make for excellent entertainment; you can only reserve a table in the renovated upstairs rooms. Friday lunch starts early and continues well into the evening. Shorts and T-shirts are never allowed; a jacket is required for dinner and all day Sunday. [S] *Average main: $27 ✉ 209 Bourbon St., French Quarter ☎ 504/525–2021 🌐 www.galatoires.com ⏲ Closed Mon. ✥ 1:D3.*

$$ ECLECTIC

🍴 **The Green Goddess.** At this cozy (read: small) restaurant in the heart of the French Quarter, diners are wowed by the inventive and globally-inspired cuisine, though the service is a bit eclectic, too. Menus change regularly but may feature apple cheddar French toast, and duck confit salad for lunch, or cucumber lemon balm soup and shrimp risotto for dinner. The staff weaves through the tight space with the grace of gymnasts, keeping the crowds both well fed and well lubricated with specialty cocktails. Tables are set outside when the weather's fine. [S] *Average main: $15* ✉ *307 Exchange Pl., French Quarter* ☎ *504/301–3347* 🌐 *www.greengoddessnola.com* ✍ *Reservations not accepted* 🕓 *Closed Tues. No dinner Mon.* ✥ *1:D3.*

SAFE SEAFOOD

The 2010 Deepwater Horizon oil disaster raised concerns about the safety of Gulf seafood. Since then, more than 10,000 pieces of seafood have been inspected and no troubling levels of contamination were detected. According to a recent statement by the U.S. Food and Drug Administration, "Gulf seafood is as safe to eat now as it was before the spill."

$ CREOLE 🍴 **Gumbo Shop.** Even given a few modern touches—like the vegetarian gumbo offered daily—this place evokes a sense of old New Orleans. The menu is chock-full of regional culinary anchors: jambalaya, shrimp creole and rémoulade, red beans and rice, bread pudding, and seafood and chicken-and-sausage gumbos, heavily flavored with tradition but easy on your wallet. The patina on the ancient painting covering one wall seems to deepen by the week, and the old tables and bentwood chairs have started to seem like museum pieces. Reservations are accepted only for groups of 10 or more. [S] *Average main: $14* ✉ *630 St. Peter St., French Quarter* ☎ *504/525–1486* 🌐 *www.gumboshop.com* ✥ *1:C4.*

$$$ SEAFOOD 🍴 **GW Fins.** If you're looking for seafood, you won't be disappointed with GW Fins, which impresses with quality and variety—the bounty of fish species from around the world is among the menu's lures. Chef Tenney Flynn's menu changes daily, depending on what's fresh, but typical dishes have included luscious lobster dumplings, Hawaiian big-eye tuna, and sautéed rainbow trout with spinach, oysters, and shiitake mushrooms. For dessert, try the baked-to-order deep-dish apple pie. The spacious dining room's attractive modern decor and the enthusiastic service make this a relaxing refuge from the French Quarter's crowds. [S] *Average main: $27* ✉ *808 Bienville St., French Quarter* ☎ *504/581–3467* 🌐 *www.gwfins.com* 🕓 *No lunch* ✥ *1:D3.*

$ CREOLE 🍴 **Hermes Bar.** The allure here is that you'll have your pick of the classic dishes that made Antoine's—founded in 1840—famous, without committing to a full-price meal in its austere dining room. Elegant bar snacks such as oysters Rockefeller, souffléed pommes de terre, and fried eggplant make just as grand a meal, with the added benefit of a front-row view of the Bourbon Street crowd. Expertly mixed old-school cocktails, such as the Sazerac and Ramos gin fizz, are a tradition here. Hermes is connected to Antoines, but there is a separate entrance next door. [S] *Average main: $11* ✉ *713 St. Louis St., French Quarter* ☎ *504/581–4422* 🌐 *www.antoines.com* ✍ *Reservations not accepted* 🕓 *No lunch* ✥ *1:C3.*

$$ ITALIAN 🍴 **Irene's Cuisine.** The walls here are festooned with enough snapshots, garlic braids, and crockery for at least two more restaurants, but it all just adds to the charm of this cozy Italian-Creole eatery. From Irene DiPietro's kitchen come succulent roasted chicken brushed with olive

oil, rosemary, and garlic; delicious, velvety soups; and fresh shrimp, aggressively seasoned and grilled before they join linguine glistening with herbed olive oil. Waits here can stretch to the 60-minute mark during peak dinner hours, which is just enough time for a bottle of wine in the convivial little piano bar. The service is easily the friendliest in the French Quarter. [S] *Average main: $18* ✉ *539 St. Philip St., French Quarter* ☎ *504/529–8811* ✍ *Reservations not accepted* ⏲ *Closed Sun. No lunch* ✥ *1:B4.*

WORD OF MOUTH

"For inexpensive local breakfasts, try Johnny's PoBoy (a greasy spoon with very good food) in the French Quarter and Camellia Grill at the end of the streetcar line in the Garden District (counter seating only, servers have probably been working there for 30 years, great omelets and milkshakes) [see the Uptown spotlight earlier in the chapter for contact info]." —sf7307

$$ AMERICAN 🍴 **Iris.** Chef Ian Schnoebelen's contemporary-American cuisine and a daily changing menu means choices like sunchoke-and-cauliflower soup, duck breast with honey-cured bacon, or shrimp with a Vietnamese-style papaya salad. The bar staff is particularly adept at matching cocktails to your meal. The thoughtful balance between meat and seafood entrées, the array of salads, and the generously portioned appetizers are all reasons to stop and smell the irises. [S] *Average main: $25* ✉ *321 N. Peters St., French Quarter* ☎ *504/299–3944* 🌐 *www.irisneworleans.com* ⏲ *Closed Sun. and Tues. No lunch Mon., Wed., and Sat.* ✥ *1:D3.*

$ CAFÉ 👍 🍴 **Johnny's Po-boys.** Strangely enough, good po' boys are hard to find in the French Quarter. Johnny's compensates for the scarcity with a cornucopia of them, even though the quality is anything but consistent, and the prices are somewhat inflated for the tourist trade. Inside the soft-crust French bread come the classic fillings, including lean boiled ham, well-done roast beef in garlicky gravy, and crisply fried oysters or shrimp. The chili may not cut it in San Antonio, but the red beans and rice are the real deal. The surroundings are rudimentary. Johnny's closes at 4:30 pm. [S] *Average main: $8* ✉ *511 St. Louis St., French Quarter* ☎ *504/524–8129* 🌐 *www.johnnyspoboy.com* ✍ *Reservations not accepted* 💳 *No credit cards* ⏲ *No dinner* ✥ *1:D4.*

$$$ CAJUN 🍴 **K-Paul's Louisiana Kitchen.** It was in this comfortable French Quarter café with glossy wooden floors and exposed brick that chef Paul Prudhomme added "Cajun" to America's culinary vocabulary and started the craze for blackening, in which a fish fillet is coated with a thick layer of herbs and spices and seared until dark. More than three decades later, many still consider a visit to New Orleans lacking without a visit to K-Paul's for his inventive gumbos, fried crawfish tails, blackened Gulf fish, and sweet potato–pecan pie. Prices are steep, but servings are generous. A casual "deli" menu, focusing more on sandwiches, is served at lunch. Although Prudhomme no longer works in the kitchen, he's still often found greeting guests at the door. [S] *Average main: $30* ✉ *416 Chartres St., French Quarter* ☎ *504/524–7394* 🌐 *www.kpauls.com* ⏲ *Closed Sun. No lunch Mon.* ✥ *1:D3.*

CLOSE UP

Mardi Gras Sweet Spotlight: The King Cake

New Orleans is known for lots of local flavor, from pralines and po' boys to beignets and chicory coffee. But for a true taste of Mardi Gras, you can't beat a King Cake.

The origins of the King Cake go back to early-12th-century Europe, when a similar type of cake was baked to represent the arrival of the biblical Three Kings on the twelfth day after Christmas. French settlers passed along the tradition in the late 19th century to the residents of New Orleans. Many years and iterations later, the King Cake lives on, and starting on January 6th, twelve days after Christmas and the first day of Mardi Gras, through Fat Tuesday, the day before Ash Wednesday, a party isn't complete without a King Cake at hand.

Traditional King Cakes are a ring-shaped, cinnamon-flavored brioche with purple, gold, and green icing for the colors of Mardi Gras. Nowadays, King Cakes come in a variety of flavors and fillings, such as cream cheese or chocolate. A small plastic toy baby, said to represent Baby Jesus, is hidden inside the cake. It's tradition that whoever gets the slice with the hidden baby must host the next Mardi Gras party or buy the King Cake for the next celebration.

You can find them all around the area in special bakeries and local grocery stores.

8

$$ AMERICAN 🍴 **Le Meritage.** One way to attract more clientele when the economy goes south is as easy as portion size. Le Meritage offers every dish in both a small- and large-plate option—for example, you can pair a small plate of lamb osso buco with horseradish mashed potatoes ($14) with mushroom risotto ($11 for the small plate, $20 for the large). The dining room is contemporary chic with a view of the hotel's lovely courtyard. Fresh, regional foods with ingredients indigenous to Louisiana populate the menu, and the wine list is well conceived and affordable. And if all of that were not reason enough to dine here, the rotating exhibits of local artists' works are the perfect accompaniment. [S] *Average main: $24* ✉ *1001 Toulouse St., Maison Dupuy hotel, French Quarter* ☎ *504/522–8800* 🌐 *www.lemeritagerestaurant.com* 🕒 *Closed Sun. and Mon. No lunch Tues.–Thurs. and Sat.* ✥ *1:C3.*

$$$ CREOLE 🍴 **Mr. B's Bistro.** Those who wonder if there really is a New Orleans restaurant that can properly cater to both tourists and locals need look no farther than Mr. B's. On one of the busiest French Quarter corners, this bistro never disappoints when it comes to consistency, culinary innovation, and full flavor. Using as many ingredients and products indigenous to Louisiana as possible on the changing menu, the chef offers a standout braised rabbit, an irresistible honey-ginger glazed pork chop, and one of the best barbecued shrimp dishes in the city. First-timers must try the "Gumbo Ya-Ya," a rich chicken and sausage gumbo, and no meal here can end without the hot buttered pecan pie. Upscale yet accessible, Mr. B's is still on the map because of its just-right seasonings, its windows on the French Quarter world, and its dedica-

tion to service. [S] *Average main: $26* ✉ *201 Royal St., French Quarter* ☎ *504/523–2078* 🌐 *www.mrbsbistro.com* ✥ *1:D3.*

$$$ CREOLE 🍴 **Muriel's Jackson Square.** Among Jackson Square's many dining spots, Muriel's is easily the most ambitious, in both atmosphere and menu. In the large downstairs rooms, architectural knickknacks and artwork evoke the city's colorful past, while diners indulge in hearty updated renderings of old Creole favorites. The upstairs balcony has views of the square, with the occasional sounds of street music wafting in. The menu is diverse, ranging from a Gorgonzola-prosciutto tart appetizer to barbecue shrimp or pecan-crusted puppy drum (a popular local fish also known as red drum) with Louisiana crabmeat relish for main courses. Sunday brunch is accompanied by live jazz. [S] *Average main: $26* ✉ *801 Chartres St., French Quarter* ☎ *504/568–1885* 🌐 *www.muriels.com* ✥ *1:C4.*

$$$ CREOLE 🍴 **Nola.** Fans of Emeril Lagasse will want to grab a seat at the food bar overlooking the open kitchen at this French Quarter restaurant. Freewheeling appetizers are among the big attractions, the standout being "Miss Hay's stuffed chicken wings" with hoisin dipping sauce. Entrées, such as the hickory-roasted duck with whiskey-caramel glaze and buttermilk-cornbread pudding, are heavy but delicious. Be warned: after a few bites of the buttermilk fried chicken with bourbon mashed sweet potatoes, you may start looking for property in New Orleans. Leave room in your tummy, and heart, for the banana-pudding layer cake. The space is arty and bright, but it can get pretty noisy. [S] *Average main: $30* ✉ *534 St. Louis St., French Quarter* ☎ *504/522–6652* 🌐 *www.emerils.com* ✍ *Reservations essential* ⏲ *No lunch Mon.–Wed.* ✥ *1:D4.*

$$ CREOLE 🍴 **Palace Café.** Occupying what used to be New Orleans's oldest music store, this Dickie Brennan stalwart is a convivial spot to try some of the more imaginative contemporary Creole dishes, such as crabmeat cheesecake, shrimp in Creole meunière sauce, and pepper-crusted duck breast with foie gras. Desserts, especially the white-chocolate bread pudding and the house-made ice creams, are luscious. Drugstore-tile floors and stained cherrywood booths set the mood. The wraparound mezzanine is lined with a large mural depicting the city's famous musicians, such as Louis Armstrong, Fats Domino, and Aaron Neville. The outdoor sidewalk café is just for small plates and wine. The Sunday jazz brunch is New Orleans all the way. [S] *Average main: $25* ✉ *605 Canal St., French Quarter* ☎ *504/523–1661* 🌐 *www.palacecafe.com* ✍ *Reservations essential* ✥ *1:D3.*

$$$ ECLECTIC 🍴 **Pelican Club.** Sassy New York flourishes permeate the menu of chef Richard Hughes's smartly decorated, eminently comfortable restaurant in the heart of the French Quarter, but there's still evidence of Hughes's Louisiana origins. He turns out what may be the best crab cakes in the city (infused with fresh shrimp) but with the surprise addition of pineapple-jalapeño chutney, served over fried green tomatoes. The whole crispy fish with diver scallops is decadent, while the Australian rack of lamb with rosemary-pesto crust is almost a spiritual experience. [S] *Average main: $32* ✉ *312 Exchange Pl., French Quarter* ☎ *504/523–1504* 🌐 *www.pelicanclub.com* ⏲ *No lunch* ✥ *1:D3.*

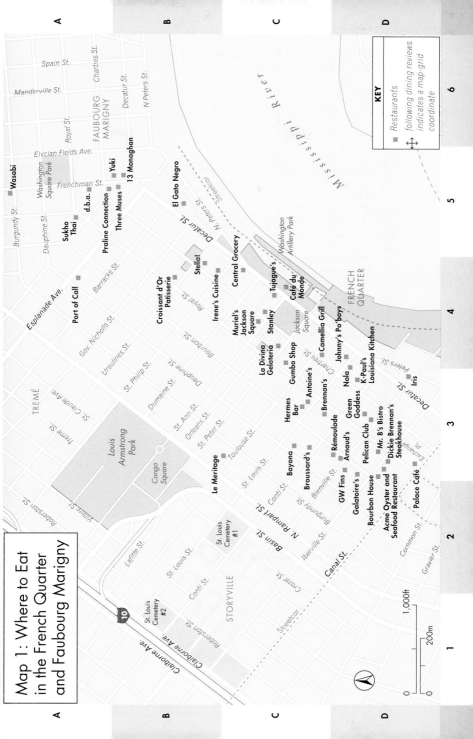

Map 1: Where to Eat in the French Quarter and Faubourg Marigny

KEY

■ Restaurants
  following dining reviews indicates a map-grid coordinate

A

Spain St.
Manderville St.
Chartres St.
Decatur St.
N Peters St.
Royal St.

FAUBOURG MARIGNY

Elysian Fields Ave.

■ Wasabi

Washington Square Park

Frenchman St.

■ Sukho Thai
■ d.b.a.
■ Yuki
■ 13 Monaghan

Burgundy St.
Dauphine St.

■ Praline Connection
■ Three Muses

Esplanade Ave.

■ Port of Call

Barracks St.

■ El Gato Negro

Gov. Nicholls St.

■ Croissant d'Or Patisserie

Ursulines St.

Decatur St.
N Peters St.

Mississippi River

Washington Artillery Park

FRENCH QUARTER

■ Stella!

■ Central Grocery

■ Irene's Cuisine

■ Muriel's Jackson Square
■ Stanley
■ Tujague's
■ Café du Monde

Jackson Square

Royal St.
Bourbon St.
Dauphine St.

St. Philip St.

TREMÉ

St. Claude Ave.
Tremé St.
Robertson St.
Villere St.

Louis Armstrong Park

Congo Square

Dumaine St.
St. Ann St.
Orleans St.
St. Peter St.

■ Le Meritage

Toulouse St.

Hermes Bar ■
■ Antoine's
■ Brennan's

■ La Divina Gelateria
■ Gumbo Shop

■ Camellia Grill
■ Johnny's Po'boys
■ Nola
■ K-Paul's Louisiana Kitchen
■ Iris

Chartres St.

■ Rémoulade
■ Arnaud's
■ Green Goddess
■ Pelican Club
■ Mr. B's Bistro
■ Dickie Brennan's Steakhouse

■ Bayona
■ Broussard's

St. Louis St.
Conti St.

■ GW Fins
■ Galatoire's
■ Bourbon House
■ Acme Oyster and Seafood Restaurant

Bienville St.
Burgundy St.

■ Palace Café

Exchange Pl.

Decatur St.

Peters St.

St. Louis Cemetery #1

STORYVILLE

Basin St.
N. Rampart St.
Crozat St.
Conti St.

Iberville St.
Canal St.

Common St.
Gravier St.

St. Louis Cemetery #2

Claiborne Ave.
Robertson St.

Lafitte St.
St. Louis St.

Streetcar

10

1,000ft
200m
0

A **B** **C** **D**

1 2 3 4 5 6

$ AMERICAN 🦆 🍴 **Port of Call.** People wait for more than an hour outside Port of Call every night, in the heavy heat of July and the downpours of September, for fist-thick burgers made from freshly ground beef, grilled to order and served with baked potatoes (there are no fries here) that are always perfectly fluffy. For the definitive experience, drink a Monsoon (Port of Call's mind-bending take on the Hurricane) while you wait, and order your potato "loaded" (with mushrooms, cheddar cheese, sour cream, butter, chives, and bacon bits). A juicy filet mignon is also available. In the afternoon and early evening, it's a fun stop for kids. Port of Call is open until midnight from Sunday through Thursday and 1 am on Friday and Saturday. [S] *Average main: $14* ✉ *838 Esplanade Ave., French Quarter* ☎ *504/523–0120* 🌐 *www.portofcallnola.com* ✍ *Reservations not accepted* ⊕ *1:A4.*

$ CREOLE 🍴 **Rémoulade.** Operated by the owners of the posh Arnaud's, Rémoulade is more laid-back and less pricey but serves the same Caesar salad and pecan pie, as well as a few of the signature starters: shrimp Arnaud in rémoulade sauce, baked oysters, turtle soup, and shrimp bisque. The marble-counter oyster bar and mahogany cocktail bar date from the 1870s; a dozen oysters shucked here, paired with a cold beer, can easily turn into two dozen, maybe three. Tile floors, mirrors, a pressed-tin ceiling, and brass lights create an old-time New Orleans environment. It's open daily until 11 pm. [S] *Average main: $10* ✉ *309 Bourbon St., French Quarter* ☎ *504/523–0377* 🌐 *www.remoulade.com* ⊕ *1:C3.*

$ CREOLE 🦆 🍴 **Stanley.** Chefs across America are ditching the white tablecloths and applying their fine-dining chops to burgers, bar food, and comfort fare. Here, chef Scott Boswell of Stella! takes this track with the already delicious food of Louisiana. In the morning, pancakes are covered in earthy Louisiana cane syrup and eggs Benedict are topped with Cajun boudin sausage. At lunch and dinner, the traditional oyster po' boy gets an extra zing from spicy remoulade dressing and the roast beef po'boy is remade as Korean barbecue with nose-clearing, spicy kimchee. Some grumble about prices too high for what is, at heart, New Orleans neighborhood fare. But this crisply decorated café sits on a coveted corner of Jackson Square, and that view is priceless. [S] *Average main: $12* ✉ *547 St. Ann St., French Quarter* ☎ *504/587–0093* 🌐 *www.stanleyrestaurant.com* ✍ *Reservations not accepted* ⊕ *1:C4.*

$$$$ MODERN AMERICAN Fodor's Choice ★ 🍴 **Stella!.** Chef Scott Boswell has evolved into one of the city's most innovative and daring culinarians, marrying wild creativity with an obsession for precision. The spicy Asian-chili prawns are an excellent start to any meal, while mains like duck five ways with foie-gras wontons, or seven-layer boneless pork with bacon, spinach, garbanzo beans, glazed carrots, and sweet-potato puree will entrance the taste buds. Desserts like the grilled cheese with dark-chocolate ganache are a playful ending to any meal. This is one of New Orleans's best and most elegant fine-dining restaurants. [S] *Average main: $36* ✉ *1032 Chartres St., French Quarter* ☎ *504/587–0091* 🌐 *www.restaurantstella.com* ✍ *Reservations essential* ⏲ *No lunch* ⊕ *1:B4.*

FAUBOURG MARIGNY, BYWATER, AND TREMÉ

FAUBOURG MARIGNY

$ CREOLE 🐤 🍴 **Praline Connection.** Down-home cooking in the southern-Creole style is the forte of this very Southern restaurant, just a few blocks from the French Quarter. The fried or stewed chicken, smothered pork chops, fried chicken livers, and collard greens are definitively done, and the soulful filé gumbo, peas with okra, and sweet-potato pie are welcome in a neighborhood otherwise in short supply of soul food. Add a congenial staff and a comfortable dining room, and the result is a fine place to enjoy a relaxing mealtime. The adjacent sweetshop holds such delights as sweet-potato cookies and Creole pralines. [S] *Average main: $15* ✉ *542 Frenchmen St., Faubourg Marigny* ☎ *504/943–3934* 🌐 *www.pralineconnection.com* ⊕ *1:A5.*

$$ THAI 🍴 **Sukho Thai.** Certainly the most extensive Thai restaurant in the area, Sukho Thai fits snugly into its arty neighborhood with servers wearing all black and a hip, art-gallery approach to decorating. You can't go wrong with any of the curries, but the whole fried fish with three spicy chili sauces is a showstopper. Creative house-made desserts take the form of barely sweetened coconut custard and black-rice pudding. The most imaginative and extensive tea menu in the area compensates for the lack of a liquor license, although you can bring your own wine for a $5 corkage fee. [S] *Average main: $18* ✉ *1913 Royal St., Faubourg Marigny* ☎ *504/948–9309* 🌐 *www.sukhothai-nola.com* 🕐 *Closed Mon.* ⊕ *1:A5.*

$ ECLECTIC 🍴 **Three Muses.** The most eclectic mix of music, food, and people can be found on Frenchmen Street, and Three Muses captures everything that makes this vibrant stretch of the Faubourg Marigny worth seeking out. The small-plates menu traverses the globe, with standout delicacies including lamb sliders, lemongrass short ribs, french fries with feta cheese, and a falafel salad. The kitchen devotes special attention to the vegetarian offerings. There's live acoustic music most nights, too. [S] *Average main: $9* ✉ *536 Frenchmen St., Faubourg Marigny* ☎ *504/252–4801* 🌐 *www.thethreemuses.com* ✍ *Reservations not accepted* 🕐 *Closed Tues. No lunch* ⊕ *1:B5.*

BYWATER

$ SOUTHERN 🍴 **Elizabeth's.** "Real food, done real good" is the motto at Elizabeth's, a real down-home Southern joint where the vinyl-print tablecloths look just like grandma's, and where breakfast is the most important meal of the day. The menu offers everything from traditional po' boys to a stellar seared duck to crispy fried chicken livers with pepper jelly. The fried-oyster po' boy is huge and irresistible. The staff is spunky, and so is the Bywater neighborhood clientele. Weekend brunch is served from 8 am to 2:30, and includes corn-bread waffles with duck hash, "red neck eggs" (fried green tomatoes with poached eggs and hollandaise), and traditional country breakfast with smoked pork chops. Weekday breakfast (Tuesday–Friday, 7 am to 2:30) has almost the same options. [S] *Average main: $15* ✉ *601 Gallier St., Bywater* ☎ *504/944–9272* 🌐 *www.elizabeths-restaurant.com* ✍ *Reservations not accepted* 🕐 *Closed Mon. No dinner Sun.* ⊕ *3:B5.*

$ SOUTHERN

🍴 **The Joint.** You can't miss this bright yellow building but it's the smell of the meat—pork shoulder, pork ribs, beef brisket, and pulled chicken—cooking in the custom-made smoker that will draw you in. In a town not really known for great barbecue, the Joint is the exception, which is why it draws hungry patrons from far and wide. The meat is the thing, but don't skip the side dishes, which go above and beyond in concept and execution, particularly the sweet-and-spicy baked beans, and the crispy-on-the-outside mac and cheese. Pecan, key lime, and peanut butter pies are fitting country desserts. [S] *Average main: $11* ✉ *701 Mazant St., at Royal St., Bywater* ☎ *504/949–3232* 🌐 *www.alwayssmokin.com* ✍ *Reservations not accepted* ⏲ *Closed Sun.* ✥ *3:B6.*

CBD AND THE WAREHOUSE DISTRICT

CBD

$$ ITALIAN

🍴 **A Mano.** Chef Adolfo García proved his mastery of Spanish cooking at Rio Mar, and at A Mano he shows equal ability with the flavors of Italy. In New Orleans, most Italian restaurants serve a crowd-pleasing Creole version of red sauce, or "red gravy" as it's known here, and local seafood. But this Warehouse District trattoria goes back to the source for authentic tastes of Italy, with options like house-cured meats, *trippa all Romana* (beef tripe with tomato, pecorino, and mint), homemade pasta, and rabbit roasted with olives and thyme. After dessert, linger a little longer with a glass of Italian *amaro* or a homemade liqueur. [S] *Average main: $21* ✉ *870 Tchoupitoulas St., Warehouse District* ☎ *504/208–9280* 🌐 *www.amanonola.com* ⏲ *Closed Sun. No lunch Sat.–Thurs.* ✥ *2:C4.*

$$ AMERICAN 🐤

🍴 **The American Sector.** Celebrity-chef John Besh has dazzled the culinary world with his prowess on the plate and his Southern-boy charm, but his most impressive feat might be this restaurant inside the National World War II Museum—worth visiting even if you skip the exhibits. The menu focuses on updated comfort fare like chicken-fried steak, heirloom tomato soup served in a can, or a sloppy Joe made from short ribs. This is also a fun spot for kids: the efficient staff wear period garb and children's meals are served in lunch pails. Accompany your meal with a seasonal milk shake or, if you're of age, a well-made retro cocktail like a Pink Squirrel or Singapore Sling. [S] *Average main: $18* ✉ *National World War II Museum, 945 Magazine St., Warehouse District* ☎ *504/528–1940* 🌐 *www.nationalww2museum.org/american-sector* ✥ *2:D3.*

$$$$ MODERN AMERICAN Fodor's Choice ★

🍴 **August.** If the Gilded Age is long gone, someone forgot to tell the folks at August, where the main dining room shimmers with masses of chandelier prisms, thick brocade fabrics, and glossy woods. Service is anything but stuffy, however, and the food showcases chef John Besh's modern techniques. Nothing is mundane on the seasonally changing menu, which might include handmade gnocchi with blue crab and winter truffle or rabbit cassoulet with andouille sausage. Expect the unexpected—like slow-roasted Kobe beef short ribs with Jerusalem artichokes. The sommelier is happy to confer with you on the surprisingly affordable wine list. [S] *Average main: $35* ✉ *301 Tchoupitoulas St.,*

CBD ☎ 504/299–9777 🌐 www.restaurantaugust.com ✍ Reservations essential ⏲ No lunch weekends ✣ 2:B4.

$$$ CAJUN ✕ **Bon Ton Café.** The Bon Ton's opening in 1953 marked the first appearance of a significant Cajun restaurant in New Orleans, and the now-famed crawfish dishes, gumbo, jambalaya, and oyster omelet continue to draw fans. The bustle in the dining room peaks at lunchtime on weekdays, when businesspeople from nearby offices come in droves for turtle soup, eggplant with a shrimp and crab étouffée, and the warm, sugary bread pudding. If you can sacrifice the afternoon for pleasure, try a Rum Ramsey cocktail. The veteran servers are knowledgeable and fleet-footed. [S] *Average main: $28 ✉ 401 Magazine St., CBD ☎ 504/524–3386 🌐 www.thebontoncafe.com ⏲ Closed weekends ✣ 2:B4.*

$$ SEAFOOD ✕ **Borgne.** It's a mystery why New Orleans doesn't have more restaurants like Borgne. The menu, overseen by celebrity-chef John Besh and former Galatoire chef Brian Landry, takes rustic Louisiana seafood dishes and adds a touch of city sophistication. Shrimp is served over white beans, a seafood-stuffed flounder comes with Meyer lemon butter, and the Gulf fish in a bag is accompanied by onions, fennel, and crab fat. Named after Lake Borgne in eastern Louisiana, the restaurant nods to that area's many Spanish settlers with items like paella, empanadas, and goat cheese with green "mojo" sauce. The one off note is the decor, which feels like a museum cafeteria furnished with stiff chairs and undersized tables. [S] *Average main: $24 ✉ 601 Loyola Ave., CBD ☎ 504/613–3860 🌐 www.borgnerestaurant.com ✣ 2:B2.*

$$ ITALIAN Fodor's Choice ★ ✕ **Domenica.** Local celebrity-chef John Besh continues to wow diners, here with rustic Italian cooking, a rarity in New Orleans's culinary landscape. In the renovated Roosevelt hotel—a 19th-century landmark—the Domenica restaurant departs from the hotel lobby's stuffy, gilded decor, opting instead for sleek black walls and chain-link curtains, warmed by jewel-box displays of house-cured meats. Friendly and knowledgeable waiters happily help patrons with lesser-known ingredients, but it doesn't take a lengthy explanation to know that the fresh pastas and wood-fired pizzas are a must. [S] *Average main: $21 ✉ 123 Baronne St., CBD ☎ 504/648–6020 🌐 www.domenicarestaurant.com ✣ 2:A3.*

$$ SOUTHERN ✕ **Grand Isle.** This Louisiana fish camp–theme restaurant gave a significant boost to the emerging entertainment district surrounding the Fulton Street corridor and Harrah's Casino. The rustic interior, reminiscent of 1920s and '30s Louisiana, is the perfect backdrop for shrimp gumbo; spicy boiled shrimp; fresh gulf fish; cold smoked-and-grilled tuna; and a lemon icebox pie that will make you fall in love with New Orleans all over again. Except for freshwater catfish and Canadian mussels, all the seafood comes straight from the Gulf of Mexico. Produce and pork all come from local farmers and purveyors, too. Grand Isle is generally packed, but it's worth the wait (which also gives you an excuse to spend some time at the elegant mahogany bar). [S] *Average main: $21 ✉ 575 Convention Center Blvd., CBD ☎ 504/520–8530 🌐 www.grandislerestaurant.com ✣ 2:B5.*

$$$ AMERICAN ✕ **The Grill Room.** With a glassed-in dining area overlooking the courtyard of the Windsor Court hotel, elegant table settings, and canvases depicting the lives of the British nobility, the Grill Room is all about

8

understated class. The equally dazzling menu, which changes daily, is filled with smart modern-American specialties with local touches. Think duck prosciutto with foie-gras mousse, striped bass with crawfish-and-hedgehog mushrooms, or scallops with butternut-squash puree, apples, and star fruit. And just when you think the best is behind, out comes the city's best cheese plate, followed by soothing cordials. The wine cellar, with its extensive collection of vintage Bordeaux reds, is awe inspiring, so don't hesitate to ask the knowledgeable staff for recommendations. [S] *Average main: $33* ✉ *Windsor Court Hotel, 2nd level, 300 Gravier St., CBD* ☎ *504/522–1994* 🌐 *www.windsorcourthotel.com* ✍ *Reservations essential* ✥ *2:B4.*

$$$ SOUTHERN Fodor's Choice ★

🍴 **Herbsaint.** Chef Donald Link (also of Cochon and Cochon Butcher) turns out food that sparkles with robust flavors and top-grade ingredients at this casually upscale restaurant. Small plates and starters such as a daily gumbo, charcuterie, and house-made pastas are mainstays. Don't overlook the rich and flavorful Louisiana shrimp and grits with tasso and okra. Also irresistible are the lamb neck with mushroom farro, and the muscovy duck-leg confit with dirty rice and citrus gastrique. For dessert, banana brown-butter tart will ensure return trips. The plates provide most of the color in the lighthearted, often noisy, rooms. The wine list is expertly compiled and reasonably priced. [S] *Average main: $27* ✉ *701 St. Charles Ave., Warehouse District* ☎ *504/524–4114* 🌐 *www.herbsaint.com* ✍ *Reservations essential* ⏲ *Closed Sun. No lunch Sat.* ✥ *2:B3.*

$$$ LATIN AMERICAN

🍴 **La Boca.** If you need a break from the bounties of the sea prevalent in New Orleans restaurants, book a table at this classic Argentine steak house. Although most steak houses are clubby, masculine, and hard on the wallet, this Warehouse District eatery feels more like a party. The kitchen excels at coaxing flavor from less expensive cuts, like flank and hanger steaks. Sides include empanadas, thick rounds of provolone grilled and sprinkled with oregano, and house-made pasta, a nod to Argentina's large Italian population. A group of four or more can order a five-course feast served family style for $50 each. After dinner at La Boca, you'll walk outside and be surprised to discover that you're not in Buenos Aires. [S] *Average main: $27* ✉ *857 Fulton St., Warehouse District* ☎ *504/525–8205* 🌐 *www.labocasteaks.com* ⏲ *Closed Sun. No lunch.* ✥ *2:C4.*

$$ SOUTHERN

🍴 **Lüke.** While Lüke is a John Besh restaurant, it tends to be inconsistent and often doesn't live up to the standards of his other properties. The atmosphere—rather hotel-restaurant banal—belies the rather pricey food. Breakfast might be the standout: the shrimp and grits are excellent, if expensive; otherwise we'd recommend you find your French- and Louisiana-influenced dishes elsewhere. [S] *Average main: $19* ✉ *333 St. Charles Ave., CBD* ☎ *504/378–2840* 🌐 *www.lukeneworleans.com* ✥ *2:A3.*

$$$ SOUTHERN

🍴 **MiLa.** Chefs Slade Rushing and Allison Vines-Rushing, from Mississippi and Louisiana, respectively, merged the names and cuisines of their home states to produce MiLa. The restaurant defines a new Southern elegance with its comfy-chic atmosphere and its culinary tributes to each chef's childhood memories of Southern cooking. The results on

Continued on page 165

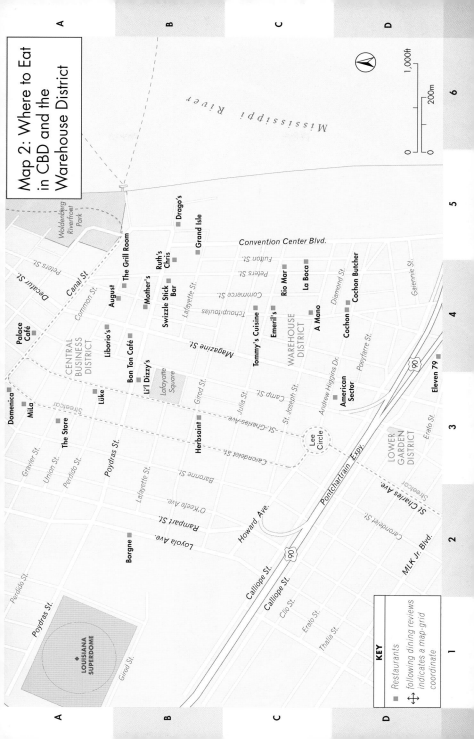

Map 2: Where to Eat in CBD and the Warehouse District

Mississippi River

Woldenberg Riverfront Park

Drago's
Grand Isle

Convention Center Blvd.

The Grill Room
Ruth's Chris
Mother's
August
Swizzle Stick Bar

Fulton St.
Peters St.
Commerce St.
Rio Mar
La Boca
Cochon Butcher

Liborio's
Bon Ton Café
Lil' Dizzy's

Tommy's Cuisine
Emeril's
A Mano
Cochon

Lafayette Square

WAREHOUSE DISTRICT

Palace Café

Domenica
Mila
The Store
Lüke

Herbsaint

Lee Circle

American Sector

Eleven 79

CENTRAL BUSINESS DISTRICT

Borgne

LOUISIANA SUPERDOME

LOWER GARDEN DISTRICT

Lafayette St.
Poydras St.
Magazine St.
Girod St.
Julia St.
Camp St.
St. Joseph St.
Andrew Higgins Dr.
Poeyfarre St.
Diamond St.
Gaiennie St.

St. Charles Ave.
Carondelet St.
Baronne St.
O'Keefe Ave.
Rampart St.
Loyola Ave.
Howard Ave.
Pontchartrain Expy.

Calliope St.
Clio St.
Erato St.
Thalia St.
MLK Jr. Blvd.
Carondelet St.
St. Charles Ave.

Perdido St.
Girod St.
Gravier St.
Union St.
Perdido St.
Poydras St.

Decatur St.
Peters St.
Canal St.
Common St.
Tchoupitoulas
Lafayette St.

1,000 ft
200 m

KEY

■ Restaurants

✦ following dining reviews indicates a map-grid coordinate

DID YOU KNOW?

Crawfish is a staple in the Louisiana diet. It is found in a number of Cajun and Creole dishes, but it is most commonly boiled and served with potatoes and corn on the cob.

THE CUISINE OF NEW ORLEANS

From humble po' boy shops to white-tablecloth temples of classic Creole cuisine, food is a major reason to visit the Crescent City. People in New Orleans love to eat, and discerning local customers support a multitude of options when it comes to dining. Innovative fine dining restaurants exist alongside more modest eateries serving red beans and rice and boiled crawfish. Whatever the cost, it's hard to find a bad meal in this culinary town.

Given New Orleans's location near the mouth of the Mississippi River and the Gulf of Mexico, it was perhaps inevitable that an outstanding food culture would develop in the area. Farmers grow an abundance of produce—locally prized Creole tomato, okra, strawberries, and chayote (locally know as mirliton)—in the fertile delta soil that surroundes the city and fishermen harvest a wealth of seafood like black drum, speckled trout, shrimp, blue crabs, oysters, and crawfish from the marshes and open waters of the Gulf of Mexico.

As a port city, New Orleans has always been something of a melting pot. The city's native Creole cuisine is a mixture of French, African, and Spanish influences; immigration from Italy and Sicily in the 19th century gave New Orleans its own version of Italian cooking. Plus, there is a lingering influence from an influx of German settlers; more recently, immigrants from Vietnam have brought their culinary traditions to New Orleans and the surrounding parishes.

Creole food is the cooking of the city, while Cajun food evolved from the rural traditions of the plains and swamps of southwest Louisiana. The Acadians, a people of French heritage, arrived in Louisiana after being expelled by the British from parts of Canada (present-day Nova Scotia and surrounding areas) in the 18th century. Like the cuisine of rural France, Cajun cooking is hearty and employs similar cooking techniques such as slow braising and the addition of a roux (a combination of flour and fat), but it features local seafood, game, and produce.

By Robert D. Peyton

(top) A café au lait and beignets served at the renowned Café du Monde.

CLASSIC CREOLE AND CAJUN FOOD

Jambalaya

Oysters Rockefeller

BEIGNETS

Beignets are fried pillows of dough, generally served with powdered sugar (and lots of it!) and steaming cups of café au lait made with New Orleans-style chicory coffee. Beignets are typically consumed for breakfast or for dessert.

ÉTOUFFÉE

Étouffée means "smothered" in French, and the dish can be made with shrimp; chicken; and, most typically, crawfish. The dish is Cajun in origin, but there are Creole versions, as well. As with many Cajun dishes, it starts with a light roux, to which chopped onion, celery, and bell pepper (called "the trinity" in South Louisiana) is added. Some versions contain tomatoes, and the sauce is finished with stock and meat, poultry, or seafood. Crawfish étouffée is best during crawfish season (March–June), but you can find it year-round.

MUFFALETTA

The Muffaletta sandwich was invented at the Central Grocery (923 Decatur St.) by Salvatore Lupo and became popular enough that it can now be found all over town. The sandwich is served on a round loaf that's stuffed with salami, ham, provolone, and a local condiment called olive salad, which typically consists of olives, celery, and pickled peppers. Some restaurants heat the sandwich, but many purists consider that heresy.

OYSTERS ROCKEFELLER

Oysters Rockefeller was invented at Antoine's, the oldest continuously operated restaurant in the United States. The dish, to this day, consists of oysters baked on the half-shell with an anise-scented puree of herbs and bread crumbs. Although the recipe Antoine's uses remains a closely guarded secret, the dish typically contains parsley, chervil, tarragon, and celery leaves. This is a dish that should be ordered while oysters are at their best, between September and April.

JAMBALAYA

Jambalaya is a hearty dish that combines rice with meat, poultry, and/or seafood with a result akin to the Spanish paella. In New Orleans, the dish usually includes tomatoes, giving it a reddish hue. Ingredients can include chicken, andouille, pork, shrimp, crawfish, duck, and even alligator. The requisite "trinity" of onion, celery, and

Shrimp gumbo

Pralines

bell pepper is cooked with or without meat or seafood, and then the rice is added with stock, and the dish is covered to finish.

GUMBO

Gumbo is yet another dish that has both Cajun and Creole variations. It is a thick soup or thin stew that can include almost any meat, poultry, sausage, or seafood found in South Louisiana. Cajuns generally cook the roux for gumbo until it is very dark, giving the dish a nutty flavor, while in New Orleans a lighter roux is employed, and okra and tomatoes are often included. A common ingredient, filé powder (dried, ground sassafras leaves), used as a thickening agent and seasoning, is considered by some as a necessary ingredient for making Cajun and Creole gumbo.

BOUDIN

Boudin is a Cajun sausage that combines rice with pork or other ingredients; some of the best can be found just outside of the city at rural gas stations, where it's frequently eaten as a roadside snack. In restaurants, the stuffing is sometimes removed from its casing, formed into balls, and fried.

TASSO

Tasso is a cured and smoked pork product that is one of the treasures of Acadian charcuterie. It is a highly spiced preparation that is used as a flavor base in many local recipes such as gumbo and red beans. Though it is sometimes called tasso ham, the meat used to prepare it is from the shoulder rather than the leg.

ANDOUILLE

Andouille is a smoked sausage made with both ground and cubed pork and flavored with garlic. It is a variation of a French sausage that in the Cajun interpretation is more highly spiced and aggressively flavored. It appears as an ingredient in many South Louisiana dishes, including gumbo and jambalaya.

PRALINES

Pralines are a sweet patty-shaped Creole treats made with caramelized sugar, cream, butter, and pecans—the latter often sourced from trees that grow locally in great abundance. Modern interpretations include chocolate, peanut butter, and bourbon pralines. Be sure to pronounce it like the locals: "PRAH-line," not "PRAY-line."

TASTEMAKERS AND THEIR RESTAURANTS

Donald Link

DONALD LINK
Donald Link was raised in Acadia Parish, and the simple, hearty food he grew up eating influences his cooking. The menu at Link's first restaurant, Herbsaint, is a mix of European and South Louisiana cooking. Link's Cajun heritage is most apparent at one of the city's best and most innovative Cajun restaurants, Cochon, which he operates with chef Steven Stryjewski. Around the corner from Cochon, Link's more casual restaurant, Cochon Butcher, offers small plates, sandwiches, and house-made charcuterie. Link also recently opened a branch of Cochon in Lafayette, the heart of Cajun country.

Emeril Lagasse

EMERIL LAGASSE
Emeril Lagasse has done more to bring the cuisine of New Orleans to the attention of modern diners than any other individual. Though he no longer has quite the omnipresence in the media he once enjoyed, his restaurants in New Orleans—Emeril's, NOLA, and Delmonico—are consistently ranked among the best in the city by locals.

John Besh

JOHN BESH
John Besh, a native of south Louisiana, has seven restaurants in New Orleans. August, his flagship, is a consistently rated top restaurant in New Orleans. Lüke, an Alsatian brasserie (with a branch in San Antonio, TX); the American Sector and the Soda Shop, both in the National WWII Museum; the Italian restaurant, Domenica; the French restaurant, La Provence; and the steakhouse, Besh Steak, round out his culinary dominance in town. Besh demonstrates his commitment to sourcing products locally by raising animals and growing produce for all of his operations.

Susan Spicer

SUSAN SPICER
Susan Spicer came to prominence when she opened the intimate Bistro at Maison de Ville in 1986. Four years later, Spicer opened Bayona in a 200-year-old converted cottage on Dauphine Street in the French Quarter. Mediterranean, Asian, North African, Indian, and other cuisines influence Spicer's cooking both at Bayona and the more casual restaurant, Mondo, in the Lakeview neighborhood. Spicer has led the way for other female chefs in the Crescent City and like the other tastemakers identified here, she has received numerous awards.

the seasonally updated menu are dishes like oysters Rockefeller "deconstructed" and sweet tea–brined rotisserie duck. For the true insider experience, take a seat at the bar and try the hot deer sausage and cheddar biscuits. Much of the restaurant's produce comes from a farm in Mount Hermon, Louisiana. ■ TIP→ **MiLa offers a very affordable ($20) three-course, prix-fixe lunch on weekdays.** [S] *Average main: $30* ✉ *817 Common St., CBD* ☎ *504/412–2580* 🌐 *www.milaneworleans.com* 🕓 *Closed Sun. No lunch Sat.* ✥ *2:A3.*

THE WAREHOUSE DISTRICT

$$ CAJUN Fodor's Choice ★ 🍴 **Cochon.** Chef-owned restaurants are common in New Orleans, but this one builds on owner Donald Link's family heritage as he, working with co-owner Stephen Stryjewski (who received a James Beard Award for his work here), prepares Cajun dishes he learned to cook at his grandfather's knee. The interior may be a bit too hip and noisy for some patrons, but the food makes up for it. The fried boudin with pickled peppers is a must—trust us on this one—then move on to black-eyed pea–and-pork gumbo, and a hearty Louisiana *cochon* (pork) with turnips, cracklings, and cabbage. All the vegetable sides are excellent. Everyone talks about the alligator, but there are more memorable dishes. [S] *Average main: $20* ✉ *930 Tchoupitoulas St., Warehouse District* ☎ *504/588–2123* 🌐 *www.cochonrestaurant.com* ✍ *Reservations essential* 🕓 *Closed Sun.* ✥ *2:D4.*

$ SOUTHERN Fodor's Choice ★ 🍴 **Cochon Butcher.** Around the corner from its big brother Cochon, Butcher packs its own Cajun punch with an upscale sandwich menu that dials up the flavor on local classics. With house-cured meats and olive salad, the muffaletta reveals exactly how delicious Creole-Italian can be, although the pork-belly sandwich also brings customers back again and again. In addition to sandwiches, there are meaty small plates and a rotating selection of wines, beers, and well-made cocktails. There are a few tall tables for dining in, or you can get your sandwich to go. Before leaving, stock up on boudin, bacon pralines, and other to-go Cajun delicacies—all much better souvenirs than anything for sale on Bourbon Street. [S] *Average main: $10* ✉ *930 Tchoupitoulas St., Warehouse District* ☎ *504/588–7675* 🌐 *www.cochonbutcher.com* ✍ *Reservations not accepted* 🕓 *No dinner Sun.* ✥ *2:D4.*

$$ ITALIAN 👶 🍴 **Drago's.** Since 1969 the Cvitanovich family restaurant has been a fixture in Metairie, just a short drive from downtown New Orleans, so when it was revealed the family would open a second location inside the Hilton Riverside hotel, locals started salivating and the word quickly spread. ■ TIP→ **The charbroiled oysters are the absolute must-order.** After that you can branch out to authentic Italian pasta dishes, Maine lobster, and fried seafood entrées. Families love the place—especially because of the kids' menu—and the warm apple cobbler is the sweet stuff legends are made of. [S] *Average main: $26* ✉ *2 Poydras St., CBD* ☎ *504/584–3911* 🌐 *www.dragosrestaurant.com* ✍ *Reservations not accepted* ✥ *2:B5.*

$$$ ITALIAN 🍴 **Eleven 79.** If the Rat Pack boys were alive today, they'd ask for a corner table at this tiny, softly lit Italian eatery, where garlic rules and red wine is revered. Dean Martin music adds a soft ambience, while candlelit tables serve as the perfect platform for tender pastas bathed

8

in perfectly seasoned sauces. The *panéed* (breaded) veal with asparagus, buffalo mozzarella, roasted red peppers, and lemon sauce is sublime, but make sure to check out the specials. Note that pasta dishes are available as half orders. Every dish is full of flavor; there is no such thing as a bad meal at Eleven 79. Ⓢ *Average main: $27* ✉ *1179 Annunciation St., Warehouse District* ☎ *504/299–1179* ⊕ *www. eleven79.com* ⊗ *Closed Sun. No lunch Sat.* ✛ *2:D4.*

$$$
AMERICAN ✕ **Emeril's.** Celebrity-chef Emeril Lagasse's urban-chic flagship restaurant is always jammed, so it's fortunate that the basket-weave-patterned wood ceiling muffles much of the clatter and chatter. The ambitious menu gives equal emphasis to Creole and modern American cooking—try the Thai-spiced lamb ribs or the barbecue shrimp, which is one one of the darkest, richest versions of that local specialty. Desserts, such as the renowned banana cream pie, verge on the gargantuan. Service is meticulous, and the wine list's depth and range mean that you shouldn't hesitate to ask your server for advice. Ⓢ *Average main: $30* ✉ *800 Tchoupitoulas St., Warehouse District* ☎ *504/528–9393* ⊕ *www. emerils.com* ⌧ *Reservations essential* ⊗ *No lunch weekends* ✛ *2:C4.*

$$
SEAFOOD ✕ **Rio Mar.** Chef Adolfo García's largely seafood menu reflects his Spanish style and Panamanian heritage. Each of his several ceviches has its own distinct marinade and combination of superfresh seafood. For entrées, try the stewlike *zarzuela* of seafood, with chunks of fish and shellfish in a peppery red broth. It's all tapas at lunch, when you tick off your selections on a small menu card: options include salty Spanish ham, roasted peppers, Manchego cheese, and marinated seafood. The dining room's low ceiling and tiled floor mean that the atmosphere can be loud and boisterous—but this, and the decor, are very reminiscent of good times in Barcelona. Ⓢ *Average main: $21* ✉ *800 S. Peters St., Warehouse District* ☎ *504/525–3474* ⊕ *www.riomarseafood.com* ⊗ *Closed Sun. No lunch Sat.* ✛ *2:C4.*

$$
ITALIAN ✕ **Tommy's Cuisine.** The upscale dining rooms here are clubby and festive, the crowd is always interesting, and the menu seamlessly blends Creole and Italian. There are several types of oyster appetizers to choose from, while mains focus on sophisticated preparations of fish and meat: make sure to find out the daily specials before you make your decision. Service is gentlemanly, the chef's dinner specials are imaginative, and the wines span all of Italy. After dinner, head next door to the cushy Tommy's Wine Bar. Ⓢ *Average main: $22* ✉ *746 Tchoupitoulas St., Warehouse District* ☎ *504/581–1103* ⊕ *www.tommysneworleans.com* ⌧ *Reservations essential* ⊗ *No lunch* ✛ *2:C4.*

Fried alligator at Cochon.

THE GARDEN DISTRICT

$$$$
CREOLE

✕**Commander's Palace.** No restaurant captures New Orleans's gastronomic heritage and celebratory spirit as well as this one, long considered the grande dame of New Orleans fine dining. Recent renovations added new life, especially upstairs, where the Garden Room's glass walls have marvelous views of the giant oak trees on the patio below. The menu's classics include a spicy and meaty turtle soup; shrimp and tasso Henican (shrimp stuffed with ham, with pickled okra); a wonderful griddle-seared Gulf fish; and poached oysters in absinthe cream sauce under a pastry dome. Among the addictive desserts is the bread-pudding soufflé: it's too good not to try, but it might ruin you for other bread puddings. The weekend brunch is a not-to-be-missed New Orleans tradition. Jackets are preferred at dinner. **$** *Average main: $39* ⊠ *1403 Washington Ave., Garden District* ☎ *504/899–8221* ⊕ *www.commanderspalace. com* ♿ *Reservations essential* ✛ *3:D4.*

$$$
CREOLE
Fodor's Choice
★

✕**Emeril's Delmonico.** Chef Emeril Lagasse bought the century-old Delmonico restaurant in 1998 and converted it into a large, extravagant restaurant serving some of the most ambitious reinterpretations of classic Creole dishes in town. The atmosphere is lush, with high-ceiling dining spaces swathed in upholstered walls and superthick window fabrics, and the food is decadent. House-cured charcuterie is a reliable option, as are crab cakes, rabbit crepes, and sautéed fish meunière. Prime dry-aged steaks with traditional sauces have emerged as a specialty in recent years, but the menu gets more ambitious by the month. Plush and polish are the bywords here, and the service is exemplary. **$** *Average main:*

Food Glossary

Barbecue shrimp. Shrimp baked in their shells in a blend of olive oil, butter, or margarine and usually seasoned with bay leaf, garlic, and other herbs and spices.

Béarnaise (pronounced bare-*nayz*). A sauce of egg yolk and butter with shallots, wine, and vinegar, used on meat and fish.

Bouillabaisse (pronounced *booey-yah*-base). A stew of various fish and shellfish in a broth seasoned with saffron and often more-assertive spices.

Boulette (pronounced *boo*-let). Minced, chopped, or pureed meat or fish shaped into balls and fried.

Café brûlot (pronounced broo-*loh*). Cinnamon, lemon, clove, orange, and sugar, steeped with strong coffee, then flambéed with brandy and served in special pedestaled cups.

Chicory coffee. The ground and roasted root of a European variety of chicory is added to ground coffee in varying proportions.

Crème brûlée (pronounced broo-*lay*). Literally meaning "burned cream," a custard with a brittle crust of browned sugar.

Dirty rice. In this cousin of jambalaya, bits of meat, such as giblets or sausage, and seasonings are added to white rice before cooking.

Dressed. A po' boy "dressed" contains lettuce, tomato, pickles, and mayonnaise or mustard.

Meunière (pronounced muhn-*yehr*). This method of preparing fish or soft-shell crab entails dusting it with seasoned flour, sautéeing it in brown butter, and using the butter with lemon juice as a sauce.

Mirliton (pronounced merl-i-*tawn*). A pale-green member of the squash family, usually identified as a vegetable pear or chayote.

Oysters Bienville (pronounced byen-*veel*). Oysters lightly baked in their shells topped with a cream sauce flavored with bits of shrimp, mushroom, and green seasonings.

Oysters en brochette (pronounced awn-bro-*shet*). Whole oysters and bits of bacon dusted with seasoned flour, skewered, and deep-fried, and traditionally served on toast with lemon and brown butter.

Panéed veal (pronounced pan-*aid*). Breaded veal cutlets sautéed in butter.

Po' boy. A hefty sandwich, made with local French bread and any number of fillings: roast beef, fried shrimp, oysters, ham, meatballs in tomato sauce, and cheese are common.

Ravigote (pronounced rah-vee-*gote*). In Creole usage, this is a piquant mayonnaise—usually made with capers—used to moisten blue crabmeat.

Rémoulade (pronounced ray-moo-*lahd*). A brick-red whipped mixture of olive oil, mustard, scallions, cayenne, lemon, paprika, and parsley, served on cold peeled shrimp or lumps of backfin crabmeat.

Souffléed potatoes. Thin, hollow puffs of deep-fried potato, produced by two fryings at different temperatures.

Sno-balls. Shaved ice topped with flavored syrup.

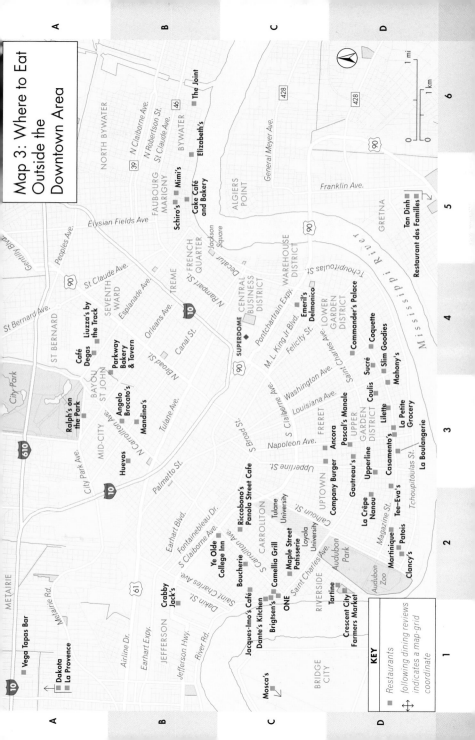

Map 3: Where to Eat Outside the Downtown Area

KEY

■ Restaurants

↔ *following dining reviews indicates a map-grid coordinate*

METAIRIE

■ Vega Tapas Bar
← ■ Dakota
■ La Provence

JEFFERSON

■ Crabby Jack's

■ Huevos

■ Ralph's on the Park

City Park

MID-CITY

■ Angelo Brocato's
■ Mandina's

■ Café Degas
■ Liuzza's by the Track

■ Parkway Bakery & Tavern

SEVENTH WARD

TREME

BAYOU ST JOHN

NORTH BYWATER

FAUBOURG MARIGNY

■ Schiro's
■ Mimi's

■ Cake Café and Bakery
■ Elizabeth's

BYWATER

■ The Joint

FRENCH QUARTER

Jackson Square

SUPERDOME

CENTRAL BUSINESS DISTRICT

WAREHOUSE DISTRICT

■ Emeril's
■ Delmonico

LOWER GARDEN DISTRICT

■ Commander's Palace

■ Sucré
■ Coquette
■ Slim Goodies
■ Mahony's

UPPER GARDEN DISTRICT

■ Coulis
■ Lilette
■ La Petite Grocery
■ La Boulangerie

■ Pascal's Manale
■ Ancora

FRERET

■ Casamento's

■ Upperline

■ Gautreau's

UPTOWN

■ Company Burger

■ La Crêpe Nanou
■ Martinique
■ Patois
■ Clancy's

■ Tee-Eva's

Magazine St.

■ Riccobono's Panola Street Cafe

S CARROLLTON

Tulane University
Loyola University

■ Ye Olde College Inn

■ Boucherie
■ Camellia Grill

■ Maple Street Patisserie
■ ONE

■ Jacques-Imo's Cafe
■ Dante's Kitchen

■ Brigtsen's

■ Tartine
■ Crescent City Farmers Market

Audubon Park

Audubon Zoo

■ Mosca's

BRIDGE CITY

RIVERSIDE

ALGIERS POINT

GRETNA

■ Tan Dinh
■ Restaurant des Familles

Mississippi River

Franklin Ave.

0 1 mi
0 1 km

A B C D

1 2 3 4 5 6

Pork cheek at Emeril's Delmonico.

$34 ✉ *1300 St. Charles Ave., Lower Garden District* ☎ *504/525–4937* 🌐 *www.emerils.com* ✍ *Reservations essential* ⏲ *No lunch* ✥ *3:C4.*

$ CAFÉ Fodor's Choice ★

🍴 **Sucré.** Do you have a sweet tooth? If so, make sure to stop in at Sucré, whether it be for a morning coffee and pastry, a late-night snack (the shop is open till midnight on Friday and Saturday), or perhaps an afternoon gelato—this stylish sweetshop offers a wide array of irresistible confections. The pastel *macarons* (airy French meringue cookies), artisanal chocolates, and gelato hold their own with even the prettiest offerings at a French patisserie. Eat your sweets here, savor them on a stroll down the shop-lined street, or pack some for later. [S] *Average main: $8* ✉ *3025 Magazine St., Garden District* ☎ *504/520–8311* 🌐 *www.shopsucre.com* ✍ *Reservations not accepted* ✥ *3:D4.*

UPTOWN AND CARROLLTON-RIVERBEND

UPTOWN

$ ITALIAN

🍴 **Ancora.** Every dish on the short menu at this Italian newcomer shows an obsessive attention to detail. The starters prominently feature the handiwork of the full-time charcuterie chef, whose sausages and other cured meats hang inside a glass room against the back wall of the restaurant. The main attraction, though, are the pizzas, which follow Neapolitan pizza rules and use only flour, water, and salt for their dough. They enter an 800°F oven—which was imported from Naples—and emerge a minute later charred and fragrant. Despite the seriousness of the kitchen, the vibe out front is casual and contemporary. Adolfo García, who also owns RioMar, La Boca, and High Hat Cafe next door, created this welcoming pizzeria which, like many other places on burgeoning Freret Street, suits the needs of neighbors but turns out food worthy of a visitor's attention. [S] *Average main: $13* ✉ *4508 Freret St., Uptown* ☎ *504/324–1636* 🌐 *www.ancorapizza.com* 🕒 *Closed Sun. No lunch Mon.–Thurs.* ✣ *3:C3.*

$ SEAFOOD 🍴 **Casamento's.** Casamento's has been a haven for Uptown seafood lovers since 1919. Family members still wait tables and staff the immaculate kitchen in back, while a reliable handful of oyster shuckers ensure that plenty of cold ones are available for the standing-room-only oyster bar. Specialties from the diminutive menu include oysters lightly poached in seasoned milk; fried shrimp, trout, and soft-shell-crab platters; and fried oysters, impeccably fresh and greaseless, served between thick slices of white toast. Everything is clean, and nothing is superfluous. Even the house plants have a just-polished look. [S] *Average main: $14* ✉ *4330 Magazine St., Uptown* ☎ *504/895–9761* 🌐 *www.casamentosrestaurant.com* ✍ *Reservations not accepted* 💳 *No credit cards* 🕒 *Closed Sun., Mon. No dinner Tues., Wed. Seasonal closure late May–late Aug.* ✣ *3:D3.*

$$ CREOLE 🍴 **Clancy's.** Understatement defines the mood at locally beloved Clancy's, and the classy but neutral decor reflects this, though the scene can get lively. The small bar is usually filled with regulars who know one another—and tourists who wish they were regulars. Most of the dishes are imaginative treatments of New Orleans favorites. Some specialties, like the seasonal smoked soft-shell crab, are exceptional. Other signs of an inventive chef are the expertly fried oysters matched with warm Brie, and a peppermint-ice-cream pie. On more festive nights you may yearn for earplugs. [S] *Average main: $22* ✉ *6100 Annunciation St., Uptown* ☎ *504/895–1111* 🌐 *www.clancysneworleans.com* ✍ *Reservations essential* 🕒 *Closed Sun. No lunch Mon.–Wed. and Fri.* ✣ *3:D2.*

$ AMERICAN Fodor's Choice ★ 🍴 **Company Burger.** At the Company Burger, you'll have it their way. The amazing signature burger comes with two fresh-ground patties, bread-and-butter pickles, American cheese, and red onions on a freshly baked bun. No lettuce, and no tomatoes, but you're free to load it up with homemade condiments like basil mayonnaise or Creole honey mustard. Other options include a lamb burger, a turkey burger, and a hot dog made with franks from Cochon Butcher. Wash it all down with a pint from one of the city's most intriguing beer lists. Owner Adam Biderman grew up in New Orleans but first earned fame for his burger at Atlanta's Holeman and Finch Public House. He's part of the wave of young transplants and returning natives who have reenergized New Orleans since Katrina. They're hip, restless, and not beholden to local traditions. [S] *Average main: $8* ✉ *4600 Freret St., Uptown* ☎ *504/267–0320* 🌐 *www.thecompanyburger.com* 🕒 *Closed Tues.* ✣ *3:C3.*

$$$ AMERICAN 🍴 **Coquette.** Every neighborhood needs a local hangout, and the dwellers of the elegant mansions in the Garden District tend to spend their time at this fabulous corner bistro. The long bar downstairs, staffed by some of the city's most creative bartenders, fuels the lively scene, and the window seats here, looking out on Magazine Street, are always in demand. Those seeking a quieter evening head to the upstairs dining room, where chef Michael Stoltzfus has created a menu of seasonal, modern-American offerings. The seafood dishes, in particular, are stellar. Stoltzfus is

8

relentlessly creative and changes the menu almost nightly, making every meal here a new adventure. Ⓢ *Average main: $26* ✉ *2800 Magazine St., Uptown* ☎ *504/265–0421* ⊕ *www.coquette-nola.com* ⌕ *Reservations essential* ☾ *No lunch Sun.–Tues.* ✛ *3:D4.*

$$$
AMERICAN

✕**Gautreau's.** This vine-covered neighborhood bistro doesn't have a sign, but that hasn't stopped the national food media from finding it. Lauded chef Sue Zemanick cooks with elegant confidence in a classic French style, but with surprising bursts of understated creativity, evidenced in dishes like wild mushroom pierogies. At Gautreau's, even the simple roasted chicken satisfies, and everyone should indulge in the caramelized banana split, at least once. An older crowd of well-dressed regulars monopolize most of the tables in this dark, quiet space that once housed a pharmacy, but if you can get a reservation, you'll feel like you've gained admittance to an elite club. Ⓢ *Average main: $30* ✉ *1728 Soniat St., Uptown* ☎ *504/899–7397* ⊕ *www.gautreausrestaurant.com* ⌕ *Reservations essential* ☾ *Closed Sun. No lunch* ✛ *3:D3.*

$$
FRENCH

✕**La Crêpe Nanou.** French chic for the budget-minded is the style at this welcoming little neighborhood bistro, where, during peak hours, there might be a half-hour wait for a table. Woven café chairs on the sidewalk and awnings that resemble metro-station architecture evoke the Left Bank of Paris, and the Gallic focus is also evident in dishes like the filet mignon, served with a choice of several classic French sauces. Other good options are the pâté maison, mussels and fries, and the lavish dessert crepes—the coffee-ice-cream crepe with chestnut cream, flamed with rum, is more than memorable. Space is a little tight in the oddly configured dining areas, but the whimsical paintings and profuse greenery combine to create an inviting room. Ⓢ *Average main: $19* ✉ *1410 Robert St., Uptown* ☎ *504/899–2670* ⊕ *www.lacrepenanou.com* ⌕ *Reservations not accepted* ☾ *No lunch Sat.–Thurs.* ✛ *3:D2.*

$$
SOUTHERN

✕**La Petite Grocery.** Flower shops sometimes bloom into intimate fine-dining establishments in New Orleans, and this one, with just-bright-enough lighting and a sturdy mahogany bar, has caught on in a big way with the locals. In the kitchen, chef Justin Devillier draws on contemporary American tastes, using Louisiana raw materials whenever he can. Signature items include the blue crab beignets and pork shank osso buco with grits and kale. Many locals, however, return to the red-leather banquettes for the signature burger. Ⓢ *Average main: $21* ✉ *4238 Magazine St., Uptown* ☎ *504/891–3377* ⊕ *www.lapetitegrocery.com* ⌕ *Reservations essential* ☾ *Closed Mon. No dinner Sun.* ✛ *3:D3.*

$$$
AMERICAN

✕**Lilette.** Proprietor-chef John Harris uses New Orleans and French culinary traditions as springboards for Lilette's inspired dishes. Look for the raw Brussels sprout salad; panéed black drum with Israeli couscous, leeks, and tomatoes; and roasted muscovy duck breast with kale and butternut squash. For dessert, the goat cheese quenelles with lavender honey are as light as sorbet but more satisfying. The wine list has been thoughtfully chosen. Framed mirrors hang along the maroon walls of the intimate front dining room–cum–bar, and there are also a few tables filling out a second room and a patio. Ⓢ *Average main: $28* ✉ *3637 Magazine St., Uptown* ☎ *504/895–1636* ⊕ *www.liletterestaurant.com* ⌕ *Reservations essential* ☾ *Closed Sun. and Mon.* ✛ *3:D3.*

$ CAFÉ 🐤

🍴 **Mahony's Po-Boy Shop.** What happens when a fine-dining chef opens a po' boy joint? You get delicious local shrimp, hand-cut french fries, and nontraditional menu items like chicken livers with coleslaw or fried oysters "dressed" with rémoulade sauce. Despite the ambitions in the kitchen, this restaurant still feels like a low-key neighborhood hangout. The crowds are equal parts working class and professional, with a good number of families. The po' boy is New Orleans's own version of fast food, but here the waits can sometimes stretch to half an hour. It's wise to avoid peak meal times, or, if you're not in a hurry, order an Abita beer and settle into a seat on the patio. [S] *Average main: $8* ✉ *3454 Magazine St., Uptown* ☎ *504/899–3374* 🌐 *www.mahonyspoboys.com* ✍ *Reservations not accepted* ⏲ *Closed Sun.* ✥ *3:D3.*

$$ FRENCH

🍴 **Martinique Bistro.** The original chef here was influenced by Caribbean flavors, hence the name of this one-room restaurant with a tropical courtyard. These days, the Martinique Bistro is known for its French cooking, including the butternut squash bisque, escargot with exotic mushrooms, and oven-roasted, cane-syrup-infused duck breast options on the menu. Make sure to budget for wine—the excellent list is continually updated. Dinner menus change every three months. The corner table in Martinique's courtyard is now a legendary marriage-proposal spot. [S] *Average main: $25* ✉ *5908 Magazine St., Uptown* ☎ *504/891–8495* 🌐 *www.martiniquebistro.com* ✍ *Reservations essential* ⏲ *Closed Mon. No lunch Tues.–Thurs.* ✥ *3:D2.*

$$ ITALIAN

🍴 **Pascal's Manale.** Barbecue shrimp is an addictive regional specialty that involves neither neither a barbecue nor barbecue sauce, and Pascal's is considered the dish's birthplace. The original recipe, introduced a half-century ago, remains unchanged: jumbo shrimp, still in the shell, are cooked in a buttery pool enhanced with just the right amount of Creole spice and pepper. The rest of the menu here is taken up with generally unexciting regional seafood and Italian-style creations, although the turtle soup and the fried eggplant are good starters, and the uppercrust scene always amuses. Most important, the atmospheric old bar might be the best place in the city to slurp raw oysters. [S] *Average main: $24* ✉ *1838 Napoleon Ave., Uptown* ☎ *504/895–4877* ✍ *Reservations essential* ⏲ *Closed Sun. No lunch Sat.* ✥ *3:D3.*

$$$ FRENCH
Fodor's Choice ★

🍴 **Patois.** Hidden away on a quiet residential corner, this bustling bistro looks like it was transported directly from Provence. The menu continues the French theme, although chef Aaron Burgau approaches the classic dishes with a Louisiana attitude. Mussels arrive in a fragrant tomato broth, sautéed sweetbreads are bathed in a country ham reduction, and the meunière sauce on the Gulf fish gets a bright burst from local citrus. Burgau developed close connections with growers and fishermen while managing a local farmers' market, so his kitchen is stocked with the best. He knows what New Orleanians like to eat, and his Uptown neighbors, an affluent mix of young and older couples, have rewarded him with a full house nearly every night. [S] *Average main: $26* ✉ *6078 Laurel St., Uptown* ☎ *504/895–9441* 🌐 *www.patoisnola.com* ⏲ *Closed Mon. and Tues. No dinner Sun. No lunch Sat., Wed., and Thurs.* ✥ *3:D2.*

$$$ CREOLE

🍴 **Upperline.** For more than 25 years, this gaily colored Uptown cottage has defined New Orleans Creole bistro fare, combining the lusty flavors of traditional items like dark gumbo or étouffée with enough elegance to make it worthy of white tablecloths. Boisterous regulars know their orders before the cocktails even arrive: perhaps crispy oysters over celery root remoulade, spicy local shrimp with jalapeño cornbread, or duck with ginger-peach sauce. **■TIP→ Order the $40 "Taste of New Orleans" menu to sample seven classic dishes.** Owner and local character JoAnn Clevenger, who filled the sprawling space with her extensive collection of regional art, presides over Upperline like the hostess of a party. [S] *Average main: $27* ✉ *1413 Upperline St., Uptown* ☎ *504/891–9822* 🌐 *www.upperline.com* ✍ *Reservations essential* 🕓 *Closed Mon. and Tues. No lunch.* ✥ *3:D3.*

CARROLLTON-RIVERBEND

$ SOUTHERN Fodor's Choice ★

🍴 **Boucherie.** Nathanial Zimet's gutsy, down-home cooking fits right in at its cozy location in a converted Uptown home. Locals first got a taste of his unique blend of Louisiana and contemporary Southern styles with the Que Crawl "barbecue truck" that used to pop up late night at music venues in the Faubourg Marigny and at Tipitina's; the food at Boucherie is a bit more refined than the street food, but every bit as delicious. The menu here is updated monthly, but it always kicks off with small plates, including every iteration of grits imaginable—fries, cakes, even crackers. Large plates pack big flavors—smoked scallops, Wagyu brisket, and pulled-pork cakes all deliver. No entrée costs more than $16. Try the Krispy Kreme bread pudding, even if you haven't saved room for it. [S] *Average main: $14* ✉ *8115 Jeannette St., Uptown* ☎ *504/862–5514* 🌐 *www.boucherie-nola.com* 🕓 *Closed Sun. and Mon.* ✥ *3:C2.*

$$$ CREOLE

🍴 **Brigtsen's.** Chef Frank Brigtsen's fusion of Creole refinement and Acadian earthiness reflects his years as a Paul Prudhomme protégé, and his dishes here represent some of the best south Louisiana cooking you'll find anywhere. Everything is fresh and filled with deep, complex tastes. The butternut shrimp bisque defines comfort food. Rabbit and duck dishes, usually presented in rich sauces and gravies, are full of robust flavor. But Brigtsen really gets to unleash his creativity on the "Shell Beach Diet," a nightly changing seafood platter. Trompe l'oeil murals add whimsy to the intimate spaces of this turn-of-the-20th-century frame cottage. Ask for a table on the enclosed front sun porch. [S] *Average main: $29* ✉ *723 Dante St., Uptown* ☎ *504/861–7610* 🌐 *www.brigtsens.com* ✍ *Reservations essential* 🕓 *Closed Sun. and Mon. No lunch* ✥ *3:C2.*

$$ SOUTHERN

🍴 **Dante's Kitchen.** Ask local chefs where they dine on their day off, and chances are a good number of them will mention Dante's Kitchen. Chef Eman Loubier, a nine-year veteran of Commander's Palace, prepares seasonal menus for those with a sense of adventure. Duck breast is served with kumquats and pickled hot-pepper sauce, pork is paired with Brie-and-pastrami mac and cheese, and every visit demands a helping of root beer–candied sweet potatoes. Desserts, such as the sweet-potato-and-white-chocolate pie, are homey and hearty. An outdoor patio is especially welcoming on cooler nights and at brunch on Saturday and Sunday. At lunch Monday through Friday, and Tuesday for dinner—When Dante's is closed—the pop-up restaurant McClure's BBQ takes over with smoked pork, brisket, and chicken. [S] *Average main: $25* ✉ *736 Dante St., Uptown* ☎ *504/861–3121* 🌐 *www.danteskitchen.com* 🕒 *No lunch; closed Tues.* ✣ *3:C2.*

$$ CAJUN 🍴 **Jacques-Imo's Cafe.** Oak Street might look like any other sleepy urban thoroughfare by day, but once the sun sets, the half-block stretch containing Jacques-Imo's Cafe feels like the center of the universe. Prepare for lengthy but festive waits in the crowded bar for a table in the boisterous, swamp-theme dining rooms (fortunately, the bartenders are skilled). Although not everyone is a fan, most say the modest-looking but innovative food is worth it: deep-fried roast beef po' boys, alligator sausage cheesecake, Cajun bouillabaisse, and smothered rabbit over grits are among the excellent only-at-Jacques-Imo's specialties. All main courses come with salad and corn muffins. Reservations are accepted for parties of five or more. [S] *Average main: $18* ✉ *8324 Oak St., Carrollton-Riverbend* ☎ *504/861–0886* 🌐 *www.jacquesimoscafe.com* 🕒 *Closed Sun. No lunch* ✣ *3:C2.*

$$ SOUTHERN 🍴 **ONE.** Intimate, neighborhoody, and chic all at once, ONE proves that fine dining and casual elegance are not mutually exclusive. The interior is sleek and sophisticated, while the kitchen is wide open. Even though the restaurant is pretty much as far uptown as you can go, it's more than worth the trip. Chef Scott Snodgrass and co-owner Lee McCullough are the perfect hosts, and seem to love every minute of it. Typical of Snodgrass's creations are pan-fried flounder atop spaghetti squash gratin and the beef tenderloin with beef rillettes and Stilton cheese. [S] *Average main: $22* ✉ *8132 Hampson St., Carrollton-Riverbend* ☎ *504/301–9061* 🌐 *www.ONE-SL.com* 🕒 *Closed Sun. No lunch Sat.–Mon* ✣ *3:C2.*

8

MID-CITY

$ CAFÉ 👶 🍴 **Angelo Brocato's.** Traditional Sicilian gelato, spumoni, cannoli, pastries, and candies are the attractions at this quaint little sweetshop, now over a century old. The crisp biscotti, traditional Sicilian desserts, and the lemon and strawberry ices haven't lost their status as local favorites. The shop closes at 10 pm weekdays (closed Monday), 10:30 pm Fridays and Saturdays, and 9 pm on Sundays. Plan to stand in line and chat with mostly locals. [S] *Average main: $4* ✉ *214 N. Carrollton Ave., Mid-City* ☎ *504/486–1465* 🌐 *www.angelobrocatoicecream.com* 🕒 *Closed Mon.* ✣ *3:B3.*

$ FRENCH 🍴 **Café Degas.** Dining at Café Degas is like being at a sidewalk café in Paris, even though the restaurant is completely covered: there's a tree growing through the center of the dining room, and the front windows overlook picturesque Esplanade Avenue. Employees are matter-of-fact, but in a relaxing, European way. The fare here is a mixture of French-bistro cooking and what you might find at a countryside inn—pâté, onion soup, steamed mussels, duck in orange sauce, steaks, crème brûlée. Daily specials are always creative and ingenious. [S] *Average main: $16* ✉ *3127 Esplanade Ave., Mid-City* ☎ *504/945–5635* 🌐 *www.cafedegas.com* 🕒 *Closed Mon. and Tues.* ✣ *3:A4.*

$ ✕ **Liuzza's by the Track.** Fried-oyster po' boys drenched in garlic butter,
CREOLE bowls of sweet-corn-and-crawfish bisque, and grilled Reuben sandwiches with succulent corned beef are some of the reasons you might
decide to tolerate the poor ventilation in this barroom near the racetrack
and Jazz Fest grounds. The Creole chicken and sausage gumbo with
shrimp is always good—thin on body, but heavy on spice (the shrimp
is cooked to order and can be left out if you have dietary restrictions).
But the pièce de résistance here is a barbecue-shrimp po' boy, for which
the shrimp are cooked in a bracing lemon-pepper butter with enough
garlic to cure a cold. The kitchen closes at 7 pm. Ⓢ *Average main: $10*
✉ *1518 N. Lopez St., Mid-City* ☎ *504/218–7888* 🍴 *Reservations not
accepted* 🕙 *Closed Sun.* ✛ *3:A4.*

$$ ✕ **Mandina's.** Although New Orleans boasts many nationally known
CREOLE restaurants, the locals here, as everywhere, tend to frequent their neigh-
🍴 borhood corner restaurant. Mandina's is just such a spot, and has been
since 1932. This fixture on Canal Street serves just the right combina-
tion of expected favorites, including étouffée, po' boys, fried seafood,
and perfect pastas. Although the restaurant has expanded over the
years, nothing has dampened the locals' love for this place, or dimin-
ished the full flavors of the house shrimp rémoulade, crawfish cakes,
turtle soup, or, on Monday, tender red beans with Italian sausage. If
you're looking for the ideal bar and restaurant to spend a football
Sunday, this is your place, complete with flat-screen TVs and the ici-
est beers in town. Ⓢ *Average main: $18* ✉ *3800 Canal St., Mid-City*
☎ *504/482–9179* ⊕ *www.mandinasrestaurant.com* ✛ *3:B3.*

$ ✕ **Parkway Bakery & Tavern.** Former contractor Jay Nix resurrected
CAFÉ more than just a dilapidated building when he reopened Parkway:
he also brought back to life a dormant community spirit. You can
find neighbors and regulars from other parts of the city sinking into
Parkway's roast beef and grilled-ham po'boys; some simply wander
in for a hot dog and beer at the bar, and to take in the New Orleans
nostalgia decorating the walls. For dessert, choose from a selection of
rum cake, bread pudding, and banana pudding—all made fresh daily.
As it's near the fairgrounds, Parkway jumps during Jazz Fest. Ⓢ *Aver-
age main: $8* ✉ *538 Hagan Ave., Mid-City* ☎ *504/482–3047* ⊕ *www.
parkwaybakeryandtavernnola.com* 🍴 *Reservations not accepted*
🕙 *Closed Tues.* ✛ *3:B4.*

$$ ✕ **Ralph's on the Park.** Seasoned restaurateur Ralph Brennan has matched
CREOLE this beautifully renovated historic building with an outstanding menu
that mixes contemporary Creole standbys with innovative twists. The
culinary staff excel with full-flavored seafood dishes like an inventive
take on oysters Rockefeller and a variety of fresh fish. By all means, try
the rib-eye wrapped scallops. For Sunday brunch, the Louisiana seafood
crepe with local crabmeat, shrimp, and fish will remind you that you're
way down South. The solid wine list is always evolving. Ⓢ *Average
main: $25* ✉ *900 City Park Ave., Mid-City* ☎ *504/488–1000* ⊕ *www.
ralphsonthepark.com* 🍴 *Reservations essential* 🕙 *No lunch Mon. and
Sat.* ✛ *3:A3.*

$ ✕ **Ye Olde College Inn.** A stalwart neighborhood joint, the age-old Col-
CREOLE lege Inn occupies a new building after decades in an older, now razed
🍴

structure next door. The flat, greasy burgers are still popular, particularly when ordered with french fries and a cold Abita beer, but the diner fare has been joined by options like lemon-thyme chicken and grilled Gulf fish over crawfish étouffée. Many of the vegetables come from the restaurant's two neighboring urban gardens. Despite all the updates, you can still get the veal cutlet that's been on the menu since 1933. [S] *Average main: $16* ✉ *3000 S. Carrollton Ave., Mid-City* ☎ *504/866–3683* 🌐 *www.collegeinn1933.com* 🕓 *Closed Sun. and Mon. No lunch* ✥ *3:C2.*

OUTSIDE CITY LIMITS

$ SOUTHERN 👶 🍴 **Crabby Jack's.** Panéed rabbit po' boys, fried-green-tomato-and-shrimp rémoulade salads, and fried chicken draw legions of urban New Orleanians out to Jefferson Parish. Crabby Jack's is a down-home, boxy joint; diners don't come for the atmosphere, they come for the smoky red beans, muffulettas, and the jambalaya, which are all first-rate and cheap, though the creative fresh-fish specials provide a more definitive experience. If you want to eat "real" New Orleans food, eat here. [S] *Average main: $11* ✉ *428 Jefferson Hwy., Jefferson* ☎ *504/833–2722* 🕓 *Closed Sun. No dinner* ✥ *3:B2.*

$$$ CREOLE 🍴 **Dakota.** Warm colors, lustrous woods, and floral accents set the scene at Dakota, one of the most reliable and consistent fine-dining experiences on the north shore. Owner-chef Kim Kringlie's inspirations may be multicultural, but his seasonal menus are solidly grounded in south Louisiana. Both the Brie and crabmeat soup and the crackly soft-shell crab stuffed with a variety of expertly seasoned shellfish are signatures. The wine list is among the most complex and well-planned in the area. [S] *Average main: $30* ✉ *629 U.S. 190, Covington* ☎ *985/892–3712* 🌐 *www.thedakotarestaurant.com* 🕓 *Closed Sun. and Mon. No lunch Sat.* ✥ *3:A1.*

$$$ FRENCH 🍴 **La Provence.** It's almost an hour's drive from central New Orleans, but the glorious French provincial food and relaxing atmosphere of this exceptional restaurant are well worth the trip. Now among the chef John Besh group of restaurants, La Provence has taken on even richer and more creative culinary stylings. Start with roasted pumpkin soup followed by ravioli of rabbit or an herb-roasted pork shoulder. Separating the two dining rooms, which are hung with pleasant Provençal landscape paintings, is a hearth that welcomes you on damp winter days. In warmer seasons, the tree-shaded deck is almost as congenial. Best of all, most of the vegetables are grown on the property right near the massive herb garden. They even raise pigs and chickens. [S] *Average main: $30* ✉ *25020 Hwy. 190, 7 miles from Lake Pontchartrain Causeway, Lacombe* ☎ *985/626–7662* 🌐 *www.laprovencerestaurant.com* ✍ *Reservations essential* 🕓 *Closed Mon. and Tues. No lunch Wed.–Sat.* ✥ *3:A1.*

$$ ITALIAN Fodor's Choice ★ 🍴 **Mosca's.** The food here—combining Louisiana ingredients and Italian ingenuity—is good enough to lure city folk to this remote spot about 30 minutes from the city. Baked oysters with bread crumbs, olive oil, garlic, and herbs approach the summit of Italian-Creole cuisine. The Italian shrimp are cooked in an herbed mix of olive oil and spices, the roasted chicken with rosemary is luscious, and the house-made Italian sausage

is full of peppery goodness. Getting a table usually means waiting at the bar, even if you have made reservations. "Worth the wait" would be an understatement. [S] *Average main: $18* ⊠ *4137 U.S. Hwy. 90, West-wego* ☎ *504/436–9942* ⊕ *www.moscasrestaurant.com* ⌕ *Reservations essential* ▭ *No credit cards* ⊘ *Closed Sun. and Mon. No lunch* ✛ *3:C1.*

$ ✕**Restaurant des Familles.** No time for a trip to Cajun country? Well,
CAJUN   this restaurant, about a 20-minute drive from central New Orleans, is the next best thing (although you'd better ask for directions when reserving a table). Just a few yards from the vast windows are the slow-moving waters of Bayou des Familles, providing a dramatic vista. Elegantly illuminated at night, the huge Acadian-style raised cottage has a kitchen that produces familiar, and locally beloved, seafood in the Creole style—shrimp rémoulade, crawfish étouffée, shrimp Diane, and crawfish-stuffed rainbow trout. The seafood gumbo is one of the best around. The restaurant closes at 6 pm on Sunday. [S] *Average main: $15* ⊠ *7163 Barataria Blvd., Crown Point* ☎ *504/689–7834* ⊕ *www. restaurantdesfamilles.com* ⊘ *Closed Mon.* ✛ *3:D5.*

$ ✕**Tan Dinh.** Serving arguably the best Vietnamese food in the area, Tan
VIETNAMESE   Dinh is a 15-minute drive from downtown New Orleans, but a world away in flavor. Curry goat stew, roasted quail with sticky-rice cakes, steamed flour cakes topped with dried shrimp, and jellyfish salad are among the more exotic menu items. Spring rolls, noodle soups, and sandwiches, all equally good, might be safer bets for Vietnamese new-comers. With cherrywood chairs and faux-marble tabletops, the res-taurant exhibits a convincing polish. [S] *Average main: $11* ⊠ *1705 Lafayette St., Gretna* ☎ *504/361–8008* ⌕ *Reservations not accepted* ⊘ *Closed Tues.* ✛ *3:D5.*

$$ ✕**Vega Tapas Café.** The small plates on the largely Mediterranean-
MEDITERRANEAN   inspired menu here are almost unfailingly good, so don't hesitate to order the more exotic-sounding dishes. Calling cards here include the Moorish pork and rare coriander tuna with avocado-tomato relish. There is an educated selection of wines, many of them Spanish, and specialty cocktails. Everything is served in a large, minimally decorated room lined with hard surfaces, which ups the noise level a couple of notches. Rotating art exhibits feature local and regional artists. [S] *Aver-age main: $21* ⊠ *2051 Metairie Rd., Metairie* ☎ *504/836–2007* ⊕ *www. vegatapascafe.com* ⊘ *Closed Sun. No lunch* ✛ *3:A1.*

Where to Stay

WORD OF MOUTH

"The French Quarter is a good place to stay, especially for a first trip to NOLA—even if [you] aren't party types. There are several blocks on Bourbon Street that are the party atmosphere that most people think of when they think of the FQ, but the rest is not really like that. There are some parts of the FQ that are downright quiet."

—november_moon

Updated
by Beth
D'Addono

Deciding where to stay in New Orleans has everything to do with what you want from your visit. Are you interested in the nightlife and architecture of the French Quarter? Do you want to be where the party is? Are you in town primarily to eat—and to eat well? Do the antebellum mansions of the Garden District pique your interest? Do you need to be close to business district and the convention center? New Orleans is a fairly compact town, but if you choose to stay Uptown, you'll need to travel a bit to reach the Quarter. Although most hotels favored by visitors are in the French Quarter, Central Business District (CBD), or Warehouse District, there are also good options that are farther afield.

The French Quarter is a destination in itself. With fascinating architecture, vibrant nightlife, shopping, and incredible restaurants, you could spend a week in New Orleans without leaving its confines.

Hotels in the CBD, many of them chains, cater to business travelers as well as tourists; most are larger than those in the French Quarter, and have more amenities. The Warehouse District harbors many hotels whose buildings were originally used to store cotton or other goods. In most cases, thoughtful renovations let the original purpose of the structures show through, making for an interesting architectural style.

Just across Esplanade Avenue on the north and east of the Quarter is the Faubourg Marigny. Originally a Creole plantation and one of the first "suburbs" of New Orleans, it remains a residential area, with its own nightlife and restaurant scene centered along Frenchmen Street.

To the west, upriver of the city's center, the Garden District and Uptown neighborhoods offer streets lined by the spreading boughs of live oaks, excellent stores, interesting architecture, and more outstanding dining and music venues. Public transportation is not one of New Orleans's strengths, but if you have a bit of patience, the streetcar line that runs the length of St. Charles Avenue from Carrollton to Canal Street is a fun way to travel.

NEW ORLEANS LODGING PLANNER

RESERVATIONS

Book your room as far in advance as possible—up to a year ahead for Mardi Gras, Jazz Fest, or other special events.

SERVICES

Most hotels have private baths, central heating, air-conditioning, and private phones. More and more major hotels have added Wi-Fi or in-room broadband Internet service, though most major chains continue to charge for in-room Wi-Fi. Smaller bed-and-breakfasts and hotels may not have all of these amenities; ask before you book your room.

Hotels that do not have pools may have agreements with nearby health clubs or other facilities to allow guests to use club facilities for a nominal fee.

Most hotels have parking available, but this can run you as much as $36 a day. Valet parking is usually available at the major hotels. If you park on the street, keep in mind that New Orleans meter attendants are relentless, and ticketing is imminent for illegally parked vehicles. The minimum fee for a parking ticket is $20.

PRICES

Properties are assigned price categories based on the rate for a standard double room during high season.

The lodgings we list are the most desirable in each price category, but rates are subject to change. Use Fodors.com to shop around for rooms before booking. Many major hotels occasionally offer Internet special rates. Be aware that room rates may be higher in October (considered peak convention season) and during the July 4 weekend (due to the annual Essence Music Festival). Rates are also high at the end of April and beginning of May during Jazz Fest. Rates are at their peak during Mardi Gras, and major hotels will require either a three- or four-night stay.

WITH KIDS

In the listings, look for the symbol, which indicates the property is particularly good for kids.

USING THE MAPS

Throughout the chapter, you'll see mapping symbols and coordinates (⊕ 3:F2) at the end of each review. The first number after the ⊕ symbol indicates the map number. Following that is the property's coordinate on the map grid.

HOTEL REVIEWS

Listed alphabetically within neighborhood. The following reviews have been condensed for this book. Please go to Fodors.com for full reviews of each property.

THE FRENCH QUARTER

$ B&B/INN 🏨 **Andrew Jackson Hotel.** This property, located on a relatively quiet part of Royal Street and within walking distance of major attractions, is one of the best deals in the French Quarter. **Pros:** free in-room Wi-Fi; comfortable rooms; balcony views; killer location. **Cons:** basic furnishings; no parking; no restaurant. **TripAdvisor:** "clean and quaint," "great location," "charming." [S] *Rooms from: $109* ✉ *919 Royal St., French Quarter* ☎ *504/561–5881 or 800/654–0224* 🌐 *www.andrewjacksonhotel.com* 🛏 *20 rooms, 2 suites* 🍴 *Breakfast* ✥ *1:D2.*

$$ HOTEL 🏨 **Astor Crowne Plaza.** Located on the edge of the French Quarter on bustling Canal Street, this large property is a good choice for both business and leisure stays: it's within walking distance of everything that counts in the Quarter and downtown. **Pros:** convenient location; large guest rooms and big fitness center; direct access to streetcar. **Cons:** Bourbon Street is right next door, which is too close for some; Internet fees. **TripAdvisor:** "perfection," "ideal location," "lovely room." [S] *Rooms from: $170* ✉ *739 Canal St., French Quarter* ☎ *504/962–0500 or 888/696–4806* 🌐 *www.astorneworleans.com* 🛏 *693 rooms, 28 suites* 🍴 *No meals* ✥ *1:C3.*

$$$$ B&B/INN 🏨 **Audobon Cottages.** This luxurious group of cottages delivers high-end amenities and tons of privacy in an enviable location that's close to just about everything in the Quarter. **Pros:** lovely pool with outdoor lounge and cabanas; lots of personal service; use of the fitness center at the nearby Dauphine Orleans Hotel. **Cons:** expensive; you have to climb steps to reach the two-story unit; some courtyards are shared. **TripAdvisor:** "a taste of New Orleans," "amazing French Quarter escape," "absolutely perfect." [S] *Rooms from: $399* ✉ *509 Dauphine St., French Quarter* ☎ *504/586–1516* 🌐 *www.auduboncottages.com* 🛏 *7 cottages* 🍴 *Breakfast* ✥ *1:C2.*

$$ HOTEL 🏨 **Bienville House Hotel.** Located near the Mississippi River, on a sliver of land between Decatur and N. **Pros:** close to the Canal Street streetcars, Jackson Square, and family-friendly attractions, including the aquarium; personalized service. **Cons:** noise can be a problem at night; standard rooms are on the small side; fitness center off-site. **TripAdvisor:** "charming," "what a pleasant surprise," "close to everything." [S] *Rooms from: $159* ✉ *320 Decatur St., French Quarter* ☎ *504/529–2345* 🌐 *www.bienvillehouse.com* 🛏 *80 rooms, 3 suites* 🍴 *Breakfast* ✥ *1:D3.*

$$ B&B/INN 🏨 **Bon Maison Guest House.** Quiet and homey accommodations lie inside the gates of this 1833 town house that's on the less touristy end of Bourbon Street. **Pros:** within walking distance of all French Quarter attractions and a block or two from lots of restaurants; Wi-Fi and cable TV. **Cons:** can be difficult to reserve; minimum stay of three nights; no parking; no breakfast. **TripAdvisor:** "romantic getaway," "can't

BEST BETS FOR
NEW ORLEANS LODGING

Fodor's offers a selective listing of quality lodging experiences in every price range, from the city's best budget motel to its most sophisticated luxury hotel. Here are our top hotel recommendations by price and experience. The very best properties—in other words, those that provide a particularly remarkable experience in their price range—are designated in the listings with the Fodor's Choice logo.

Fodor's Choice ★

Chimes Bed and Breakfast, $$, p. 202

Edgar Degas House, $$, p. 203

Grand Victorian Bed & Breakfast, $$$, p. 201

Harrah's New Orleans Hotel, $$$, p. 195

Hotel Monteleone, $$$, p. 189

Loews New Orleans Hotel, $$$, p. 197

Ritz-Carlton New Orleans, $$$$, p. 191

Royal Sonesta Hotel New Orleans, $$$, p. 191

Soniat House, $$$, p. 191

Windsor Court Hotel, $$$$, p. 198

By Price

$

Hotel Royal, p. 189

Lion's Inn, p. 194

$$

Bon Maison Guest House, p. 182

Chimes Bed and Breakfast, p. 202

Edgar Degas House, p. 203

$$$

Grand Victorian Bed and Breakfast, p. 201

Harrah's New Orleans Hotel, p. 195

Hotel Le Marais, p. 185

Hotel Monteleone, p. 189

Loews New Orleans Hotel, p. 197

Royal Sonesta Hotel New Orleans, p. 191

Soniat House, p. 191

$$$$

Ritz-Carlton New Orleans, p. 191

W Hotel New Orleans French Quarter, p. 193

Windsor Court Hotel, p. 198

Best By Experience

BEST FOR KIDS

Embassy Suites New Orleans-Convention Center, $$$, p. 195

Hilton New Orleans Riverside, $$$$, p. 195

Homewood Suites by Hilton New Orleans, $$, p. 195

BEST FOR ROMANCE

Claiborne Mansion, $$, p. 194

Hotel Mazarin, $$$, p. 185

Loft 523, $$, p. 197

W Hotel New Orleans French Quarter $$$$, p. 193

BEST B&BS

Chimes Bed and Breakfast, $$, p. 202

Edgar Degas House, $$, p. 203

1896 O'Malley House, $$, p. 203

Grand Victorian Bed and Breakfast, $$$, p. 201

Lion's Inn, $, p. 194

Maison Perrier Bed & Breakfast, $$, p. 202

Sully Mansion, $, p. 202

BEST GRANDE DAME HOTELS

Hotel Monteleone, $$$, p. 189

The Roosevelt Hotel New Orleans, $$$, p. 197

Royal Sonesta Hotel New Orleans, $$$, p. 191

BEST HOTEL BARS

Hotel Modern, $$, p. 201

Hotel Monteleone, $$$, p. 189

International House, $$, p. 196

Loews New Orleans Hotel, $$$, p. 197

Renaissance Pere Marquette, $$$, p. 197

The Roosevelt Hotel New Orleans, $$$, p. 197

BEST POOLS

Bourbon Orleans Hotel, $$$, p. 184

Hotel Monteleone, $$$, p. 189

Omni Royal Orleans, $$$, p. 190

The Saint Hotel, $$, p. 191

9

WHERE SHOULD I STAY?

NEIGHBORHOOD	VIBE	PROS	CONS
The French Quarter	The tourist-focused main event is action packed, but still charming. Lodging runs from small inns to luxury hotels.	Lots of visitor attractions and nationally acclaimed restaurants. Everything is within walking distance of your hotel.	Crowded, high-traffic area. If you're sound sensitive, request a room that does not face a main street, or find a hotel some distance from Bourbon.
Faubourg Marigny	Residential area just to the east of the French Quarter with a bohemian feel.	Balanced residential–commercial community. Close to French Quarter nightlife, and with an eclectic nightlife scene of its own. The area is a more peaceful alternative to the Quarter.	Can be confusing to navigate for newcomers. Don't forget your map!
CBD and Warehouse District	The Warehouse District is also known as New Orleans's arts district. It's a great area for visitors who want to stay in luxurious high-rise hotels or smaller boutique properties.	Good retail and restaurants, and some of the best galleries and museums in the city. Within walking distance of the French Quarter.	Crowded; traffic can be a problem for pedestrians.
Garden District/ Uptown	Residential, upscale, and fashionable, this neighborhood is a slower-paced alternative to staying downtown.	Beautiful and right on the historic St. Charles Ave. streetcar line. Traffic here is not as heavy as downtown. Excellent shopping opportunities on Magazine St.	Far from the French Quarter and tourist attractions; must drive or take public transportation.
Mid-City	This is primarily an urban–residential area, with few lodging options.	Many local businesses and mid-price owner-operated restaurants. Home to City Park, one of the largest urban parks in the country.	More challenging for tourists to navigate—some distance from tourist attractions. You'll need a car; public transportation is not convenient.

beat the location or character," "great atmosphere." [S] *Rooms from: $175* ✉ *835 Bourbon St., French Quarter* ☎ *504/561–8498* 🌐 *www.bonmaison.com* 🛏 *2 rooms, 2 suites* 🍴 *No meals* ✥ *1:D2.*

$$ HOTEL 🏨 **Bourbon Orleans Hotel.** In the center of the French Quarter, this hotel also has lots of attractions inside as well. **Pros:** meticulous renovation done in 2011, with upgraded bedding and furnishings; free Wi-Fi and gym; beautiful courtyard and pool. **Cons:** lobby level is often crowded and noisy due to curious passersby; hotel is steps from loud, 24-hour Bourbon Street bars; no breakfast. **TripAdvisor:** "royal treatment," "a class in itself," "great staff." [S] *Rooms from: $169* ✉ *717 Orleans Ave.,*

French Quarter ☎ 504/523–2222 ⊕ *www.bourbonorleans.com* ⤳ *218 rooms, 28 suites* ⊠ *No meals* ✛ *1:D2.*

$$ 🏨 **Chateau LeMoyne.** A great location just one block off Bourbon Street,
HOTEL surprisingly large rooms, and period touches are all great reasons to stay at this distinctive branch of the Holiday Inn chain. **Pros:** great location; large pool; affordable rates; the moderately priced hotel restaurant serves authentic Southern breakfast; kids eat free. **Cons:** no room service or meals beyond breakfast; beds are doubles, not queens; some bathrooms are small. **TripAdvisor:** "perfect location," "nice property and professional staff," "charming and delightful." Ⓢ *Rooms from: $162* ⊠ *301 Dauphine St., French Quarter* ☎ *504/581–1303 or 800/465–4329* ⊕ *www.hiclneworleanshotelsite.com* ⤳ *160 rooms, 11 suites* ⊠ *No meals* ✛ *1:C3.*

$$ 🏨 **Dauphine Orleans.** Within walking distance of the action but removed
HOTEL enough to make it a secluded respite, this French Quarter hotel has a lot of charm. **Pros:** good location in a relatively quiet section of the Quarter; free in-room Wi-Fi; charming French Quarter architecture; saltwater pool. **Cons:** some rooms require climbing stairs; some rooms can be noisy. **TripAdvisor:** "romantic," "very pleasant stay," "charming and clean." Ⓢ *Rooms from: $179* ⊠ *415 Dauphine St., French Quarter* ☎ *504/586–1800 or 800/521–7111* ⊕ *www.dauphineorleans.com* ⤳ *107 rooms, 3 suites* ⊠ *Breakfast* ✛ *1:C3.*

$ 🏨 **Holiday Inn New Orleans French Quarter.** This family-friendly, 20-story
HOTEL chain hotel is close to Canal Street and within walking distance of
☺ Royal Street shopping, French Quarter restaurants, and the Central Business District. **Pros:** moderately priced by French Quarter standards; near popular bars and restaurants; kids eat free. **Cons:** a bit generic; slow elevators. **TripAdvisor:** "great location," "clean and comfortable," "very average." Ⓢ *Rooms from: $144* ⊠ *124 Royal St., French Quarter* ☎ *504/529–7211 or 800/448–2296* ⊕ *www.hifrenchquarterhotel.com* ⤳ *374 rooms* ⊠ *No meals* ✛ *1:C3.*

$$$ 🏨 **Hotel Le Marais.** This well-located hotel is an anomaly in the French
HOTEL Quarter, with modern furnishings and a lobby that combines urban chic with an artsy New Orleans vibe. **Pros:** modern furnishings; free in-room Wi-Fi; quiet despite location near Bourbon Street. **Cons:** not for those who want a traditional-looking hotel; no in-hotel restaurant. **TripAdvisor:** "perfect location," "can't wait to go back," "excellent service and staff." Ⓢ *Rooms from: $200* ⊠ *717 Conti St., French Quarter* ☎ *504/525–2300* ⊕ *www.hotellemarais.com* ⤳ *66 rooms* ⊠ *Breakfast* ✛ *1:C3.*

$$$ 🏨 **Hotel Mazarin.** Opened at the end of 2011, the former St. Louis is
HOTEL now a boutique hotel with lots of local charm, including a picture-
Fodor's Choice perfect courtyard with a fountain and sophisticated, well-appointed
★ guest rooms. **Pros:** outstanding breakfast; great location; excellent guest service. **Cons:** rooms facing the street can be noisy. **TripAdvisor:** "beautiful courtyard," "great service," "wonderful cozy hotel." Ⓢ *Rooms from: $209* ⊠ *730 Bienville St., Downtown* ☎ *504/581–7300 or 800/535–9111* ⊕ *www.hotelmazarin.com/* ⤳ *102 rooms, 3 suites* ⊠ *Breakfast* ✛ *1:C3.*

9

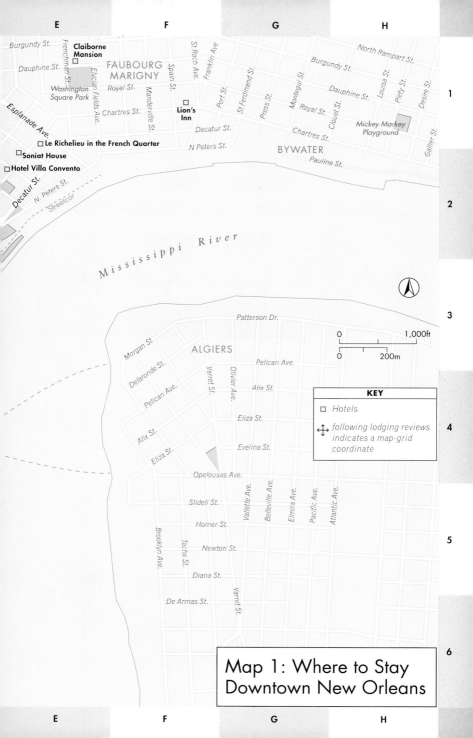

Map 1: Where to Stay
Downtown New Orleans

Hotel Monteleone

Ritz-Carlton New Orleans

$$$
HOTEL
Fodor's Choice
★

Hotel Monteleone. In this grand hotel from 1886, the rooms are well sized and luxurious, and the ornate baroque facade, liveried doormen, shimmering lobby chandeliers, and nightly live jazz warm many a traditionalist's heart. **Pros:** great location for French Quarter, Royal Street shopping, and CBD locations; civilized, with attentive service. **Cons:** no in-room coffeemaker; the lobby and entranceway can get crowded. **TripAdvisor:** "beautiful historic hotel," "perfect location," "New Orleans atmosphere." $ Rooms from: $229 ⊠ 214 Royal St., French Quarter ☎ 504/523–3341 or 800/535–9595 ⊕ www.hotelmonteleone.com ⇌ 600 rooms, 55 suites ⦿| No meals ✛ 1:C3.

$$$
HOTEL

Hotel Provincial. The next time you want to stay in a "real New Orleans hotel," consider this secluded option: the bright, good-size, traditionally furnished rooms have 19th-century touches that include exposed-brick walls, and many overlook a lush courtyard with iron grillwork. **Pros:** quaint; quiet surroundings (in a residential section of the French Quarter); destination restaurant. **Cons:** suites are pricey. **TripAdvisor:** "perfect," "lots of charm," "stunning historic hotel." $ Rooms from: $249 ⊠ 1024 Chartres St., French Quarter ☎ 504/581–4995 or 800/535–7922 ⊕ www.hotelprovincial.com ⇌ 93 rooms, 6 suites ⦿| Breakfast ✛ 1:D2.

$
HOTEL

Hotel Royal. Think of the coolest big-city boutique hotel, mix in some authentic New Orleans elegance and a good location, and this is your place. **Pros:** central location; pastries served in the courtyard on weekends and Monday. **Cons:** some rooms are small; no elevator, steps to reach upper floors. **TripAdvisor:** "old French Quarter meets modern accommodations," "clean and comfortable," "charming." $ Rooms from: $125 ⊠ 1006 Royal St., French Quarter ☎ 504/524–3900 or 800/776–3901 ⊕ www.frenchquarterhotelgroup.com ⇌ 43 rooms ⦿| No meals ✛ 1:D2.

$
HOTEL

Hotel Villa Convento. The Campo family provides around-the-clock service in this four-story 1833 Creole town house on quaint, quiet street close to the Old Ursuline Convent, but just blocks from the Quarter's tourist attractions, shopping, and restaurants. **Pros:** located in the quieter residential section of the French Quarter; true New Orleans flavor; personal service. **Cons:** rooms on the small side; no children under 10; Wi-Fi only available in courtyard and lobby area. **TripAdvisor:** "friendly staff," "quintessential New Orleans charm," "very accommodating." $ Rooms from: $109 ⊠ 616 Ursulines St., French Quarter ☎ 504/522–1793 ⊕ www.villaconvento.com ⇌ 25 rooms ⦿| No meals ✛ 1:E2.

$$$
HOTEL

The Inn on Bourbon. Located on the site of New Orleans's original French opera house, this property is well-kept and fairly priced, given its in-demand location. **Pros:** ideal for those who want to be in the heart of the French Quarter; free WI-Fi. **Cons:** the high-traffic location means the party outside your front door never ends. **TripAdvisor:** "great location if you want to party," "nice facility," "peace and quiet." $ Rooms from: $249 ⊠ 541 Bourbon St., French Quarter ☎ 504/524–7611 or 800/535–7891 ⊕ www.innonbourbon.com ⇌ 179 rooms, 7 suites ⦿| No meals ✛ 1:C2.

9

$$ HOTEL 🏨 **Le Richelieu in the French Quarter.** Close to the Old Ursuline Convent and the French Market, Le Richelieu combines the friendly personal charm of an old-fashioned small hotel with some luxe touches (upscale toiletries)—at a moderate rate. **Pros:** great value; some rooms have balconies; reasonably priced on-site parking. **Cons:** café only open for breakfast and lunch; bathrooms are small, and rooms could use updating. **TripAdvisor:** "great French Quarter hotel," "the perfect location," "lovely stay away from the madness." [S] *Rooms from: $159* ✉ *1234 Chartres St., French Quarter* ☎ *504/529–2492 or 800/535–9653* 🌐 *www.lerichelieuhotel.com* 🛏 *69 rooms, 17 suites* 🍴 *No meals* ✣ *1:E2.*

$$ HOTEL 🏨 **The Maison Dupuy.** Just two blocks from Bourbon Street, these seven restored 19th-century town houses contain rooms that are all good-sized; some have balconies. **Pros:** quiet yet still close to French Quarter action; excellent hotel restaurant. **Cons:** lobby can be cramped at check-in; guests should be aware of surroundings if walking late at night. **TripAdvisor:** "superb location," "classic," "quaint." [S] *Rooms from: $159* ✉ *1001 Toulouse St., French Quarter* ☎ *504/586–8000 or 800/535–9177* 🌐 *www.maisondupuy.com* 🛏 *187 rooms, 13 suites* 🍴 *No meals* ✣ *1:C2.*

$$ B&B/INN 🏨 **Melrose Mansion.** A few minutes from the French Quarter, this Victorian mansion, heavily renovated in late 2011, turns on the granduer with antique furnishings, hardwood floors, and cathedral ceilings with large chandeliers. **Pros:** freshly renovated; private and luxurious, with lots of pampering. **Cons:** seven-day cancellation policy; one night's stay is charged prior to arrival, and full bill is charged at check-in; small daily fee for continental breakfast, Wi-Fi, and use of the 24-hour gym. **TripAdvisor:** "modern," "like a home," "amazing place." [S] *Rooms from: $125* ✉ *937 Esplanade Ave., French Quarter* ☎ *504/944–2255 or 800/650–3323* 🌐 *www.melrosemansion.com* 🛏 *11 rooms, 3 suites* 🍴 *Multiple meal plans* ✣ *1:D1.*

$$$ HOTEL 🏨 **New Orleans Marriott Hotel.** This skyscraper hotel has a fabulous view of the Quarter, the CBD, and the river; it's an easy walk from the Canal Place mall, the Riverwalk, and the Convention Center. **Pros:** excellent chef-driven restaurant; good location; stunning city and river views. **Cons:** typical chain hotel; inconsistent service; lacks charm; daily charge for Wi-Fi and phone calls. **TripAdvisor:** "well maintained and clean," "great location and service," "one of the best choices for NOLA." [S] *Rooms from: $264* ✉ *555 Canal St., French Quarter* ☎ *504/581–1000 or 800/228–9290* 🌐 *www.neworleansmarriott.com* 🛏 *1,274 rooms, 55 suites* 🍴 *No meals* ✣ *1:C4.*

$$$ HOTEL 🏨 **Omni Royal Orleans Hotel.** At this elegant white-marble hotel, a replica of the grand St. Louis Hotel of the 1800s, with sconce-enhanced columns, gilt mirrors, fan windows, and three magnificent chandeliers, you get a central location with the traditional elegance. **Pros:** old-world grandeur; central location. **Cons:** can be crowded in the lobby and pool areas; some rooms are small. **TripAdvisor:** "beautiful stay," "excellent location and service," "stylish." [S] *Rooms from: $217* ✉ *621 St. Louis St., French Quarter* ☎ *504/529–5333 or 800/843–6664* 🌐 *www.omnihotels.com* 🛏 *346 rooms, 16 suites* 🍴 *No meals* ✣ *1:D3.*

$$$$ **Ritz-Carlton New Orleans.** In an
HOTEL artful conversion, the landmark
Fodor's Choice Maison Blanche department store
★ is now a luxury hotel filled with
local antiques, a lush courtyard,
and many other nods to the city's
past. **Pros:** great location for either
business or pleasure; luxurious
rooms and suites; outstanding
modern New Orleans fare at M
Bistro; afternoon tea in Davenport
Lounge is one of the most civilized
traditions in the city. **Cons:** sometimes feels a like a chain; rates are
some of the highest in town. **TripAdvisor:** "old school luxury,"
"very nice," "comfortable as you
would expect." Ⓢ *Rooms from:
$429* ✉ *921 Canal St., French
Quarter* ☎ *504/524–1331* ⊕ *www.
ritzcarlton.com* ⇱ *527 rooms, 38
suites* ⊙| *No meals* ✛ *1:B3.*

> **CLIMBERS BEWARE!**
>
> One of the best Mardi Gras
> parade-viewing spots in town is
> the **Royal Sonesta Hotel** balcony.
> To keep revelers from climbing up
> from the street below, the staff
> greases all the support poles with
> petroleum jelly. The media turns
> out in droves, and the hotel turns
> the event into a party. For many
> New Orleanians, this odd event
> signifies the true beginning to
> Mardi Gras weekend. Festivities
> start at 10 am the Friday before
> Mardi Gras; after the poles are
> greased, many attendees flood
> into the hotel for a lavish seafood
> buffet.

$$$ **Royal Sonesta Hotel New Orleans.** Step from the revelry of Bourbon
HOTEL Street into the marble elegance of this renowned hotel, where the lobby's
Fodor's Choice lush plants enhance a cool, serene atmosphere, and the guest rooms are
★ equally restful. **Pros:** outstanding service; bustling, cavernous lobby;
great balcony views of the Quarter. **Cons:** consistent high occupancy
can lead to slow elevator service; rooms facing Bourbon are noisy. **Tri-
pAdvisor:** "perfect location and excellent accommodations," "oasis in
French Quarter," "don't judge from outside appearance." Ⓢ *Rooms
from: $249* ✉ *300 Bourbon St., French Quarter* ☎ *504/586–0300 or
800/766–3782* ⊕ *www.sonesta.com/royalneworleans* ⇱ *483 rooms, 35
suites* ⊙| *No meals* ✛ *1:C3.*

$$ **The Saint Hotel.** With a beaux arts building, a stellar Canal Street loca-
HOTEL tion, and up-to-the-minute style, the Saint made a big, scene-stealing
impression when it opened in early 2012. **Pros:** on the Canal streetcar line and parade route; a few blocks from French Quarter action;
marble baths; free Wi-Fi. **Cons:** may be too edgy and stark for some
guests; lacks traditional New Orleans ambience and charm. **TripAdvisor:** "quiet rooms," "great location and décor," "chic." Ⓢ *Rooms
from: $199* ✉ *931 Canal St., French Quarter* ☎ *504/522–5400* ⊕ *www.
thesainthotelneworleans.com* ⇱ *166 rooms* ⊙| *No meals* ✛ *1:B3.*

$$$ **Soniat House.** Many regular New Orleans visitors consider this hand-
B&B/INN some oasis with elegant rooms the city's finest hotel. **Pros:** very refined;
Fodor's Choice expert service; afternoon wine service that is as civilized as it gets; use
★ of off-site New Orleans Athletic Club included in rates. **Cons:** break-
fast is delicious, but it costs extra, and menu options are limited; sev-
eral rooms are accessible by steps only. **TripAdvisor:** "charming," "old
New Orleans style," "quiet romance in the French Quarter." Ⓢ *Rooms
from: $245* ✉ *1133 Chartres St., French Quarter* ☎ *504/522–0570 or*

9

Royal Sonesta Hotel New Orleans

Harrah's New Orleans

CLOSE UP

Haunted Hotels

In New Orleans, reminders of human mortality are never far from view. Because most of the city is at or below sea level, graves were built aboveground, and walled cemeteries are common tourist destinations. As a port city, New Orleans has always been a boisterous place, where pirates, prostitutes, gamblers, and characters of all manner could find a comfortable home. The city's reputation as a home for voodoo is well founded; it is the birthplace of legendary voodoo priestess Marie Laveau. Unsurprisingly, many of the city's hotels are purportedly home to restless spirits. Guests at the **Dauphine Orleans** (✉ *415 Dauphine St., French Quarter* ☎ *504/586–1800 or 800/521–7111*) report seeing a dancing woman in the courtyard and the spirit of a patron roaming the grounds, a reminder of the days when there was a brothel here. The grandfather clock in the lobby of the **Hotel Monteleone** (✉ *214 Royal St., French Quarter* ☎ *504/523–3341 or 800/535–9595*) is said to be haunted by the ghost of its maker, and in the Garden District's **Columns Hotel** (✉ *3811 St. Charles Ave., Uptown* ☎ *504/899–9308 or 800/445–9308*), the former owner—who died in 1898—is occasionally still seen by guests. Hurricane Katrina was only the most recent catastrophe to befall New Orleans; yellow fever was a scourge on the city in the 18th and 19th centuries. The **Lafitte Guest House** (✉ *1003 Bourbon St., French Quarter* ☎ *504/581–2678 or 800/331–7971*) is only one hotel in which victims of the disease still linger. Of course you can't talk about the haunted hotels of New Orleans without mentioning the **Bourbon Orleans Hotel** (✉ *717 Orleans Ave., French Quarter* ☎ *504/523–2222*). Once a ballroom, and then convent, the storied building is said to house apparitions of former tenants, like the Confederate soldier roaming the sixth and seventh floors, and the dancer seen swaying underneath the crystal chandelier in the hotel's ballroom. There are a number of tour operators that cater to those with an interest in the supernatural, but if you stay at the right hotel, you may not need their services.

800/544–8808 🌐 *www.soniathouse.com* 🛏 *18 rooms, 12 suites* 🍴 *No meals* ✥ *1:E2.*

$$$$ HOTEL 🏨 **W Hotel New Orleans French Quarter.** This modern hotel has one of the best locations in the Quarter; rooms designed with fun jazz and tarot themes are in the main building, and many of them have balconies that overlook either the courtyard or Chartres Street. **Pros:** a 2011–12 renovation created spruced-up rooms and public areas; beautiful courtyard and pool; excellent service. **Cons:** lacks traditional New Orleans ambience; small driveway area can get crowded with valet activity. **TripAdvisor:** "quiet boutique hotel," "great stay," "great location." [S] *Rooms from: $305* ✉ *316 Chartres St., French Quarter* ☎ *504/581–1200 or 888/627–8260* 🌐 *www.wfrenchquarter.com* 🛏 *97 rooms, 6 suites* 🍴 *No meals* ✥ *1:C4.*

9

$$$ HOTEL 🏨 **The Westin New Orleans Canal Place.** This large convention hotel was designed with great views in mind; two-story arched lobby windows overlook the French Quarter and the great bend in the Mississippi River. **Pros:** luxurious rooms and suites; fabulous views of the Mississippi River and the French Quarter; close to shopping. **Cons:** lobby is on the 11th floor and can be a bit cumbersome to access; hotel has a big-box chain feel; groups can overwhelm lobby; large daily charge for Internet access. **TripAdvisor:** "nice stay," "great staff," "amazing views." [S] *Rooms from: $214* ✉ *100 Iberville St., French Quarter* ☎ *504/566–7006 or 800/996–3426* 🌐 *www.starwoodhotels.com/westin* 🛏 *438 rooms, 40 suites* 🍴 *No meals* ✣ *1:D4.*

FAUBOURG MARIGNY, BYWATER, AND TREMÉ

FAUBOURG MARIGNY

$$ B&B/INN 🏨 **Claiborne Mansion.** Enormous rooms with high ceilings, canopy or four-poster beds, polished hardwood floors, and rich fabrics distinguish this handsome 1859 mansion in the Faubourg Marigny, on the fringe of the French Quarter. **Pros:** big rooms; very private and relaxing; within walking distance of several great restaurants and jazz clubs. **Cons:** limited parking on the premises. **TripAdvisor:** "awesome historical mansion," "favorable," "peaceful retreat." [S] *Rooms from: $150* ✉ *2111 Dauphine St., Faubourg Marigny* ☎ *504/949–7327* 🌐 *www.claibornemansion.com* 🛏 *2 rooms, 5 suites* 🍴 *Breakfast* ✣ *1:E1.*

$ B&B/INN 🏨 **Lion's Inn.** From the swimming pool and hot tub in the private garden to the singularly elegant, Old South room decor, this B&B resembles a traditional Louisiana mansion, and its location makes it handy for visiting the many nightspots and restaurants on Frenchmen Street. **Pros:** gracious owners; private courtyard; lovely neighborhood feel. **Cons:** a 10-minute walk to the Quarter or Frenchmen Street means that you may want to take a cab at night. **TripAdvisor:** "very cool place," "the garden is amazing," "absolutely lovely." [S] *Rooms from: $120* ✉ *2517 Chartres St., Faubourg Marigny* ☎ *800/485–6846 or 504/945–2339* 🌐 *www.lionsinn.com* 🛏 *10 rooms* 🍴 *Breakfast* ✣ *1:F1.*

CBD AND THE WAREHOUSE DISTRICT

CBD

$$$ HOTEL 👶 🏨 **Courtyard New Orleans Downtown Near the French Quarter.** A central CBD location, modern amenities, and some nods to period charm help make this family-friendly hotel a good option—it combines modern niceties like free Wi-Fi with architectural elements that recall the 19th century. **Pros:** central CBD location that's close to the French Quarter, the World War II Museum, and Harrah's Casino. **Cons:** significant street noise at all hours. **TripAdvisor:** "great location," "friendly staff," "clean rooms." [S] *Rooms from: $209* ✉ *124 St. Charles Ave., CBD* ☎ *504/581–9005 or 800/321–2211* 🌐 *www.marriott.com* 🛏 *140 rooms* 🍴 *No meals* ✣ *1:C3.*

$$ HOTEL 🏨 **DoubleTree by Hilton Hotel New Orleans.** This chain hotel with open, airy rooms is close to the river, across the street from the Canal Place mall, and a block from the French Quarter. **Pros:** close to the French

Quarter and Riverfront attractions; across the street from the Canal Place shops and kid-friendly Insectarium. **Cons:** some rooms could use an update; restaurant is average at best; chain hotel vibe. **TripAdvisor:** "nice room," "super staff," "great location." [S] *Rooms from: $179* ✉ *300 Canal St., CBD* ☎ *504/581–1300 or 800/222–8733* 🌐 *www.doubletree.com* 🛏 *364 rooms, 6 suites* 🍴 *No meals* ✣ *1:C4.*

$$$ HOTEL 👶 🏨 **Embassy Suites New Orleans-Convention Center.** If your primary destination is the convention center (three blocks away) or the restaurants, galleries, and museums in the Warehouse District, then this high-rise on Gallery Row is a great choice. **Pros:** spacious, well-maintained rooms; friendly service. **Cons:** lackluster restaurant and room service; a significant distance from the French Quarter. **TripAdvisor:** "friendly staff," "great rooms," "excellent service." [S] *Rooms from: $212* ✉ *315 Julia St., CBD* ☎ *504/525–1993 or 800/362–2779* 🌐 *www.embassyneworleans.com* 🛏 *346 suites, 24 rooms* 🍴 *Breakfast* ✣ *1:C5.*

$ HOTEL 🏨 **Hampton Inn Downtown.** This well-priced facility is one of several office buildings that have been converted into hotels; the lobby, with lavish furnishings and decor, is an oasis in the midst of the bustling CBD, and the rooms are large, comfortable, and pleasant but a little generic. **Pros:** spacious rooms; particularly nice breakfast; free Wi-Fi; convenient to French Quarter (but be careful when walking at night). **Cons:** rooms that face the street can be noisy, typical chain hotel. **TripAdvisor:** "relaxing," "convenient setting," "friendly staff." [S] *Rooms from: $149* ✉ *226 Carondelet St., CBD* ☎ *504/529–9990 or 800/426–7866* 🌐 *www.neworleanshamptoninns.com* 🛏 *185 rooms* 🍴 *Breakfast* ✣ *1:D6.*

$$$ HOTEL Fodor's Choice ★ 🏨 **Harrah's New Orleans Hotel.** Odds are that you'll be comfortable at this well-appointed 26-story hotel, which is directly across the street from Harrah's New Orleans Casino and near the Convention Center and Riverfront attractions. **Pros:** well-trained staff provides above-average service; guests without cars can easily walk to Riverfront, CBD, and French Quarter attractions. **Cons:** the hustle and bustle of this part of town means peace and quiet can be in short supply; casino marketing is ever present. **TripAdvisor:** "Southern charm," "good location," "well equipped." [S] *Rooms from: $269* ✉ *Poydras St. at Fulton St., CBD* ☎ *504/533–6000 or 800/847–5299* 🌐 *www.harrahsneworleans.com* 🛏 *450 rooms, 94 suites* 🍴 *No meals* ✣ *1:D4.*

$$$$ HOTEL 👶 🏨 **Hilton New Orleans Riverside.** The sprawling multilevel Hilton complex sits right on the Mississippi, with superb views. **Pros:** well-maintained facilities; hotel runs like a well-oiled machine; great security. **Cons:** the city's biggest hotel; typical chain service and surroundings; groups can overwhelm lobby. **TripAdvisor:** "very nice," "nice river view," "convenient location." [S] *Rooms from: $279* ✉ *2 Poydras St., CBD* ☎ *504/561–0500 or 800/445–8667* 🌐 *www.hilton.com* 🛏 *1,600 rooms, 60 suites* 🍴 *No meals* ✣ *1:D5.*

$$ HOTEL 👶 🏨 **Homewood Suites by Hilton New Orleans.** A stay in one of this hotel's huge apartment-like suites—about 625 square feet—means that you'll be just three blocks from the Superdome and near Warehouse District museums and restaurants. **Pros:** friendly; huge rooms; near Lafayette Square's live music offerings. **Cons:** no in-hotel restaurant or room

service; expect a 5- to 10-minute walk to nearby restaurants; about a half mile from French Quarter. **TripAdvisor:** "modern accommodating style," "oasis in the middle of the city," "excellent service." $\boxed{s}$ *Rooms from: $170* ✉ *901 Poydras St., CBD* ☎ *504/581–5599* ⊕ *www. homewoodsuitesneworleans.com* ⤳ *166 suites* ❑ *Breakfast* ✛ *1:B4.*

$$ ⌂ **The Hyatt Regency New Orleans.** Everything about this 32-story busi-
HOTEL ness and convention hotel is huge: its cavernous lobby and glass stair-way, its mega-ballroom, its acres of meeting space, and its spacious and well-appointed guest rooms, with natural stone baths and iPod docking stations. **Pros:** next door to the Superdome; excellent service and amenities; close to Tulane University Hospital and the New Orleans BioInnovation Center. **Cons:** lacks New Orleans charm: it could be anywhere; in a high-traffic area complicated by construction of the Loyola streetcar line (which may be finished in 2012); not pedestrian friendly. **TripAdvisor:** "big and comfortable," "very nice staff," "chic." $\boxed{s}$ *Rooms from: $179* ✉ *601 Loyola Ave., CBD* ☎ *504/561–1234 or 888/591–1234* ⊕ *neworleans.hyatt.com* ⤳ *1,193 rooms, 95 suites* ❑ *No meals* ✛ *1:A4.*

$$ ⌂ **InterContinental New Orleans.** One of the major convention hotels,
HOTEL this modern rose-granite structure overlooking St. **Pros:** superior ser-vice; club-level rooms are among the best in town; perfect location for Mardi Gras; streetcar is just out front. **Cons:** located on one of the city's busiest downtown streets, which can be noisy; large big-box hotel. **TripAdvisor:** "what a gem," "downtown luxury," "nice room." $\boxed{s}$ *Rooms from: $184* ✉ *444 St. Charles Ave., CBD* ☎ *504/525–5566 or 800/445–6563* ⊕ *www.intercontinental.com* ⤳ *479 rooms, 31 suites* ❑ *No meals* ✛ *1:C4.*

$$ ⌂ **International House.** Stylish and contemporary, this boutique hotel
HOTEL pairs lots of creature comforts with a location that's just two blocks from the French Quarter. **Pros:** great downtown location; ideal if you thrive in cool, sophisticated surroundings; scene-making hotel bar. **Cons:** small rooms; hotel faces busy downtown street with heavy traffic. **TripAdvisor:** "great location," "wonderful experience," "New Orleans' finest." $\boxed{s}$ *Rooms from: $199* ✉ *221 Camp St., CBD* ☎ *504/553–9550 or 800/633–5770* ⊕ *www.ihhotel.com* ⤳ *117 rooms, 5 suites* ❑ *No meals* ✛ *1:C4.*

$$ ⌂ **Lafayette Hotel.** This small brick building has housed the Lafayette
HOTEL since it was built in 1916; handsome millwork, brass fittings, and mar-ble baths adorn the property throughout. **Pros:** streetcar stops right outside the front door; within walking distance of Riverfront and French Quarter attractions; pet-friendly. **Cons:** not a great area for walking late at night. **TripAdvisor:** "hospitable place to stay," "very helpful staff," "great service and location." $\boxed{s}$ *Rooms from: $189* ✉ *600 St. Charles Ave., CBD* ☎ *504/524–4441 or 800/366–2743* ⊕ *www. thelafayettehotel.com* ⤳ *24 rooms, 20 suites* ❑ *No meals* ✛ *1:B5.*

$$$$ ⌂ **Le Pavillon Hotel.** You'll feel like royalty at this sumptuous hotel, where
HOTEL the rooms are romantic and the service is attentive. **Pros:** elegant French ambience; attentive staff; lovely restaurant. **Cons:** guest rooms could use some updating; not a fit if you're after something contemporary; on a busy street. **TripAdvisor:** "classy," "excellent personal service,"

"beautiful hotel." [S] *Rooms from: $309* ✉ *833 Poydras St., CBD* ☎ *504/581–3111 or 800/535–9095* 🌐 *www.lepavillon.com* 🛏 *219 rooms, 7 suites* 🍴 *No meals* ✥ *1:B4.*

$$$ Fodor's Choice ★ 🏨 **Loews New Orleans Hotel.** Stellar service; a Brennan-family restaurant; and bright, oversize rooms are what you'll find in this plush downtown hotel. **TripAdvisor:** "great layout," "classy and convenient," "pure Zen." [S] *Rooms from: $249* ✉ *300 Poydras St., CBD* ☎ *504/595–3300 or 800/235–6397* 🌐 *www.loewshotels.com/en/New-Orleans-Hotel* 🛏 *285 rooms, 12 suites* 🍴 *No meals* ✥ *1:C4.*

$$ HOTEL 🏨 **Loft 523.** If you're after contemporary and chic loft-life digs, look no further. **Pros:** sexy setting; inviting lounge; top-shelf amenities. **Cons:** some guests may be put off by the trendiness of it all; no restaurant. **TripAdvisor:** "personal service above and beyond," "quiet and comfortable," "hippest hotel in New Orleans." [S] *Rooms from: $179* ✉ *523 Gravier St., CBD* ☎ *504/200–6523* 🌐 *www.loft523.com* 🛏 *16 rooms, 2 penthouses* 🍴 *No meals* ✥ *1:C4.*

$$ HOTEL 🏨 **Pelham Hotel.** In a 19th-century building close to CBD sights like the Riverwalk and the casino, the Pelham offers a less hectic alternative to the convention hotels. **Pros:** centrally located, but far from heavily traveled tourist streets; free Wi-Fi. **Cons:** rooms can be small and some lack windows; no on-site fitness area; interior noise from downtown traffic. **TripAdvisor:** "best kept secret in New Orleans," "great location," "great service." [S] *Rooms from: $150* ✉ *444 Common St., CBD* ☎ *504/522–4444 or 800/659–5621* 🌐 *www.thepelhamhotel.com* 🛏 *60 rooms* 🍴 *No meals* ✥ *1:C4.*

$$$ HOTEL 🏨 **Renaissance Pere Marquette Hotel.** A block from Canal Street, this boutique Marriott delivers comfort with large rooms that are quiet—in spite of a CBD location. **Pros:** lobby-level MiLa Restaurant is outstanding; excellent service. **Cons:** standard chain property; location is not pedestrian friendly; additional fee for Wi-Fi. **TripAdvisor:** "absolutely wonderful," "chic hotel," "perfect location." [S] *Rooms from: $209* ✉ *817 Common St., CBD* ☎ *504/525–1111 or 800/372–0482* 🌐 *www.renaissancehotels.com* 🛏 *268 rooms, 4 suites* 🍴 *No meals* ✥ *1:B3.*

9

$$$ HOTEL Fodor's Choice ★ 🏨 **The Roosevelt Hotel New Orleans.** From its glittering lobby to each beautiful, traditionally furnished guest room, the Roosevelt offers an iconic and very grand New Orleans experience. **Pros:** exquisite lobby; location near downtown and French Quarter; outstanding bar and restaurants; streetcar just outside. **Cons:** pricey fees for parking and in-room Wi-Fi. **TripAdvisor:** "beautiful property," "a class act," "wonderful people." [S] *Rooms from: $249* ✉ *123 Baronne St., CBD* ☎ *504/648–1200* 🌐 *www.therooseveltneworleans.com* 🛏 *504 rooms, 135 suites* 🍴 *No meals* ✥ *1:B3.*

$ HOTEL 🏨 **St. Christopher Best Western.** Combining good rates and a location that's just a block from the French Quarter, this former office building, built in the 1890s, makes a very good base for exploring the city. **Pros:** good location for the Convention Center and the French Quarter; free Wi-Fi; friendly service; no two rooms exactly alike. **Cons:** generic breakfast room—and breakfast; bar only open Thursday–Saturday. **TripAdvisor:** "excellent location," "very nice," "good service." [S] *Rooms from: $129* ✉ *114 Magazine St., Central Business District*

☎ 800/645–9312 or 504/648–0444 🌐 www.stchristopherhotel.com 🛏 108 rooms 🍴 Breakfast ✥ 1:C4.

$$$ HOTEL **Sheraton New Orleans Hotel.** After a $45 million stem-to-stern renovation that's set to end in early 2013, this hotel will be more ready then ever to please the corporate groups and conventions it caters to. **Pros:** large hotel with lots of rooms; experienced staff; great service; central location. **Cons:** typical corporate convention property; lacks the warmth of some of its competitors; can be crowded during peak season; renovations may cause some inconvenience. **TripAdvisor:** "good base for crazy NOLA," "in the heart of things," "great for a conference." [S] *Rooms from: $215 ✉ 500 Canal St., CBD ☎ 504/525–2500 or 800/253–6156 🌐 www.sheratonneworleans.com 🛏 1,100 rooms, 53 suites 🍴 No meals ✥ 1:C4.*

$$ HOTEL **Staybridge Suites New Orleans French Quarter/Downtown.** A great option for extended-stay business travelers, families, or friends staying together, this all-suites hotel is well located and comfortable. **Pros:** convenient location; spacious rooms; a good-size pool. **Cons:** a bit generic; no restaurant; located on a very busy intersection in the CBD. **TripAdvisor:** "fabulous," "even better than we hoped," "great location." [S] *Rooms from: $182 ✉ 501 Tchoupitoulas St., CBD ☎ 504/571–1818 or 800/541–4998 🌐 wwwstaybridge.com 🛏 182 suites 🍴 Breakfast ✥ 1:C4.*

$$$$ HOTEL ★ **W Hotel New Orleans.** A sleek blend of East Coast sophistication and Southern charm gives way to inspired accommodations at the W. **Pros:** great for those looking for contemporary, hip quarters. **Cons:** beautifully designed chain hotel, but lacking the warmth of comparable properties in the city; walkway into the property is extremely slick when wet. **TripAdvisor:** "cool hotel in a good location," "excellent service," "friendly staff." [S] *Rooms from: $279 ✉ 333 Poydras St., CBD ☎ 504/525–9444 or 888/627–8389 🌐 www.whotels.com 🛏 423 rooms, 23 suites 🍴 No meals ✥ 1:C4.*

$$ HOTEL **The Whitney, A Wyndham Historic Hotel.** A great choice if you're looking to stay away from the Bourbon Street fray, this European-style hotel has top-notch service as well as eminently comfortable rooms with comfy pillow-top mattresses, upscale toiletries and amenities, and ergonomic chairs. **Pros:** L'il Dizzy's Café—known for authentic soul food and New Orleans cuisine —is on the lobby level; free Wi-FI; near the Convention Center, the French Quarter, and the Superdome. **Cons:** it's at one of the busiest downtown intersections in the city; narrow lobby can be difficult to navigate when the hotel is busy. **TripAdvisor:** "excellent location and staff," "all you could ask for," "very nice." [S] *Rooms from: $179 ✉ 610 Poydras St., CBD ☎ 504/581–4222 or 800/996–3426 🌐 www.wyndham.com 🛏 70 rooms, 23 suites 🍴 No meals ✥ 1:C4.*

$$$$ HOTEL Fodor's Choice ★ **Windsor Court Hotel.** Plush carpeting, marble vanities, and mirrored dressing areas are just a few of the luxurious features in the very large rooms of this exquisite hotel, which is just four blocks from the French Quarter. **Pros:** old-world elegance; superior service; location near the French Quarter but not in the thick of it. **Cons:** location close to casino can mean traffic outside. **TripAdvisor:** "contemporary," "great customer service," "a flawless visit." [S] *Rooms from: $275 ✉ 300 Gravier St.,*

Loews Hotels

Chimes Bed and Breakfast

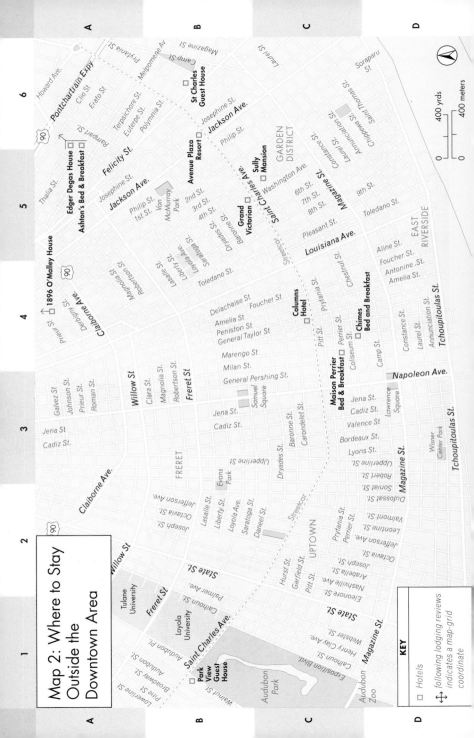

Map 2: Where to Stay Outside the Downtown Area

A

Howard Ave.
Pontchartrain Expy
90
Thalia St.
Clio St.
Erato St.
Terpsichore St.
Euterpe St.
Polymnia St.
Felicity St.
Rampart St.
Prieur St.
Edgar Degas House □
Ashton's Bed & Breakfast □
1896 O'Malley House □ ↑
90
Claiborne Ave.

B

Magazine St.
Camp St.
Prytania St.
Melpomene Av.
St Charles Guest House □
Josephine St.
Jackson Ave.
Philip St.
Avenue Plaza Resort □
2nd St.
3rd St.
4th St.
Van McMurray Park
Grand Victorian □
Josephine St.
Jackson Ave.
Philip St.
1st St.
Baronne St.
Dryades St.
Saratoga St.
Loyola Ave.
Liberty Ave.
Leslie St.
Toledano St.
Magnolia St.
Robertson St.
Magnolia St.
Clara St.
Willow St.
Freret St.
Claiborne Ave.
Galvez St.
Johnson St.
Prieur St.
Roman St.
Jena St.
Cadiz St.
Jena St
Cadiz St.
FRERET
Jena St.
Cadiz St.
Upperline St.
Dryades St.
Baronne St.
Carondelet St.

C

Laurel St.
Saint Thomas St.
GARDEN DISTRICT
Jackson Ave.
Annunciation St.
Laurel St.
Constance St.
Chippewa St.
Washington Ave.
Saint Charles Ave.
Sully Mansion □
6th St.
7th St.
8th St.
9th St.
Magazine St.
Toledano St.
Pleasant St.
Louisiana Ave.
Streetcar
Chestnut St.
Prytania St.
Columns Hotel □
Pitt St.
Perrier St.
Chimes Bed and Breakfast □
Coliseum St.
Camp St.
Maison Perrier Bed & Breakfast □
Delachaise St.
Foucher St.
Amelia St.
Peniston St
General Taylor St.
Marengo St.
Milan St.
General Pershing St.
Samuel Square
Napoleon Ave.
Jena St.
Cadiz St.
Valence St
Bordeaux St.
Lyons St.
Upperline St.
Robert St.
Soniat St.
Dufossat St.
Valmont St.
Leontine St.
Jefferson Ave.
Octavia St.
Prytania St.
Perrier St.
Magazine St.
Lawrence Square
Wisner Center Park
Jena St.
Cadiz St.

D

Soraparu St.
Chippewa St.
Saint Thomas St.
EAST RIVERSIDE
Aline St.
Foucher St.
Antonine St.
Amelia St.
Magazine St.
Constance St.
Laurel St.
Annunciation St.
Tchoupitoulas St.
Tchoupitoulas St.

Tulane University
Freret St.
Loyola University
Willow St.
State St.
Palmer Ave.
Calhoun St.
Audubon Pl.
Audubon St.
Broadway St.
Pine St.
Lowerline St.
Joseph St.
Octavia St.
Jefferson Ave.
Saratoga St.
Loyola Ave.
Liberty St.
Lasalle St.
Evans Park
Danee St.

Park View Guest House □
Saint Charles Ave.
Audubon Park
Exposition Blvd.
Calhoun St.
Henry Clay Ave.
Webster St.
State St.
Magazine St.
Audubon Zoo
Walnut St.
Hurst St.
Garfield St.
Pitt St.
Eleanore St.
Nashville Ave.
Arabella St.
Joseph St.
Prytania St.
Perrier St.
Leontine St.
Octavia St.
UPTOWN
Magazine St.

6 **5** **4** **3** **2** **1**

⊕
0   400 yrds
0   400 meters

KEY

□ Hotels

⊕ following lodging reviews
indicates a map-grid
coordinate

CBD ☎ *504/523–6000 or 800/262–2662* 🌐 *www.windsorcourthotel.com* 🛏 *58 rooms, 266 suites, 1 penthouse* 🍴 *No meals* ✥ *1:C4.*

THE WAREHOUSE DISTRICT

$ HOTEL 🏨 **Hampton Inn and Suites–Convention Center.** Two century-old warehouses have been converted into a French colonial–style hotel that is comfortable, architecturally distinctive, and moderately priced, with large, airy rooms. **Pros:** architecturally stunning; minutes from Convention Center. **Cons:** extremely busy area; can be daunting to both pedestrians and drivers; no restaurant on-site. **TripAdvisor:** "beautiful place and friendly staff," "just perfect," "what a gem." [S] *Rooms from: $149* ✉ *1201 Convention Center Blvd., Warehouse District* ☎ *504/566–9990 or 800/292–0653* 🌐 *www.neworleanshamptoninns.com* 🛏 *288 rooms* 🍴 *Breakfast* ✥ *1:D6.*

$$ HOTEL 🏨 **Hotel Modern.** Close to galleries and museums, this chic boutique hotel on Lee Circle delivers a bit of attitude along with its eclectic selection of rooms. **Pros:** on the St. Charles streetcar line and parade route; hipster vibe; excellent service, restaurant, and bar. **Cons:** hallways can be cramped; you're a 15-minute walk from the French Quarter; some rooms are tiny, with small windows; not a traditional New Orleans stay. **TripAdvisor:** "good room," "great staff," "unique property." [S] *Rooms from: $149* ✉ *936 St. Charles Ave., Warehouse District* ☎ *504/962–0900 or 800/684–9525* 🛏 *135 rooms* 🍴 *No meals* ✥ *1:B5.*

$$ HOTEL 🏨 **Renaissance Arts Hotel.** Art lovers looking to stay close to downtown but not in the CBD should check out this circa-1910 warehouse-turned-hotel; the huge windows now make for great views from the guest rooms. **Pros:** modern, well-appointed facilities; beautiful artwork. **Cons:** not suitable for those who want a traditional New Orleans hotel or to spend lots of time in the French Quarter; daily fee for Wi-Fi. **TripAdvisor:** "all the amenities," "excellent location," "beautiful property." [S] *Rooms from: $199* ✉ *700 Tchoupitoulas St., Warehouse District* ☎ *504/613–2330 or 800/431–8634* 🌐 *www.marriott.com* 🛏 *210 rooms, 7 suites* 🍴 *No meals* ✥ *1:C5.*

9

THE GARDEN DISTRICT

$$ HOTEL 🏨 **Avenue Plaza Resort.** If you're looking for real local charm off the French Quarter grid, this suites-only hotel with an impessive courtyard and pool is ideal. **Pros:** Garden District location; delightful private pool; reasonable on-site parking. **Cons:** not convenient to French Quarter or CBD; lobby is small and can get crowded during busy times. **TripAdvisor:** "great time," "perfect place to stay," "good rooms." [S] *Rooms from: $190* ✉ *2111 St. Charles Ave., Garden District* ☎ *504/566–1212 or 800/439–6493* 🌐 *www.avenueplazahotel.com* 🛏 *264 suites* 🍴 *No meals* ✥ *2:B6.*

$$$ B&B/INN Fodor's Choice ★ 🏨 **Grand Victorian Bed & Breakfast.** A block and a half from Commander's Palace Restaurant, the Grand Victorian more than lives up to its lofty name; each lavishly appointed, romantic room evokes old Louisiana through period pieces and distinctive private baths. **Pros:** true elegance; rooms are exquisitely appointed; possibly the best bed-and-breakfast value in the area; on the streetcar line. **Cons:** limited parking; not

within easy walking distance of French Quarter or the CBD. **TripAdvisor:** "peaceful Victorian home," "great accommodations and perfect location," "unmatched hospitality." [S] *Rooms from: $200* ✉ *2727 St. Charles Ave., Garden District* ☎ *504/895–1104 or 800/977–0008* 🌐 *www.gvbb.com* 🛏 *8 rooms* 🍴 *Breakfast* ⊕ *2:B5.*

$ B&B/INN 🏨 **St. Charles Guest House.** Simple and affordable, this 125-year-old bed-and-breakfast is convenient to the St. **Pros:** very affordable rates; within walking distance of the St. Charles streetcar line; well run. **Cons:** furnishing and surroundings are in need of an update; no elevator or restaurant; credit cards not accepted. **TripAdvisor:** "homey," "taste of old Garden District," "something special." [S] *Rooms from: $85* ✉ *1748 Prytania St., Garden District* ☎ *504/523–6556* 🌐 *www.stcharlesguesthouse.com* 🛏 *30 rooms, 24 with bath* 💳 *No credit cards* 🍴 *Breakfast* ⊕ *2:B6.*

$ HOTEL 🏨 **Sully Mansion.** The stunning art-filled setting and the personal attention you get from the responsive owners set this B&B apart. **Pros:** old-world charm; individualized attention to guests. **Cons:** it's a mile or so from the French Quarter. **TripAdvisor:** "a magic garden," "wonderful stay," "great accommodations." [S] *Rooms from: $149* ✉ *2631 Prytania St., Garden District* ☎ *504/891–0457 or 800/364–2414* 🌐 *www.sullymansion.com* 🛏 *8 rooms, 2 suites* 🍴 *Breakfast* ⊕ *2:C5.*

UPTOWN

$$ B&B/INN Fodor's Choice ★ 🏨 **Chimes Bed and Breakfast.** This charming Uptown B&B's rooms, in a main house and a converted carriage house, are homey but also have all the conveniences of a hotel: hair dryers, irons, stereos, coffeemakers, Wi-Fi, and private entrances. **Pros:** everything sparkles; just three blocks from the streetcar and Magazine Street; laptop and printer for guest use. **Cons:** noise carries easily from room to room; 3 miles from the French Quarter, which might be too far for some. **TripAdvisor:** "peaceful," "welcome hospitality," "couldn't be better." [S] *Rooms from: $150* ✉ *1146 Constantinople St., Uptown* ☎ *504/899–2621* 🌐 *www.chimesneworleans.com* 🛏 *5 rooms* 🍴 *Breakfast* ⊕ *2:C4.*

$$ HOTEL 🏨 **Columns Hotel.** The large though somewhat sparsely furnished rooms here could use an update, but the rest of this white-columned 1883 Victorian hotel drips with local charm. **Pros:** exquisite architecture; the veranda's perfect for watching the St. Charles parades during Mardi Gras; on the streetcar line. **Cons:** lobby area feels tired, and second-floor rooms feel a bit stale (try to book on the third floor); transportation necessary to French Quarter and CBD. **TripAdvisor:** "still great," "Victorian splendor," "wonderful experience." [S] *Rooms from: $170* ✉ *3811 St. Charles Ave., Uptown* ☎ *504/899–9308 or 800/445–9308* 🌐 *www.thecolumns.com* 🛏 *20 rooms* 🍴 *Breakfast* ⊕ *2:C4.*

$$ B&B/INN 🏨 **Maison Perrier Bed & Breakfast.** This 1890s Victorian mansion is filled with antiques, gorgeous local art, and many extra comforts, including Abita on draft for guests. **Pros:** personalized service; lovely residential setting; the periwinkle "Dolly's Room" is one of the most beautiful places to stay in New Orleans. **Cons:** not well located if you prefer to spend most of your time in the French Quarter; no elevator. **TripAdvisor:**

"a neighborhood jewel," "perfect in every way," "calming." [S] *Rooms from: $199* ✉ *4117 Perrier St., Uptown* ☎ *504/897–1807 or 888/610–1807* 🌐 *www.maisonperrier.com* 🛏 *9 rooms* 🍴 *Breakfast* ✣ *2:C4.*

$$ B&B/INN 🏨 **Park View Guest House.** Adjacent to beautiful Audubon Park, this Victorian guesthouse has graced St. **Pros:** great views; easy access to public golf course; close to St. Charles streetcar line; good restaurants nearby. **Cons:** not walkable to downtown or the French Quarter. **TripAdvisor:** "an amazing stay in a historical home," "comfortable and convenient," "Southern charm and hospitality." [S] *Rooms from: $150* ✉ *7004 St. Charles Ave., Uptown* ☎ *504/861–7564 or 888/533–0746* 🌐 *www.parkviewguesthouse.com* 🛏 *21 rooms* 🍴 *Breakfast* ✣ *2:B1.*

MID-CITY

$$ B&B/INN 🏨 **1896 O'Malley House.** Best for those seeking a less touristy New Orleans experience, this elegant bed-and-breakfast is near the intersection of Canal Street and North Carrollton Avenue, an area that has seen multiple new restaurants open in the last several years. **Pros:** complimentary snacks, wine, and beer available; walking distance to entertainment and restaurants. **Cons:** roughly 3 miles from the French Quarter and the Garden District; not for guests wanting to be in the middle of the action. **TripAdvisor:** "splendor in Midcity," "charming gentility," "we wouldn't stay anywhere else." [S] *Rooms from: $169* ✉ *120 S. Pierce St., Mid-City* ☎ *504/488–5896 or 866/226–1896* 🌐 *www.1896omalleyhouse.com* 🛏 *8 rooms* 🍴 *Breakfast* ✣ *2:A4.*

$$ B&B/INN 🏨 **Ashton's Bed & Breakfast.** Few details have been missed in re-creating this sumptuous 1861 mansion, nine blocks from the French Quarter. **Pros:** exquisitely decorated and spacious rooms; nice location that's not far from New Orleans City Park; convenient to Jazz Fest. **Cons:** if you don't have a car, you need to take a taxi or city bus to reach the French Quarter. **TripAdvisor:** "an oasis," "just perfect," "great Southern hospitality." [S] *Rooms from: $169* ✉ *2023 Esplanade Ave., Mid-City* ☎ *504/942–7048 or 800/725–4131* 🌐 *www.ashtonsbb.com* 🛏 *8 rooms* 🍴 *Breakfast* ✣ *2:A6.*

$$ B&B/INN Fodor's Choice ★ 🏨 **Edgar Degas House.** Once home to French impressionist Edgar Degas, this mansion from 1852 retains its original floor plan and colors; the spacious second-floor rooms have chandeliers that hang from 14-foot ceilings (three have whirlpool baths and balconies). **Pros:** meticulously maintained and expertly operated; luxe amenities and extras; on the National Register of Historic Places; close to Jazz Fest. **Cons:** not in the middle of the action; if you don't have a car, you'll be taking the city bus on Esplanade Avenue to the Quarter, or cabbing it at night. **TripAdvisor:** "lovely breakfast," "classic old New Orleans," "beautiful." [S] *Rooms from: $199* ✉ *2306 Esplanade Ave., Mid-City* ☎ *504/821–5009 or 800/755–6730* 🌐 *www.degashouse.com* 🛏 *9 rooms* 🍴 *Breakfast* ✣ *2:A6.*

Nightlife

WORD OF MOUTH

"Just got back from a trip to New Orleans. My first trip and I think that if I lived there I would be dead in a year. Wow! . . . [My] favorite thing: seeing every type of person—gay, straight, young, old, handicapped, and highfalutin—just enjoying themselves . . . . Oh, and being able to carry your cocktail with you on the street. Hope my liver recovers soon."

—SharonG

COCKTAIL CULTURE

In the early 1800s, the Creole apothecary Antoine Amadie Peychaud ran a pharmacy in the French Quarter. He concocted a cherry-colored bitters that is still an essential ingredient of the Sazerac, New Orleans's favorite cocktail.

(above) Ingredients for New Orleans's official cocktail, at the Sazerac Bar. (top right) Tales of the Cocktail festival. (bottom right) The Museum of the American Cocktail.

According to legend, Peychaud mixed his bitters with brandy, water, and sugar, then served the drink in a traditional French eggcup called a "coquetier." Soon English speakers mangled the French word and called the drink a "cocktail." It's a good story, except that Peychaud was three years old when the word "cocktail" first appeared in print. But even if the cocktail wasn't invented in New Orleans, no other city has embraced it with more passion. From Peychaud's now-famous bitters to the iconic Hurricane and beyond, New Orleans is home to many of the greatest inventions in cocktail history. In recent years, a new generation of bartenders has reinvigorated the Crescent City's cocktail culture with elaborate techniques and farm-fresh ingredients. —by Todd A. Price

NEW ORLEANS'S OFFICIAL DRINK

Conservative legislators were concerned that naming the Sazerac Louisiana's official cocktail would cause people to associate the state with drinking. New Orleans, presumably, was already a lost cause. So on June 2008 the potent blend of rye whiskey, sugar, and Peychaud's bitters became the official cocktail of New Orleans, the only city in the country to have an official drink written into legislation.

COCKTAIL EVENTS AND EXHIBITS

The Museum of the American Cocktail. An extensive collection of rare spirits, books, Prohibition-era literature and music, vintage cocktail shakers, glassware, tools, gadgets, and all manner of cocktail memorabilia and photographs culled from the collections of museum founders and patrons are on display in this small exhibit. ⊠ *Southern Food and Beverage Museum, Riverwalk Marketplace, 1 Poydras St., Suite 169, Warehouse District* ☎ *504/569–0405* ⊕ *www.museumoftheamericancocktail.org.*

New Orleans Original Cocktail Tour. The Gray Line walking tour leads you through the saloons and wine cellars of the French Quarter. Frequent stops for libations along the route guarantee that you'll get firsthand experience of the city's best drinks. The 2½-hour tours depart daily at 4 pm from the Lighthouse ticket office at Toulouse St. and the Mississippi River. ⊠ *Warehouse District* ☎ *504/569–1401* ⊕ *www.graylineneworleans.com/cocktail-tour.html.*

New Orleans Wine and Food Experience. Serious wine drinkers skip the beach for this five-day celebration of Bacchus over Memorial Day weekend. Popular events include a series of vintner dinners at local restaurants, a wine-fueled stroll through the shops of Royal Street, and the two-day Grand Tasting, where nearly 75 restaurants serve food

and 1,000 different wines are poured. ☎ *504/529–9463* ⊕ *www.nowfe.com.*

Old New Orleans Rum Distillery. Founded in 1995, this craft distillery is the oldest maker of rum in the continental United States. Tours start with a cocktail and end with a tasting of four different rums. Complimentary transportation from the French Quarter is available during the week—make reservations for it in advance. ⊠ *2815 Frenchmen St., Gentilly* ☎ *504/945–9400* ⊕ *www.neworleansrum.com.*

Tales of the Cocktail. Each July the annual Tales of the Cocktail, billed as "the most spirited event of the summer," brings thousands of experts and enthusiasts together for an internationally acclaimed, five-day celebration dedicated to the artistry and science of making drinks. In addition to enjoying some of "the best cocktails ever made," attendees participate in dinners, demonstrations, tastings, competitions, seminars, book signings, tours, and parties. ☎ *504/948–0511* ⊕ *www.talesofthecocktail.com.*

10

TOP FIVE ICONIC NEW ORLEANS COCKTAILS

Sazerac: Rye whiskey, Peychaud's bitters, and sugar served in a rocks glass rinsed with absinthe or Herbsaint, a local absinthe substitute

Claim to Fame: Official drink of New Orleans

Best Place to Try One: Tujague's

Ramos Gin Fizz: Gin, cream, orange flower water, and lemon and lime juice shaken with an egg white and topped with club soda

Claim to Fame: Huey P. Long's favorite eye-opener

Best Place to Try One: Sazerac Bar at the Roosevelt Hotel

Hurricane: Blend of rum, grenadine, and tropical juices

Claim to Fame: The start of many a lost weekend

Best Place to Try One: Pat O'Brien's

Vieux Carré: Brandy, rye whiskey, sweet vermouth, Bénédictine, and a dash each of Peychaud's and Angostura bitters

Claim to Fame: A perfectly balanced tribute to the French Quarter

Best Place to Try One: Carousel Bar at the Hotel Monteleone, where it was invented

Pimm's Cup: Pimm's No. 1 topped with lemon-lime soda and garnished with a cucumber

Claim to Fame: A British thirst quencher embraced by the Crescent City

Best Place to Try One: Napoleon House

THE "NEW" NEW ORLEANS COCKTAILS

Bar Tonique: *Blanche DuBois* (Death's Door gin, curacao, orgeat, lemon juice, mint, and strawberries)

Cure: *Union Jack Rose* (Tanqueray gin, bonded apple brandy, pomegranate reduction, lime juice, orange bitters, and mint)

Loa: *Potation* (ingredients change seasonally. Previous example: shochu, lemongrass syrup, muddled fresh clover, and Chartreuse Elixir Vegetal)

Twelve Mile Limit: *The Baudin* (bourbon, honey, lemon, and hot sauce)

By Robert
Peyton

There are many iconic images that come to mind when people think of New Orleans nightlife, including the neon glitz of Bourbon Street and the lone jazzman playing his horn beneath an old French Quarter gas lamp. But this is only the start of what New Orleans nightlife is all about. Whether you're looking for the simple pleasures of a perfectly constructed cocktail with a balcony view, or something entirely more adventurous, you've come to the right place.

No American town places such a premium on pleasure as New Orleans. From swank hotel lounges and refined jazz halls to sweaty dance clubs and raucous Bourbon Street bars, this city is serious about frivolity—and famous for it. Partying is more than an occasional indulgence in this city; it's a lifestyle. The bars and clubs that pulse with music are the city's lifeblood, and are found in every neighborhood. Like stars with their own gravity, they draw people through their doors to belly up to the bars or head feet first onto the dance floors. Blues, jazz, funk, R&B, rock, roots, Cajun, and zydeco—there are almost too many kinds of music and nightlife experiences to cover in one chapter. On any day or night of the year, the city is brimming with musical possibilities.

10

The French Quarter and Faubourg Marigny are the easiest places to find great music and nightspots. The venues are numerous and all within easy walking distance of each other. In the nearby Warehouse District, New Orleans institutions like Howlin' Wolf, Mulate's, and Circle Bar have been joined by scores of new bars, clubs, and restaurants. Moving upriver through the Garden District and Uptown, you'll find some of the most famous music spots in the city, such as Tipitina's and Maple Leaf. The Bywater, Mid-City, and Tremé are residential neighborhoods with fewer commercial strips, but they too have their crown jewels, like Vaughan's, Bullet's, and Rock 'n Bowl.

FRENCH QUARTER

The old square, with its scrolling Spanish architecture and narrow, French-named streets, is the hub of the Crescent City, and remains the beating heart of New Orleans's nightlife. Live music comes at you from all directions—from bars, clubs, concert halls, restaurants, and even from the streets themselves, and many of the neighborhood's restaurants, shops, cafés, and galleries stay open late to accommodate the night crowd. Although mostly fueled by tourists, the French Quarter remains the city's premiere nightlife destination because of its diversity and convenience.

BARS AND LOUNGES

Bar Tonique. One of the eclectic nightspots on North Rampart Street, this wine-and-cocktail bar harkens back to bygone eras, serving modern masterpieces alongside absinthe drinks and 19th-century Sazeracs. The brick-walled lounge has private nooks and crannies and a beautiful outdoor courtyard. It draws an eclectic crowd, from theatergoers to neighborhood hipsters. ⊠ *820 N. Rampart St., French Quarter* ☎ *504/324–6045.*

Bombay Club. A longtime favorite for its martinis, Bombay Club has become equally known for its upscale dinner menu. It's a rather swanky place for the French Quarter, with leather chairs and dark paneling, and one of the few places in the city that enforces a dress code, although it's not overly formal: no shorts, no jeans. Tucked away from the street, this bar in the Prince Conti Hotel hosts live music on many nights. ⊠ *830 Conti St., French Quarter* ☎ *504/586–0972.*

★ **Carousel Revolving Bar.** This revolving hotel bar has been one of New Orleans' favorite drinking destinations since 1949. Its nationally-revered bartenders serve thirsty patrons (primarily tourists) the classics. The adjoining piano bar hosts live music on weekends, and the venue comes with a literary pedigree: Tennessee Williams, Truman Capote, and Ernest Hemingway, among many others, drank here. ⊠ *Hotel Monteleone, 214 Royal St., French Quarter* ☎ *504/523–3341.*

Cat's Meow. You'll hear this Bourbon Street landmark before you see it—it's New Orleans's most popular karaoke bar. Occupying an ideal corner location, the tall doors and windows open onto two streets, beckoning people to the dance floor and the spotlit stage. High energy MCs and DJs keep the night spinning along, but be sure to get on the sign-up sheet early if you want a chance at French Quarter fame. ⊠ *701 Bourbon St., French Quarter* ☎ *504/523–2788.*

Chart Room. Unpretentious even by New Orleans standards, this little bar not far from Canal Street draws a good number of locals from the Quarter and beyond—they're drawn by the inexpensive drinks and the wide-open doorways that offer table seating just off the sidewalk. ⊠ *300 Chartres St., French Quarter* ☎ *504/522–1708.*

Cosimo's. Few tourists make their way to this hip neighborhood bar, which is in a far corner of the Lower Quarter. A short flight of stairs leads to a pool and dart room. Quirky chandeliers, ample windows, and a decent wine selection lend the street-level bar a touch of class. Food

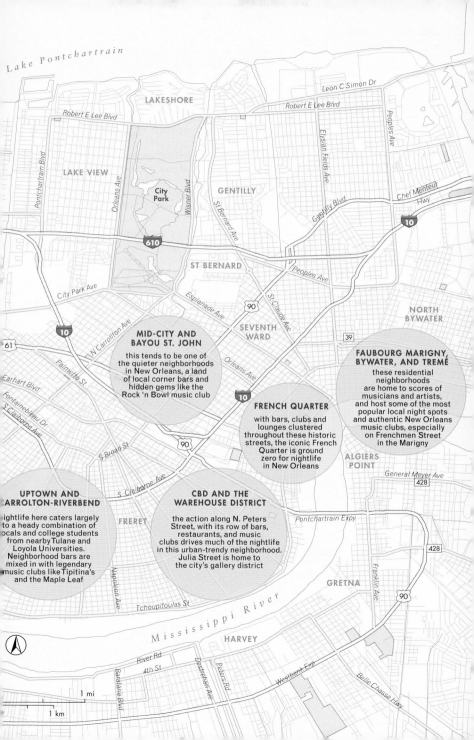

Lake Pontchartrain

LAKESHORE

Leon C Simon Dr

Robert E Lee Blvd

Robert E Lee Blvd

Peoples Ave

LAKE VIEW

City Park

GENTILLY

Chef Menteur Hwy

Pontchartrain Blvd

Orleans Ave

Wisner Blvd

St Bernard Ave

Elysian Fields Ave

Gentilly Blvd

610

ST BERNARD

City Park Ave

Peoples Ave

NORTH BYWATER

N Carrollton Ave

Esplanade Ave

90

SEVENTH WARD

St Claude Ave

39

Palmetto St

61

10

Earhart Blvd

MID-CITY AND BAYOU ST. JOHN
this tends to be one of the quieter neighborhoods in New Orleans, a land of local corner bars and hidden gems like the Rock 'n Bowl music club

Orleans Ave

FAUBOURG MARIGNY, BYWATER, AND TREMÉ
these residential neighborhoods are home to scores of musicians and artists, and host some of the most popular local night spots and authentic New Orleans music clubs, especially on Frenchmen Street in the Marigny

Fontainebleau Dr
S Claiborne Ave

10

FRENCH QUARTER
with bars, clubs and lounges clustered throughout these historic streets, the iconic French Quarter is ground zero for nightlife in New Orleans

S Broad St

90

ALGIERS POINT

General Meyer Ave

428

S Claiborne Ave

Pontchartrain Expy

UPTOWN AND CARROLLTON-RIVERBEND
nightlife here caters largely to a heady combination of locals and college students from nearby Tulane and Loyola Universities. Neighborhood bars are mixed in with legendary music clubs like Tipitina's and the Maple Leaf

FRERET

CBD AND THE WAREHOUSE DISTRICT
the action along N. Peters Street, with its row of bars, restaurants, and music clubs drives much of the nightlife in this urban-trendy neighborhood. Julia Street is home to the city's gallery district

Franklin Ave

428

Napoleon Ave

GRETNA

90

Tchoupitoulas St

Mississippi River

HARVEY

River Rd

4th St

Barataria Blvd

Destrehan Ave

Peters Rd

Westbank Exp

Belle Chasse Hwy

1 mi

1 km

PRACTICAL MATTERS

Little about New Orleans can actually be described as practical, but here are some general guidelines to help you navigate the scene.

Bars tend to open in the early afternoon and stay open well into the morning hours. Live music usually begins around 6 in a handful of clubs that host early sets, but **things really get going between 9 and 11 pm**. Bear in mind that many venues operate on "New Orleans time," meaning that if a show is advertised for 10 pm then it might kick off closer to 11.

If you're a night owl, plenty of clubs have **late-night sets**, some not starting until 1 am.

Dress codes are as rare as snow in this city. On any given night in the French Quarter, and especially during the Carnival season, you'll see everything from tuxedoes to tutus, T-shirts to fairy wings, and everything in between. Wear whatever is easiest to dance in.

Many bars on Bourbon Street entice visitors by presenting bands with no cover charge. They make their money by imposing a **one- or two-drink minimum**, with draft beer or soft drinks costing $5 to $8 apiece. In general, prices for beer, wine, and cocktails range from $4 to $9, unless you land in a good neighborhood dive bar, and then the prices can drop by as much as half. Music clubs generally charge a flat cover between $5 and $20, with the high-end prices usually reserved for national touring artists, holidays, and special occasions.

Bring cash to live-music clubs; **many bands play for tips alone**. Expect the hat (or the bucket, or the old coffee can, or the empty goldfish bowl) to be passed around once per set.

Although much of New Orleans is safe, especially in the French Quarter, it's always a good idea to **keep an eye out and be aware of your surroundings**, especially late at night, or if it's readily apparent that you've been hitting the Hurricanes a little too hard. Pickpockets and muggers do exist, but an ounce of prevention in the form of awareness goes a long way toward avoiding any kind of incident. In the French Quarter and downtown, it's usually fine to walk from place to place, but if you're traveling through outlying neighborhoods late at night it's best to take a car or taxi.

A great source for concert, event, and local information is **WWOZ**, the jazz and heritage community radio station, which broadcasts worldwide over the Internet at ⊕ *www. wwoz.org*. Local musicians, music historians, and personalities make up the all-volunteer corps of DJs, and they broadcast live 24/7 out of the French Quarter.

For more detailed event listings, check out **Gambit Weekly** (⊕ *www. bestofneworleans.com*), the alternative weekly available free in many bars, cafés, and stores. The monthly **OffBeat** (⊕ *www.offbeat.com*) magazine has in-depth coverage of local music and venues and is available at many hotels, stores, and restaurants as well.

options include pizzas, burgers, sandwiches and Asian-inspired items like the Thai noodle salad and pork pot stickers. ✉ *1201 Burgundy St., French Quarter* ☎ *504/522–9715.*

Crescent City Brewhouse. The only microbrewery in the French Quarter, this convivial pub and restaurant makes four specialty beers on the premises and one seasonal selection. The atmosphere can get a little touristy, but oysters on the half shell, live jazz in the evenings, and a second-floor riverview balcony make a visit more than worthwhile. ✉ *527 Decatur St., French Quarter* ☎ *504/522–0571.*

The Dungeon. A dark narrow alley is not normally where you want to find yourself in New Orleans—unless it's on the way to The Dungeon. This skull-and-chain-theme bar, which opens at midnight, has become a cult destination of sorts where the rich and famous might turn up shaking it on the goth/industrial dance floor alongside the regulars. It's not to be confused with the Front of the Dungeon, a more traditional bar next door. ✉ *738 Toulouse St., French Quarter* ☎ *504/523–5530.*

★ **French 75.** This bar is a must-visit for any who love to submerge themselves in old-time elegance. Adjoining Arnaud's, the classic New Orleans Creole restaurant, French 75 offers a terrific selection of beer, wine, fine liquors, and drinks in a French-style setting with leather-backed chairs. Bartender Chris Hannah works magic with his encyclopedic knowledge of cocktails and arsenal of ingredients. Be sure to venture upstairs to the Germaine Wells Mardi Gras Museum (free), a slightly bizarre showcase for memorabilia and ball gowns worn by the original owner's daughter. ✉ *813 Bienville St., French Quarter* ☎ *504/523–5433.*

Hermes Bar. This classy but laid-back destination is an offshoot of Antoine's, one of the oldest and most revered New Orleans restaurants. Bow-tied bartenders, who happen to be some of the most knowledgeable mixologists in the city, serve up classics like Sazeracs, sidecars, and Pimms cups in an elegant but unpretentious style. With live music on Fridays and Saturdays, great happy hour specials, and a divine food menu, this spot just off Bourbon Street is a favorite with many downtowners. ✉ *725 Rue St. Louis, French Quarter* ☎ *504/581–4422.*

Kerry Irish Pub. This comfortably well-worn pub has a pool table, a jukebox stocked with the Pogues and Flogging Molly, and, of course, Guinness on draft. A small stage at the back hosts Irish musicians, singer-songwriters and R&B or jazz musicians most evenings, with no cover charge. It's one of the last venues for Irish music in the Quarter. ✉ *331 Decatur St., French Quarter* ☎ *504/286–5862.*

★ **Lafitte's Blacksmith Shop.** Probably the most photographed building in the Quarter after St. Louis Cathedral, this 18th-century cottage was, according to legend, once a blacksmith shop that served as a front for the eponymous pirate's less legitimate business ventures. Today, it's a popular and atmospheric piano bar with a rustic, candlelit interior and a small outdoor patio that has banana trees and a sculpture by the late Enrique Alferez (whose work also decorates City Park). Despite the addition of a few flat-screen TVs, a drink here just after sundown, when the place is lit only by candles, lets you slip back in time for an hour or so. ✉ *941 Bourbon St., French Quarter* ☎ *504/593–9761.*

10

French Quarter Nightlife

Molly's at the Market. One of the best-known and most popular bars along this stretch of lower Decatur Street, Molly's is a great place to grab a perch almost any time of day. Perfect pints of Guinness, generously poured cocktails, and great bartenders make this a good spot to pull up a window seat and do some people watching, from the afternoon crowds of shop goers

> **ONE FOR THE ROAD**
>
> Although bottles and glasses are officially banned on the street, New Orleans is one of the few places where it's perfectly legal to carry a drink in public. Ready to move on? Ask the bartender for a "go cup."

and sightseers to late-night revelers. Everyone from politicians to punk rockers drifts though these doors at some point. ⌂ *1107 Decatur St., French Quarter* ☎ *504/525–5169.*

Fodor'sChoice
★
Napoleon House Bar and Cafe. This vintage restaurant and watering hole has long been popular with writers, artists, and other free spirits. It's a living shrine to what may be called the semiofficial New Orleans school of decor: faded grandeur. Chipped wall paint, diffused light, and a tiny courtyard with a trickling fountain and lush banana trees create a timeless escapist mood. The house specialty is a Pimm's Cup (here they top Pimm's No. 1 with lemonade and 7-Up). Even locals who don't venture often into the French Quarter will make an exception for Napoleon House. ⌂ *500 Chartres St., French Quarter* ☎ *504/524–9752.*

Old Absinthe House. A low-key oasis in the middle of Bourbon Street's excess, the building that houses this popular watering hole has had some illustrious visitors over its 200-year history, including Oscar Wilde, Mark Twain, Franklin Roosevelt, and Frank Sinatra. It's now mostly frequented by tourists and casual local characters who appreciate a good brewski or cocktail to go. Thousands of business cards stapled to the wall serve as interesting wallpaper. ⌂ *240 Bourbon St., French Quarter* ☎ *504/523–3181.*

Pat O'Brien's. Sure, it's touristy, but there are reasons Pat O's has been a must-stop on the New Orleans cocktail trail for so long. For one thing, there's plenty of room to spread out, from the elegant side bar and piano bar that flank the carriageway entrance to the lush (and in winter, heated) patio. Friendly staff, an easy camaraderie among patrons, and a signature drink—the pink, fruity, and extremely potent Hurricane, which comes with a souvenir glass—make this French Quarter stalwart a pleasant afternoon diversion. Expect a line on weekend nights, and remember to return your glass to get back the deposit if you don't want to keep it. ⌂ *718 St. Peter St., French Quarter* ☎ *504/525–4823.*

10

Patrick's Bar Vin. Before Katrina hit, Patrick Van Hoorebeek was the beloved longtime maître d' at the now-shuttered Bistro at Maison de Ville. In 2011 he opened this elegant hotel bar, where he holds court in a clubby atmosphere of dark wood and wine-red upholstery. The bar specializes in wines by the glass, but there's also an excellent selection of cocktails and beers, including choices from Van Hoorebeek's own Belgium. There's a limited selection of small plates from the hotel's kitchen, and wine lockers are available for major oenophiles. The bar is only a few steps from Bourbon Street, but it can feel like another world entirely. It's a perfect stop for an after-dinner drink or as an oasis from the occasional insanity of the Quarter—it opens at 2 pm on Friday to catch the after-lunch crowd. ⊠ *730 Bienville St., French Quarter* ☎ *504/200–3180* ⊕ *patricksbarvin.com.*

Pravda. With its dim lighting, run-down elegance, and plush red velvet decor, Pravda is a small timeless universe of its own. With a Soviet-themed motif and array of absinthes and vodkas from around the world, it's not hard to imagine you're in some clandestine speakeasy at the edge of the empire. An eclectic clientele includes everyone from businesspeople and tourists to artists and tattooed goth kids. There's a nice courtyard out back if you'd rather lighten up. ⊠ *1113 Decatur St., French Quarter* ☎ *504/581–1110.*

Tujague's. Open since 1856, Tujague's has been a landmark of the French Quarter culinary and bar scenes for generation upon generation. A gathering place for everyone from dock workers to U.S. presidents, the fine service and traditional menu have helped Tujague's survive the dark days of world wars, the Great Depression, and Prohibition. Almost unchanged to this day, with its limited seating and vintage stand-up bar (shipped from Paris in 1856), the no-frills barroom harkens back to a bygone era with a delicious menu of old-school cocktails. ⊠ *823 Decatur St., French Quarter* ☎ *504/525–8676.*

GAY BARS AND CLUBS

★ **Bourbon Pub.** It's impossible to miss this 24-hour video bar at the corner of St. Ann and Bourbon, especially in early evenings, when the doors are open and the dance crowd spills into the street. There's usually a cover charge on Friday and Saturday nights after 10 pm; Sunday afternoon is devoted to vintage videos by assorted gay icons. ⊠ *801 Bourbon St., French Quarter* ☎ *504/529–2107.*

Café Lafitte in Exile. A Bourbon Street stalwart, Lafitte attracts a somewhat older and very casual group of gay men. The bar has a second floor with a pool table and wraparound balcony with a bird's-eye view of the street scene below. Sunday afternoon, when the oldies spin and the paper-napkin confetti flies, is especially popular. ⊠ *901 Bourbon St., French Quarter* ☎ *504/522–8397.*

Corner Pocket. Filmmaker John Waters reportedly counts the Pocket as a New Orleans favorite, and with skinny, tattooed strippers on the bar and an inebriated drag queen emceeing the show, it's easy to see why. Sleazy fun on a good night, but keep your wits about you. ⊠ *940 St. Louis St., French Quarter* ☎ *504/568–9829.*

Golden Lantern. The Lower Quarter has become a lot more upscale since this neighborhood gay haunt's heyday, but the Lantern soldiers on. The bartender's whims determine the music, the drinks are strong, and the 4–9 pm happy hour is one of the city's longest. The bar is best known as ground zero for the annual Southern Decadence drag parade, when a throng gathers out front for the kickoff. ⊠ *1239 Royal St., French Quarter* ☎ *504/529–2860* ⊕ *www.tubbysbarneworleans.com.*

Good Friends. With its tasteful decor and reasonable volume level, Good Friends provides a slightly more upscale, sedate alternative to the blasting

Gay Scene in New Orleans

Southern Decadence festival

New Orleans has a laissez-faire attitude about many things, and that includes sexual orientation. The city has one of the oldest and most vibrant gay, lesbian, and transgender communities in the nation, which is just part of the reason that New Orleans has long been a popular destination for gay travelers. Another key factor is the parties. The GBLT community is famous for their mega-celebrations around holidays like Mardi Gras and Southern Decadence (held Labor Day weekend). Social clubs, often organized around bars or other gay-owned business sponsors, join forces to throw parades, costume balls, and themed parties. The street party at Bourbon and St. Anne streets in the French Quarter is always a popular event. This intersection tends to be a main hub of the gay social scene, with **Bourbon Pub** and **Oz** perched on each side of the street, pumping out music from the techno-club-style dance floors. Great crowds also turn out for Halloween, and for

Easter, when a gay Easter parade rolls through the Quarter. The city celebrates Gay Pride in October, but it actually tends to be a fairly low-key affair compared to these other more lavish parties. It's probably because the gay pride is evident 365 days a year.

Most of the social scene is focused in the French Quarter, but the Faubourg Marigny neighborhood offers some great gay bars, restaurants, and other destinations.

Stop in **FAB—Faubourg Marigny Art and Books** (✉ *600 Frenchmen St.* ☎ *504/947–3700*), one of the oldest (and funkiest) gay bookstores in the nation, and pick up a copy of *Ambush Magazine*, the alternative biweekly. Or visit ⊕ *www.gayneworleans.com*, another great resource.

10

disco bars down the street. The Queen's Head Pub on the second floor, open weekends, has darts, a wraparound balcony, and respectable martinis. Brush up on your show tunes at the popular Sunday afternoon piano sing-along. ⊠ *740 Dauphine St., French Quarter* ☏ *504/566–7191.*

Napoleon's Itch. The only gay bar in New Orleans that's also attached to a large hotel, this narrow space is in the heart of St. Ann–and–Bourbon gay central; it's a must-visit during the annual Southern Decadence festival. The comfy sofas and handsome bartenders are a plus, and the crowd tends to be a bit dressier than at similar venues. ⊠ *734 Bourbon St., French Quarter.*

★ **Oz.** A spacious dance club that mainly attracts young gay men, Oz also draws straight men and women, largely because of the scarcity of good dance floors in the French Quarter. It's open around the clock and tends to peak very late. ⊠ *800 Bourbon St., French Quarter* ☏ *504/593–9491.*

Parade Disco. High-energy disco rules at this dance club above the Bourbon Pub. If it gets to be too much, a quieter back bar and a balcony offer retreat. The crowd is mostly male and young, but women are welcome. ⊠ *801 Bourbon St., above Bourbon Pub, French Quarter* ☏ *504/529–2107.*

Rawhide. As the name indicates, this is a rowdy—and sexually charged—leather-and-Levi's gay bar. It's two blocks from Bourbon Street and is open around the clock. ⊠ *740 Burgundy St., French Quarter* ☏ *504/525–8106.*

MUSIC CLUBS

Davenport Lounge. Set amid the swanky, split-level digs of the Ritz Carlton Hotel and overlooking famous Canal Street, the Davenport Lounge is home to its namesake Jeremy Davenport, a Grammy-nominated musician and performer who harkens back to the great crooners like Sinatra and Crosby. With a hot trumpet and a swinging dance floor, Davenport performs Thursday through Saturday, and draws a mixed crowd of visitors and locals. ⊠ *The Ritz Carlton New Orleans, 921 Canal St., French Quarter* ☏ *504/524–1331.*

Fritzel's European Jazz Pub. An old-school gem in the midst of Bourbon Street mayhem, this music club is built in the style of the old American and European jazz halls, with tight rows of seating close to the stage and floating barmaids. Drinks will cost you a little more here, particularly mixed drinks, but there's never a cover charge and the stage is home to some great trad, European, Dixieland, and old time jazz bands. They play several sets a day, 7 days a week. ⊠ *733 Bourbon St., French Quarter* ☏ *504/586–4800.*

★ **House of Blues.** Despite its name, blues is a relatively small component in the booking policy at this Decatur Street club, which also embraces rock, jazz, country, soul, funk, and world music, performed by everyone from local artists to international touring acts. The adjoining restaurant has an eclectic menu, with classic Southern cuisine, served in ample portions at reasonable prices. The **Parish,** a smaller, more intimate offshoot upstairs from the main house, hosts local and touring groups. ⊠ *225 Decatur St., French Quarter* ☏ *504/529–2583 concert line* ⊕ *www.houseofblues.com.*

★ **Irvin Mayfield's Jazz Playhouse.** A terrific destination for serious music lovers, this intimate lounge combines a modern aesthetic with the laid-back class of old New Orleans. Irvin Mayfield, one of the city's great musicians and performers and winner of both Grammy and Billboard awards, was determined to bring topflight jazz back to Bourbon Street, which has largely been overtaken by loud rock and blues cover bands. He succeeded, providing an incredible lineup of local talent for multiple sets every day with no cover and shows starting between 5 and 8 pm. ⊠ *Royal Sonesta Hotel, 300 Bourbon St., French Quarter* ☎ *504/586–0300.*

Margaritaville Café. Ever-popular with tourists and Jimmy Buffett fans, Margaritaville offers regional blues, rock, and zydeco performances, with sets starting as early as 3 pm and going into the night. Menu items, most notably the "Cheeseburger in Paradise," are derived from Buffett songs, and several varieties of the salt-rimmed signature drink are served. Whimsical island-themed decor includes an airplane emerging from a wall and a tire swing bar. ⊠ *1104 Decatur St., French Quarter* ☎ *504/592–2565.*

One Eyed Jack's. This former Toulouse Street theater plays host to touring modern rock acts as well as local up-and-comers. The 19th-century saloon interior provides an appropriately decadent backdrop for Fleur de Tease, a resident burlesque troupe. ⊠ *615 Toulouse St., French Quarter* ☎ *504/569–8361.*

Palm Court Jazz Café. Banjo player Danny Barker immortalized this restaurant in his song "Palm Court Strut." The best of traditional New Orleans jazz is presented in a classy setting with tile floors, exposed-brick walls, and a handsome mahogany bar. There are decent creature comforts here; regional cuisine is served, and you can sit at the bar and rub elbows with local musicians. A wide selection of records, tapes, and CDs are on sale. ⊠ *1204 Decatur St., French Quarter* ☎ *504/525–0200.*

Fodor's Choice **Preservation Hall.** The jazz tradition that flowered in the 1920s is
★ enshrined in this cultural landmark by a cadre of distinguished New Orleans musicians, most of whom were schooled by an ever-dwindling group of elder statesmen. There is limited seating on benches—many patrons end up squatting on the floor or standing in back—and no beverages are served or allowed. Nonetheless, the legions of satisfied customers regard an evening here as an essential New Orleans experience. Cover charge is $10, but can run a bit higher for special appearances. Call ahead for performance times; sometimes the show ends before you even begin prepartying. ⊠ *726 St. Peter St., French Quarter* ☎ *504/522–2841 or 504/523–8939* ⊕ *www.preservationhall.com.*

10

FAUBOURG MARIGNY, BYWATER, AND TREMÉ

Frenchmen Street in the Marigny is the hottest music strip in town, and is also known for its food and street life. Much of Frenchmen's activity is within a three-block area (between Decatur and Dauphine streets), where fun seekers crawl bars and people-watch outside on the sidewalk. Some clubs along this strip charge a $5–$10 cover for music, but many charge nothing at all. Along St. Claude Avenue, a diverse cluster of bars and clubs offers everything from brass-band jams to death metal to experimental, avant-garde, indie rock.

Continued on page 228

by Alison Fensterstock
and Jennifer Odell

Above and opposite, French Quarter jazz clubs, Maison Bourbon and Preservation Jazz Hall.

NEW ORLEANS NOISE

The late local R&B star Ernie K-Doe once said, "I'm not sure, but I think all music comes from New Orleans." He wasn't far off. The Crescent City has crafted American music for hundreds of years— from Jelly Roll Morton's Storyville jazz piano to the siren sound of Louis Armstrong's genre-defining trumpet; from Little Richard's first French Quarter rock 'n'roll recording session to Lil Wayne's hip-hop domination.

Right, New Orleans' musical legend, Louis Armstrong.

THE SOUNDS OF THE BIG EASY

JAZZ

The roots of New Orleans jazz reach back to the 17th century, when slaves sang traditional songs in Congo Square. As their African and Caribbean polyrhythms blended with European styles, new sounds were born.

In the Storyville red-light district in 1895, cornetist Buddy Bolden played what is considered to be the first jazz. It was a march-meets-syncopation sound that drew from the city's numerous fraternal and societal brass marching bands, from ragtime, and from blues.

Pianist Jelly Roll Morton, who also got his start playing in Storyville's bordellos, helped transition ragtime into jazz with his more flamboyant playing style. In 1915 he published the first jazz composition, "Jelly Roll Morton Blues."

But it was the cornet and trumpet players of the day who really sounded off. Joe "King" Oliver, Louis Armstrong's mentor, changed his cornet's sound by holding a plunger over the bell. Sidney Bechet revolutionized soloing with his radical fingering. Louis Armstrong made jazz a phenomenon with his skill, improvisational style, and showmanship. These men were the originators of New Orleans Dixieland, which rapidly spread across the nation and was itself transformed—here and elsewhere—through the decades.

Today, young New Orleans musicians benefit from the work of contemporary jazz players and educators like pianist Ellis Marsalis. His students have included Terence Blanchard, Donald Harrison, Jr., and Nicholas Payton, as well as his own talented sons: Wynton (trumpet), Branford (sax), Delfeayo (trombone), and Ellis III (drums).

LISTEN TO: King Oliver, Louis Armstrong, Sidney Bechet, Jelly Roll Morton, Kid Ory, Donald Harrison, Jr., Nicholas Payton.
GO TO: Preservation Hall and Palm Court Jazz Café (traditional; French Quarter). Snug Harbor and the Blue Nile (contemporary; Faubourg Marigny).
EXPERIENCE IT: on Historic New Orleans, Inc.'s (www.tourneworleans. com) daily New Orleans Music tour; during ranger-led talks and walks at the Jazz National Historic Park (www. nps.gov/jazz).

Far left, clockwise from left, jazz at Bourbon Street, Jelly Roll Morton, Louis Armstrong. Below right, Zydeco accordionist. Left, Soul Rebel Brass Band.

BRASS BANDS

To lay down those 2/4 and 4/4 rhythms, traditional New Orleans Dixieland was greatly influenced by the format of the city's brass bands: trumpet or coronet for melody; clarinet for countermelody and harmony; trombone to emphasize the chord-change notes; banjo (later replaced by guitar); tuba (later, the piano); and drums.

In the 1970s and '80s, young brass bands like Rebirth and Dirty Dozen updated the traditional rollicking drum-and-horn street parade sound with funk and hip-hop. Now they're the elder statesmen of a thriving scene.

LISTEN TO: Hot 8, Stooges, Rebirth, Soul Rebels.
GO SEE: Rebirth at the Maple Leaf (Tues., Uptown); Stooges at the Hi Ho Lounge (Thurs., Marigny).
EXPERIENCE IT: at the Backstreet Cultural Museum (www.backstreetmuseum.org), with artifacts from the Mardi Gras Indian, brass band, and second-line traditions.

CAJUN AND ZYDECO

Most purveyors of plaintive French-language balladry and squeeze-box and fiddle-driven dancehall rhythms play a few hours outside of the city. But some bands, like the Grammy-nominated Lost Bayou Ramblers, do make their way into *la ville*. The same is true of zydeco, accordion and washboard-driven music that evolved from the rural black-Creole sounds and urban R&B.

LISTEN TO: Cajun—Beausoleil, Feufollet, Pine Leaf Boys, Les Freres Michot, Savoy Family Cajun Band. Zydeco—Clifton Chenier, Chubby Carrier, Terrance Simien, Rockin' Dopsie Jr.
GO TO: For Cajun, Mulate's the Original Cajun (Warehouse District); Tropical Isle and One Eyed Jacks (the Quarter); dba (the Marigny). For zydeco, Bruce Daigrepont's Sunday *fais do do* at Tipitina's (Uptown) or Zydeco Thursday at Rock 'n' Bowl (Mid-City).
EXPERIENCE IT: at mid-June's Louisiana Cajun-Zydeco Festival (www.jazzandheritage.org/cajun-zydeco) in the French Quarter.

Above, performers at Congo Square, New Orleans, Jazz Fest.
Below, Allen Toussaint.
Top right, Dr. John.
Below right, Partners-N-Crime.

SOUL AND R&B

In the 1950s and '60s, producers like Allen Toussaint and Dave Bartholomew laid the groundwork for rock 'n' roll with funky, groove-based R&B that captured the gritty, fun-loving rhythm of New Orleans.

LISTEN TO: Professor Longhair, Fats Domino, Irma Thomas, Ernie K-Doe, Allen Toussaint, Neville Brothers, Dr. John, Guitar Lightnin' Lee, Little Freddie King.

GO SEE: Veterans like Al "Carnival Time" Johnson and Ernie Vincent still perform around town, most often at festivals, but occasionally at the Rock 'n' Bowl, dba, or neighborhood bars.

BOUNCE AND HIP-HOP

The danceable, hard-driving party rap known as bounce originated in New Orleans housing projects and neighborhood bars in the late 1980s. In the 1990s, No Limit and Cash Money Records put New Orleans hip-hop on the map.

LISTEN TO: Big Freedia, Truth Universal, Partners-N-Crime, Mystikal, Juvenile, Lil' Wayne

GO SEE: Big-name acts like Juvenile and Mystikal play at the House of Blues (the Quarter) or Howlin' Wolf (Warehouse District). Look for bounce performers at small rock venues around town and hip-hop artists at Dragon's Den in the Marigny.

SECOND LINES AND JAZZ FUNERALS

Second line parade in the French Quarter.

If you encounter a marching band parading down the streets of New Orleans, chances are it's a second line, a type of parade historically associated with jazz funerals. The term second line refers specifically to the crowd that marched behind the "first line" of the brass band and family of the deceased. During the early 20th century, the New Orleans second line served an important community function; African Americans were not allowed to buy insurance, so they formed mutual-aid societies—called Social Aid and Pleasure Clubs—to help members through tough times. The tradition continues to this day; different Social Aid and Pleasure Clubs parade in all neighborhoods of the city every weekend of the year, outside of the hottest summer months. If you get wind of an authentic second line, go, but use caution. Stick to the safer-looking streets, and be prepared to make an exit if things start to get edgy.

The website www.blogofneworleans.com posts routes and schedules for the weekend's second lines each Thursday.

Sylvester Francis has spent the better part of a lifetime documenting second-line parades and jazz funerals; his **Backstreet Cultural Museum** (*1116 St. Claude Ave., Tremé, 504/522-4806, www. backstreetmuseum.org*) is a repository of second-line mementos and tons of photographs. Call ahead to be sure they're open.

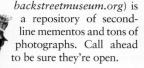

Uncle" Lionel Batiste of the Tremé Brass Band.

JAZZ AND HERITAGE FESTIVAL

Above, crowds and performers at Jazz Fest. Opposite page, Mr. Okra vending truck.

A sprawling, rollicking celebration of Louisiana music, food, and culture, Jazz Fest is held annually the last weekend in April and the first weekend in May at the historic Fair Grounds Race Course. The grounds reverberate with rock, Cajun, zydeco, gospel, rhythm and blues, hip-hop, folk, world music, country, Latin, and, yes, traditional and modern jazz. Throw in world-class arts and crafts, exhibitions and lectures, and an astounding range of local food, and you've got a festival worthy of America's premiere party town.

Over the years, Jazz Fest lineups have come to include mainstream performers—Bruce Springsteen, Tom Petty, and My Morning Jacket topped the bill in 2012—but at its heart the festival is about the hundreds of Louisiana musicians who live, work, and hone their chops in the Crescent City. Many New Orleans musicians are still recovering from the effects of Hurricane Katrina, and Jazz Fest is their chance to show a huge, international audience that the music survives.

HISTORY

Veterans of the first Jazz Fest, which took place in 1970 in what's now Armstrong Park, talk about it with the same awe and swagger of those who rolled in the mud at Woodstock in 1969. The initial lineup included such legendary performers as Mahalia Jackson, Duke Ellington, Fats Domino, The Meters, and the Olympia Brass Band, who played for a small audience of about 350 people, approximately half the number of performers and production staffers it took to put the event on. In 2006 the first post-Katrina festival drew 350,000 people from all over the world and showcased the talents of some 6,000 performers, artisans, and chefs. Many of the musicians who performed at the first Jazz Fest came back to play the emotional 2006 festival. In 2011 the festival welcomed more than 400,000 attendees.

Official Logo of Jazz and Heritage Festival.

MUSIC

Each of the 12 stages has its own musical bent. The Congo Square stage hosts hip-hop and world music, the Fais-Do-Do stage specializes in Cajun and zydeco performers, fans of traditional jazz head for the Economy Hall Tent, and everyone spends at least a few minutes in the Gospel Tent soaking up the exuberant testimony.

FOOD

Cooks from all over Louisiana turn out dishes both familiar (shrimp po'boys and jambalaya) and exotic (alligator sausage, anyone?). Favorites include gumbo, soft-shell-crab or cochon de lait po'boys, and Crawfish Monica, a creamy pasta dish. Beer and wine are available, but hard liquor is taboo.

CRAFTS

Craft areas at Jazz Fest include Contemporary Crafts, near the Gospel Tent, which sells wares from nationwide artists; the Louisiana Marketplace, near the Fais-Do-Do stage and Louisiana Folklife Village, which showcase area folk art; and a Native American Village, which spotlights indigenous culture. Surrounding the Congo Square stage are stands with African and African-influenced artifacts items. ■ TIP→ Many artists have a spot for only part of the fest; ask about their schedule before putting off any purchases.

A tent beside Economy Hall sells CDs by festival performers, as well as other New Orleans and Louisiana artists; nearby is the official merchandise, including limited-edition Jazz Fest posters, which range in price from about $70 for a numbered silkscreen to several hundred dollars for a signed and numbered remarque print. In the Books Tent, local authors sign works on Louisiana music and culture. ■ TIP→ You don't need to bring a lot of cash. ATMs are located throughout the site.

10

JAZZ FEST TIPS

■ Book hotels as early as possible.

■ Thursdays on the second weekend are the least-packed day, and a local favorite.

■ You can purchase a full program once you arrive at the festival, with detailed schedules and maps, or tear the "cubes" out of the *Gambit* weekly paper, *Offbeat* monthly, or the *Times-Picayune's* weekly Lagniappe pullout. Free iPhone apps are also available.

■ Don't stress out trying to catch all the big names; inevitably, the obscure local musicians provide the most indelible Jazz Fest memories.

■ For a break from the heat and sun (plus air-conditioned indoor restrooms), visit the Grandstand, which hosts exhibits, cooking demonstrations (often with free samples), and musician interviews.

■ Longtime fest goers bring flags to let friends know where they're located. These make great markers when trying to find your friends in the crowd.

■ Cool, casual, and breathable fabrics, along with a wide-brim hat and plenty of sunscreen, are your best bets for the long day outdoors. Wear comfortable shoes, and ones that can get dirty. The grounds are a racetrack, after all, and by the end of Jazz Fest the ground is a mix of dust, straw, mud, and crawfish shells.

Perhaps the edgiest local scene is in Bywater, home to a dozen low-key bars. Past the corner of Royal and Franklin streets a smattering of bars cater to a varied crowd. At the far end of the Bywater, local idol Kermit Ruffins (of *Treme* fame) plays Vaughan's every Thursday. Ruffins also plays the Seventh Ward's Bullet's Sports Bar, usually on Tuesday nights.

Tremé, which has found new popularity in the wake of the HBO series, is one of the oldest musical neighborhoods in the nation. Largely residential, Tremé is home to some great local nightclubs and music venues. Be careful traveling after dark, however, as the neighborhood remains rough.

BYWATER

BARS AND LOUNGES

★ **Bacchanal Fine Wine & Spirits.** Although technically a wineshop, Bacchanal, in the far reaches of Bywater, is also part tasting room, part neighborhood hangout. Among the wine racks in the old New Orleans building are two big round tables, as well as seating in the courtyard. You can have a bottle uncorked on the premises or order by the glass. High-end Scotches, bourbons, and rums are also on the menu. Sunday afternoons are especially fun, when a local band (and often a chef with a grill) sets up on the courtyard. ⊠ *600 Poland Ave., Bywater* ☎ *504/948–9111.*

BJ's Lounge. This gritty corner bar has long been a stalwart neighborhood joint, but the new owners have developed a terrific musical lineup, featuring old-school "swamp pop" and New Orleans rhythm and blues. Regular acts like Little Freddie King (most Fridays) and King James and the Special Men (Mondays) blow the top off the place. ⊠ *4301 Burgundy Street, Bywater* ☎ *504/945–9256.*

Country Club New Orleans. If you're looking for a nontouristy, out-of-the-way experience, check out this "restaurant, lounge, pool, Jacuzzi, cabana bar." Set in a handsome 19th-century Bywater mansion, this onetime gay club now offers an elegant retreat from the hustle and bustle of the city, with a lounge area; an up-and-coming restaurant; and large, clothing-optional outdoor pool and deck bar hidden away behind lush vegetation and high walls. ⊠ *634 Louisa St., Bywater* ☎ *504/945–0742* ⊕ *www.thecountryclubneworleans.com.*

MUSIC CLUBS

Vaughan's. Jazz trumpeter Kermit Ruffins's Thursday-night sets (served up with free red beans and rice) are the big draw at this ramshackle place in Bywater's farthest reaches; at other times, it's a picturesque and exceptionally friendly neighborhood bar with live music two or three nights a week and boiled seafood or barbecue in the back. ⊠ *800 Lesseps St., at Dauphine St., Bywater* ☎ *504/947–5562.*

FAUBOURG MARIGNY

BARS AND LOUNGES

AllWays Lounge & Theatre. This lounge/theater combo has become one of the centerpieces of the local indie, avant-garde, and art scenes. Bringing to mind 1930s Berlin, the lounge has a black-and-red color scheme and frayed-at-the-edges art deco aesthetic. Musicians, burlesque dancers, clowns, artists, and jacks-of-all-trades take to the stage here most nights of the week. Meanwhile, in the back of the house, the 100-seat AllWays Theatre hosts weekend plays and other performances. ⊠ *2240*

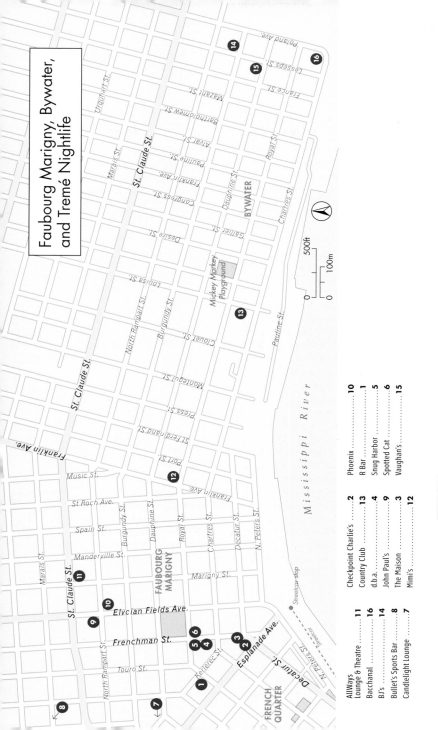

Faubourg Marigny, Bywater, and Tremé Nightlife

BYWATER

Mississippi River

10

Saint Claude Ave., Faubourg Marigny ☎ *504/218–5778* ⊕ *theallwayslounge.net/.*

Checkpoint Charlie's. This bustling corner bar draws young locals who shoot pool and listen to blues and rock, whether live or from the jukebox—24 hours a day, seven days a week. Weekends often feature hard rock, punk, and metal bands as well. There's also a paperback library, a menu of bar grub, and a fully functioning Laundromat. ✉ *501 Esplanade Ave., Faubourg Marigny* ☎ *504/281–4847.*

John Paul's. This bar is famous for its special events, themed nights, and performances. There's a big-screen TV for football games, drag shows on Friday and Saturday, frequent performances by Marcy Marcell, DJs, and a large selection of vodkas and top-shelf bourbons. ✉ *940 Elysian Fields Ave, Faubourg Marigny* ☎ *504/948–1888.*

> ### FRENCHMEN STREET PERSONALITIES
>
> Street life on Frenchmen can be as entertaining as anything going on inside the clubs and bars. Street artists and brass bands gather on corners and in doorways on most weekends and turn intersections and sidewalks into impromptu, open-air galleries, boutiques, and dance parties. A poet selling custom love sonnets typed up on a vintage typewriter and a shopping cart turned mechanical bull with built-in music and smoke machine are just some of the characters you'll encounter on an average night.

The Maison. This historic building has been rescued from near-crumbling decay to become one of the most popular destinations on Frenchmen Street. With a sprawling three-story floor plan, interior balconies, a terrific kitchen, multiple bars, stages, and dance floors, it's easy to see how the venue has become party central. Live music every night of the week and no cover make it inviting, and the managers skillfully weave local and touring DJs and electronic music into their lineup of parties and events. ✉ *508 Frenchmen St., Faubourg Marigny* ☎ *504/371–5543.*

Mimi's. A popular destination among locals citywide, this two-story nightspot perches over the corner of Franklin and Royal streets, and the big windows stay open most evenings. Downstairs is a bar with table seating, couches, and pool table, while upstairs is home to the tapas-styled kitchen/restaurant, the dance floor where bands and DJ's play most nights of the week (packed on weekends, and especially Saturday night when DJ Soul Sister gets her groove on), and wraparound balcony. ✉ *2601 Royal St., Faubourg Marigny* ☎ *504/872–9868.*

Phoenix. The Phoenix bills itself as a "Leather/Levi Neighborhood Alternative Bar," and that's a pretty apt description. The downstairs bar is a popular Marigny nightspot, with a calendar of special events and themed parties, including the International Mr. Leather Contest. The upstairs bar, called the Eagle, caters to the cruising crowd of gay men, and is notorious for its "anything goes" atmosphere. ✉ *941 Elysian Fields Ave., Faubourg Marigny* ☎ *504/945–9264.*

R Bar. This neighborhood corner bar turns into something of a hipster hangout and social hub at night and during holiday weekends. Tinted windows and red vinyl provide a throwback ambience, and classic New

Wave (and pitchers of local Abita Beer) is always on tap. In addition to crawfish boils on Friday afternoons (during season), the place likes to run some offbeat specials—on Monday night, for example, 10 bucks will get you a shot and a haircut—and it's prime real estate on costume holidays like Mardi Gras and Halloween. ⊠ *1431 Royal St., Faubourg Marigny* ☎ *504/948–7499.*

MUSIC CLUBS

Bullet's Sports Bar. For a real taste of New Orleans, drop by this neighborhood joint on a Tuesday night, when Kermit Ruffins is playing. Not just the soul of the city, but the soul food, too, emerges as Kermit and friends serve up their famous barbeque and fixin's in between sets. Featured in the HBO series *Treme*, Bullets has become something of a New Orleans hot spot, but remember that if the neighborhood around the bar looks a little scary, that's because it *is* a little scary. Use caution when traveling here, but be prepared for a warm and welcoming musical experience when you arrive. Technically Bullet's is in the Seventh Ward neighborhood. ⊠ *2441 A.P. Tureaud Ave., Tremé* ☎ *504/948–4003.*

Fodor'sChoice
★
d.b.a. At this southern outpost of a popular bar in New York's East Village, the selection of drinks—including international beers on tap, aged Scotches, and obscure tequilas, all listed on chalkboards above the bar—is reason enough to visit. Live music most nights and the Marigny's best people-watching make it a neighborhood favorite. ⊠ *616 Frenchmen St., Faubourg Marigny* ☎ *504/942–3731.*

★ **Snug Harbor.** This intimate club is one of the city's best rooms for soaking up modern jazz, blues, and R&B. It is the home base of such esteemed talent as vocalist Charmaine Neville and pianist-patriarch Ellis Marsalis (father of Wynton and Branford). The dining room serves good local food but is best known for its burgers. Note that you can listen to the band through speakers in the bar without paying the rather high cover charge. ⊠ *626 Frenchmen St., Faubourg Marigny* ☎ *504/949–0696.*

Fodor'sChoice
★
The Spotted Cat. Jazz, old time, and swing bands perform nightly at this rustic club right in the thick of the Frenchmen Street action. Weekends feature afternoon sets as well. Drinks cost a little more at this cash-only destination, but there's never a cover charge and the entertainment is great—from the the popular bands to the cadres of young, rock-step swing dancers. ⊠ *623 Frenchmen St., Faubourg Marigny* ☎ *504/943–3887* ⊕ *spottedcatmusicclub.com.*

TREMÉ
MUSIC CLUBS

Bullet's Sports Bar. For a real taste of New Orleans, drop by this neighborhood joint on a Tuesday night, when Kermit Ruffins is playing. Not just the soul of the city, but the soul food, too, emerges as Kermit and friends serve up their famous barbeque and fixin's in between sets. Featured in the HBO series *Treme*, Bullets has become something of a New Orleans hot spot, but remember that if the neighborhood around the bar looks a little scary, that's because it *is* a little scary. Use caution when traveling here, but be prepared for a warm and welcoming musical experience when you arrive. Technically Bullet's is in the Seventh Ward neighborhood. ⊠ *2441 A.P. Tureaud Ave., Tremé* ☎ *504/948–4003.*

10

Candlelight Lounge. This small, old school joint draws the crowds on Wednesday nights to hear the Treme Brass Band. If you're lucky, neighborhood legend Uncle Lionel Batiste will make an appearance any night of the week, and dance with all the ladies; despite his frail appearance and the cane, he can be pretty lively. We recommend taking a cab out here. ✉ *925 N. Robertson St., Tremé* ☎ *504/571–1021.*

CBD AND WAREHOUSE DISTRICT

With the many apartment buildings built from converted 19th-century warehouses and cotton mills as backdrop, the Warehouse District has turned into a great draw for locals and visitors alike with numerous bars, restaurants, and clubs that cater to hip professionals. It's also home to the contemporary-art scene, with dozens of galleries arranged through the district that host their own series of parties and celebrations.

The Central Business District (CBD) is mostly quiet at night, but closer to Canal Street and the French Quarter are some terrific nightspots, like the Sazerac Bar and the swanky Club Ampersand.

CBD

BARS AND LOUNGES

12 Bar on Fulton Street. Named after the 12-bar guitar chord progression made famous by blues artists, this downtown club features an array of the city's finest jazz, blues, R&B, funk, and rock. Set in an 1800s building with a prime location adjoining the French Quarter and the CBD, the bar draws a mixed crowd of happy hour enthusiasts and music lovers. It also features comedy on Tuesday nights and a modern "antebellum-styled ultralounge" with acoustic acts during the early evening. ✉ *608 Fulton St., CBD* ☎ *504/212–6476.*

Handsome Willy's. Sandwiched between a forlorn stretch of the Interstate 10 overpass and the Medical District, Handsome Willy's—named for a dapper repeat customer of the notorious brothel that used to be on the site—is one of a tiny collection of historic buildings remaining on this block. (One other is the writer Lafcadio Hearn's New Orleans home.) Willy's offers daily drink and menu specials, happy hour cookouts on the back patio, and at night there's a rotating cast of DJs, frequent (and irreverent) literary events, and the occasional live band. It's not on many tourist maps, but it's casually hip and worth seeking out. ✉ *218 S. Robertson St., CBD* ☎ *504/525–0377.*

Loa. In voodoo tradition, *loa* are the divine spirits, and this bar just off the lobby of the chic International House hotel certainly strives for an extraordinary experience with its modern upscale decor. Well-heeled downtown professionals mingle with international jet setters gathering for the evening and sipping on inventive, high-end cocktails. Try the loa'tini, which comes garnished with edible flowers. ✉ *221 Camp St., CBD* ☎ *504/553–9550.*

Rusty Nail. Nestled in between the overhead highway and a series of converted 18th-century warehouses, this discreet neighborhood bar can be difficult to find but is worth the trip. With live music most nights of the week, a great selection of scotches, and a gorgeous renovated patio,

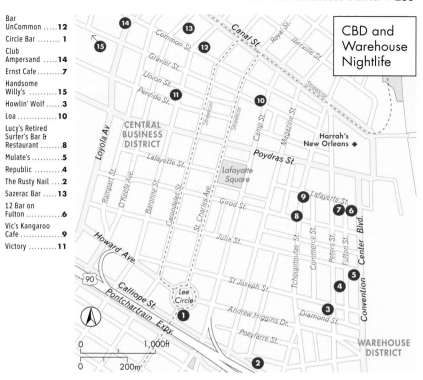

the Rusty Nail is a great place to get the night started or to spend a low-key evening relaxing outdoors. Catering to professionals, the bar also plays host to the popular Opera on Tap performance series, in which local opera performers spend the evening delivering rousing scenes to a packed barroom. ⊠ *1100 Constance St., CBD* ☏ *504/525–5515.*

★ **The Sazerac Bar.** This is one of the most famous bars in Louisiana, providing libations and inspiration since 1893. Drawn to the signature Sazerac cocktails and Ramos Gin Fizzes, a famous and intriguing clientele has graced this hotel bar over the years, including Governor Huey P. Long, who in the 1930s built a 90-mile highway between New Orleans and the state capital, so, many believe, he could get directly to the hotel lounge for his signature drink. ⊠ *Roosevelt Hotel, 123 Baronne St., CBD* ☏ *504/648–1200.*

Victory. On an unassuming block in the CBD stands another entry in the growing list of craft cocktail bars. It's named for Daniel Victory, one of the bar's owners, who also happens to be one of the city's best mixologists. Young urban dwellers and head to this darkly lit, vaguely industrial space for drinks that push the boundaries of traditional cocktails. Many of the ingredients are prepared in-house by bar chefs whose enthusiasm for bitters, reductions, and flavored ices borders on evangelical. Small plates like bacon-wrapped scallops, Korean lettuce wraps, and chicken satay are available from the kitchen. ⊠ *339 Baronne St., CBD* ☏ *504/522–8664* ⊕ *www.victorycocktails.com.*

CASINOS

Harrah's New Orleans. Commanding the foot of Canal Street, this beaux arts–style casino is the largest in the South. Its 100,000 square feet hold 2,900 slots and 120 gaming tables. There's an upscale steak restaurant run by local celebrity-chef John Besh. Valet parking is available. ⊠ *4 Canal St., CBD* ☏ *504/533–6000 or 800/427–7247* ⊕ *www.harrahs.com.*

MUSIC CLUBS

Club Ampersand. New Orleans has very few dedicated electronic music dance clubs; this converted bank building is one of the biggest and nicest in the city. It features two levels, a large dance floor, VIP Suite, a balcony, courtyard, and several cozy sitting rooms, one of which used to be the bank's vault. Regularly featuring local DJs, the venue also boasts performances by many of the most famous names in electronic and hip-hop music. ⊠ *1100 Tulane Ave., CBD* ☏ *504/587–3737.*

WAREHOUSE DISTRICT

BARS AND LOUNGES

Bar UnCommon. Cool installations of local, national, and international artwork adorn the Renaissance Pere Marquette Hotel's sleek and chic bar. One of the bartenders is Laura McMillian, a major player in the local cocktail scene. ⊠ *Renaissance Pere Marquette Hotel, 817 Common St., Warehouse District* ☏ *504/525–1111.*

Ernst Cafe. Ernst has been operating as a bar since the first years of the 20th century, and the classic interior and upstairs balcony provide a welcome respite for conventioneers, lawyers from nearby firms, and service-industry folks finishing shifts at surrounding hotels. The classic menu include local bar-food staples like fried green tomatoes, po'boys, wraps, and burgers. ⊠ *600 S. Peters St., Warehouse District* ☏ *504/525–8544.*

Lucy's Retired Surfer Bar & Restaurant. Space can get tight in this out-of-its-element urban beach bar, especially when the young professionals arrive in search of happy hour cold beer and cocktails. The other half of the place is a restaurant that serves tasty sandwiches, fish tacos, and brunch on weekends; upstairs, a secondary club hosts occasional open-mike comedy shows. ⊠ *701 Tchoupitoulas St., Warehouse District* ☏ *504/523–8995.*

MUSIC CLUBS

Circle Bar. Like something out of a Tim Burton film, this teetering old Victorian house that straddles the concrete jungles of downtown and the Warehouse District is home to one of the hippest indie rock clubs in the city. Around 10 pm, scenesters descend on the venue, but earlier in the evening this is a laid-back haunt. If you can't squeeze into the room that holds what might be the world's tiniest stage, you can watch the action on a monitor over the bar. ⊠ *1032 St. Charles Ave., Warehouse District* ☏ *504/588–2616.*

Howlin' Wolf. This New Orleans favorite has long been a premier venue and anchor of the Warehouse District club and music scene. With a great corner location in a converted warehouse, they host larger rock,

Enjoying New Orleans Music with Your Kids

Bourbon Street's entertainment options are largely off-limits to children, but younger music fans need not feel excluded. Dozens of options exist outside of barrooms and traditional clubs, and several of the most prestigious clubs offer all-ages shows.

Preservation Hall and **Palm Court Jazz Café**, both legendary jazz venues, welcome underage patrons. **Tipitina's** and **Howlin' Wolf** occasionally host all-ages shows as well. Around **Jackson Square**, talented street musicians perform most days of the week, and the **French Market** hosts a regular series of concerts as well as a separate busking stage for local and visiting performers to play for tips. The **Louisiana Music Factory** (⊠ *210 Decatur St.* ☎ *504/586–1094* ⊕ *www.louisianamusicfactory.com*),

an excellent New Orleans music and record store, regularly hosts in-store performances. And kids are always welcome at the free shows staged by the National Park Service's **New Orleans Jazz Historical Park**, both at the park's visitor center (⊠ *419 Decatur St.* ☎ *504/589–4841* ⊕ *www.nps.gov/jazz*) and the Tuesday–Saturday afternoon shows at 916 North Peters Street, in the French Market.

---

funk, blues, Latin, and hip-hop shows on the main stage. Meanwhile, the side bar called the Den hosts more intimate events and popular weekly parties like Brass Band Sundays. ⊠ *907 S. Peters St., Warehouse District* ☎ *504/522–9653*.

Mulate's. Across the street from the Convention Center, this large restaurant seats 400, and the dance floor quickly fills with couples twirling and two-stepping to authentic Cajun bands from the countryside. Regulars love to drag first-timers to the floor for impromptu lessons. The home-style Cajun cuisine is quite good, and the bands play until 10:30 or 11 pm. ⊠ *201 Julia St., Warehouse District* ☎ *504/522–1492*.

Republic. Part of the new generation of music venues in the Warehouse District, this rock club retains the rough-timbered feel of the cotton-and-grain warehouse it used to be. The club books touring rock bands as well as local acts, and DJs take over the sound system late at night for popular dance parties. ⊠ *828 S. Peters St., Warehouse District* ☎ *504/528–8282*.

THE GARDEN DISTRICT

Near downtown and right on the streetcar line, the Garden District is relatively easy to reach and offers numerous options for dining and going out, especially along St. Charles Avenue, which is the main thoroughfare. Running parallel, just a few blocks toward the river, Magazine Street is another corridor rich with restaurants, bars, and nightspots. St. Charles Avenue tends to offer a more upscale and elegant version of nightlife, with historic venues and a touch of haute couture, while Magazine Street caters to a younger crowd of students and young professionals looking for vibrant neighborhood hangouts, beer gardens, and sidewalk cafés.

BARS AND LOUNGES

The Avenue Pub. Given that this place has one of the best beer selections in New Orleans with some of the best pub grub, you can see how this has become one of the city's top destinations for beer lovers: being right on the streetcar line doesn't hurt either. Specializing in craft beers, whisky, and scotch, the pub also offers a great New Orleans neighborhood vibe with pressed tin ceilings, bars located on two floors, and a wraparound balcony that's terrific for watching Carnival parades roll by. ⊠ *1732 St. Charles Ave, Garden District* ☎ *504/586–9243.*

Bayou Bar. Step back in time at this historic New Orleans destination, which was once a favorite of Ginger Rogers, Betty Davis, Jack Benny, Bob Hope, and other Hollywood legends. Still catering to a well-heeled crowd, the bar, inside a senior-living facility that used to be a famed hotel, features live music on Friday and Saturday and is the perfect place to get nostalgic with a signature Moscow Mule, a chocolate martini, wine, or aged Scotch while nibbling on free appetizers. ⊠ *The Pontchartrain, 2031 St. Charles Ave., Garden District* ☎ *504/524–0581.*

Bridge Lounge. At the Bridge Lounge it's mostly youngish professionals you'll find kicking back, many with their dogs in tow. The drinks are good, the light flattering, and the owners' oenophilia is reflected in the bar's extensive list of wines by the glass. ⊠ *1201 Magazine St., Garden District* ☎ *504/299–1888.*

The Bulldog. A beautiful brick patio is the main draw of this neighborhood institution, allowing patrons to gather in droves for happy hour and evening sessions overlooking the hustle and bustle of this lively stretch of Magazine Street. The dog-friendly venue calls itself "Uptown's International Beer Tavern," offering 50 different brews on tap and more than 100 selections in bottles. A surprisingly good selection of bar food keeps patrons fueled for evenings out, and during crawfish season boiled mudbugs are a popular option from the corner seafood market across the street. ⊠ *3236 Magazine St., Garden District* ☎ *504/891–1516.*

Garden District Pub. Just down the block from some of Magazine Street's best boutiques, you'll find the Garden District Pub. With its exposed brick walls and a copper-top bar, this neighborhood haunt exudes the ambience of a 19th-century pub, complete with Sazeracs and absinthe on a terrific drink menu. It's a great place to end a day of exploring or to get the evening started while mingling among the neighborhood denizens. ⊠ *1916 Magazine St., Garden District* ☎ *504/267–3392.*

Parasol's Restaurant & Bar. Po' boy devotees practically genuflect at the mention of this hole-in-the-wall, which has been serving the sloppy sandwiches, along with Guinness on tap, for more than 50 years. The annual St. Patrick's Day party at Parasol's spills out into the surrounding neighborhood of the Lower Garden District; it's grown so large that police have to erect barricades to keep traffic out—or keep the revelers in. ✉ *2533 Constance St., Garden District* ☎ *504/897–5413.*

UPTOWN AND CARROLLTON-RIVERBEND

Uptown is rich in clubs, although they are far less concentrated than the ones downtown. They tend to be tucked down residential side streets or scattered along one of the main drags, and they mostly cater to the large populations of college students and young professionals who dwell in this part of town. Local institutions like Tipitina's and Le Bon Temps Roulez are ever-popular destinations for music lovers drawn to the beats of funk, brass, blues, and rock.

Farther uptown, the Carrollton-Riverbend area is a favorite among Loyola and Tulane university students and is home to citywide favorites like the famous Maple Leaf club, which hosts live music every night of the week. Around the corner, Carrollton Station is a more laid-back option, with bands on weekends and some weeknights. Uptown bars tend to warm up with after-work crowds and then go late into the night. Late-night destinations like the F&M Patio Bar offer dance parties 'til the sun comes up.

CARROLLTON-RIVERBEND
MUSIC CLUBS
Carrollton Station. This cozy neighborhood bar keeps unfolding the farther back you go—from the front bar to the stage to the backyard. The live music that's performed most nights of the week is mainly local roots, rock, and acoustic acts. It's two blocks off the Carrollton streetcar line, and close to the Oak Street commercial district as well with its clubs and restaurants. ✉ *8140 Willow St., Carrollton-Riverbend* ☎ *504/865–9190.*

Fodor's Choice
★
Maple Leaf. The phrase "New Orleans institution" gets thrown around a lot, but this place deserves the title. It's wonderfully atmospheric, with pressed-tin walls and a lush tropical patio, and it's also one of the city's best venues for blues, New Orleans–style R&B, funk, zydeco, and jazz. On Sunday, the bar hosts the South's longest-running poetry reading, and Walter "Wolfman" Washington starts his set around 10:30. It's a long haul from the French Quarter, but worth the trip, especially if combined with a visit to one of the restaurants clustered near this commercial stretch of Oak Street. ✉ *8316 Oak St., Carrollton-Riverbend* ☎ *504/866–9359.*

UPTOWN
BARS AND LOUNGES
Fodor's Choice
★
Columns Hotel. An evening cocktail on the expansive front porch of the Columns, shaded by centuries-old oak trees and overlooking the St. Charles Avenue streetcar route, is one of the more romantic New Orleans experiences. The Victorian Lounge, with period decor and a fireplace, and plenty of decaying elegance, draws a white-collar crowd. Live jazz combos play Sunday through Thursday evenings. ✉ *3811 St. Charles Ave., Uptown* ☎ *504/899–9308.*

Cure. An early part of the movement that made Freret Corridor a destination, this elegant bar and restaurant dropped a touch of urban chic

10

Maple Leaf, a New Orleans institution.

into a historic rambling neighborhood. A doorman waits to welcome guests into a custom-designed interior, with 20-foot ceilings, a lovely patio, and doors salvaged from a 19th-century bank. Knowledgeable bartenders serve up happy-hour specials and a full cocktail menu that combines traditional classics with modern twists on the form. ✉ *4905 Freret St., Uptown* ☎ *504/302–2357* ⊕ *www.curenola.com.*

Delachaise. A charming sliver of a building on a busy stretch of St. Charles Avenue, Delachaise looks as if it was air-dropped straight from Paris. Offering a carefully chosen (and reasonably priced) selection of beer, liquor, and wines by the glass, the menu also includes brasserie fare—mussels, french fries, cheese platters—in appetizer-size portions, and the long, slender room and plush banquettes make you feel like you've wandered into the lounge car of a particularly elegant train. ✉ *3442 St. Charles Ave., Uptown* ☎ *504/895–0858.*

F&M Patio Bar. For some people, an all-nighter in New Orleans isn't complete until they've danced on top of the pool table at this late-night hangout. There's a loud jukebox, a popular photo booth, and a late-night kitchen (it gets going around 8 pm and keeps serving until early in the morning). The tropical patio can actually be peaceful at times. You'll need a car or a taxi to get here. ✉ *4841 Tchoupitoulas St., Uptown* ☎ *504/895–6784.*

The Kingpin. Deep-red walls and a velvet Elvis lend this Uptown spot a touch of kitsch, but it's the friendly atmosphere, a jukebox stocked with vintage soul and modern rock, and a young, attractive crowd that draw people in nightly. Stop in on a Sunday during football season for barbecue and a chance to cheer on the beloved Saints. ✉ *1307 Lyons St., Uptown* ☎ *504/891–2373.*

St. Joe's. This popular nightspot is known for its religious-themed decor and its mixed drinks. The narrow front bar draws inspiration from Latin American churches; the back patio, strung with Chinese lanterns and decorated with statues of Asian deities, is a "Caribbean Zen temple," in the owner's words. Drinks are made with real juice, and the mojitos are especially popular. ✉ *5535 Magazine St., Uptown* ☎ *504/899–3744.*

MUSIC CLUBS

★ **Le Bon Temps Roulé.** Local acts from a wide range of genres—rock, jazz, blues, or funk—take the stage nightly at this lovably ramshackle Magazine Street nightspot. The music gets started after 10 pm; pool tables and a limited bar-food menu keep the crowd, which includes a lot of students from nearby Tulane and Loyola universities, entertained until then. ✉ *4801 Magazine St., Uptown* ☎ *504/897–3448.*

★ **Tipitina's.** A bust of legendary New Orleans pianist Professor Longhair, or "Fess," greets visitors at the door of this Uptown landmark, which takes its name from one of his most popular songs. As the concert posters pinned to the walls attest, Tip's hosts a wide variety of touring bands and local acts. The long-running Sunday-afternoon Cajun dance still packs the floor. The Tipitina's Foundation has an office and workshop upstairs, where local musicians affected by Hurricane Katrina can network, gain access to resources, and search for gigs. Although the neighborhood's not especially dangerous, it's probably most convenient to take a cab to this slightly out-of-the-way location. ✉ *501 Napoleon Ave., Uptown* ☎ *504/895–8477.*

MID-CITY AND BAYOU ST. JOHN

Spread out around City Park and Bayou St. John, this mostly residential area is almost like a small town: it's got neighborhood joints unknown to most tourists. From Finn McCool's, which might just be the best Irish pub in New Orleans, to Rock 'n Bowl, which is definitely the greatest bowling alley–meets–concert hall in the city, the area has lots to offer if you know where to look. Venues are spread out, so a car or taxi is recommended at night.

BAYOU ST. JOHN

BARS AND LOUNGES

Pal's. Tucked away in a quiet Bayou St. John neighborhood, this little gem is a surprisingly hip hangout with a carefully crafted, Rat Pack–era louche vibe, right down to the pinup girl wallpaper in the men's room. ✉ *949 N. Rendon St., Bayou St. John* ☎ *504/488–7257.*

MID-CITY

BARS AND LOUNGES

Bayou Beer Garden. The best feature here is the sprawling multilevel outdoor patio. Combine that with a great selection of beers, multiple screens for sports games, live bands on weekends, and warm Mid-City hospitality, and you've got a terrific stopover on any trip through the neighborhood. ✉ *326 N. Jefferson Davis Pkwy., Mid-City* ☎ *504/302–9357.*

10

Finn McCool's Irish Pub. Run by devoted soccer fans, this popular and expansive neighborhood bar beams in European games via live satellite feed for devout expats. Pool and darts tournaments are a regular feature as well, and a kitchen serves delicious fish-and-chips. On Monday night, there's a popular and competitive trivia quiz; prizes include sacks of potatoes, and if you happen to be in town for St. Patrick's Day, don't miss their rollicking day-long festival. ⊠ *3701 Banks St., Mid-City* ☎ *504/486–9080.*

Twelve Mile Limit. This neighborhood joint might be off the beaten path, but it's worth the trip for its unlikely combination of an innovative cocktail menu and . . . barbecue. Compared favorably to swanky wine and cocktail bars like Cure or Delachaise, Twelve Mile Limit offers a decidedly down-home vibe with its pulled pork and brisket, its run-down exterior (a contrast with the nicely done interior), and reasonable prices. On Monday the bar offers a free "family meal," such as spaghetti with or without meat sauce or barbecue chicken. ⊠ *500 Telemachus St., Mid-City* ☎ *504/488–8114.*

MUSIC CLUBS

Banks Street Bar and Grill. Over the past few years, this comfortable Mid-City nightspot has become one of the city's most reliable venues for local music, with live shows—sometimes two—every night of the week. The bill of fare tends to blues and funk. ⊠ *4401 Banks St., Mid-City* ☎ *504/486–0258.*

Chickie Wah Wah. Right on the Canal Street streetcar line, this neighborhood music club is unassuming from the outside but hosts some of the city's most popular acts on its well-respected stage. With happy hour and early evening music sets, a covered patio, a delicious menu of designer pub grub, and a clean, comfortable environment, this destination is a favorite among more low-key New Orleanians who want to step out for a good time but aren't into the late night crowds or hours. ⊠ *2828 Canal St., Mid-City* ☎ *504/304–4714.*

★ **Rock 'n' Bowl.** Down-home Louisiana music, rockabilly, R&B, New Orleans swing, and swamp pop in a bowling alley? Go ahead, try not to have fun. This iconic venue has a terrific lineup of music Tuesday through Saturday. Thursday is Zydeco Night, when some of the best musicians from rural Louisiana take the stage. ⊠ *3000 S. Carrollton Ave., Mid-City* ☎ *504/861–1700.*

11

Shopping

WORD OF MOUTH

"First stop: window shopping on Royal Street. I had forgotten how much I love dawdling along Royal and seeing the artworks in the windows. Love the antiques, too. Some of the old estate items are just incredible! You would not believe the corkscrews we saw in one shop . . . silver capped horn from the 1800's . . . Wow."

—otherfootloose

Updated
by Susan
Langenhennig

Shopping in New Orleans is like opening a treasure chest in which everything you want is at your fingertips, from rare antiques to novelty T-shirts, artwork, jewelry, and foods that represent the city's flavors and culture. Old-world influences intersect with modern trends, creating a singular shopping experience, and making it easy to find something for even the pickiest person on your souvenir list.

New Orleanians have a deep love and devotion for the Crescent City and the varied ethnic components that make up its unique cultural gumbo. For shoppers, this translates into merchandise that reflects that pride, including jewelry and clothing bearing city icons such as the fleur-de-lis—a French symbol associated with the city since its early days—Mardi Gras masks, tributes to its world-class food and culture, black-and-gold Saints symbols, and unique and often humorous statements about political issues and local personalities. Residents also strongly support local entrepreneurs, which means fewer big-name chains in favor of homegrown stores selling items and artwork produced in the city.

Make sure you take home some of the city's artwork, including the posters designed around New Orleans's special events such as Mardi Gras and Jazz Fest (which often become collector's items). In the city's thriving arts districts, you'll find contemporary works by local artists alongside renowned names in the art world. The special sounds of New Orleans—Dixieland and contemporary jazz, rhythm and blues, Cajun, zydeco, rap, hip-hop, and the city's unique bounce beat—are available in music stores like Louisiana Music Factory and Peaches Records and at live-music venues such as Preservation Hall, Snug Harbor, and House of Blues. Independent bookstores and major chains stock a plethora of local cookbooks, photography, history, and local literature and lore. Clothing stores focus on items that wear well in New Orleans's often-intense heat and humidity, with styles ranging from the latest runway fashions and high-end designer clothes to vintage frocks and styles by local designers.

Lake Pontchartrain

LAKESHORE

Robert E Lee Blvd

Leon C Simon Dr

Robert E Lee Blvd

Peoples Ave

LAKE VIEW

City Park

GENTILLY

Elysian Fields Ave

Genefly Blvd

Chef Menteur Hwy

10

Orleans Ave

Wisner Blvd

St Bernard Ave

610

ST BERNARD

Peoples Ave

NORTH BYWATER

City Park Ave

Esplanade Ave

90

St Claude Ave

61

N Carrollton Ave

Tulane Ave

N Broad St

SEVENTH WARD

39

MID-CITY AND BAYOU ST. JOHN
great wine and spirits stores supply liquid goods to enjoy in City Park or along Bayou St. John

FAUBOURG MARIGNY, BYWATER, AND TREMÉ
a historic New Orleans-meets-hipster aesthetic is reflected at stores in this haven for artists and musicians.

Palmetto St

Earhart Blvd

Fontainebleau Dr

S Claiborne Ave

10

Orleans Ave

90

FRENCH QUARTER
high-end art and antique retailers epitomize Old World opulence—it's window shopping at its finest

ALGIERS POINT

General Meyer Ave

428

S Broad St

S Claiborne Ave

CBD AND THE WAREHOUSE DISTRICT
a thriving arts district defines this urban chic part of town, chockablock with contemporary arts galleries

Pontchartrain Expy

428

UPTOWN AND CARROLTON-RIVERBEND
a quaint, small-town vibe permeates au courant boutiques and food shops

FRERET

GARDEN DISTRICT
trendy, funky stores and galleries beckon strollers, especially on Magazine Street, in this picturesque neighborhood

Tchoupitoulas St

GRETNA

Franklin Ave

90

Mississippi River

HARVEY

Barataria Blvd

River Rd

4th St

Destrehan Ave

Peters Rd

Westbank Expy

Belle Chasse Hwy

1 mi

1 km

WHAT'S WHERE

The main shopping areas in the city are the **French Quarter**, with narrow, picturesque streets lined with gift, fashion, home decor, and antiques shops and art galleries; the **Central Business District (CBD)**, populated mostly with specialty and department stores; the **Warehouse District**, best known for contemporary art galleries and cultural museums; **and Magazine Street**, the city's 6-mile boutique strip filled with trendy and designer clothing, accessories, locally made jewelry, and antiques shops, art galleries, and specialty stores. Magazine Street stretches from the **Garden District** to the Uptown area. Nearby, the **Carrollton-Riverbend** neighborhood is another hot spot for finding women's clothing, jewelry, antiques, art galleries, and bookstores. You also can find a few noteworthy galleries and shops in the **Tremé**, **Marigny**, and **Bywater** areas.

> ### PRIDE IN BLOOM
>
> The fleur-de-lis, historically an emblem of French royalty, has long been an icon of New Orleans. Since Hurricane Katrina, however, locals have fallen in love with it all over again, and artists have found creative and beautiful ways to use it to adorn a range of items including jewelry, T-shirts, artwork, candles, glassware, and even wrought-iron home decor. You can find many examples of the quintessential New Orleans symbol at stores all over the city.

FRENCH QUARTER

The shops that line the French Quarter's streets are filled with an array of clothing, jewelry, novelties, artwork, home decor, and antique furniture, mostly from the 17th to 20th centuries. Browsing through the picturesque storefronts in this compact area is as much a cultural experience as a shopping excursion. Royal Street, known for its antiques stores, is great for a stroll and some window-shopping. Along both Royal and Chartres streets, you'll find clusters of high-end fine-art galleries displaying traditional, contemporary, and New Orleans–centric works. Many stores sell traditional Carnival masks—great for a costume, to give as a gift, or use as decorative art—that range from simple feather and ceramic styles available for about $10 to handcrafted, locally made varieties that carry much heftier price tags. Jewelry stores feature curated selections of estate and antique jewelry alongside new creations in a variety of styles. Souvenir shops are around every corner, especially as you approach the heavily trafficked areas near the river. If your energy lags, plenty of cafés, coffee shops, candy stores, and bistros will provide a boost.

SHOPPING CENTERS AND MARKETS

French Market. Vendors have been selling their wares on this spot since 1791, making it one of the oldest public marketplaces in the country. Today, the market includes a large flea market, small produce stands, and retail shops. For the daily flea market, dozens of vendors set up tables inside and outside the covered pavilion, selling jewelry, handbags, T-shirts, and curios as well as vintage and used items, clothing, and collectibles. The market generally is open daily from about 7 to

Antiques shops are one of New Orleans's specialties.

7, but hours can vary depending on the weather. ⊠ *1200 block of N. Peters St., French Quarter* ☎ *504/522–2621* ⊕ *www.frenchmarket.org.*

Jax Brewery. A historic building that once was a factory for Jax beer now holds an upscale mall filled with local shops and a few national chain stores, such as Chico's, along with a food court and balcony overlooking the Mississippi River. Shops carry souvenirs, clothing, books, and more, with an emphasis on New Orleans–themed items. The mall is open daily, and during summer days serves as an air-conditioned refuge. ⊠ *600 Decatur St., French Quarter* ☎ *504/566–7245* ⊕ *www. jacksonbrewery.com.*

ANTIQUES AND COLLECTIBLES

Brass Monkey. A small but charming shop, Brass Monkey's specialty is Limoges boxes ranging from small red beans—a favorite food in New Orleans—to baby carriages. It also has antique walking sticks, Venetian glass, and English Staffordshire porcelain. ⊠ *407 Royal St., French Quarter* ☎ *504/561–0688.*

French Antique Shop. One of the largest collections of European crystal and bronze chandeliers in the country glitters over gilded mirrors, authentic 18th- and 19th-century hand-carved and marble mantels, French and Continental furniture, porcelain, and objets d'art in this shop, which originally opened in 1947 and is run by a second generation of the founding family. ⊠ *225 Royal St., French Quarter* ☎ *504/524–9861* ⊕ *www.gofrenchantiques.com.*

Greg's Antiques. This giant, 8,000-square-foot retail wonderland is filled with interesting antiques, lighting fixtures, salvaged items, and art. The antiques come from England, France, and Belgium, and are high quality

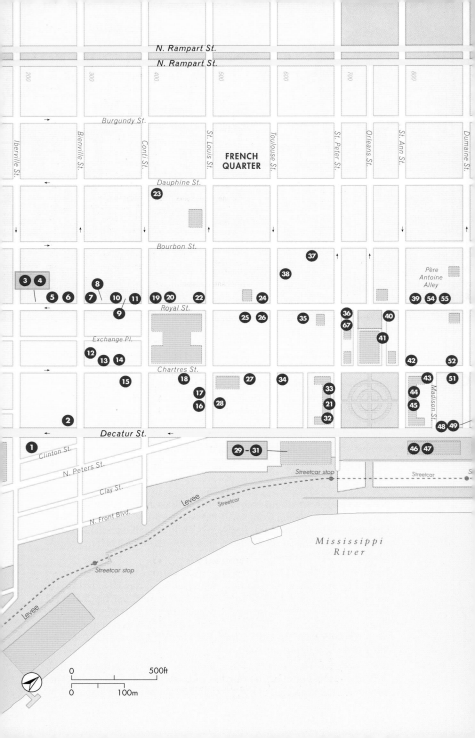

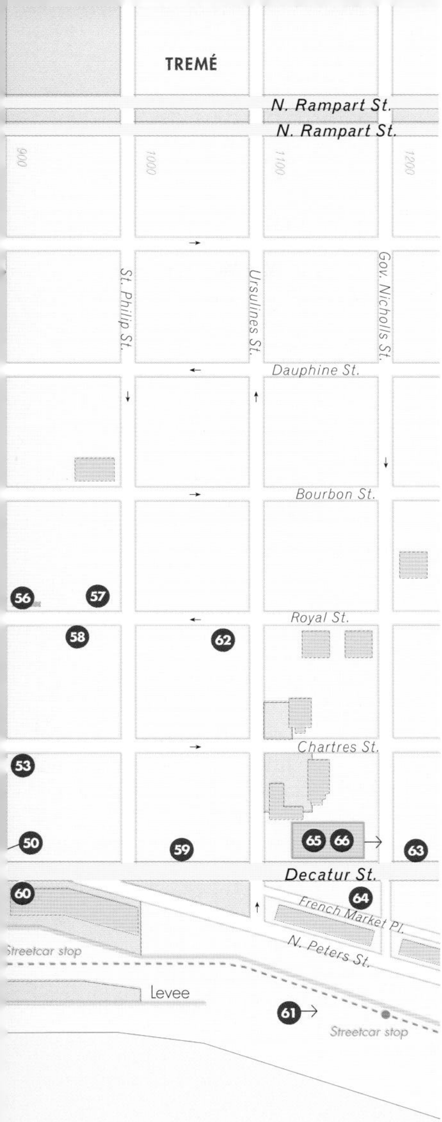
TREMÉ
N. Rampart St.
N. Rampart St.
900
1000
1100
1200
St. Philip St.
Ursulines St.
Gov. Nicholls St.
Dauphine St.
Bourbon St.
Royal St.
Chartres St.
Decatur St.
French Market Pl.
N. Peters St.
Streetcar stop
Levee
Streetcar stop
56
57
58
62
53
50
59
65
66
63
60
64
61

French Quarter Shopping

but affordable. The store's selection of salvaged elements, mostly from old New Orleans houses, and art from emerging local artists allows shoppers to take home a unique part of the city. ✉ *1209 Decatur St., French Quarter* ☎ *504/202–8577* ⊕ *www.gregsantiques.net.*

Harris of Royal. Locals as well as visitors are drawn to this shop for its two floors of 19th-century paintings, 18th- and 19th-century French and English furniture, trumeau mirrors, estate jewelry, bronze sculptures, and chandeliers. ✉ *233 Royal St., French Quarter* ☎ *504/523–1605* ⊕ *www.harrisantiques.com.*

James H. Cohen & Sons Inc. Pick up a piece of history in this shop, opened in 1898, which sells many one-of-a-kind antique firearms, swords, and currency, including coins from as early as 319 BC. There also are obsolete bank notes, jewelry made from rare coins, and collectibles such as antique telescopes and opera glasses. ✉ *437 Royal St., French Quarter* ☎ *504/522–3305 or 800/535–1853* ⊕ *www.cohenantiques.com.*

Keil's Antiques. Leave yourself plenty of time to browse through the three floors of 18th- and 19th-century furniture, chandeliers, estate jewelry, art, statuary, and other furnishings at this business, run by the fourth generation of the family that started it in 1899. It's a favorite stop for interior designers looking for the perfect pieces for their clients. ✉ *325 Royal St., French Quarter* ☎ *504/522–4552* ⊕ *www.keilsantiques.com.*

Fodor'sChoice
★
Lucullus. The entire store is focused on the art of food—preparing it, serving it, and eating it—and is filled with French tables, English china, cooking and serving utensils, linens, lighting, food-related art, snuff boxes, and more, including oddities like Lady Sarah Churchill's picnic set. Items are mainly from the 18th and 19th centuries. The shop is owned by Patrick Dunne, author of *Epicurean Collector.* ✉ *610 Chartres St., French Quarter* ☎ *504/528–9620* ⊕ *www.lucullusantiques.com.*

Fodor'sChoice
★
M.S. Rau. Historically significant items, such as furniture and other pieces from royal families, are spotlighted among 18th- and 19th-century French, American, and English furniture, sterling silver, cut glass, statuary, and jewelry in this 30,000-square-foot store, which opened in 1912. ✉ *630 Royal St., French Quarter* ☎ *504/523–5660 or 866/349–0705* ⊕ *www.rauantiques.com.*

Moss Antiques. Specialties include French and English antiques from the early 19th century, including period jewelry, wooden boxes, furniture with inlaid woods, porcelain oyster plates, sculpture, objets d'art, walking sticks, and silver services. ✉ *411 Royal St., French Quarter* ☎ *504/522–3981* ⊕ *www.mossantiques.com* ☾ *Closed Sun.*

DO YOU VOODOO?

Voodoo souvenirs are available all over the French Quarter, including voodoo dolls with pins, special hex or prayer candles, and gris-gris bags. Pick yours with care. Gris-gris bags, for example, are not created equal; they are prepared according to your needs—attracting love, bringing luck or ending bad luck, or protection from the evil eye. They are prepared with an even number of items, and you have to add something personal of your own. Follow the instructions that come with the bag for best results.

Oh Susannah. Many shops in the French Quarter carry collectible dolls, but this one has one of the largest and highest-quality selections. The store also sells children's clothing and accessories. ✉ *518 St. Peter St., French Quarter* ☎ *504/586–8701.*

Royal Antiques. French, English, and Continental antique furniture as well as Biedermeier pieces can be found in this 113-year-old shop, alongside chandeliers, sconces, trumeau mirrors, accessories, and estate jewelry. ✉ *309 Royal St., French Quarter* ☎ *504/524–7033* ⊕ *www.royalantiques.com.*

SHOPPING TOUR

If you want a personal guide, local art-and-antiques shopping consultant **Macon Riddle** (☎ *504/899–3027* ⊕ *www. neworleansantiquing.com*) conducts half- and full-day personalized shopping expeditions by appointment. She can sometimes gain access to antiques warehouses that are not normally open to the public.

Sword and Pen. This store stocks beautifully crafted and hand-painted miniature armies, from sword- and spear-wielding ancient Roman and Greek soldiers to World War II troopers. It also has a selection of war memorabilia, including Civil War hats and uniform insignia from a variety of conflicts. ✉ *528 Royal St., French Quarter* ☎ *504/523–7741* ⊕ *www.swordandpenorleans.com.*

Vintage 329. An essential stop for memorabilia collectors, the store carries items autographed by celebrities, including a framed photo signed by Gene Autry, a music sheet autographed by Fred Astaire and Ginger Rogers, a guitar signed by the Allman Brothers band, posters from performances, first-edition signed books, and more. New items arrive every week. ✉ *329 Royal St., French Quarter* ☎ *504/525–2262* ⊕ *www. vintage329.com.*

Waldhorn & Adler. Founded in 1881, one of the city's oldest antiques stores specializes in French, Italian, and English furniture from the 18th, 19th, and early 20th centuries, but also has new and estate jewelry. ✉ *343 Royal St., French Quarter* ☎ *504/581–6379* ⊕ *www. waldhornadlers.com* ⊙ *Closed Mon.*

Whisnant Galleries. Antique weapons and armor are the real eye-catchers here and range from the Gothic to art deco periods, but the shop also carries a large selection of antique gilded furniture, lighting, and mirrors; paintings from the 18th, 19th, and 20th centuries; African and ethnic art and jewelry; religious items; objets d'art; and statuary. ✉ *229 Royal St., French Quarter* ☎ *504/524–9766* ⊕ *www.whisnantgalleries.com.*

ART GALLERIES

Fodor's Choice ★

A Gallery for Fine Photography. The rare books and photographs here include works from emerging local artists like Josephine Sacabo and Jerry N. Uelsmann; luminaries such as E.J. Bellocq, Ansel Adams, and Henri Cartier-Bresson; and more-contemporary giants, including Annie Leibovitz, Walker Evans, Helmut Newton, and local Herman Leonard. ✉ *241 Chartres St., French Quarter* ☎ *504/568–1313* ⊕ *www.agallery.com.*

Angela King Gallery. Gallery owner Angela King renovated an 1850s jewelry store into a modern gallery that exhibits oil paintings, prints,

MARDI GRAS SHOPPING BLITZ

New Orleans during Mardi Gras may seem chaotic, but it's actually very organized. To orient yourself, attend a few evening parades before you jump into the all-day celebration on Fat Tuesday, and you'll soon find you can catch beads and other coveted throws like a pro. The best way to experience the joys of Carnival is to go in costume. To find the perfect getup, start at the top with a custom-made wig from Fifi Mahony's on Royal Street in the French Quarter. Feel free to turn to the store's expert staff for all manner of costume advice, from how to properly apply glitter eye shadow and how to ensure your false eyelashes stay put to how to replicate Lady Gaga's platinum bow-tied hairdo. For the rest of your outfit, stroll down to the French Market, where you can find cheap sunglasses, feather boas, and all sorts of other accessories, or continue to the **Artist's Market**, where you'll find an assortment of masks you'll want to keep long after Mardi Gras has faded into Lent. For a one-stop costume experience, travel to Magazine Street and **Funky Monkey**, where you can find handmade costumes, stockings, wigs, and accessories in one place, or the **Encore Shop**, where you can choose from affordable ball gowns, suits, and more. The important thing to remember about Mardi Gras is that it is meant to be fun for all ages. So dress the part, enjoy the sardonic humor of Carnival krewes' floats, and have a ball.

and metal and cast-glass sculptures from about 25 contemporary artists including Marlene Rose, Peter Max, Andy Baird, Terri Hallman, and Frederick Hart. ✉ *241 Royal St., French Quarter* ☎ *504/524–8211* ⊕ *www.angelakinggallery.com.*

Artist's Market. This co-op of regional artists showcases a wide variety of works, including handmade masks, photography focusing on New Orleans personalities and scenes, ceramics, blown-glass, paintings, wrought-iron architectural accents, turned-wood bowls and vases, prints, jewelry, beads, and more. ✉ *1228 Decatur St., French Quarter* ☎ *504/561–0046* ⊕ *www.artistsmarketnola.com.*

Elliott Gallery. Pioneers of modern and contemporary art are represented, including a large selection of prints and paintings by Theo Tobiasse, Max Papart, Nissan Engel, James Coignard, Garrick Yrondi, David Schneuer, Petra Seipel, Marc Chagall, Picasso and others. ✉ *540 Royal St., French Quarter* ☎ *504/523–3554* ⊕ *www.elliottgallery.com.*

Great Artists' Collective. More than 50 regional artists display their works in this double-shotgun house in the middle of the French Quarter. You'll find paintings, metalwork mirrors, a vast array of earrings, blown glass, ceramics, wood sculptures, handmade clothing, hats, ironwork, masks, vignettes in oyster shells, and more. ✉ *815 Royal St., French Quarter* ☎ *504/525–8190* ⊕ *www.greatartistscollective.com.*

Harouni Gallery. David Harouni, a favored artist among locals and businesses who decorate their walls with fine art, displays his take on neo-Expressionism in his paintings of faces, figures, and streetscapes, created in this gallery-studio space. He also sells silk screens. ✉ *933 Royal St.,*

French Quarter ☎ *504/299–4393* ⊕ *www.harouni.com.*

Kurt E. Schon, Ltd. In the hushed atmosphere of an art museum, and with a well-educated staff, this gallery showcases high-end European paintings from the 18th and 19th centuries. A sister gallery at 520 Royal Street displays contemporary art. ✉ *510 St. Louis St., French Quarter* ☎ *504/524–5462* ⊕ *www. kurteschonltd.com* ☉ *Closed Sun.*

La Belle Galerie & the Black Art Collection. Global themes from Russian art to African-American experiences in music, history, contemporary life, and culture are portrayed through limited-edition graphics, photographs, posters, paintings, furniture, ceramics, textiles, and sculpture. ✉ *309 Chartres St., French Quarter* ☎ *504/529–5538.*

Michalopoulos. Local artist James Michalopoulos showcases his abstract visions of New Orleans's architecture, street scenes, and personalities in oil paintings, lithographs, prints, posters, and serigraphs. ✉ *617 Bienville St., French Quarter* ☎ *504/558–0505* ⊕ *www.michalopoulos.com.*

★ **Rodrigue Studios.** One of Louisiana's most successful artists, George Rodrigue is best known for his series featuring the Blue Dog, which has become a local icon. But it's the images of his Cajun ancestors in stylized Acadiana settings that get the most praise from art critics. His work is available in original paintings and signed and numbered silk-screen prints. He also sells sculpture and jewelry. ✉ *730 Royal St., French Quarter* ☎ *504/581–4244* ⊕ *www.georgerodrigue.com.*

BOOKS

Dauphine Street Books. Stocking both new and used books, this store specializes in local history, the arts, modern fiction, and out-of-print titles. Bibliophiles will delight in its selection of antique books and rare titles. ✉ *410 Dauphine St., French Quarter* ☎ *504/529–2333* ☉ *Closed Wed.*

Faulkner House Books. Named for William Faulkner, who rented a room here in 1925, this bookstore is designated a National Literary Landmark. It specializes in first editions, rare and out-of-print books, mostly by Southern authors, but also carries new titles. The store, which keeps thousands of additional books at an off-site warehouse, hosts an annual Words & Music Festival that salutes Faulkner and new Southern writers and musicians. ✉ *624 Pirate's Alley, French Quarter* ☎ *504/524–2940* ⊕ *www.faulknerhouse.net.*

★ **Librairie Book Shop.** Set up like a library with well-stocked shelves of old, new, and hard-to-find volumes, this spot carries one of the Quarter's largest selections of books, posters, and postcards of local lore. ✉ *823 Chartres St., French Quarter* ☎ *504/525–4837.*

CLOTHING

Cajun Clothing Co. A smaller version of the locally owned Perlis boutique on Magazine Street, this shop carries clothing for men, women, and children, with a focus on polo shirts, boxers, and ties with crawfish logos, as well as everything from Hawaiian shirts to boxers printed with images of Tabasco products. ⊠ *Jax Brewery, 600 Decatur St., Suite 104, French Quarter* ☎ *504/523–6681* ⊕ *www.perlis.com.*

Fodor's Choice ★ **Trashy Diva Boutique.** Boutique owner-designer Candice Gwinn puts a retro-romantic spin on the women's fashions she creates. Inspired by styles from the 1920s to the 1950s, she makes dresses, blouses, skirts, coats, jewelry, and upscale shoes with vintage flair but modern fit. The Trashy Diva Lingerie Boutique next door (831 Chartres Street) features corsets and romantic evening wear. ⊠ *829 Chartres St., French Quarter* ☎ *504/581–4555* ⊕ *www.trashydiva.com.*

★ **United Apparel Liquidators.** Label-loving locals as well as celebrities in town shooting movies are known to shop this 30-year-old designer clothing liquidator. The tiny boutique is busting with deeply discounted apparel, shoes, and accessories by major designers, such as Marni, Balenciaga, Michael Kors, Phillip Lim, and Prada. Contemporary lines, such as Serfontaine Denim, Steven Alan, Yigal Azrouel, and Alexander Wang also fill the racks. The stylish, friendly, and eminently helpful sales staff has created a loyal cult of frequent shoppers, and many of them visit the store several times a week. ⊠ *518 Chartres St., French Quarter* ☎ *504/301–4437.*

Violet's. Girly girls rule at this boutique, which caters to the softer side of feminine dresses, skirts, sexy blouses, handbags, jewelry, and accessories, with styles ranging from contemporary to retro romantic. ⊠ *808 Chartres St., French Quarter* ☎ *504/569–0088.*

The Voluptuous Vixen. This contemporary women's boutique, just a short stroll from Jackson Square, is a must-visit destination for stylish women with curves. Owner Jaclyn McCabe sources hip, trendy apparel, undergarments, and accessories designed to fit and flatter fuller figures sizes 12 and up. Word about the boutique has gotten out, and Hollywood stylists (including the one working with Oscar-nominated actress Gabourey Sidibe) have come calling when they need a dress that rocks a woman's shape even when it's not stick straight. ⊠ *818 Chartres St., French Quarter* ☎ *504/529–3588* ⊕ *www.thevoluptuousvixen.com.*

FOOD

Aunt Sally's Praline Shop. Satisfy your sweet tooth with an array of pralines made while you watch. The traditional version is concocted from cane sugar spiked with pecans, but newer treatments include chocolate and other ingredients. You also can buy prepackaged tomato gravy, muffuletta mix, Bourbon Street glaze, and Italian salad dressing, as well as art and books about New Orleans, zydeco CDs, and logo cups and aprons. ⊠ *French Market, 810 Decatur St., French Quarter* ☎ *504/524–3373 or 800/642–7257* ⊕ *www.auntsallys.com.*

Café du Monde. This open-air café and New Orleans landmark serves café au lait (half coffee, half hot milk) and beignets (holeless doughnuts sprinkled liberally with powdered sugar). Take-home products from

GLUTTONY TO GO

There are lots of treats to sample while you're in the Big Easy—but you don't have to eat them all while you're here, since many of the city's famous tastes come in easy-to-pack (or ship) forms. In the French Quarter, you can pick up classic pralines at **Aunt Sally's Praline Shop** or **Laura's Candies,** which also sell other to-go items. Don't forget beignet mix and chicory coffee to re-create breakfast at **Café du Monde.** In the Warehouse District, **Riverwalk Marketplace** has candy shops that will make fudge and pralines while you watch, then package them for you to take home. Stores like the **New Orleans School of Cooking and Louisiana General Store** not only provide the ingredients you need to create local dishes in your own kitchen, they'll even give you cooking classes to help you do it right. All the city's bookstores and many gift shops are stocked with a variety of cookbooks by local chefs and tomes about the area's foods. In the Garden District, Sucré sells artisanal chocolates featuring New Orleans flavors such as Bananas Foster and Coffee and Chicory.

the café include prepackaged chicory coffee and beignet mix, coffee mugs, prints, and posters depicting the spot. The café's store across the street also sells logo T-shirts, aprons, and other souvenirs. ⊠ *800 Decatur St., French Quarter* ☎ *504/525–4544 or 800/772–2927* ⊕ *www.cafedumonde.com.*

Evans Creole Candy Factory. The smell of candy being made on-site will draw you in to this shop, established in 1900. You'll find a variety of pralines, pecan logs, and New Orleans's own Cuccia Chocolates, as well as coffee and gift baskets. ⊠ *848 Decatur St., French Quarter* ☎ *504/522–7111 or 800/637–6675* ⊕ *www.evanscreolecandy.com.*

Laura's Candies. In the candy-making business since 1913, this shop sells sweet pralines as well as chocolate specialties—including its signature Mississippi mud, made with milk or dark chocolate laced with caramel. ⊠ *331 Chartres St., French Quarter* ☎ *504/525–3880 or 800/992–9699* ⊕ *www.laurascandies.com.*

New Orleans School of Cooking and Louisiana General Store. Learn how to make a roux and other Louisiana cooking techniques at this school located in a renovated 1800s molasses warehouse. Lessons are spiced with history and tales about the state's famous cuisine. The store also stocks all kinds of regional spices, condiments, sauces, snacks, gift baskets, and cookbooks. ⊠ *524 St. Louis St., French Quarter* ☎ *504/525–2665 or 800/237–4841* ⊕ *www.neworleansschoolofcooking.com.*

Tabasco Country Store. Named for the famous Louisiana-produced hot sauce, this store also offers spices, cookbooks, New Orleans– and cooking-themed clothing and aprons, kitchen accoutrements, ties, posters, pewter items, and more. ⊠ *537 St. Ann St., French Quarter* ☎ *504/539–7900* ⊕ *countrystore.tabasco.com.*

JEWELRY AND ACCESSORIES

Currents Fine Jewelry. Owners Terry and Sylvia Weidert create a variety of chic, art deco–inspired designs in 14- and 18-karat gold and platinum. ✉ *627 Royal St., French Quarter* ☎ *504/522–6099* ☼ *Closed Sun.*

Dashka Roth Contemporary Jewelry and Judaica. The handmade, contemporary jewelry on display is created by designer Dashka Roth and 80 other American artists. Necklaces, rings, and bracelets can be found downstairs; the second-floor features contemporary Judaica, including kiddush cups, mezuzahs, menorahs, and dreidels. The store is closed for all Jewish holidays. ✉ *332 Chartres St., French Quarter* ☎ *504/523–0805 or 877/327–4523* ⊕ *www.dashkaroth.com.*

Fifi Mahony's. Anyone with a passion for playing dress up and a flair for the dramatic will love this place, filled with custom wigs, wild accessories, makeup, and hair products. The shop provides essential resources for Mardi Gras and Halloween costume accoutrement as well as ample creative advice. ✉ *934 Royal St., French Quarter* ☎ *504/525–4343* ⊕ *www.fifimahonys.com.*

Quarter Smith. Gemologist and gold- and silversmith Ken Bowers designs contemporary jewelry in gold, silver, and platinum and carries a selection of antique pieces. ✉ *535 St. Louis St., French Quarter* ☎ *504/524–9731* ⊕ *www.quartersmith.com* ☼ *Closed Sat.–Mon.*

Sterling Silvia. Silvia and Juan Asturias operate this business near the French Market, where Silvia's fleur-de-lis and flower-inspired jewelry designs share space with other silver jewelry from Chile, Mexico, Indonesia, Russia, Thailand, and elsewhere. There's also jewelry made from coral beads, gift items, ceramic dolls, and more. ✉ *41 French Market Pl., French Quarter* ☎ *504/299–9225 or 504/299–9229* ⊕ *www.sterlingsilvia.com.*

MASKS

Mask Gallery. One of the treats of visiting this shop is watching the artist Dalili fabricate his intricate but wearable masks out of leather at a workstation in the front of the store. There also are masks made by other local artists, as well as Venetian and feather versions, pewter sculptures, jewelry, and figurines. ✉ *636 Royal St., French Quarter* ☎ *504/523–6664 or 888/278–6672* ⊕ *www.neworleansmask.com.*

Serendipitous Masks. With masks mingled with elaborately dressed dolls, the layout of this shop evokes the playroom of royalty. The masks are made by local artists using exotic feathers, jewels, ceramics, and leather. ✉ *831 Decatur St., French Quarter* ☎ *504/522–9158* ☼ *Closed Tues. and Wed.*

Yesteryear's. Elaborate feather masks made by owner Teresa Latshaw and other artists comprise most of the inventory, but voodoo dolls and

---

HEALTHY JAVA

Local coffee brands like Community, French Market, Luzianne, and Café Du Monde add up to 30% chicory to the coffee they sell. Chicory is caffeine-free and reportedly healthful for your liver, helps control blood sugar and reduce cholesterol, and boosts bone-mineral density.

folklore objects are also available. ⊠ *626 Bourbon St., French Quarter* ☏ *504/523–6603.*

MUSIC

Louisiana Music Factory. A favorite resource for New Orleans and regional music—new and old—this retail store has records, tapes, CDs, DVDs, sheet music, and books as well as listening stations, music-oriented T-shirts, original art of musicians, and a stage that hosts frequent live concerts. ⊠ *210 Decatur St., French Quarter* ☏ *504/586–1094* ⊕ *www.louisianamusicfactory.com.*

Peaches Records. This locally owned music shop specializes in vinyl records as well as CDs, with a focus on New Orleans rap, hip-hop, and bounce. But you'll also find jazz, gospel, classic soul, and a few music accessories. Live shows are sometimes presented in a café at the front of the store. ⊠ *408 N. Peters St., French Quarter* ☏ *504/282–3322* ⊕ *peachesrecordsneworleans.com.*

NOVELTIES AND GIFTS

Erzulie's Authentic Voudou. If the food, music, and architecture of New Orleans hasn't cast its spell on you, then step inside this voodoo shop. Altars display good-luck charms and other ritual items, as well as spell kits, elixirs and potions, body-care products, voodoo dolls, gris-gris bags, and gift items. Tarot readings also are available. ⊠ *807 Royal St., French Quarter* ☏ *504/525–2055 or 866/286–8368* ⊕ *www.erzulies. com* ☉ *Closed Tues. and Wed.*

Esoterica Occult Goods. Calling itself "the one-stop shop for all your occult needs," this store is a place to pick up potions, gris-gris goods, jewelry, spell kits, incense, altar and ritual items, as well as books on magic and the occult arts. Tarot reading and astrological consultations are available by appointment. ⊠ *541 Dumaine St., French Quarter* ☏ *504/581–7711* ⊕ *www.onewitch.com.*

Forever New Orleans. It's all about the Crescent City in this small shop filled with New Orleans–themed items, including glassware adorned with pewter fleur-de-lis, affordable jewelry that boasts local icons, stationery, tiles, clocks, ceramics, framed crosses, charms, bottle stoppers, frames, candles, cookbooks, and more. This is a place to pick up upscale souvenirs and gifts. ⊠ *700 Royal St., French Quarter* ☏ *504/586–3536.*

Idea Factory. Wood becomes art at the hands of craftspeople who carve functional clocks, clipboards, and jewelry boxes as well as more whimsical whirligigs, hand-carved board games, puzzles, kaleidoscopes, and toys, proving that not all playthings need to be plugged in. ⊠ *838 Chartres St., French Quarter* ☏ *504/524–5195* ⊕ *www. ideafactoryneworleans.com.*

A RELAXING SCENT

Take home the scents of New Orleans with soaps, room sprays, candles, and perfumes in sweet olive or vetiver. The latter was a staple in proper Creole households, where it was used to keep moths away from fabrics and add a pleasant scent to bed linens and clothing stored in armoires. Oil extracted from the roots of the grassy plant is popular among aromatherapy enthusiasts, who claim the scent relieves stress and increases energy.

Nadine Blake. Quirky gifts, gorgeous design books, handmade note cards, vintage furniture, and a slew of cool whatnots fill this small boutique run by one of friendliest shopkeepers in the French Quarter. New Orleans native Nadine Blake worked in interior design in New York before moving home to the Crescent City and setting up shop. Her delightful store reflects her varied travels and eclectic interests. ⊠ *1036 Royal St., French Quarter* ☎ *504/529–4913* ⊕ *www.nadineblake.com.*

Rendezvous Inc. A throwback to the days of Southern belles, this shop on Jackson Square has linens and lace ranging from christening outfits for babies to table runners, napkins, women's handkerchiefs, and more. It also offers a charming array of antiques and reproductions such as perfume bottles, tea sets, fleur-de-lis, and crosses. ⊠ *522 St. Peters St., French Quarter* ☎ *504/522–0225.*

Santa's Quarters. It's Christmas year-round at this shop, which displays a diverse range of traditional and novelty ornaments and decorations, Santa Clauses of all kinds, and a host of Louisiana-themed holiday items. ⊠ *1027 Decatur St., French Quarter* ☎ *504/581–5820 or 888/599–9693* ⊕ *www.santasquarters.com.*

What's New. Everything in this store carries a New Orleans theme, making it a great place to buy souvenirs people will actually want to keep and use, including fleur-de-lis–clad flasks, decorative pillows, nightlights with shades made from photographs of city scenes, glassware, ceramics, jewelry, and other works by local artists. ⊠ *French Market, 824 Decatur St., French Quarter* ☎ *504/586–2095* ⊕ *www.whatsnew-nola.com.*

SPA AND BEAUTY

Bourbon French Parfums. Opened in 1843, this old-world-style shop offers about three dozen fragrances for men and women, including a 200-year-old formula for men's cologne. It will custom blend perfumes for individuals based on assessments of body chemistry, personality, and scent preferences. The shop also sells perfume bottles and toiletries. ⊠ *805 Royal St., French Quarter* ☎ *504/522–4480 or 800/476–0303* ⊕ *www. neworleansperfume.com.*

★ **Hové Parfumeur, Ltd.** A must-visit for perfume lovers, this store has been blending fragrances since 1931. Scented oils, soaps, sachets, and potpourri have been made to order on-site for three generations and are sold all over the world. There are 52 fragrances for men and women, as well as bath salts, anti-aging treatments, massage and body oils, antique shaving and dressing-table accessories, new and antique perfume bottles, and bed and bath items. ⊠ *434 Chartres St., French Quarter* ☎ *504/525–7827* ⊕ *www.hoveparfumeur.com.*

TOYS

☾ **Kite Shop.** The ceiling is thick with hanging wind socks. Kites of all designs, including an assortment of stunt kites, line one wall; another is stocked with hand and finger puppets, marionettes, flying toys, and other fanciful playthings. ⊠ *542 St. Peter St., French Quarter* ☎ *504/524–0028* ⊕ *www.kiteshopneworleans.com.*

☾ **Little Toy Shop.** There's a mix of New Orleans souvenirs, miniature die-cast metal cars from the Model T to the Hummer, character lunch boxes, puppets, plastic animals, costume hats, and collectible Madame

Alexander dolls in a dozen different costumes at this 50-year-old business. ⊠ *900 Decatur St., French Quarter* ☎ *504/522–6588.*

FAUBOURG MARIGNY AND BYWATER

Stores in these neighborhoods reflect the area's bohemian spirit by selling relatively affordable, unique, and locally made products. The shops on or around Frenchmen Street are easily walkable, but it may be wise to bring a map or knowledgeable local along while exploring the Bywater, where stores and other businesses are sparser. There are plenty of cafés and restaurants in the area to refuel during shopping trips.

ANTIQUES AND COLLECTIBLES

The Junque Shop. An eclectic selection of furniture, jewelry, and collectibles fill this delightful store, where you'll find solid wood antiques, glassware, lighting, and small knickknacks. For things a little too big for your suitcase, the friendly staff will ship. ⊠ *421 Frenchmen St., Faubourg Marigny* ☎ *504/952–5651* ⊕ *www.thejunqueshop.com.*

BOOKS

Beth's Books. A favorite place for Bywater residents to grab a good read and a cup of joe, this cozy bookstore, attached to the Sound Cafe coffeehouse, emphasizes local authors, artists, and works about New Orleans. You'll find new and used books as well as magazines and stationery. ⊠ *2700 Chartres St., Bywater* ☎ *504/947–4477* ⊙ *Closed Mon. and Tues.*

CBD AND WAREHOUSE DISTRICT

This area between the French Quarter and the Magazine Street shopping district is filled with boutique hotels, locally owned and national chain stores, and (in the Warehouse District) museums and art galleries displaying a variety of artwork and crafts from local, regional, and nationally known artists. Julia Street in particular is a cornucopia of small art galleries, many of them artist-owned.

The *Times-Picayune,* the local daily newspaper, and the *Gambit,* the weekly newspaper, publish listings that detail openings of new exhibits, which generally are accompanied by wine, hors d'oeuvres, and sometimes music. Because many of the galleries are artist owned and operated, hours and days of operation can vary. It's best to call and confirm gallery hours; many owners are also happy to set up special appointments for you to view their art.

SHOPPING CENTERS AND MARKETS

Canal Place. This high-end shopping center focuses on national chains, including Saks Fifth Avenue, Michael Kors, Anthropologie, Banana Republic, Coach, J.Crew, and BCBG Max Azria. But the mall also includes quality local shops, such as the artists co-op RHINO (which stands for Right Here in New Orleans), Jean Therapy denim boutique, Wehmeier's Belt Shop, and Saint Germain shoes. A highlight is the Mignon Faget jewelry store, which carries the local designer's full line of upscale, Louisiana-inspired creations. ⊠ *333 Canal St., CBD* ☎ *504/522–9200* ⊕ *www.theshopsatcanalplace.com.*

Riverwalk Marketplace. Built in what was once the International Pavilion for the 1984 World's Fair, the Riverwalk Marketplace offers a few national chain stores, such as the Gap, Chico's, and Ann Taylor Loft, as well as shops filled with souvenirs, jewelry, shoes, and merchandise with local themes. There's a food court, a Café du Monde, and a balcony overlooking the Mississippi River that provides a picturesque place to take a break from shopping. Appropriately placed next to the food court is the Southern Food and Beverage Museum, which explores the food and culture of local cuisine. Outside the mall is Spanish Plaza, the scene of frequent outdoor concerts and special events. ⊠ *1 Poydras St., Warehouse District* ☎ *504/522–1555* ⊕ *www.riverwalkmarketplace.com.*

ART GALLERIES

Ariodante. Mostly local and Gulf Coast artists are represented in this gallery, which has custom-made cases displaying high-end and reasonably priced contemporary crafts and fine art, including jewelry, blown glass, sculpture, furniture, photography, paintings, ceramics, and decorative accessories. ⊠ *535 Julia St., Warehouse District* ☎ *504/524–3233* ⊕ *www.ariodantegallery.com* ☉ *Closed Sun.*

Fodor's Choice
★

Arthur Roger Gallery. One of the most respected local names among art aficionados, Arthur Roger has compiled a must-see collection of local contemporary artwork by Lin Emery, Jacqueline Bishop, and Willie Birch, as well as national names such as glass artist Dale Chihuly and filmmaker-photographer John Waters. ⊠ *432–434 Julia St., Warehouse District* ☎ *504/522–1999* ⊕ *www.arthurrogergallery.com.*

★ **Callan Contemporary.** This sleek gallery specializes in modern sculpture and paintings from both local and internationally renowned artists, including Pablo Atchugarry, Eva Hild, Raine Bedsole, Keysook Geum, Adrian Deckbar, and Sibylle Peretti. ⊠ *518 Julia St., Warehouse District* ☎ *504/525–0518* ⊕ *www.callancontemporary.com* ☉ *Closed Sun. and Mon.*

George Schmidt Gallery. History, particularly New Orleans's rich past, is the passion of artist George Schmidt. His gallery displays and sells paintings and narrative art, from small-scale monotypes to mural-size depictions of historic moments. He also sells signed and numbered prints of his work. ⊠ *626 Julia St., Warehouse District* ☎ *504/592–0206 or 504/524–8137* ⊕ *www.georgeschmidt.com* ☉ *Closed Sun. and Mon.*

Heriard-Cimino Gallery. The front gallery holds a changing solo exhibit, and a second gallery displays abstract and figurative paintings, sculptures, drawings, photos, and prints from contemporary artists—most based in New York, Miami, and Louisiana. ⊠ *440 Julia St., Warehouse District* ☎ *504/525–7300* ⊕ *www.heriardcimino.com* ☉ *Closed Sun. and Mon.*

Jean Bragg Gallery of Southern Art. Aficionados call it one of the city's best sources for collectible pottery from Newcomb and George Ohr, but the gallery also carries 19th- and 20th-century Louisiana paintings. Contemporary artist exhibits are presented each month. ⊠ *600 Julia St., Warehouse District* ☎ *504/895–7375* ⊕ *www.jeanbragg.com* ☉ *Closed Sun.*

Jonathan Ferrara Gallery. Cutting-edge art with a message is standard at this gallery's monthly exhibits. Contemporary paintings, photography, mixed-media artworks, sculpture, glass and metalwork by local and international artists are displayed. ⊠ *400-A Julia St., Warehouse District* ☏ *504/522–5471* ⊕ *www.jonathanferraragallery.com.*

LeMieux Gallery. Gulf Coast artists from Louisiana to Florida display art and crafts here alongside work by the late New Orleans abstract artist Paul Ninas. ⊠ *332 Julia St., Warehouse District* ☏ *504/522–5988* ⊕ *www.lemieuxgalleries.com* ☉ *Closed Sun.*

☾ **New Orleans ArtWorks at New Orleans Glassworks and Printmaking Studio.** The South's largest glassblowing and printmaking studio has a viewing room where visitors can watch glassblowers at work. The gallery also displays and sells functional and decorative art and sculptures. ⊠ *727 Magazine St., Warehouse District* ☏ *504/529–7277* ⊕ *www. neworleansglassworks.com* ☉ *Closed Sun.*

Ogden Museum of Southern Art. You don't have to pay admission to enter the museum's Center for Southern Craft and Design store, where you can buy ceramics, glasswork, decorative pieces, books, scarves, and jewelry by Southern artists. The museum is filled with contemporary and folk paintings, mixed-media, photography, and sculpture. ■**TIP**➔ Live music and after-hours events are held on Thursday. ⊠ *925 Camp St., Warehouse District* ☏ *504/539–9600* ⊕ *www.ogdenmuseum.org* ☉ *Closed Tues.*

RHINO Contemporary Crafts Co. The name stands for Right Here In New Orleans, which is where most of the artists involved in this co-op live and work. You'll find original paintings in varying styles, metalwork, sculpture, ceramics, glass, functional art, jewelry, fashion accessories, and artwork made from found objects. The gallery also holds art classes for children. ⊠ *Shops at Canal Place, 333 Canal St., CBD* ☏ *504/523–7945* ⊕ *www.rhinocrafts.com.*

Soren Christensen. More than 40 local, national, and international artists working in a diverse range of mediums and aesthetics showcase at this gallery. Popular artists include Gretchen Weller Howard, Michael Marlowe, Tony Hernandez, and Saskia Ozols Eubanks. ⊠ *400 Julia St., Warehouse District* ☏ *504/569–9501* ⊕ *www.sorengallery.com* ☉ *Closed Sun. and Mon.*

CLOTHING

Fodor'sChoice
★
Rubensteins. Known as one of the city's premier men's stores, this locally owned clothier has been selling high-end suits, tuxedos, casual wear, and made-to-measure apparel since 1924. Brands range from Brioni and Zegna to Ralph Lauren, Prada, Hugo Boss, and Paul Smith. ⊠ *102 St. Charles Ave., CBD* ☏ *504/581–6666* ⊕ *www.rubensteinsneworleans.com.*

FOOD AND WINE AND SPIRITS

Southern Food & Beverage Museum. The museum that documents and celebrates Southern culinary heritage has a gift shop with food-related and New Orleans–centric items. There's a big selection of Southern cookbooks, cooking utensils, and both vintage and modern cocktail tools and books. The shop features works by Dr. Bob, a local artist whose "Be Nice or Leave" signs are all over New Orleans, as well as pieces by

CAFE ROSE NICAUD

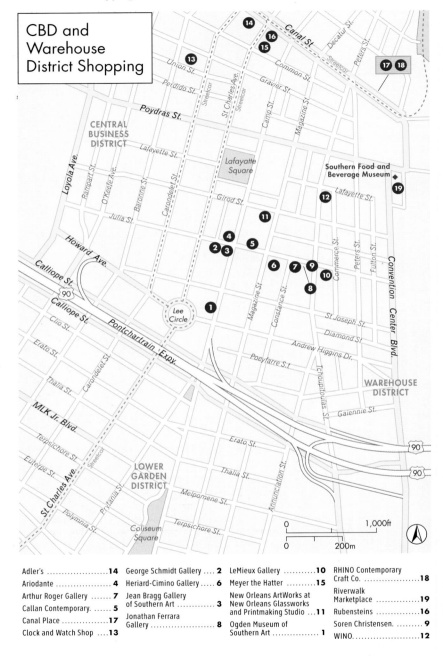

CBD and Warehouse District Shopping

other artists and a small selection of packaged foods from local brands Jazzmen Rice and PJ's coffee. The store is open to the public without paid museum admission. ⊠ *Riverwalk Marketplace, 500 Port of New Orleans Pl., Suite 169, Warehouse District* ☏ *504/569–0405.*

★ **Wine Institute of New Orleans.** There's little swishing and spitting involved with wine tasting at WINO. Walk around with a glass and sample the shop's more than 120 wines, available to taste by the ounce, half glass, or full glass using the Enomatic serving systems (the machines resemble fountain soda or beer taps). Buy the wines you like by the bottle, or just continue to taste to your heart's content—just make sure you keep tabs on your credit card tally, as it's easy to get carried away. Owner Bryan Burkey offers regular wine-tasting events and classes at the store. ⊠ *610 Tchoupitoulas St., Warehouse District* ☏ *504/324–8000* ⊕ *www. winoschool.com.*

JEWELRY AND ACCESSORIES

Adler's. This century-old, locally owned jewelry store carries upscale watches, engagement rings, jewelry with gemstones, wedding gifts, top-of-the-line silver, and more. ⊠ *722 Canal St., CBD* ☏ *504/523–5292 or 800/925–7912* ⊕ *www.adlersjewelry.com.*

Clock and Watch Shop. Master clock maker Josef Herzinger repairs and restores all types of new, vintage, and antique watches and clocks at his two-story shop. The store also sells more than 15 brands of new watches and clocks, ranging from miniature and mantle styles to large grandfather clocks. ⊠ *824 Gravier St., CBD* ☏ *504/523–0061 or 504/525–3961* ⊕ *www.clockwatchshop.com* ⊙ *Closed weekends.*

Meyer the Hatter. One of the South's largest hat stores, Meyer the Hatter has been in operation for more than a hundred years and is run by a third generation of the Meyer family. A favorite of locals and out-of-towners, the shop carries a large selection of fedoras, tweed caps, Kangols, cowboy hats, and just about any type of topper you can put on your head. ⊠ *120 St. Charles Ave., CBD* ☏ *504/525–1048 or 800/882–4287* ⊕ *www.meyerthehatter.com* ⊙ *Closed Sun.*

THE GARDEN DISTRICT AND MAGAZINE STREET

A winding, 6-mile strip of kitsch, commerce, funk, and fashion that winds from Uptown through the Garden District to downtown, Magazine Street is a shopper's mecca, a browser's paradise, and a perch for prime people-watching. Young professionals, college students, and hipsters flock to the area's funky vintage shops, cafés, boutiques, restaurants, and casual bars. Trendy local shops, with a few notable national chain stores like American Apparel, and Free People mixed in, make Magazine Street one of the most popular, bustling spots in the city. Clothing stores here run the gamut, offering everything from on-trend casual wear to vintage and consignment goods to high-end designer apparel. Antiques and home furnishing shops are also peppered throughout. There are also Magazine Street shops listed in the Uptown neighborhood.

City buses provide transportation to and along Magazine Street, and streetcars travel along St. Charles Avenue, parallel to Magazine Street and a short walk away. Walking the 6-mile length of Magazine Street is possible, but you're best off looking at a map and deciding where you want to focus. Detailed maps are available from the Magazine Street Merchants Association.

Magazine Street Merchants Association. The Magazine Street Merchants Association publishes a free brochure with maps and descriptions of the myriad stores, galleries, restaurants, and shops that line the city's boutique strip; it's available in hotels and stores, or you can request one from the association's website. ☎ *866/679–4764 or 504/342–4435* ⊕ *www.magazinestreet.com.*

ANTIQUES AND COLLECTIBLES

Antiques Magazine. Lighting is the specialty here, with nearly 200 lighting fixtures hanging from the ceiling, some dating back to the 1850s. The store also carries Victorian furniture, rare oyster plates, and accessories. ⊠ *2028 Magazine St., Garden District* ☎ *504/522–2043* ☉ *Closed Sun.*

As You Like It Silver Shop. Everything you'd want in silver is available here, with a bounty of discontinued, hard-to-find, and obsolete American sterling-silver tea services, trays, and flatware. Victorian pieces, art nouveau and art deco items, and engraved pillboxes round out the selection. The store also offers monogramming, repair, and sterling silver pattern identification. ⊠ *3033 Magazine St., Garden District* ☎ *800/828–2311* ⊕ *www.asyoulikeitsilvershop.com* ☉ *Closed Sun.*

★ **Bush Antiques.** Antique beds are the specialty, but you'll also find religious artifacts, Continental furniture, architectural elements, ironwork, and lighting. The shop displays its beds, furniture, and accessories in vignettes in rooms on two floors. A courtyard in the back holds a bounty of antique garden accoutrements. ⊠ *2109 Magazine St., Garden District* ☎ *504/581–3518* ⊕ *www.bushantiques.com* ☉ *Closed Sun.*

La Belle Nouvelle Orleans. Elaborate stained-glass windows are mounted to the ceiling because the rest of the ample space is devoted to European antique furniture, artwork, porcelain, sculpture, and oddities from the 18th to 20th century. An open-air patio outfitted with garden benches, fountains, and other outdoor decor is linked to the main showroom by a warehouse-type gallery stacked almost floor to ceiling with furniture, salvaged doors, and other architectural items. ⊠ *2112 Magazine St., Garden District* ☎ *504/581–3733* ⊕ *www.labellenouvelle.com* ☉ *Closed Sun.*

Magazine Antique Mall. If you are easily intimidated, you should take a deep breath before you walk into this expansive shop, where every possible inch of counter and shelf space is filled with antiques and vintage goods. You will find an array of costume and fine jewelry, vintage photographs, antique clocks, home decor, glassware, clothing, silver, furniture, collectible china and ceramics, and a variety of other collectibles from a number of vendors. ⊠ *3017 Magazine St., Garden District* ☎ *504/896–9994.*

If you're in town for Mardi Gras, buy a mask at one of the city's many costume shops.

ART GALLERIES

Derby Pottery. Fragments of wrought ironwork and other architectural details form the inspiration for many of Mark Derby's beautiful mugs, vases, and handmade Victorian reproduction tiles. His tile work can be seen on Oak Street, St. Claude Avenue, and Magazine Street, and his clocks and plaques, fashioned from reproductions of New Orleans's historic art deco water-meter covers, have earned cult popularity. ⊠ *2029 Magazine St., Lower Garden District* ☏ *504/586–9003* ⊕ *www. derbypottery.com* ☾ *Mon.–Sat. 10–5.*

★ **Thomas Mann Gallery I/O.** The handmade jewelry of Thomas Mann, known for his "technoromantic" pins, earrings, bracelets, and necklaces (often featuring industrial-style hearts), is showcased here alongside work by a changing slate of other artists. The result is an eclectic mix of contemporary jewelry, housewares, sculpture, and unique gifts. ⊠ *1812 Magazine St., Garden District* ☏ *504/581–2113 or 800/875–2113* ⊕ *www.thomasmann.com* ☾ *Closed Sun.*

BOOKS

Garden District Book Shop. This small bookstore at the Rink shopping center is packed with works of history, fiction, and cookbooks by local, regional, and national authors; it was the first stop on novelist Anne Rice's book tours when she lived in New Orleans. Autographed copies and limited editions of her titles are usually in stock, and the store hosts frequent author events. ⊠ *The Rink, 2727 Prytania St., Garden District* ☏ *504/895–2266* ⊕ *www.gardendistrictbookshop.com.*

Magazine Street Shopping:
Garden District and Uptown

Magnolia St.
Robertson St.
Freret St.
Lasalle St.
Liberty St.
Loyola Ave.
Saratoga St.
Daneel St.
Dryades St.
Baronne St.
Carondelet St.
Philip St.
2nd St.
1st St.
3rd St.
4th St.
Felicity St.
Coliseum St.
Josephine St.
Jackson Ave.
Saint Charles Ave.
Prytania St.
Toledano St.
Louisiana Ave.
Harmony St.
Amelia St.
Foucher St.
Penison St.
General Taylor St.
Marengo St.
Baronne St.
Streetcar
6th St.
7th St.
Washington Ave.
Magazine St.
Laurel St.
UPTOWN
Pitt St.
Prytania St.
Perrier St.
Coliseum St.
Chestnut St.
Penison St.
8th St.
9th St.
Harmony St.
Pleasant St.
GARDEN DISTRICT
Constance St.
Annunciation St.
Chippewa St.
Saraparu St.
1st St.
Philip St.
Camp St.
Aline St.
Foucher St.
Antonine St.
Amelia St.
Delachaise St.
Toledano St.
Chippewa St.
Saint Thomas St.
Livaudais St.
Division St.
Saraparu St.
3rd St.
Rousseau St.
Constance St.
Laurel St.
Annunciation St.
EAST RIVERSIDE
Tchoupitoulas St.

(44) (35) (34) (29) (28) (30 – 33) (26) (27) (21) (23) (25) (19) (20) (24) (22) (18)

(42) (41) (43) (36) (38) (37) (39) (40)

Mississippi River

0 _____ 400 yrds
0 _____ 400 meters

CLOTHING

Funky Monkey. Popular with local college students, the clothing exchange mixes new, used, and vintage apparel for men and women with hipster couture, custom-made T-shirts, handmade costumes, and lots of quirky accessories, all at affordable prices. ✉ *3127 Magazine St., Garden District* ☎ *504/899–5587.*

Green Serene. This is a store for women who love stylish, trendy clothes but want their wardrobes to reflect their values. Green Serene sells only clothing and accessories made with environmentally friendly practices. Owner Jamie Menutis has an expert eye for sourcing chic, affordable dresses, shirts, skirts, and pants made with organic cotton, soy silk, hemp, alpaca, and other eco-fabrics, including—and this is something you should really feel—surprisingly soft recycled plastics. Cool, locally made tote bags, candles, and other accessories also keep with the green theme. ✉ *2041 Magazine St., Garden District* ☎ *504/252–9861* ⊕ *www. greenserene.biz.*

RagDoll. The affordable, chic, vintage-inspired dresses, skirts, and tops in this adorable boutique focus on a retro look with modern-day fit. Styles from the 1940s, '50s, and '60s get an update for contemporary bodies by indie brands from California, England, and Spain. Shoes and accessories round out the offerings, with most everything priced under $100. ✉ *5235 Magazine St., Garden District* ☎ *504/304–5073.*

Storyville. This T-shirt shop not only has its own collection of "Storyville Originals," but also solicits the work of local designers. Shirts depict everything from fleurs-de-lis to local catchphrases to Louisiana State University–theme gear. The store also offers custom screen-printing services. A Storyville kids' shop across the street (3118 Magazine Street) sells clothing, hats, and blankets for little hipsters. ✉ *3029 Magazine St., Garden District* ☎ *504/304–6209.*

★ **Style Lab for Men.** Geared toward the trim, trendy guy, this men's clothing shop aims to work hard and play hard. The store stocks styles commonly found in New York and Los Angeles, with an eye toward mostly casual wear, hipster brands, and a small assortment of accessories, including shoes, belts, and wallets. ✉ *3326 Magazine St., Garden District* ☎ *504/304–5072* ⊕ *www.stylelabformen.com.*

FOOD

★ **Sucré.** Elaborate cakes on display in the window lure Magazine Street strollers inside this pastel-painted café and confectionary. The sweets live up to their colorful environs: the artisanal chocolates, pillowy marshmallows, French macaroons, and other treats crafted by executive pastry chef Tariq Hanna and his team are among the best in the city. You can buy chocolates individually, mix and match to create your own box, or purchase a pre-assembled box organized by theme. ✉ *3025 Magazine St., Garden District* ☎ *504/520–8311* ⊕ *www.shopsucre.com.*

HOUSEWARES

Cameron Jones for Your Home. Contemporary furniture, local art, home accessories, rugs, art glass, lighting, and a cadre of gift items here have a distinctly West Coast attitude melded with New Orleans flair. ✉ *1305 Decatur St., French Quarter* ☎ *504/524–3119* ☼ *Closed Sun.*

Loisel Vintage Modern. Take a step back to the atomic age in this retro furniture and accessories store, which carries sofas, chairs, tables, clocks, lamps, and glasses from the 1940s to the 1970s. ✉ *2855 Magazine St., Garden District* ☎ *504/899–2444* ⊕ *www.loiselvintagemodern.com.*

Fodor's Choice
★

perch. Eclectic, feminine, and contemporary, this store's collection of furnishings is the sort you'd find in a high-end home decor magazine. If you love the look but don't have the decorating gene, the staff provides interior design services. ✉ *2844 Magazine St., Garden District* ☎ *504/899–2122* ⊕ *www.perch-home.com* ☾ *Closed Sun. and Mon.*

Spruce Eco-Studio. Even if you aren't looking for environmentally friendly furniture and accessories, this chic home decor store is worth a visit for its well-curated collection of Jonathan Adler ceramics and lamps, John Robshaw bedding, and Greenform outdoor items. The owners have a sharp eye for design, but also an environmental consciousness that makes going green seem smart and easy. ✉ *2043 Magazine St., Garden District* ☎ *504/265–0946* ⊕ *www.sprucenola.com* ☾ *Closed Mon.*

LINGERIE

Fodor's Choice
★

House of Lounge. Nestled in a Magazine Street row house, this upscale lingerie shop makes high art out of lacy, pretty undies. Merchandise includes high-quality bustiers, bras, slips, panties, hosiery, gowns, and sexy accessories. The store periodically holds special events, often featuring burlesque dancers. ✉ *2044 Magazine St., Garden District* ☎ *504/671–8300* ⊕ *www.houseoflounge.com* ☾ *Closed Sun.*

SPA AND BEAUTY

Fodor's Choice
★

Aidan Gill for Men. Merging the attentiveness of a spa with the old-world charm of a barbershop, this high-end men's salon caters to guys who prefer getting a hot-towel shave and a haircut while enjoying a whiskey. The front of the store is devoted to manly diversions, with shaving sets, contemporary and New Orleans–theme cuff links, cutting-edge pocket knives, wallets, bow ties (a specialty), grooming products for face and hair, and gifts. ✉ *2026 Magazine St., Garden District* ☎ *504/587–9090* ⊕ *www.aidangillformen.com.*

> **LOOKING FOR LAGNIAPPE**
>
> Lagniappe (pronounced lan-yap), or a little something extra, is a tradition in New Orleans, whether it's getting a free taste of fudge at the candy store, free whipped cream on your latte, or an unexpected balloon animal from the clowns who entertain visitors on Jackson Square.

UPTOWN AND MAGAZINE STREET, WITH CARROLLTON-RIVERBEND

Trendy clothing boutiques, upscale home stores, contemporary art galleries, and restaurants housed in turn-of-the-century cottages create a pleasant, small-town feel to the area closest to Tulane and Loyola universities. Reflecting the area's family-friendly vibe, you'll find something for every age: toys and novelties, locally made jewelry, books,

contemporary art, and New Orleans–centric T-shirts. The Uptown end of Magazine Street, a popular haunt for college students, is the main shopping drag. On Maple Street, boutiques cover about six blocks, from Carrollton Avenue to Cherokee Street, and in the Riverbend, they dot the streets behind a shopping center on Carrollton Avenue. Oak Street, a burgeoning boutique corridor and one of the city's up-and-coming dining destinations, has several of the city's newest cafés and restaurants serving up everything from barbecue to sushi.

ANTIQUES AND COLLECTIBLES

Kevin Stone Antiques & Interiors. Unusual European antiques, most from the 18th and early 19th centuries, fill this shotgun house; the collection includes many large, very ornate pieces from the Louis XIV and XV eras. The inventory ranges from small decorative bowls and ornate sconces to a large grand piano and armoires. ✉ *3420 Magazine St., Uptown* ☎ *504/891–8282 or 504/458–7043* ⊕ *www.ksantiquer.com.*

ART GALLERIES

Carol Robinson Gallery. This two-story Uptown house is home to contemporary paintings and sculpture by U.S. artists, with a special nod to those from the South, includng Jere Allen, David Goodman, Nell C. Tilton, and Jean Geraci. ✉ *840 Napoleon Ave., at Magazine St., Uptown* ☎ *504/895–6130* ⊕ *www.carolrobinsongallery.com.*

Cole Pratt Gallery. Contemporary paintings and sculptures by more than 40 midcareer Southern artists are displayed at this modern gallery. Opening receptions are held the first Saturday of every month. ⊠ *3800 Magazine St., Uptown* ☎ *504/891–6789* ⊕ *www.coleprattgallery.com.*

Highwater Gallery. Located slightly off Oak Street's main drag, this gallery and retail space is a hidden gem. The gallery features fair-trade folk art from indigenous communities, as well as mixed media, textile works, stained glass, paintings, and sculpture from local artists. A highlight is proprietor Forrest Bacigalupi's handmade jewelry, made of mixed media ranging from antiques to animal bones. ⊠ *7800 Oak St., Carrollton-Riverbend* ☎ *504/309–5535* ⊕ *www.artskinetic.com* ⊗ *Closed weekends.*

Nuance/Louisiana Artisans Gallery. Mostly local and regional handblown-glass artists are represented in this Riverbend neighborhood studio, which also carries an eclectic mix of jewelry, pewter, ceramics, lamps, T-shirts, and more. ⊠ *728 Dublin St., Uptown* ☎ *504/865–8466* ⊕ *www.nuanceglass.com* ⊗ *Closed Sun.*

Octavia Art Gallery. This quaint gallery space showcases a number of established, midcareer, and emerging local artists and ones from around the world who work in a variety of mediums. Alex Beard, the New Orleans–based author and artist whose childlike, whimsical paintings are popular among locals, is one of the many artists represented by the gallery. ⊠ *4532 Magazine St., Uptown* ☎ *504/309–4249* ⊕ *www. octaviaartgallery.com* ⊗ *Closed Sun. and Mon.*

BOOKS

⟳ **Maple Street Book Shop.** Local authors and touring ones stop here frequently to catch up on literary trade news, give readings, and autograph their works. The popular store's motto is "Fight the Stupids." Its focus is on New Orleans and Louisiana literature, but you'll also find most new titles in its well-stocked stacks. The store also carries children's books and frequently hosts storytellers. A rare- and used-books section is located in an adjacent house. ⊠ *7523–7529 Maple St., Carrollton-Riverbend* ☎ *504/866–4916* ⊕ *www.maplestreetbookshop.com.*

Octavia Books. The building's contemporary architecture gets attention, and the attractive layout inside invites leisurely book browsing. The collection includes a strong selection of architecture, art, and fiction as well as books of local interest. The store hosts frequent book signings. ⊠ *513 Octavia St., Uptown* ☎ *504/899–7323* ⊕ *www.octaviabooks.com.*

CLOTHING

Angelique. This upscale women's clothing store provides on-trend apparel, shoes, and accessories from contemporary labels such as Diane von Furstenburg, Badgley Mischka, Theory, Red Valentino, and Alice & Olivia. ⊠ *7725 Maple St., Carrollton-Riverbend* ☎ *504/866–1092* ⊗ *Closed Sun.*

Basics Underneath. The ladies at Basics Underneath are focused on ridding the world of sagging bra straps and overflowing cups. With a sharp eye for measurement, the staff at this upscale lingerie store specializes in finding the right fit for intimates, whether it's something to wear under work clothes or a bra for a more romantic occasion. The store also carries sleepwear, swimwear, and gifts. ⊠ *5513 Magazine St., Uptown* ☎ *504/894–1000* ⊘ *Closed Sun.*

C. Collection. Geared toward fashion-forward young adults, this store resembles a sorority-house closet jammed with hip, flirty, affordable clothes, shoes, handbags, and accessories, ranging from casual to dressy, by brands such as Kensie and Tulle. ⊠ *8141 Maple St., Carrollton-Riverbend* ☎ *504/861–5002* ⊕ *www.ccollectionnola.com* ⊘ *Closed Sun.*

Encore Shop. This fund-raising resale shop supports the local symphony orchestra by selling high-quality, previously owned designer clothes, from casual to formal wear, as well as shoes, handbags, and jewelry. The shop takes consignment as well as donated items. ⊠ *7814 Maple St., Carrollton-Riverbend* ☎ *504/861–9028* ⊘ *Closed Sun. and Mon.*

Gae-Tana's. The racks of this popular boutique are filled with a mix of natural fabrics and stylish-but-comfortable clothing, as well as the latest trendy styles, making this a favorite stop for fashion-conscious mature women as well as college students looking for skirts, jeans, shorts, dresses, blouses, casual shoes, handbags, and jewelry. ⊠ *7732 Maple St., Carrollton-Riverbend* ☎ *504/865–9625* ⊘ *Closed Sun.*

Jean Therapy. Popular among locals for its diverse range of denim brands—the shop carries more than 100 styles of jeans for men and women—Jean Therapy also offers a small collection of tops, jackets, and accessories, as well as T-shirts emblazoned with New Orleans–proud slogans and local lingo. ⊠ *5505 Magazine St., Uptown* ☎ *504/897–5535* ⊕ *www.jeantherapy.com.*

Perlis. The bottom floor of this venerable New Orleans retail institution is devoted to outfitting men with classic suits (white linen and seersucker are popular), sportswear, shoes, ties, and accessories, as well as the store's signature crawfish-logo polo shirts. Upstairs is dressy, casual, and formal apparel for women. ⊠ *6070 Magazine St., Uptown* ☎ *504/895–8661 or 800/725–6070* ⊕ *www.perlis.com.*

Swap. You're likely to find designers such as Diane von Furstenberg and Dolce & Gabbana as well as Ann Taylor and J.Crew on the racks of this upscale consignment store. New consignors come in every day, adding fresh inventory. A children's store, Swap for Kids (7722 Maple Street), is next door, selling children's clothes and accessories, maternity apparel, strollers, diaper bags, and other high-end accessories. ⊠ *7716 Maple St., Carrollton-Riverbend* ☎ *504/304–6025* ⊕ *www.swapboutique.com* ⊘ *Closed Sun.*

Total Woman. Local women flock to this shop for its upscale designer labels and personalized shopping experience. The store carries the kind of clothes that are perfect for gallery openings and cocktail parties, from contemporary lines such as Diane Von Furstenburg, Tracy Reese, Milly, and Trina Turk. The staff offers personal shopping services, including after-hours shopping for "fashion emergencies." ⊠ *3964 Magazine St., Uptown* ☎ *504/891–3964* ⊕ *www.totalwomanla.com* ⊘ *Closed Sun.*

Yvonne LaFleur. Though the clothes are stylish and contemporary, this beloved local boutique's approach is decidedly old-world and elegant. Owner Yvonne LaFleur custom designs hats for all occasions, and her store is always infused with the sweet scent of her signature perfume line. The romantic fashions here run the gamut, from casual dresses and flirty skirts to lingerie, ball gowns, and a whole room filled with wedding dresses in a variety of styles. ⊠ *8131 Hampson St., Carrollton-Riverbend* ☎ *504/866–9666* ⊕ *www.yvonnelafleur.com* ☾ *Closed Sun.*

FOOD

Blue Frog Chocolates. Chocolates and other confections from all over the world are sold from an old-fashioned display case in this decadent store, which also carries truffles, cocoa, and a host of other sweet treats. Many of the candies come in novel shapes; chocolate-covered almonds, for example, form flower petals for sweet bouquets. ⊠ *5707 Magazine St., Uptown* ☎ *504/269–5707* ⊕ *www.bluefrogchocolates.com.*

★ **St. James Cheese Company.** Inspired by cheese shops in Europe, this yummy emporium is stocked with massive wheels and wedges of Gruyère, Brie, cheddar, blue, and exotic cheeses from around the globe. Owners Danielle and Richard Sutton pride themselves on the select inventory, which also includes specialty meats and a variety of great foodie gifts, such as cutting boards, preserves, pastas, cutlery, crackers, and more. Sandwiches and salads are served daily, making this a popular, and crowded, spot at lunchtime. ⊠ *5004 Prytania St., Uptown* ☎ *504/899–4737* ⊕ *www.stjamescheese.com.*

JEWELRY AND ACCESSORIES

Dominique Giordano Jewelry. Local designer Dominique Giordano creates handmade contemporary jewelry in sterling silver and 18-karat gold with semiprecious and precious stones, pearls, and resin inlay. Styles range from casual to elegant. ⊠ *5420 Magazine St., Magazine Street* ☎ *504/895–3909* ⊕ *www.dgiordano.com* ☾ *Closed Sun.*

Fleur D'Orleans. Silver jewelry adorned with the fleur-de-lis is the main attraction here, but you'll also find items that carry other New Orleans icons such as crowns, masks, hearts, and architectural details. In addition to jewelry, the store sells handbags, handmade paper, glassware, wood and ceramic boxes, batik scarves, ironwork, and more. ⊠ *3701-A Magazine St., Magazine Street* ☎ *504/899–5585* ⊕ *www.fleurdorleans.com* ☾ *Closed Sun.*

Gogo Jewelry. You can't help but be in a good mood after spending a few minutes in this store surrounded by Gogo Borgerding's brightly colored jewelry designs. Her vibrant cuff bracelets, made of sterling silver and anodized aluminum, are the store's signature. The boutique also carries her sterling silver necklaces, rings, and other items, as well as work by a few local artists. A quirky blend of kitsch and high-end, the shop features offbeat items like paint-by-numbers sets and taxidermy. ⊠ *2036 Magazine St., Suite A, Lower Garden District* ☎ *504/529–8868* ⊕ *www.ilovegogojewelry.com* ☾ *Closed Sun.*

Jezebel's Art and Antiques. Inside this Magazine Street cottage is an impressive collection of antique and estate jewelry by famous designers as well as more-affordable reproductions and new pieces by local artists. The store also carries new and vintage furs, coats, and hats. ⊠ *4606 Magazine St., Uptown* ☎ *504/895–7784* ⊕ *www.jezebelscloset.com* ☾ *Closed Sun.*

CLOSE UP

Museum Shops

For souvenirs that go beyond the typical snow globe and T-shirt, visit the gift shops in New Orleans's many museums and cultural institutions. The stores, which help support the organizations' missions, often are open to shoppers without having to pay museum admission. The gift shop in the **New Orleans Museum of Art** (*1 Collins C. Diboll Circle, Mid-City*), for example, has a wealth of books on art, photography, and Louisiana cooking, as well as scarves, puzzles, and locally made crafts, such as jewelry by local designer Mignon Faget made specifically for the museum. The **Ogden Museum of Southern Art** (*925 Camp St., Warehouse District*) includes the beautifully curated Center

for Southern Craft and Design store, where you'll find ceramics, glasswork, decorative items, jewelry, and books on and by Southern artists. The **Historic New Orleans Collection**'s (*533 Royal St., French Quarter*) gift shop is the place to find such items as a reproduction of a 1916 railroad map of Louisiana and a NOVA documentary DVD on Hurricane Katrina. The **Aquarium of the Americas** (*1 Canal St., French Quarter*), the **Audubon Insectarium** (*423 Canal St., French Quarter*), and the **Audubon Zoo** (*6500 Magazine St., Uptown*), all part of the Audubon Nature Institute, all have gift shops stocked with colorful, quirky, educational, and fun items for children and adults.

Mon Coeur. Handmade jewelry crafted by Janet Bruno-Small from antique and vintage pieces is a specialty, but the showroom also has an assortment of distinctive pieces by contemporary designers as well as antique and estate jewelry. ⊠ *3952 Magazine St., Uptown* ☎ *504/899–0064* ⊕ *www.moncoeurfinejewelry.com* ⊗ *Closed Sun.*

Symmetry Jewelers. Designer Tom Mathis creates custom wedding and engagement rings and other in-house designs and performs jewelry repairs at this full-service shop, which also offers a variety of contemporary jewelry by local, national, and international craftspeople. ⊠ *8138 Hampson St., Carrollton-Riverbend* ☎ *504/861–9925 or 800/628–3711* ⊕ *www.symmetry-jewelers.com* ⊗ *Closed Sun. and Mon.*

NOVELTIES AND GIFTS

Aux Belles Choses. This dreamy cottage of French and English delights has richly scented soaps, vintage and new linens, antique enamelware, collectible plates, and decorative accessories. ⊠ *3912 Magazine St., Uptown* ☎ *504/891–1009* ⊕ *www.abcneworleans.com.*

Dirty Coast. T-shirts and bumper stickers brandishing the phrase "Be a New Orleanian. Wherever you are" deeply resonated with displaced residents after Hurricane Katrina. Since then, locals leave it to Dirty Coast to say whatever they're feeling in a clever, artful, and sometimes sarcastic way. The store's shirts, stickers, and hats satirize (a popular design says "New Orleans: So far behind, we're ahead") and celebrate local culture through eye-catching designs. ⊠ *5631 Magazine St., Uptown* ☎ *504/324–3745* ⊕ *www.dirtycoast.com.*

Fleurty Girl. Owned by the ebullient Lauren Thom, Fleurty Girl—its title a play on the fleur-de-lis—is a place to go for New Orleans–centric T-shirts and other apparel. The store is known for its T-shirts displaying the humorous catchphrases and iconography of local "Yat" culture and pride for the New Orleans Saints. There's also affordable jewelry, children's books, colorful rain boots, Carnival-themed gear, and fleurs-de-lis in every imaginable form. ✉ *3117 Magazine St., Upper Garden District* ☎ *504/304–5529* ⊕ *www.fleurtygirl.net* ✉ *632 St. Peter St., French Quarter* ☎ *504/301–2557* ⊕ *www.fleurtygirl.net.*

Hazelnut. Founded by stage and television actor Bryan Batt (he played Salvatore Romano on *Mad Men*) and his partner Tom Cianfichi, this jewel box of a shop carries gorgeous home accessories and gifts, including New Orleans toile pillows, decorative items, stemware, tableware, accent furniture, frames, and more. ✉ *5515 Magazine St, Uptown* ☎ *504/891–2424* ⊕ *www.hazelnutneworleans.com.*

Orient Expressed Imports. Imported porcelain, vases, ceramics, jewelry, and the store's own line of smocked children's clothing are popular gift items. The store also has a showroom of home furnishings, including accent furniture, lamps, and antique accessories. ✉ *3905 Magazine St., Uptown* ☎ *504/899–3060* ⊕ *www.orientexpressed.com* ☾ *Closed Sun.*

Scriptura. Fitting tributes to the arts of writing and communication are evident in the Italian leather address books and journals, hand-decorated photo albums, specialty papers and stationery, handmade invitations, and a varied selection of glass and high-quality fountain pens sold here. ✉ *5423 Magazine St., Uptown* ☎ *504/897–1555* ⊕ *www.scriptura.com* ☾ *Closed Sun.*

Shadyside Pottery. Master potter Charles Bohn's shop is filled with the functional and decorative stoneware, raku, and pottery he creates on-site as well as his custom wood tables and male and female torso sculptures. ✉ *3823 Magazine St., Uptown* ☎ *504/897–1710* ⊕ *www.shadysidepottery.com.*

Skip 'N Whistle. This shop gained notoriety around the 2010 Super Bowl for its *Where the Wild Things Are*–inspired New Orleans Saints-themed T-shirts, and it remains popular for its clever shirt designs and accessories. The store also offers custom screen printing. For those baffled by the local lingo on the shirts, there's a selection of trendy, affordable clothing and accessories, as well as jewelry by local artists. ✉ *8123 Oak St., Carrollton-Riverbend* ☎ *504/862–5909* ⊕ *www.skipnwhistle.com.*

SHOES

Victoria's Shoes. Jimmy Choo, Giuseppe Zanotti, Hoss Intropia, and Marni are just a few of the high-end brands available at this upscale shoe emporium, which also carries handbags and jewelry. ✉ *4858 Magazine St., Uptown* ☎ *504/899–8878.*

SPA AND BEAUTY

Bamboo. Amid the old shotgun-style, 19th-century houses that line Magazine Street, Bamboo's modern, minimalist facade stands out. Architect Perry Pool's design helped the spa and retailer get highlighted as one of *New Orleans Magazine*'s top 10 buildings. The cosmetic and skin care brands sold inside the spa have the same modern sensibility. The high-end lines include Laura Mercier, Molton Brown, Clarisonic, Red Flower, and Natura Bisse, and these products usually complement spa services. ⊠ *4112 Magazine St., Uptown* ☎ *504/895–1664* ☾ *Closed Sun.*

TOYS

☾ **Magic Box.** This toy store loved by both children and adults sells the
★ kind of items you won't find in big box places. While the shop carries popular items by LEGO and Playskool, Magic Box emphasizes toys by independent brands. You'll find everything from baby toys to pretend play items for older children to party games for adults. The staff goes above and beyond with customer service, offering shipping and assembly. ⊠ *5508 Magazine St., Uptown* ☎ *504/899–0117* ⊕ *www.magicbox neworleans.com* ☾ *Closed Mon.*

MID-CITY

This neighborhood isn't known as a shopping destination; however, the store NOMA goes beyond a regular museum gift shop, and small wine stores provide perfect companions for picnics at the area's many outdoor locales. A streetcar runs along Canal Street and then down North Carrollton Avenue, ending at City Park Avenue, right by the park, NOMA, and Esplanade Avenue.

NOVELTIES AND GIFTS

New Orleans Museum of Art. Well stocked with art and photography books, children's items, puzzles, jewelry, and locally made crafts, the New Orleans Museum of Art's gift shop is well worth a visit, even if you're not browsing the museum's exhibits. The shop has its own cookbook, as well as items created exclusively for it by local favorite jewelry designer Mignon Faget. You don't have to pay museum admission to enter the shop; just say you are shopping at the front desk, and you will receive a special pass. ⊠ *1 Collins C. Diboll Circle, Mid-City* ☎ *504/658–4100* ⊕ *www.noma.org* ☾ *Closed Mon.*

Side Trips from New Orleans

WORD OF MOUTH

"[I've] been to Laura, Oak Alley, and Nottoway, and liked all three . . . Laura is the plainest, being typical of a Creole-style plantation, but the tour has a lot of personal family information . . . Oak Alley has nice grounds . . . and a very good house—the tour is done by in-costume guides and is the most polished. Nottoway has the most impressive house and the least polished of the three tours."

—bachslunch

SIDE TRIPS FROM NEW ORLEANS

TOP REASONS TO GO

★ **Jam to Cajun and zydeco music.** Ensembles of fiddles, accordions, and guitars produce eminently danceable folk music, with songs sung in a mélange of English and Cajun French. Zydeco, closely related to Cajun music, adds washboard and drums to the mix and has more of a blues-rock feel.

★ **Marvel at plantation homes.** These stately homes will have you reenacting your favorite scenes from *Gone with the Wind*. Some of them now stand in the shadow of massive chemical plants and oil refineries that now operate on the Mississippi River; some plantation ruins appear in the middle of cow fields or alongside bayous, further testifying to the clash between old and new.

★ **Take a swamp tour.** Ride through the beautiful wetlands surrounding New Orleans and Baton Rouge. You'll see alligators, snakes, nutria, and more in their natural habitat.

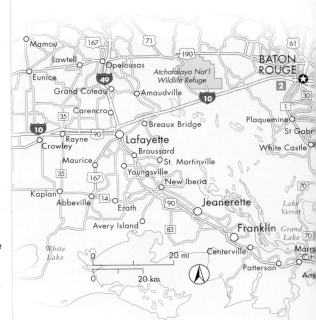

1 Plantation Country.
Take a journey into the past and see some of the South's most beautiful antebellum homes. Within an hour's drive of New Orleans you will see dozens of plantation homes in various states of repair scattered along either side of the Mississippi, heading west towards the state's capital, Baton Rouge. The views these days also include sights of the heavy industry that is scattered along the river west of New Orleans.

12

GETTING ORIENTED

Baton Rouge, the state's capital and second-largest city, is about an hour west of New Orleans. Plantation homes are scattered between the two cities, within a two-hour drive if you take the scenic Great River Road. Lafayette, about two hours west of New Orleans if you take Interstate 10, is a good post for exploring Cajun Country. Smaller Cajun towns surround the small city in all directions.

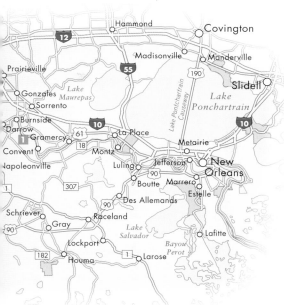

2 Cajun Country. French Louisiana, spread across the bayous, rice paddies, and canebrakes to the west of New Orleans, is famous for two things: its food (jambalaya and blackened fish) and its music (Cajun and zydeco). You'll also find excellent antiques shopping, ecotourism, and historical sights. Here you'll find much of what the Big Easy has to offer, but in a family-friendly, small-town setting.

Updated by
Ian McNulty

New Orleans has never been a typical old Southern city. But look away to the west of town, and you can find the antebellum world conjured by the term *Dixieland,* which was coined here in the early 19th century. Between New Orleans and Baton Rouge, the romantic ruins of plantation homes alternate with the occasional restored manor. Anyone with an interest in the history of the Old South or a penchant for a picturesque drive along country roads should spend at least half a day along the winding Great River Road.

Popular day trips include tours of the swamps and bayous that surround New Orleans. *Bayou* comes from a Native American word that means "creek." The brackish, slow-moving waters of south Louisiana were once the highways and byways of the Choctaw, Chickasaw, Chitimacha, and Houma. Two centuries ago Jean Lafitte and his freebooters easily hid in murky reaches of swamp, which were covered with thick canopies of subtropical vegetation; it's said that pirate gold is still buried here. The state has a wild alligator population of about 1.5 million, and most of them laze around in the meandering tributaries and secluded sloughs of south Louisiana. A variety of tour companies, large and small, take groups to swampy sites a half-hour to two hours away from the city center. Guides steer you by boat through still waters, past ancient gnarled cypresses with gray shawls of Spanish moss, explaining the state's flora and fauna and the swamp traditions of the trappers who settled here. (⇨ *For swamp tour operators, see Cajun Encounters.)*

South Louisiana, cradle of the Cajun population, is decidedly French in flavor. In small communities along the coast and in the upland prairie, Cajun French is still spoken, although just about everyone also speaks English. After a hard day's work fishing or working crawfish ponds, rural residents of Cajun Country often live up to the motto *Laissez les bons temps rouler!,* which means "Let the good times roll!"

PLANNING

WHEN TO GO

Summer is full of small-town festivals that are big fun for city folk and families. In late September and October, temperatures cool off, making it a great time for plantation exploration and swamp tours (however, it's also the tail end of hurricane season). In December, plantation homes are decked out for the holidays.

ABOUT THE RESTAURANTS

Part of the considerable charm of the region west of New Orleans is the Cajun food, popularized by Cajun chef Paul Prudhomme, a native of Opelousas. This is jambalaya, crawfish pie, and filé gumbo country, and nowhere else on Earth is Cajun food done better than where it originated. Cajun food is often described as the robust, hot-peppery country kin of Creole cuisine. It's a cuisine built upon economy—heavy on the rice and the sauces, lighter on the meats—and strongly influenced by African as well as French cooking traditions. Indigenous sea creatures turn up in étouffées, bisques, and pies, and on almost every Acadian menu are jambalaya, gumbo, and blackened fish. Alligator meat is a great favorite, as are sausages like andouille and boudin (stuffed with pork and rice). Cajun food is very rich, and portions tend to be ample. Biscuits and grits are breakfast staples, and many an evening meal ends with bread pudding.

Cajun cuisine extends beyond Cajun Country itself, and into many of the restaurants along River Road. North of Baton Rouge, however, in St. Francisville, more-typical Southern fare prevails. Here you will still find po' boys and sometimes gumbo, but barbecue is more common than boudin. (⇨ *For explanations of many Cajun foods, see Chapter 8.*)

ABOUT THE HOTELS

Some of the handsome antebellum mansions along River Road are also bed-and-breakfasts in which you may roam the high-ceiling rooms before retiring to a big four-poster or canopied bed. The greatest concentration of accommodations in Cajun Country is in Lafayette, which has an abundance of chain properties as well as some B&Bs. Charming B&Bs are also abundant in other nearby towns, including St. Francisville, which is considered one of the best B&B towns in the South.

PLANTATION COUNTRY

The area designated Plantation Country envelops a parade of plantations along the Great River Road leading west from New Orleans, plus a reservoir of fine old homes north of Baton Rouge, around the town of St. Francisville. Louisiana plantation homes range from the grandiose Nottoway on River Road to the humbler, owner-occupied Butler Greenwood near St. Francisville. Some sit upon an acre or two; others, such as Rosedown, are surrounded by extensive, lush grounds.

The River Road plantations are closely tied to New Orleans's culture and society: it was here that many of the city's most prominent families made their fortunes generations ago, and the language and tastes here are historically French. The St. Francisville area, on the other hand, received a heartier injection of British-American colonial culture during the antebellum era, evidenced in the landscaped grounds of homes such as Rosedown and the restrained interior of Oakley House, where John James Audubon lived while in the area. Baton Rouge, the state capital, provides a midpoint between the River Road plantations and St. Francisville and has some interesting sights of its own.

GETTING HERE AND AROUND

AIR TRAVEL

Baton Rouge Metropolitan Airport, 7 miles north of downtown, is served by American, Continental, Delta, and U.S. Airways. New Orleans International Airport is off Interstate 10, 20 minutes from Destrehan Plantation.

Airport Information **Baton Rouge Metropolitan Airport** (*BTR*). ⊠ *9430 Jackie Cochran Dr.* ☎ *225/355–0333* ⊕ *www.flybtr.com.*

BUS TRAVEL

Greyhound Southeast Lines has frequent daily service from New Orleans to Baton Rouge and Lafayette, and limited service to surrounding areas.

Bus Information **Greyhound Southeast Lines** ☎ *800/231–2222* ⊕ *www. greyhound.com.*

CAR TRAVEL

From New Orleans, the fastest route to the River Road plantations is Interstate 10 west to Interstate 310 to Exit 6, River Road. Alternatives to the Great River Road are to continue on either Interstate 10 or U.S. 61 west; both have signs marking exits for various plantations. Route 18 runs along the west bank of the river, Route 44 on the east.

Interstate 10 and U.S. 190 run east–west through Baton Rouge. Interstate 12 heads east, connecting with north–south Interstate 55 and Interstate 59. U.S. 61 leads from New Orleans to Baton Rouge and north. Ferries across the Mississippi cost $1 per car; most bridges are free. Route 1 travels along False River, which is a blue "oxbow lake" created ages ago when the Mississippi changed its course and cut off this section. The drive along Interstate 10 will take one hour from New Orleans to Baton Rouge. Expect the drive to take two hours if you take either Route 18 or 44, which wind around the river.

TIMING

Don't try to visit every plantation listed here—your trip will turn into a blur of columns. If you can, spend the night at one of the plantations, such as Oak Alley or Nottoway, and then tour the region. Oak Alley and Laura plantations are just a few miles from each other and provide a nice contrast in architectural styles and approaches. St. Francisville is a weekend trip in its own right. If you're visiting from New Orleans and are strapped for time, Destrehan, one of the state's oldest plantations, might fit the bill; it's 23 miles from the city.

TOURS

Allons à Lafayette. Guided tours of the River Road plantations and swamp tours are available from this company, which is based in Lafayette. ☎ *800/264–5465* ⊕ *www.allonsalafayette.com.*

Cajun Encounters Tour Co. From Cajun Encounters you can get guided tours to Oak Alley and Laura Plantations, as well as personal tours of Honey Island Swamp. ☎ *866/928–6877 or 504/834–1770* ⊕ *www. cajunencounters.com.*

VISITOR INFORMATION

Baton Rouge Area Convention and Visitors Bureau ⊠ *359 3rd St., Baton Rouge* ☎ *225/383–1825 or 800/527–6843* ⊕ *www.visitbatonrouge.com.* **Louisiana Visitor Information Center** ⊠ *900 N. 3rd St., Baton Rouge* ☎ *225/342–7317* ⊕ *www.louisianatravel.com.* **West Feliciana Parish Tourist Commission** ⊠ *1157 Ferdinand St., St. Francisville* ☎ *225/635–4224 or 800/789–4221* ⊕ *www.stfrancisville.us.*

THE GREAT RIVER ROAD

Between New Orleans and Baton Rouge, beautifully restored antebellum plantations along the Mississippi are filled with period antiques, ghosts of former residents, and tales of Yankee gunboats. Industrial plants share the scenery now, and the man-made levee, constructed in the early 20th century in an attempt to keep the mighty Mississippi on a set course, obstructs the river views that plantation residents once enjoyed. Still, you can always park your car and climb up on the levee for a look at Ol' Man River.

Between the Destrehan and San Francisco plantations you will drive through what amounts to a deep bow before the might of the Mississippi: the Bonnie Carre Spillway is a huge swath of land set aside specifically to receive the river's periodic overflow, thus protecting New Orleans, 30 miles downriver.

The Great River Road is also called, variously, Route or LA 44 and 75 on the east bank of the river and Route or LA 18 on the west bank. "LA" and "Route" are interchangeable; we use Route throughout this chapter. Alternatives to the Great River Road are Interstate 10 and U.S. 61; both have signs marking exits for various plantations. All the plantations described are listed on the National Register of Historic Places, and some of them are B&Bs. Plantation touring can take anywhere from an hour to two days, depending upon how many houses you want to see—and how much talk of moonlight and magnolias you'd like to hear.

PLANTATION HOMES

For convenience, we've listed the following plantations according to distance from New Orleans: the closest to the farthest.

Destrehan Plantation. The oldest plantation left intact in the lower Mississippi Valley, this simple West Indies–style house, built in 1787 by a free man of color, is typical of the homes built by the earliest planters in the region. The plantation is notable for the hand-hewn cypress timbers that were used in its construction and for the insulation in its walls, made of *bousillage,* a mixture of horsehair, Spanish moss, and mud. Some days bring period demonstrations of indigo dying, candle making, or open-hearth cooking; an annual fall festival with music, crafts, and food is held during the second weekend in November. A costumed guide leads you on a 45-minute tour through the house, which is furnished with

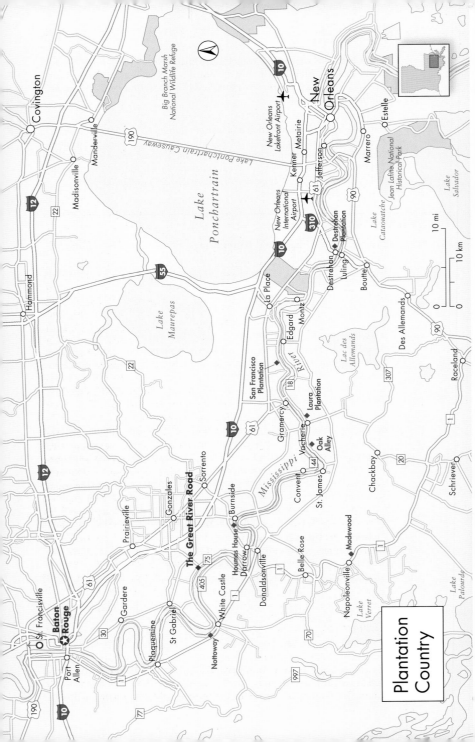

Plantation Country

period antiques and some reproductions. You are free to explore the grounds, where there are several smaller structures and massive oak trees borne down by their weighty old branches. ✉ *13034 River Rd., Destrehan ✛ 23 miles west [upriver] of New Orleans* ☎ *985/764–9315 or 877/453–2095* ⊕ *www.destrehanplantation.org* ▨ *$18* ⊗ *Daily 9–4.*

San Francisco Plantation. Completed in 1856, the elaborate San Francisco house presents an intriguing variation on the standard plantation styles, with galleries resembling the decks of a ship—hence the term for it architectural style, Steamboat Gothic. The house was once called St. Frusquin, a pun on the French slang term, *sans fruscins*, which means "without a penny in my pocket"—the condition its owner, Valsin Marmillion, found himself in after paying exorbitant construction costs. Valsin's father, Edmond Bozonier Marmillion, had begun the project. According to lore his design for the house was inspired by the steamboats he enjoyed watching along the Mississippi. Upon his father's death, Valsin and his German bride, Louise von Seybold, found themselves with a plantation on their hands. Unable to return to Germany, Louise brought German influence to south Louisiana instead. The result was an opulence rarely encountered in these parts: ceilings painted in trompe l'oeil, hand-painted toilets with primitive flushing systems, and cypress painstakingly rendered as marble and English oak. Tour guides impart the full fascinating story on the 45-minute tour through the main house. An authentic one-room schoolhouse and a slave cabin have been installed on the grounds, which you can tour at your leisure. Louisiana novelist Frances Parkinson Keyes used the site as the model for her novel *Steamboat Gothic.* ✉ *2646 River Rd., Garyville ✛ 18 miles west of Destrehan Plantation, 35 miles west of New Orleans* ☎ *985/535–2341 or 888/322–1756* ⊕ *www.sanfranciscoplantation.org* ▨ *$15* ⊗ *Nov.– Mar., daily 9:40–4; Apr.–Oct., daily 9:40–4:40.*

★ **Laura Plantation.** This is a more intimate and better-documented presentation of Creole plantation life than any other property on River Road. The narrative of the guides is built on first-person accounts, estate records, and original artifacts from the Locoul family, who built the simple, Creole-style house in 1805. Laura Locoul, whose great-grandparents founded the estate, wrote a detailed memoir of plantation life, family fights, and the management of slaves. The information from Laura's memoir and the original slave cabins and other outbuildings (workers on the plantation grounds lived in the cabins into the 1980s) provide rare insights into slavery in south Louisiana. The plantation gift shop stocks a large selection of literature by and about slaves and slavery in southern Louisiana and the United States. Senegalese slaves at Laura are believed to have first told folklorist Alcee Fortier the tales of Br'er Rabbit; his friend Joel Chandler Harris used the stories in his Uncle Remus tales. ✉ *2247 Hwy. 18(aka River Rd.), Vacherie ✛ 10 miles west of San Francisco Plantation, 57 miles west of New Orleans* ☎ *225/265–7690 or 888/799–7690* ⊕ *www.lauraplantation. com* ▨ *$18* ⊗ *Daily 10–4.*

★ **Oak Alley.** Built between 1837 and 1839 by Jacques T. Roman, a French-Creole sugar planter from New Orleans, Oak Alley is the most famous of all the antebellum homes in Louisiana—you may recognize if from

San Francisco Plantation stands out for its over-the-top "Steamboat Gothic" exterior.

its appearance in many a movie and TV show. It's also an outstanding example of Greek Revival architecture. The 28 gnarled oak trees that line the drive and give the columned plantation its name were planted in the early 1700s by an earlier settler. A guided tour introduces you to the grand interior of the manor, furnished with period antiques. Be sure to take in the view from the upper gallery of the house and to spend time exploring the expansive grounds. A number of late-19th-century cottages behind the main house provide simple overnight accommodations, and a restaurant is open daily for breakfast (8:30–10:30) and lunch (11–3). ⊠ *3645 River Rd.(Rte. 18), Vacherie* ✣ *3 miles west of Laura Plantation, 60 miles west of New Orleans* ☎ *225/265–2151 or 888/279–9802* ⊕ *www.oakalleyplantation.com* 🖃 *$18* ☉ *Weekdays 9:30–4:30, weekends 9:30–5.*

Houmas House. Surrounded by majestic 200-year-old oaks, Houmas House l a classic Louisiana plantation house—grand white pillars and all, although it's actually two buildings, of quite different styles, joined together. In 1770 Alexander Latil built the smaller rear house in the French–Spanish Creole style that was becoming popular in New Orleans. The Greek Revival mansion was added to the grounds in 1828 by Wade Hampton, who eventually connected the two structures with an arched carriageway. ⊠ *40136 Hwy. 942, ½ mile off Rte. 44, Darrow* ✣ *29 miles northwest from San Francisco Plantation, 58 miles west of New Orleans* ☎ *225/473–7841 or 225/473–9380* ⊕ *www. houmashouse.com* 🖃 *Guided home and garden tour $20, self-guided garden tour $10* ☉ *Mon. and Tues. 9–5, Wed.–Sun. 9–8.*

Madewood. This galleried, 21-room Greek Revival mansion with massive white columns was designed by architect Henry Howard and completed in 1854. The house, across the road from Bayou Lafourche, has an enormous freestanding staircase and 25-foot-high ceilings, and is best experienced overnight in the bed-and-breakfast. Guests can arrange a tour with the owners; call for appointments. ✉ *4250 Rte. 308, 2 miles south of town, Napoleonville* ✣ *20 miles south of Houmas House, 74 miles west of New Orleans* ☎ *985/369–7151* 🌐 *www.madewood.com* 🎫 *$15 tour, reservations necessary* 🕘 *Daily 10–4.*

Fodor's Choice ★ **Nottoway.** The South's largest plantation house, Nottoway, makes a very impressive sight. Built in 1857, the mansion is of Italianate style, with 64 rooms, 22 columns, and 200 windows. The crowning achievement of architect Henry Howard, it was saved from destruction during the Civil War by a Northern officer (a former guest of the owners, Mr. and Mrs. John Randolph). An idiosyncratic, somewhat rambling layout reflects the individual tastes of the original owners and includes a grand ballroom, famed in these parts for its crystal chandeliers and hand-carved columns. You can stay here overnight, and a formal restaurant serves breakfast, lunch, and dinner daily. The plantation is 2 miles north of its namesake, the town of White Castle (you'll understand when you see the vast white planation, which looks like a castle). ✉ *31025 Hwy. 1, White Castle* ✣ *33 miles northwest of Madewood, 70 miles west of New Orleans* ☎ *225/545–2730 or 866/527–6884* 🌐 *www.nottoway.com* 🎫 *$20* 🕘 *Daily 9–4.*

EXPLORING

River Road African American Museum. This museum explores the contributions of African-Americans in Louisiana's rural Mississippi River communities through exhibits that explore their cuisine, the Underground Railroad, free people of color, and jazz. ✉ *406 Charles St., Donaldsonville* ☎ *225/474–5553* 🌐 *www.africanamericanmuseum.org* 🎫 *$5* 🕘 *Wed.–Sat. 1–5, Sun. 9–5.*

WHERE TO EAT

$ SOUTHERN 🍴 **B&C Seafood.** This small shop and deli serves the tastiest seafood gumbo ever ladled into a Styrofoam bowl. Try it with a dash of hot sauce and a sprinkle of filé, or sample the alligator and garfish po' boys. Finish with a scoop of rich, dense bread pudding. The deli has fresh and frozen catfish, crawfish, alligator, and turtle meat harvested from the nearby swamps. You can buy seafood packed to travel. [$] *Average main: $10* ✉ *2155 Rte. 18, beside Laura Plantation, Vacherie* ☎ *225/265–8356* 🕘 *Closed Sun.*

$$$$ CAJUN 🍴 **Latil's Landing Restaurant and Café Burnside.** Set in the rear wing of Houmas House Plantation, Latil's Landing Restaurant is furnished with period antiques and reproductions that put you in the mood for its "nouvelle Louisiana" food, a mélange of traditional ingredients with more contemporary cooking techniques and flavors. Try the roasted oysters with local Creole cream-cheese sauce, the foie gras beignets, or the duck with praline sauce. Café Burnside is open for lunch with a menu of salads and sandwiches. [$] *Average main: $35* ✉ *Houmas*

Nottoway Plantation, our Fodor's Choice pick for best plantation home.

House Plantation, 40146 Hwy. 942, Darrow ☎ *225/473–9380 or 888/323–8314* ✍ *Reservations essential* ⏲ *No dinner Sun.–Tues.*

$ SOUTHERN 🍴 **Spuddy's Cajun Foods.** Midway between Laura and Oak Alley plantations, downtown Vacherie is short on sights but long on flavor, thanks in no small part to this down-home lunchroom. Photos and murals on the walls tell tales of local history, while po' boys, jambalaya, and fried catfish fill the tables. You can also pick up some house-made sausage as an edible souvenir. [S] *Average main: $10* ✉ *2644 Hwy. 20, Vacherie* ☎ *225/265–4013* ✍ *Reservations not accepted* ⏲ *No dinner. Closed Sun.*

$ 🍴 **Wayne Jacob's Smokehouse Restaurant.** LaPlace is known as the andouille capital of the world, and the spicy, smoky, Cajun-style sausage is deservedly popular here. In this butcher shop that doubles as a functional, straightforward restaurant, you can get andouille in burgers, in gumbo, made into chips for dipping, or worked into white beans and rice. A jazz brunch on Sunday expands the offerings to include omelets, pancakes, and other comforting fare. [S] *Average main: $10* ✉ *769 W. 5th St., near San Francisco plantation, LaPlace* ☎ *985/652–9990* 🌐 *www.wjsmokehouse.com* ✍ *Reservations not accepted* ⏲ *No dinner Sat.–Wed.*

WHERE TO STAY

For expanded hotel reviews, visit Fodors.com.

$$$$ B&B/INN 🏨 **Madewood.** Expect gracious hospitality, lovely antiques, and canopied beds in both the 21-room main house and Charlet House, a smaller structure on the plantation grounds that holds three of the inn's eight rooms for guests. **Pros:** quiet; beautiful; staying here is like

stepping back in time—though with Wi-Fi and other modern amenities. **Cons:** some may find it too quiet; no TV; dinner is a group affair. **TripAdvisor:** "super friendly," "fun and relaxing," "old-world living in a stately home." [S] *Rooms from: $259* ✉ *4250 Rte. 308, Napoleonville* ☎ *985/369–7151* 🌐 *www.madewood.com* 🛏 *8 rooms* 🍴 *Some meals.*

$$$$ B&B/INN 🏨 **Nottoway.** The largest antebellum plantation in the South, this stunner is fun for wandering around at night, when all the tours are over. **Pros:** sleeping in history. **Cons:** with so many rooms and a busy schedule of tours and events, this isn't the place to get away from it all. **TripAdvisor:** "Southern hospitality at its best," "awesome experience," "gorgeous mansion and grounds." [S] *Rooms from: $229* ✉ *31025 Hwy. 1, White Castle* ☎ *225/545–8632 or 866/428–4748* 🌐 *www.nottoway.com* 🛏 *40 rooms, 2 suites* 🍴 *Breakfast.*

$$$ B&B/INN ★ 🏨 **Oak Alley.** These 100-year-old one- and two-bedroom cottages on Oak Alley Plantation's grounds are furnished with country charm that includes brass beds and antiques or reproductions. **Pros:** spectacular sunrise views from the levee in front of the plantation; serene quiet; charming rooms with comfortable beds. **Cons:** few nearby options for supplies and food. **TripAdvisor:** "beautiful grounds," "stunning," "a step back in time." [S] *Rooms from: $150* ✉ *3645 River Rd.(Rte. 18), Vacherie* ☎ *225/265–2151 or 800/442–5539* 🌐 *www.oakalleyplantation.com* 🛏 *6 cottages* 🍴 *Multiple meal plans.*

BATON ROUGE

80 miles northwest of New Orleans via I–10.

Hemmed in as it is by endless industrial plants, Baton Rouge doesn't look like much from the road. Yet government-history enthusiasts will want to stop here on their way through the south Louisiana countryside. Baton Rouge, the state capital, has several interesting and readily accessible sights, including the attractive capitol grounds and an educational planetarium. This is the city from which the colorful, cunning, and often corrupt Huey P. Long ruled the state; it is also the site of his assassination. Even today, more than 80 years after Long's death, legends about the controversial governor and U.S. senator abound.

The parishes to the north of Baton Rouge are quiet and bucolic, with gently rolling hills, high bluffs, and historic districts. John James Audubon lived in West Feliciana Parish in 1821, tutoring local children and painting 80 of his famous bird studies. In both terrain and traits, this region is more akin to north Louisiana than to south Louisiana—which is to say, the area is very Southern.

EXPLORING

TOP ATTRACTIONS

🐤 **Louisiana Arts & Science Museum and Irene W. Pennington Planetarium.** Housed in a 1925 Illinois Central railroad station near the Old State Capitol, this idiosyncratic but high-quality museum brings together a contemporary-art gallery and an Egyptian tomb exhibit featuring a mummy from 300 BC. Also here are a children's museum and a kid-friendly planetarium. The planetarium presents regular shows, as does the ExxonMobil Space Theater. The museum hosts traveling exhibits, and houses the nation's second-largest collection of sculptures by 20th-century Croatian artist Ivan Mestrovic, many of which adorn the entrance hall. ✉ *100 S. River Rd.* ☎ *225/344–5272* ⊕ *www.lasm. org* ✑ *$7, $9 including planetarium show* ⊙ *Tues.–Fri. 10–3, Sat. 10–5 (planetarium 10–8), Sun. 1–4.*

Louisiana State Museum—Baton Rouge. This museum showcases the history of Louisiana through two exhibits. "Grounds for Greatness: Louisiana and the Nation" relates Louisiana history to the nation and the world, from the Louisiana Purchase to World War II; the "Louisiana Experience: Discovering the Soul of America," a road-trip-like exhibit that courses through the different regions of the state. The exhibit also showcases Mardi Gras traditions throughout the state. There is also a gallery for changing exhibits. ✉ *660 N. 4th St.* ☎ *225/342–5428* ⊕ *www.crt.state.la.us/ museum* ✑ *Free* ⊙ *Tues.–Fri. 10–5, Sat. 9–5.*

USS *Kidd* & Veterans Memorial Museum. This World War II survivor has been restored to its V-J Day configuration. A self-guided tour takes in more than 50 inner spaces of this ship and also the separate **Nautical Center** museum. Among the museum's exhibits are articles from the United States' 175 Fletcher-class destroyers, a collection of ship models, and a restored P-40 fighter plane hanging from the ceiling. The Louisiana Memorial Plaza lists more than 7,000 Louisiana citizens killed during combat, including the 127 citizens killed in the recent Iraq and Afghanistan wars. An A-7E Corsair plane pays tribute to the veterans of the Vietnam War. ✉ *305 S. River Rd.(Government St. at levee)* ☎ *225/342–1942* ⊕ *www.usskidd.com* ✑ *$8* ⊙ *Daily 9–5.*

Rural Life Museum and Windrush Gardens. Run by Louisiana State University (LSU), this outdoor teaching and research facility aims to represent the rural life of early Louisianians. Three major areas—the Barn, the Working Plantation, and Folk Architecture—contain more than 32 rustic 19th-century structures over 25 acres. A visitor center adjoins the Barn, which holds a collection that includes old farm tools, quilts, 19th-century horse-drawn carriages, slave items, and much more. The plantation section's buildings include a gristmill, a blacksmith's shop, and several outbuildings. The gardens were created by the late landscape designer Steele Burden. ✉ *4650 Essen La., off I–10* ☎ *225/765–2437* ⊕ *www.rurallife.lsu.edu* ✑ *$7* ⊙ *Daily 8:30–5.*

Shaw Center for the Arts. This arts facility houses the LSU Museum of Art, Manship Theatre, Hartley/Vey Studio and Workshop Theatres, the LSU Museum Store, LSU School of Art Glassell Gallery, two sculpture gardens, and rooftop terraces with great views of the Mississippi River. On-site restaurants include Tsunami, Capital City Grill, PJ's Coffee, and Stroubes Chophouse. ✉ *100 Lafayette St.* ☎ *225/346–5001* ⊕ *www. shawcenter.org* ✉ *Museum: $5* ☉ *Center: Tues.–Sat. 9 am–11 pm, Sun. 11–5, Mon. 9–4. Museum: Tues., Wed., Fri., and Sat. 10–4, Thurs. 10–8, Sun. 1–5.*

WORTH NOTING

Old Governor's Mansion. This Georgian-style house was built for Governor Huey P. Long in 1930, and eight governors have since lived there. The story goes that Long instructed the architect to design it to resemble the White House, representing Long's unrealized ambition to live in the real one. Notable features on the guided tour include Long's bedroom and a secret staircase. This historic house museum also houses the Foundation for Historical Louisiana headquarters and functions as a venue for special events. ✉ *502 North Blvd.* ☎ *225/387–2464* ⊕ *www. oldgovernorsmansion.org* ✉ *$7* ☉ *Tues.–Sat. 10–4.*

Old State Capitol. When this turreted Gothic Victorian castle was constructed between 1847 and 1852, it was declared by some a masterpiece, by others a monstrosity. No one can deny that the restored building is colorful and dramatic. In the entrance hall a stunning pink, gold, and green spiral staircase winds toward a stained-glass atrium. The building now holds the Louisiana Center for Political and Governmental History, an education and research facility with audiovisual exhibits. The "assassination room," an exhibit covering Huey Long's final moments, is a major draw. The Ghost of the Castle Exhibit is a 12-minute video that tells the history of the building, as narrated by Sarah Morgan, whose father donated the land the building was built on. ✉ *100 North Blvd., at River Rd.* ☎ *225/342–0500 or 800/488–2968* ⊕ *www.louisianaoldstatecapitol.org* ✉ *Free* ☉ *Tues–Sat. 9–4.*

State Capitol Building. Still called the "New State Capitol," this building has housed the offices of the governor and Congress since 1932. It is a testament to the personal influence of legendary Governor Huey Long that the funding for this massive building was approved during the Great Depression, and that the building itself was completed in a mere 14 months. You can tour the first floor, richly decked with murals and mosaics, and peer into the halls of the Louisiana legislature. Huey Long's colorful personality—and autocratic ways—eventually caught up with him: he was assassinated in 1935, and the spot where he was shot (near the rear elevators) is marked with a plaque. At 34 stories, this is America's tallest state capitol; an observation deck on the 27th floor affords an expansive view of the Mississippi River, the city, and the industrial outskirts. ✉ *900 N. 3rd St.* ☎ *225/342–7317* ✉ *Free* ☉ *Daily 8–4:30 (tower until 4).*

WHERE TO EAT AND STAY

For expanded hotel reviews, visit Fodors.com.

$$$

SOUTHERN

★

✕ **Juban's.** This upscale bistro with a lush courtyard and walls adorned with art is about 3 miles from the LSU campus. Tempting main courses of seafood, beef, and veal dishes, as well as roasted duck, rabbit, and quail highlight the menu. The Hallelujah Crab (soft-shell stuffed with seafood and topped with "creolaise" sauce) is a specialty, and Juban's own mango tea is delicious. The warm bread pudding makes a memorable end to meals here. [S] *Average main: $30* ✉ *Acadian Perkins Shopping Center, 3739 Perkins Rd.* ☎ *225/346–8422* 🌐 *www.jubans.com* 🕑 *Closed Sun. No lunch Mon. and Sat.*

$$ SEAFOOD 🍴 **Mike Anderson's.** This busy seafood spot manages to be a lot of things to a lot of people: first-daters, families, groups of friends, and solo diners all find a warm welcome here. Locals of every stripe praise the seafood, and it is true that the food is good, fresh, served in large portions, and consistent. The South Louisiana Combo—fried shrimp, oysters, crawfish tails, catfish, and stuffed crab served with french fries, hush puppies, and a choice of salad of various coleslaws—is your best bet. [S] *Average main: $20* ✉ *1031 W. Lee Dr.* ☎ *225/766–7823* 🌐 *www.mikeandersons.com.*

$ JAPANESE 🍴 **Tsunami.** On the roof of the Shaw Center for the Arts, the sleek, modern dining room of this Japanese restaurant commands one of the best views in town, with tables overlooking the busy Mississippi River (an open-air patio is available too). In addition to the usual sushi-bar fare, the chefs here prepare creative Louisiana-style variations: try the panko-crusted alligator roll or the tempura oysters, for instance. Weekday happy-hour specials draw a young and chatty crowd. [S] *Average main: $15* ✉ *Shaw Center for the Arts, 100 Lafayette St., 6th fl., Baton Rouge* ☎ *225/346–5100* 🌐 *www.servingsushi.com* 🕑 *Closed Sun. and Mon.*

$$$$ HOTEL 🏨 **Hilton Baton Rouge Capitol Center.** The former Heidelberg Hotel is centrally located along the river in downtown Baton Rouge, less than a mile from the capitol. **Pros:** spectacular view of the river; near all the downtown sites. **Cons:** can get crowded when conventions are in town. **TripAdvisor:** "great folks," "fabulous service," "excellent location." [S] *Rooms from: $165* ✉ *201 Lafayette St.* ☎ *225/344–5866* 🌐 *www.hiltoncapitolcenter.com* 🛏 *290 rooms, 8 suites* 🍽 *No meals.*

$$ HOTEL 🏨 **Marriott Baton Rouge.** This high-rise hotel has somewhat formal rooms and public spaces with traditional furnishings. **Pros:** accommodating to large groups; full-service hotel; lots of comforts. **Cons:** not that close to downtown sights. **TripAdvisor:** "top notch," "super friendly staff," "great rooms." [S] *Rooms from: $109* ✉ *5500 Hilton Ave.* ☎ *225/924–5000 or 800/228–9290* 🌐 *www.marriott.com* 🛏 *300 rooms* 🍽 *Multiple meal plans.*

$$$ B&B/INN 🏨 **The Stockade B&B.** It's named for the Civil War–era military prison that once occupied the site, though you definitely won't feel like a prisoner in this pleasant, tile-roofed, contemporary, brick house on the winding, oak-lined Highland Road. **Pros:** Southern hospitality and country elegance. **Cons:** the downtown sights can feel far away. **Trip-Advisor:** "beautiful and romantic," "fantastic setting," "art-filled comfort." [S] *Rooms from: $135* ✉ *8860 Highland Rd., Baton Rouge* ☎ *225/769–7358 or 888/900–5430* 🌐 *www.thestockade.com* 🛏 *6 rooms* 🍽 *Breakfast.*

ST. FRANCISVILLE

25 miles north of Baton Rouge on U.S. 61.

A cluster of plantation homes all within a half-hour drive; a lovely, walkable historic district; renowned antiques shopping; and a wealth of comfortable B&Bs draw visitors and locals from New Orleans to overnight stays in St. Francisville. The town is a two-hour drive from New Orleans, so it's also possible to make this a day trip.

St. Francisville's historic district, particularly along Royal Street, is dotted with markers identifying basic histories of various structures, most of them dating to the late 18th or early 19th century. The region's Anglo-Protestant edge, in contrast to the staunchly French-Catholic tenor of the River Road plantations, is evident in the prominent **Grace Episcopal Church,** sitting atop a hill in the center of town and surrounded by a peaceful, Spanish moss–shaded cemetery. The smaller (though older) Catholic cemetery is directly across a small fence from the Episcopal complex.

EXPLORING

Butler Greenwood Plantation. This home has been occupied by the same family since its construction in the 1790s, and the ninth generation owns it today. Its appearance is much simpler than that of the Greek Revival mansions, whose style was prevalent in the 1830s and '40s. Original family documents provide an intimate picture of day-to-day life. The tour focuses on details such as dress (several items of clothing worn by the family's ancestors are on display) and china (a beautiful set has been in the family for generations). The home remains family owned and operated, and the tour is run by a member of the Butler family. Eight cottages are available for overnight stays. ⊠ *8345 U.S. 61* ☎ *225/635–6312* ⊕ *www.butlergreenwood.com* 🖃 *$5* ⊙ *Daily 9–5.*

OFF THE BEATEN PATH

Angola Museum. The 18,000 acres that make up the notorious Angola prison are a half-hour drive from St. Francisville, at the dead end of Highway 66. With a prison population of about 5,200 inmates, this is one of the largest prisons in the United States. Nicknamed "The Farm," Angola was once a working plantation, with prisoners for field hands. Now, it produces 4 million pounds of vegetables each year that feed 11,000 inmates across the state. The prison has been immortalized in countless songs and several films and documentaries, including *Dead Man Walking* and *Angola Prison Rodeo—the Wildest Show in the South.* The prison runs a biannual rodeo in April and October, offering visitors a rare look inside the grounds of the prison. Inmates set up stands where they sell their arts and crafts during the rodeo. A small museum outside the prison's front gate houses a fascinating, eerie, and often moving collection of photographs documenting the people and events that have been a part of Angola. Items such as makeshift prisoner weapons and the electric chair used for executions until 1991 are also on display. ⊠ *Hwy. 66* ☎ *225/655–2592* ⊕ *www.angolamuseum. org* 🖃 *Free* ⊙ *Nov.–Sept., weekdays 8–4:30, Sat. 8–4; Oct., weekdays 8–4:30, Sat. 8–4, Sun. 10–5.*

The Myrtles. A 110-foot gallery with Wedgwood-blue cast-iron grillwork makes a lovely setting for the weddings and receptions frequently held at the Myrtles. The house, built around 1796, has elegant formal parlors with rich molding and faux-marble paneling. Because the upper floor is used as a bed-and-breakfast, the scope of the daytime guided tour is limited. The house is reputedly haunted, and the fun mystery tours, held at night, are more of a draw than the day tours (reservations are a good idea). The Carriage House Restaurant, beside the house, is a fine place for lunch or dinner. ✉ *7747 U.S. 61, about 1 mile north of downtown St. Francisville* ☎ *225/635–6277 or 800/809–0565* 🌐 *www.myrtlesplantation.com* 🎟 *$8 day tours, $10 mystery tours* 🕓 *Daily 9–5; mystery tours Fri. and Sat. nights at 6, 7, and 8.*

OFF THE BEATEN PATH

Audubon State Historic Site and Oakley Plantation House. John James Audubon did a major portion of his *Birds of America* studies in this 100-acre park. The three-story Oakley Plantation House on the grounds is where Audubon tutored the young Eliza Pirrie, daughter of Mr. and Mrs. James Pirrie, owners of Oakley. The simple, even spartan, interior contrasts sharply with the extravagances of many of the River Road plantations and demonstrates the Puritan influence in this region. The grounds, too, are reminiscent of the English penchant for a blending of order and wilderness in their gardens. You must follow a short path to reach the house from the parking lot. A state-run museum at the start of the path provides an informative look at plantation life as it was lived in this region 200 years ago. ✉ *11788 L.A. Hwy. 965, 2 miles south of St. Francisville off U.S. 61* ☎ *225/635–3739 or 888/677–2838* 🌐 *www.crt.state.la.us* 🎟 *Park and plantation $4* 🕓 *Daily 9–5, guided tours 10–4 pm on the hour.*

Fodor's Choice ★

Rosedown Plantation and Gardens. The opulent, beautifully restored house at Rosedown dates from 1835. The original owners, Martha and Daniel Turnbull, spent their honeymoon in Europe; Mrs. Turnbull fell in love with the gardens she saw there. She had the land at Rosedown laid out even as the house was under construction, and she spent the rest of her life lovingly maintaining some 374 acres of excuisite formal gardens. The state of Louisiana owns Rosedown, and the beauties of the restored manor, including 90% of the original furniture, can be appreciated during a thorough one-hour tour led by park rangers. Be sure to allow ample time for roaming the grounds after the tour. ✉ *12501 Hwy. 10, off U.S. 61* ☎ *225/635–3332 or 888/376–1867* 🌐 *www.crt.state.la.us* 🎟 *$10, grounds only $5* 🕓 *Daily 9–5.*

WHERE TO EAT AND STAY

For expanded hotel reviews, visit Fodors.com.

$$ CAJUN

🍴 **Carriage House Restaurant.** Located in the shadow of the Myrtles Plantation, the Carriage House is a boon to overnighters in the St. Francisville area. The dining room is elegant and intimate. The contemporary cuisine draws from a wealth of culinary traditions, with a mix of classic Southern cuisine and a dash of Creole. The baked oysters Bienville and the buttery barbecue shrimp are both worth keeping an eye out for, and the Sunday brunch is a favorite. [S] *Average main: $20* ✉ *Myrtles Planta-*

tion, 7747 U.S. 61 ☎ *225/635–6278* 🌐 *www.themyrtlesrestaurant.com* 🕒 *Closed Tues. No dinner Sun.*

$ AMERICAN 🍴 **The Magnolia.** This low-key and unassuming dining establishment turns into a St. Francisville hot spot on weekend nights. During the day, locals and tourists flock to "The Mag" for sandwiches, pizza, steaks, and Southern and Mexican dishes. At night, go for cocktails or dinner; on Friday evening there's always a live band. [S] *Average main: $15* ✉ *5689 Commerce St.* ☎ *225/635–6528* 🌐 *www.themagnoliacafe.net* 🕒 *No dinner Sun.–Wed.*

$ SOUTHERN ★ 🍴 **Roadside BBQ & Grill.** Looking for Southern barbecue? Here it is—ribs, pork, and chicken, all perfectly grilled. If you're not in the mood for 'cue, they also have hamburgers, salads, and fried seafood po' boys. There's a seafood buffet for lunch on Sunday. A children's menu is also available. [S] *Average main: $8* ✉ *Colonial Dr. and U.S. 61, 9 miles south of St. Francisville* ☎ *225/658–9669* 🕒 *Closed Mon. No dinner Tues. and Sun.*

$$$ B&B/INN 🏨 **Barrow House & Printer's Cottage.** Fittingly located on St. Francisville's historic Royal Street, these two old houses hold some of the most comfortable bed-and-breakfast accommodations in the area, with antique furnishings in most of the rooms. **Pros:** good location in downtown St. Francisville; comfortable atmosphere; friendly staff. **Cons:** if you don't like antiques, you may feel as if you're in a museum or your grandmother's home. **TripAdvisor:** "lovely," "very nice and relaxing," "elegant." [S] *Rooms from: $150* ✉ *9779 Royal St.* ☎ *225/635–4791* 🌐 *www.topteninn.com* 🛏 *4 rooms, 4 suites* 🍽 *Breakfast.*

$$$$ B&B/INN 🏨 **The Myrtles.** If you don't mind a deep legacy of hauntings, the Myrtles is a pleasant and convenient place to stay, just a few miles beyond the center of St. Francisville. **Pros:** historical property oozes atmosphere; ghost hunters' paradise; next door to Carriage House Restaurant. **Cons:** feels like it's in the middle of nowhere; easily spooked travelers might want to stay elsewhere. **TripAdvisor:** "interesting and unique," "great history," "Southern charm." [S] *Rooms from: $200* ✉ *7747 U.S. 61* ☎ *225/635–6277 or 800/809–0565* 🌐 *www.myrtlesplantation.com* 🛏 *10 rooms, 1 suite* 🍽 *Breakfast.*

CAJUN COUNTRY

French Louisiana, lying amid the bayous, rice paddies, and canebrakes to the west of New Orleans, has become famous in the rest of the country for its food—"jambalaya and a crawfish pie and filé gumbo," as Hank Williams put it—and its rollicking Cajun and zydeco music. The Cajun culture has its roots far from these parts in the present-day Canadian provinces of Nova Scotia and New Brunswick, where French settlers colonized a region they called l'Acadie at the start of the 17th century. After the British seized control of the region in the early 18th century, the French were expelled. Their exile was described by Henry Wadsworth Longfellow in his epic poem "Evangeline." Many Acadians eventually settled in 22 parishes of southwestern Louisiana. Their descendants are called "Cajun," a corruption of "Acadian"; some con-

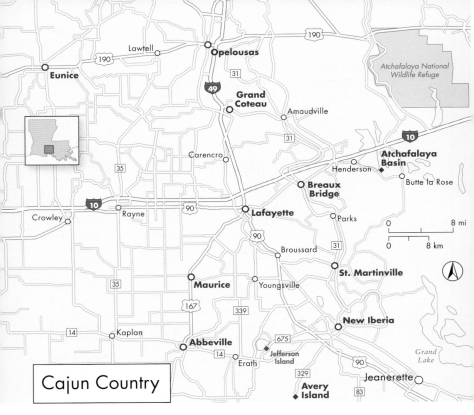

Cajun Country

tinue the traditions of the early French settlers, living by fishing and fur trapping.

Cajun culture is decidedly rural, rooted in a smattering of tiny towns and in the swamps and bayous that wind among them. Driving from one village to the next, antiques shoppers and nature lovers alike will find bliss. Live oaks with ragged gray buntings of Spanish moss form canopies over the bottle-green bayous. Country roads follow the contortions of the Teche (pronounced *tesh*), the state's longest bayou, and meander through villages where cypress cabins rise up out of the water on stilts and moored fishing boats and canoelike pirogues scarcely bob on the sluggish waters. At the centers of these same villages are wonderful bakeries, historic churches, fresh oyster bars, and regional antiques for sale in small, weathered shops.

Many visitors to this region are surprised to hear the dialect for the first time. Cajun French is an oral tradition in which French vocabulary and grammar encounter the American accent, and it differs significantly from what is spoken in France. English is also spoken throughout Cajun Country, but you will hear Gallic accents and see many signs that read "Ici on parle français" (French spoken here).

12

GETTING HERE AND AROUND

BUS TRAVEL

Greyhound has numerous daily departures from New Orleans to Lafayette. The trip takes 3–3½ hours.

Bus Information **Greyhound** ☎ *800/231–2222* ⊕ *www.greyhound.com.*

CAR TRAVEL

Interstate 10 runs east–west across the state and through New Orleans. Take Interstate 10 west to the Lafayette exit, 136 miles from New Orleans. The interstate route takes about two hours and 15 minutes. Return to New Orleans via U.S. 90, down through Houma, for scenic stopovers. This route will take close to three hours.

TRAIN TRAVEL

Amtrak connects New Orleans and Lafayette via the *Sunset Limited*. Trains make the three- to four-hour scenic trip each way once daily.

Train **Amtrak** ☎ *800/872–7245* ⊕ *www.amtrak.com.*

TOURS

Allons à Lafayette. Guides for customized tours are available from this company. ☎ *800/264–5465* ⊕ *www.allonsalafayette.com.*

24-Hour Pharmacy **CVS** ✉ *1920 Kaliste Saloom Rd., Lafayette* ☎ *337/984–1092.*

VISITOR INFORMATION

Contacts **Lafayette Convention and Visitors Commission** ☎ *337/232–3737* or *800/346–1958* ⊕ *www.lafayettetravel.com.* **St. Martin Parish Tourism Commission** ☎ *800/565–5939* ⊕ *www.cajuncountry.org.* **St. Landry Parish Tourist Commission** ☎ *337/948–8004* ⊕ *www.cajuntravel.com.*

LAFAYETTE

136 miles west of New Orleans

Lafayette (pronounced lah-fay-*ette*), with a population of about 120,000 (the largest city in Cajun Country), is a major center of Cajun life and lore. It's an interesting and enjoyable city, with some worthwhile historical and artistic sights. The simulated Cajun villages at **Vermilionville** and **Acadian Village** provide evocative introductions to the traditional Cajun way of life. Excellent restaurants and B&Bs make Lafayette a good jumping-off point for exploring the region. The city has also had an infusion of new restaurants and nightclubs—particularly downtown.

EXPLORING

Alexandre Mouton House and Lafayette Museum. Built in 1800 as the *maison dimanche,* or "Sunday house," of town founder Jean Mouton, this galleried town house with a mid-19th-century addition now preserves local history. The older section is an excellent example of early Acadian architecture and contains artifacts used by settlers. The main museum contains Civil War–era furnishings and memorabilia and an exhibit on Mardi Gras. ✉ *1122 Lafayette St.* ☎ *337/234–2208* 🖾 *$5* ⏱ *Tues.–Sat. 10–4.*

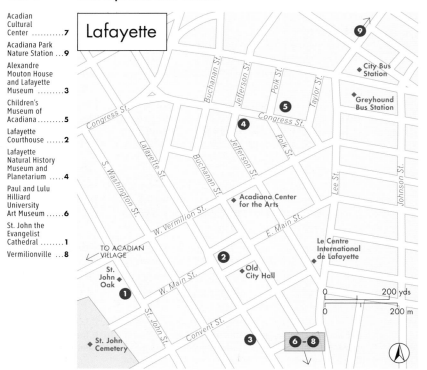

Lafayette

★ **Children's Museum of Acadiana.** Good on a rainy day or to burn off extra energy in the kids, this museum is basically a large indoor playground, with educational games and interactive exhibits such as a grocery store, a kid-size TV news studio, a bubble exhibit, and a pet exhibit. ✉ *201 E. Congress St.* ✆ *337/232–8500* ⊕ *www.childrensmuseumofacadiana. com* ➔ *$5* ☉ *Tues.–Sat. 10–5.*

Lafayette Courthouse. The courthouse contains an impressive collection of more than 2,000 historical photographs of life in the Lafayette area. There are images of famous politicians such as Dudley LeBlanc and Huey Long working the stump and scenes from the great flood of 1927. ✉ *800 S. Buchanan St.* ✆ *337/233–0150* ☉ *Weekdays 8:30–4:30.*

★ **Lafayette Natural History Museum and Planetarium.** This sparkling natural-history museum includes changing exhibitions and lots of fun hands-on science for kids. The most popular permanent attraction is the planetarium, upgraded in 2012 to include high-definition digital equipment. ✉ *433 Jefferson St.* ✆ *337/291–5544* ⊕ *www.lafayettesciencemuseum. org* ➔ *$5* ☉ *Tues.–Fri. 9–5, Sat. 10–6, Sun. 1–6.*

St. John the Evangelist Cathedral. This cathedral, completed in 1916 (construction began in 1912), is a Dutch Romanesque structure with Byzantine touches. Union troops camped on the grounds during the Civil War. In the cemetery behind the church are aboveground tombs

12

that date back to 1820; interred here are town founder Jean Mouton, Civil War hero General Alfred Mouton, General Alfred Gardiner, and Cidalese Arceneaux. Next to the cathedral is a nearly 500-year-old St. John Oak, one of the charter members of the silent but leafy Louisiana Live Oak Society. Call two weeks in advance to schedule a tour. ⊠ *914 St. John St.* ☎ *337/232–1322* ⊕ *www.saintjohncathedral. org* ☉ *Museum: Mon.–Thurs. 9–noon and 1–4, Fri. 9–noon.*

OUTSIDE DOWNTOWN

Acadian Cultural Center. A unit of the National Park service, the center traces the history of the area through numerous audiovisual exhibits of food, music, and folklore. Be sure to watch the introductory film, which is a dramatization of the Acadian exile. Black-and-white clips from the 1929 movie *The Romance of Evangeline* are incorporated in the film; film buffs will love it. Ranger-guided boat tours of Bayou Vermilion take place March through June and September through November in a traditional Cajun boat. ⊠ *501 Fisher Rd.* ☎ *337/232–0789* ⊕ *www.nps.gov/jela* ⌑ *Free* ☉ *Daily 8–5.*

> **MURALS**
>
> There are several outdoor murals by the local artist Robert Dafford in the center of Lafayette, including a 100-foot-wide Louisiana swamp scene, titled *"Till all That's Left is a Postcard,"* which is across from Dwyer's Café. Another work, titled "Ex-Garage" and full of splashy cars and TVs with vignettes of Cajun life, is on the Jefferson Tower Building. The reflections in the bumpers of the cars reveal area musicians and traditions.

OFF THE BEATEN PATH

Acadian Village. A re-creation of an early-19th-century bayou settlement, this park is on 10 wooded acres with a meandering bayou crisscrossed by wooden footbridges. Most structures here were constructed during the early 19th century; they were moved here to create this representative "village," though they actually represent a broad range of Acadian architectural styles. Each house is decorated with antique furnishings. The rustic general store, blacksmith shop, and chapel are replicas of 19th-century buildings. The weeks in December before Christmas bring "Noel Acadian au Village," with later hours, musicians, food, and buildings covered in lights. ⊠ *200 Greenleaf Dr., south of downtown* ☎ *337/981–2364 or 800/962–9133* ⊕ *www.acadianvillage.org* ⌑ *$8* ☉ *Late Dec.–Nov., Tues.–Sat. 10–4; Dec. 1–23 also open, Tues.–Sat. 5:30–9.*

Acadiana Center for the Arts. This multicultural arts center hosts art exhibits, musical performances, lectures, and children's programs. Film screenings are occasionally held at the in-house movie theater. ⊠ *101 W. Vermilion St.* ☎ *337/233–7060* ⊕ *www.acadianacenterforthearts. org* ☉ *Tues.–Sat. 10–5.*

Acadiana Park Nature Station. Naturalists are on hand in the interpretive center at this three-story cypress structure, which overlooks a 42-acre park of natural forest. Discovery boxes help children get to know the wildflowers, birds, and other outdoorsy things they'll see on the 3-mile nature trail. Free guided trail tours take place every Saturday and Sunday at 1 pm. There is a guided evening hike on the last Saturday of the month ($3 per person). ⊠ *1205 E. Alexander St.* ☎ *337/291–8448* ⊕ *www.naturestation.org* ⊠ *Free* ☉ *Weekdays 8–5, weekends 11–3.*

Paul and Lulu Hilliard University Art Museum. Inside a gleaming glass-clad box built in 2003, this museum features world-class works, including works by Deborah Butterfield and Robert Rauschenberg. ⊠ *710 E. St. Mary Blvd.* ☎ *337/482–2278* ⊕ *www.louisiana.edu/uam* ⊠ *$5* ☉ *Tues.– Thurs. 9–5, Fri. 9–noon, Sat 10–5, closed Sun.*

☼ **Vermilionville.** Directly behind the Acadian Cultural Center, a living-history village re-creates the early life of the region's Creoles, Cajuns and Native Americans, focusing on the late 1800s to the early 1900s. On select days visitors can see a blacksmith demonstration or weavers. There are exhibits in 19 Acadian-style structures, including a music hall where live Cajun or zydeco music is played every Saturday afternoon. A large rustic restaurant serves Cajun classics. Check ahead for live cooking demonstrations from their on-site cooking school. ⊠ *300 Fisher Rd., off Surrey St.* ☎ *337/233–4077 or 866/992–2968* ⊕ *www. bayouvermilion.org* ⊠ *$10* ☉ *Tues.–Sun. 10–4.*

WHERE TO EAT

$$$
CAJUN
✕ **Café Vermilionville.** This 19th-century inn with crisp white linens and old-brick fireplaces serves French and Cajun fare to a well-dressed crowd. Among the specialties are Gulf fish Acadien and grilled duck breast. This is a favorite spot for special occasions among Lafayette residents. ⓢ *Average main: $30* ⊠ *1304 W. Pinhook Rd.* ☎ *337/237–0100* ⊕ *www.cafev.com* ☉ *Closed Sun. No lunch Sat.*

$
SOUTHERN
✕ **Crawfish Time.** From roughly December through June, when Louisiana crawfish are in season, local families pack into boiled-seafood specialists like Crawfish Time to partake in the outrageous abundance. The simple, stripped-down room is filled with big tables, and crawfish, oysters, and a few sides like sausage links and boiled potatoes, plus cold beer, are essentially the whole menu. Use the drive-through window for orders to go and create your own crawfish picnic. ⓢ *Average main: $15* ⊠ *320 Ridge Rd., Lafayette* ☎ *337/216–9955* ⊕ *www.lacrawfishtime.com* ☉ *Closed June–Nov. No lunch.*

$
SOUTHERN
✕ **Johnson's Boucaniere.** This *boucaniere* (Cajun French for smoke-house) is run by the next generation of the same family that operated the iconic Johnson's Grocery, which closed in 2005. It's a laid-back, friendly place with a refreshing blend of tradition and modern style. Music from young local bands plays over the sound system (their

CREOLE VS. CAJUN

Cajun cuisine relies on locally available ingredients, including pork, seafood, smoked meats, yams, and rice. Most dishes have the "holy trinity" of sautéed celery, bell pepper, and onion as a base; traditional examples include boudin and *maque choux* (a corn stew, usually served with crawfish tails). Creole cuisine is more cosmopolitan, incorporating French, Spanish, Italian, African, and French Caribbean influences. While many dishes use the same holy trinity, Creole dishes, like their French counterparts, are defined by their sauces. Examples include shrimp Creole, crawfish bisque, and oysters Rockefeller.

Dropping in on a jam session is a must-do in Cajun country.

CDs line the shelves next to barbecue sauces for sale); customers sit on the covered porch and dig into boudin, sandwiches, and the heartily recommended barbecue, which is smoked in-house and rubbed with Cajun-style seasonings. [S] *Average main: $7* ✉ *1111 St. John St., Lafayette* ☎ *337/269–8878* 🌐 *www.johnsonsboucaniere.com* ⏲ *Closed Mon. No dinner Tues.–Thurs.*

$$ CAJUN Fodor's Choice ★

🍴 **Prejean's.** Original artwork lines the walls of this local favorite along Interstate 49, north of central Lafayette. Three meals are served in this cypress house decorated with swamp trees and a large stuffed alligator at the entrance. People gather at tables with red-and-white-check cloths to chow down on some of Prejean's classics: crawfish and alligator sausage cheesecake, Cajun-style venison, or any of the kitchen's four distinctive gumbos. Grilled seafood provides some lighter options. At breakfast, try the house rendition of eggs Benedict, made here with boudin patties, poached eggs, and crawfish étouffée over a biscuit. There's live Cajun music, and usually dancing, nightly. [S] *Average main: $18* ✉ *3480 N.E. Evangeline Throughway* ☎ *337/896–3247* 🌐 *www.prejeans.com.*

$ CAJUN

🍴 **T-Coon's Café.** This often-busy diner serves a hearty Cajun breakfast and lunch, which include daily specials such as smothered rabbit, short-rib fricassee or crawfish omelets. More Southern fare includes fried chicken and seafood dishes. [S] *Average main: $8* ✉ *1900 W. Pinhook Rd.* ☎ *337/233–0422* 🌐 *www.tcoons.com* ⏲ *No dinner.*

WHERE TO STAY

For expanded hotel reviews, visit Fodors.com.

$$$ B&B/INN ★ **Bois des Chênes Inn.** This bed-and-breakfast is housed in the 19th-century Mouton Plantation, in a quiet residential area of Lafayette. **Pros:** nice owners; pretty grounds; glass of wine and tour of the house included in rates. **Cons:** rooms can be a little stuffy. **TripAdvisor:** "comfortable," "wonderful hospitality," "charming hosts." [S] *Rooms from: $150* ✉ *338 N. Sterling St.* ☎ *337/233–7816* 🌐 *www.boisdechenes.com* 🛏 *5 rooms* 🍴 *Breakfast.*

$$$ B&B/INN **Buchanan Lofts.** Staying in one of these nine rooms is like subletting a seriously stylish apartment—each has a different size and layout, but they're also quite spacious. **Pros:** close to everything downtown; huge rooms filled with stylish furnishings. **Cons:** not much local character. [S] *Rooms from: $140* ✉ *403 S. Buchanan St., Lafayette* ☎ *337/534–4922* 🌐 *www.buchananlofts.com* 🛏 *9 rooms* 🍴 *No meals.*

$$ B&B/INN **Juliet Boutique Hotel.** This modern hotel is one of the few boutique properties in downtown Lafayette. **Pros:** great location; extremely comfortable beds; you'll feel as if you're staying in your own private hotel. **Cons:** some rooms have structural poles; bathrooms have shuttered windows (and don't feel very private); checkout can take a while (since there's only one person at the front desk). **TripAdvisor:** "charming," "well located," "beautiful and elegant rooms." [S] *Rooms from: $107* ✉ *800 Jefferson St.* ☎ *337/261–2225* 🛏 *20 rooms* 🍴 *No meals.*

$$ B&B/INN **T'Frere's House.** Built in 1880 of native cypress and handmade bricks, "little brother's house" has been a bed-and-breakfast since 1985. **Pros:** charming decor; owners like to feed their guests well; great if you are looking to get away from it all but still want to be near 21st-century amenities. **Cons:** it feels a bit far from everything; not a good option if you're on a diet. **TripAdvisor:** "great Southern charm," "beautiful old house," "lots of personality and hospitality." [S] *Rooms from: $105* ✉ *1905 Verot School Rd.* ☎ *337/984–9347 or 800/984–9347* 🌐 *www.tfreres.com* 🛏 *8 rooms* 🍴 *Breakfast.*

NIGHTLIFE AND THE ARTS

Pick up a copy of the *Times of Acadiana* or the trendier *Independent* to find listings for *fais-do-dos*, zydeco dances, and other events. These free weeklies are available in hotels, restaurants, and shops.

Blue Moon Saloon. This cottage doesn't look like much from the street, but after you pay your cover at the garden gate, you'll soon find yourself on a large covered deck packed with a young crowd dancing to the hottest local Cajun, zydeco, and roots music acts. ✉ *215 E. Convent St., Lafayette* ☎ *337/234–2422* 🌐 *www.bluemoonpresents.com.*

El Sid–o's. This family-run zydeco club hosts music on Friday and Saturday nights. Sid Williams manages the club, and his brother's band, Nathan and the Zydeco Cha-Chas, performs frequently—as does Nathan's son's band—Lil Nathan and the Zydeco Big Timers. ✉ *1523 N. St. Antoine* ☎ *337/235–0647.*

Randol's. This good Cajun restaurant is also a "salle de danse," with music and dancing nightly. ✉ *2320 Kaliste Saloom Rd.* ☎ *337/981–7080 or 800/962–2586* 🌐 *www.randols.com.*

12

Scotty's Icehouse. The beers are cold and the music from local bands is hot at this nightspot near the University of Louisiana at Lafayette's campus. ✉ *1043 Johnston St., Lafayette* ☎ *337/534–8612.*

FESTIVALS

ArtWalks. Downtown galleries are open and the streets are hopping during this popular event, which is held on the second Saturday of each month. ☎ *337/291–5566* ⊕ *www.downtownlafayette.org.*

Downtown Alive!. On Friday evenings from mid-March through June and from September through November, dancing crowds converge on downtown Lafayette, where bands play on an open-air stage. ✉ *Jefferson St. at Main St.* ☎ *337/291–5566* ⊕ *www.downtownlafayette.org.*

Festival Acadiens et Creoles. This huge music-and-food fest is held in mid-October. The admission's free, and the food is outstanding. ☎ *337/232–3737 or 800/346–1958* ⊕ *www.festivalsacadiens.com.*

★ **Festival International de Louisiane.** Taking place on the last weekend of April, this free music festival may rival the New Orleans Jazz and Heritage Festival; it fills the streets with entertainers, artisans, and chefs from French-speaking nations and communities. ☎ *337/232–8086* ⊕ *www.festivalinternational.com.*

Mardi Gras. The biggest bash in this neck of the woods is in February or March, depending on when Lent occurs. Up to a dozen different parades take to the streets over five days, culminating on "Fat Tuesday," and a festival atmosphere fills the city. ⊕ *www.gomardigras.com.*

SHOPPING

ANTIQUES

Sans Souci Gallery. If you are looking for authentic Louisiana crafts, you've come to the right place. Pottery; furniture; items made out of gourds, metal, and wood; and cornhusk dolls and jewelry are all created by members of the Louisiana Crafts Guild, which is housed here. ✉ *219 E. Vermilion St.* ☎ *337/266–7999* ⊕ *www.louisianacrafts.org* ☉ *Closed Sun. and Mon.*

FOOD

Don's Specialty Meats & Grocery. Fill your cooler with boudin, cracklings, stuffed pork chops, quail, and a variety of sausages at Don's two locations—both are just outside Lafayette. ✉ *730 I–10 S. Frontage Rd., Scott* ☎ *337/234–2528 or 337/896–6370* ⊕ *www.donsspecialtymeats.com* ✉ *104 Hwy. 1252, Carencro* ☎ *337/896–6370.*

Poupart's Bakery. The fresh French bread and pastries baked here are outstanding. It also sells specialty sauces and preserves, as well as king cakes, available during the carnival season. ✉ *1902 West Pinhook Rd.* ☎ *337/232–7921* ⊕ *www.poupartsbakery.com* ☉ *Closed Mon.*

GRAND COTEAU

11 miles north of Lafayette.

The tiny village of Grand Coteau may be the most serene place in south Louisiana. Nestled against a sweeping ridge that was a natural levee of the Mississippi River centuries ago ("grand coteau" means big hill), the town is oriented around a core of grand and beautiful religious institutions. Covering the hill itself is a peaceful cemetery, behind the stately St. Charles College, a Jesuit seminary. When the Mississippi overflowed its banks during the cataclysmic flood of 1927, the water stopped at the base of Grand Coteau's ridge, and the town was preserved. Today the entire town center is listed on the National Register of Historic Places, with dozens of historical structures including Creole cottages, early Acadian-style homes, and the grand Academy and Convent of the Sacred Heart. Martin Luther King Drive (Route 93) is the main thoroughfare. Antiques stores line the main street.

EXPLORING

Academy and Convent of the Sacred Heart. A magnificent avenue of pines and moss-hung oaks leads to the entrance of the first international branch of Sacred Heart schools (founded in 1821), and the site of the only Vatican-certified miracle to occur in the United States. The miracle occurred when nuns at the convent said novenas to St. John Berchmans, a 15th-century Jesuit priest, on behalf of Mary Wilson, a very ill novice. St. John Berchmans subsequently appeared to Mary twice, and she was suddenly and unexpectedly cured. St. John Berchmans was canonized in 1888. You may enter a shrine on the exact site of the miracle and (by appointment only) tour a museum with artifacts dating from the school's occupation by Union troops during the Civil War. ✉ *1821 Academy Rd., end of Church St.* ☎ *337/662–5275* 🌐 *www.ashcoteau.org* 🕒 *Weekdays 9–3.*

WHERE TO EAT

$$ ECLECTIC 🍴 **Catahoula's.** This stylish yet simple restaurant serves dishes that integrate French classics, Louisiana favorites, and Mediterranean influences. Locally made Creole cream cheese and caramelized onions fill the flaky, buttery tarte à l'oignon, for instance, while grilled fish, eggplant medallions, and crab cake are stacked for a seafood napoleon—which is then topped with fried oysters and a Chardonnay-and-Tabasco cream sauce. The spare decor inside this renovated former dry-goods store highlights artistic representations of the Catahoula Hound, Louisiana's state dog. [S] *Average main: $20* ✉ *234 Martin Luther King Dr.* ☎ *337/205–0578* 🌐 *www.catahoulasgrandcoteau.com* 🕒 *Closed Mon.–Thurs.*

SHOPPING

Kitchen Shop. In one of Grand Coteau's historic cottages, the Kitchen Shop specializes in regional cookbooks and cooking supplies, in addition to a wide range of gifts and other merchandise. It also has prints and greeting cards by famed local photographer John Slaughter. In the tearoom, scones, cookies, and a specialty pecan torte called gateau-nana are served. ✉ *296 Martin Luther King Dr., at Cherry St.* ☎ *337/662–3500* 🕒 *Tues.–Sat. 10–5, Sun. 1–5.*

OPELOUSAS

15 miles north of Grand Coteau.

In the heart of St. Landry Parish, Opelousas is the third-oldest town in the state—Poste de Opelousas was founded in 1720 by the French as a trading post with the Opelousas Indians. It's a sleepy spot with a historic central square, a provincial museum, and several excellent zydeco clubs in town and on its outskirts. Look for two murals located in a pocket park–parking lot adjacent to the St. Landry Bank & Trust Co. building. One depicts the history of the area and historical monuments in St. Landry Parish and the other depicts the legend of the Seven Brothers Oak, which is located south of Washington, a charming nearby town.

WEEKEND ANTIQUES HUNTING

Antiques lovers will want to stop in **Washington**, a short, 2-mile diversion from the main route if you're traveling from Opelousas to Ville Platte. Settled in 1720, Washington has many buildings on its main street that are on the National Register of Historic Places. More than 10 antiques stores cluster within walking distance of one another. Most of these stores are open only Friday to Sunday. For more information, contact the town's **museum and tourist information center** (☎ *337/826-3626* 🌐 *www.townofwashingtonla.org*).

Opelousas Tourist Information Center. At the intersection of Interstate 49 and U.S. 190, look for the Opelousas Tourist Information Center, where you can get plenty of information, arrange for tours of historic homes, and see memorabilia pertaining to Jim Bowie, the Alamo hero who spent his early years in Opelousas. ☎ *337/948–6263* 🕒 *Weekends 9–4, weekdays 8–4:30.*

EXPLORING

Louisiana Orphan Train Museum. Between 1854 and 1929, more than 2,000 orphans from New York were transplanted via train to Louisiana. The museum, housed in an old depot building, has more than 200 photos and articles of clothing of the orphans who made the journey. ✉ *233 S. Academy* ☎ *337/948–9922* 🌐 *www.laorphantrain.com* 🎟 *$5* 🕒 *Tues.–Fri. 10–3, Sat. 10–2.*

Opelousas Museum and Interpretive Center. This museum traces the history of Opelousas from prehistoric times to the present and includes an exhibit on the town's brief stint as state capital, during the Civil War, and a collection of more than 400 dolls. The museum is also home to the Louisiana Video Library and the Southwest Louisiana Zydeco Festival archives. ✉ *315 N. Main St.* ☎ *337/948–2589* 🎟 *Free* 🕒 *Weekdays 8–4:30, Sat. 10–3.*

WHERE TO EAT

$ DINER ★ 🍴 **Palace Café.** On the town square, you can step back in time at this old-style diner. Be sure to get the biscuits at breakfast, and try one of the six different types of gumbo at lunch or dinner. [S] *Average main: $10* ✉ *135 W. Landry St.* ☎ *337/942–2142* 🕒 *Closed Sun.*

NIGHTLIFE AND THE ARTS

The roads surrounding Opelousas are *the* place to catch authentic, sweaty zydeco music.

Slim's Y-Ki-Ki. This long, low, somewhat musty dance hall is a legend among zydeco lovers: it's been here since the 1940s. All the big regional acts perform here, and during festival times the club is packed wall-to-wall with dancers. ✉ *8410 Hwy. 182, Opelousas* ☎ *337/942–6242* ⊕ *www.slimsykiki.com.*

Southwest Louisiana Zydeco Music Festival. Plaisance, on the outskirts of Opelousas, holds this event in a melon patch on the Saturday before Labor Day. A parade, jam session, and breakfast are all part of the festivities. ☎ *337/942–2392* ⊕ *www.zydeco.org.*

Zydeco Hall of Fame. Known for generations as Richard's, this classic zydeco dance hall has a long history. Its schedule can be sporadic, but when the sign lights up, the zydeco faithful pour in. ✉ *11154 U.S. 190, Lawtell.*

SHOPPING

Floyd's Record Shop. Come here for recordings of Cajun, zydeco, and "swamp pop"—a mix of rock, R & B, and Cajun music that's big in the area. ✉ *434 E. Main St., Ville Platte* ☎ *337/363–2185* ⊕ *www.floydsrecordshop.com.*

EUNICE

20 miles southwest of Opelousas.

As home to some of Cajun music's most prominent proponents and establishments, tiny Eunice lays claim to some heft within the Cajun music world. Saturday is the best time to visit: spend the morning at a jam at the **Savoy Music Center;** at midday move on to see Tante Sue de Mamou at **Fred's Lounge;** end the day at the variety show *Rendez-Vous des Cajuns,* in Eunice's **Liberty Theatre.**

Courir de Mardi Gras. The area surrounding Eunice is the major stomping ground for an annual event, Courir de Mardi Gras, French for Fat Tuesday Run, which takes place on Mardi Gras Day. Costumed horseback riders dash through the countryside, stopping at farmhouses along the way to shout, "*Voulez-vous recevoir cette bande de Mardi Gras* (Do you wish to receive the Mardi Gras krewe)?" The answer is always yes, and the group enlarges and continues, gathering food for the street festivals that wind things up. .

EXPLORING

Eunice Depot Museum. This museum, in a former railroad depot, contains modest displays on Cajun culture, including Cajun music and Cajun Mardi Gras. ✉ *220 S. C. C. Duson Dr.* ☎ *337/457–6540 or 337/457–2565* 🎟 *Free* ⊙ *Tues.–Sat. 8–noon, 1–5.*

Prairie Acadian Cultural Center. Part of the Jean Lafitte National Historical Park, this impressive center has well-executed exhibits tracing the history and culture of the Prairie Acadians, whose lore and customs differ from those of the Bayou Acadians south of Lafayette. Food, crafts, and music demonstrations are held on Saturday. ✉ *250 W. Park Ave.* ☎ *337/457–8499* ⊕ *www.nps.gov/jela* 🎟 *Free* ⊙ *Tues.–Fri. 8–5, Sat. 8–6.*

Fodor's Choice ★   **Savoy Music Center and Accordion Factory.** Part music store, part Cajun accordion workshop, proprietor Marc Savoy's factory turns out about five specialty accordions a month for people around the world. On

CLOSE UP

Cajun and Zydeco Music

12

It's 9 am on a typical Saturday morning in the Cajun prairie town of Mamou, and Fred's Lounge (⇨ *Nightlife and the Arts in Eunice)* is already so full that people are spilling out the door. Inside, Cajun singer Donald Thibodeaux gets a nod from the radio announcer, squeezes his accordion, and launches into a bluesy rendition of "Pine Grove Blues." Oblivious to the posted warning that says "This is not a dancehall," the packed bar begins to roll. Fred's Lounge may not be a "formal" dance hall, but plenty of dancing is done here; it gets especially lively during Mamou's Mardi Gras and July 4 celebrations. And every Saturday morning for more than 40 years, live Cajun radio shows have been broadcast from the late Fred Tate's lounge. Things get revved up at 8 am and keep going till 1 pm, and the show is aired on Ville Platte's KVPI radio (1050 AM).

Music has been an integral expression of Cajun culture since early Acadian immigrants unpacked stringed instruments and gathered in homes for singing and socializing. With the growth of towns, these house parties—called *fais-do-dos* (pronounced *fay*-doh-doh, from "go to sleep" in French. The term *fais-do-do* comes from words mothers murmured to put their babies to sleep while the fiddlers tuned up before a dance.)—were supplanted by dance halls. Accordions, steel guitars, and drums were added

and amplified to be heard over the noise of crowded barrooms.

Cajun music went through some lean years in the 1940s and '50s when the state attempted to eradicate the use of the Cajun-French language, but today Cajun music is enjoyed at street festivals and restaurants such as Randol's and Prejean's, which serve equal portions of seafood and song. These places not only keep the music and dance tradition alive but also serve as magnets for Cajun dance enthusiasts from around the world.

Zydeco, the dance music of rural African Americans of south Louisiana, is closely related to Cajun music, but with a slightly harder, rock-influenced edge. The best place to find the music is in one of the roadside dance halls on weekends. Modern zydeco and Cajun music are both accordion based, but zydeco tends to be faster and uses heavy percussion and electric instruments; electric guitars and washboards (called a *frottoir*), largely absent from Cajun music, are staples of zydeco. Zydeco bands often play soul- and rhythm and blues–inflected tunes sung in Creole French.

Dance is the universal language of Cajun Country, but don't worry if you're not fluent—there's always someone happy to lead you around the floor and leave you feeling like a local.

Saturday morning, accordion players and other instrumentalists head here for jam sessions; musicians from all over the area drop in. ⊠ *U.S. 190, 3 miles east of town* ☎ *337/457–9563* ⊕ *www.savoymusiccenter. com* 🖃 *Free* ☉ *Tues.–Fri. 9–noon and 1:30–5, Sat. 9–noon.*

Savoy Family Band jamming in their famous store.

NIGHTLIFE AND THE ARTS

★ **Fred's Lounge.** This place is hopping on Saturday from about 8 am until about 2 pm, or for as long as the Cajun band jams and dancers crowd the tiny dance floor. A regular radio broadcast (on KVPI 1050 AM) captures the event. Drive north from Eunice on Route 13 to the tiny town of Mamou. ⊠ *420 6th St., Mamou* ☎ *337/468–5411* 🖃 *Free.*

Rendez-Vous des Cajuns. In addition to showcasing the best Cajun and zydeco bands, this two-hour variety program presents local comedians and storytellers and even a "Living Recipe Corner." The show, mostly in French, has been dubbed the Cajun Grand Ole Opry; it's held every Saturday at 6 pm in a 1924 movie house and is broadcast on local radio and TV. ⊠ *Liberty Center for the Performing Arts, 200 W. Park Ave., at 2nd St.* ☎ *337/457–7389* 🖃 *$5.*

BREAUX BRIDGE

10 miles northeast of Lafayette, 20 miles southeast of Grand Coteau.

A dyed-in-the-wool Cajun town, Breaux Bridge is known as the Crawfish Capital of the World. During the first full weekend in May, the Crawfish Festival draws more than 100,000 visitors to this little village on Bayou Teche. The town has attracted a small arts community that includes renowned Louisiana photographer Debbie Fleming Caffery and has traded its honky-tonks for B&Bs, antiques shops, and restaurants.

Chamber of Commerce. You can pick up a city map and information at the Chamber of Commerce, at the foot of the bridge that gives Breaux

Bridge its name, about ½ mile south of Interstate 10. ✉ *314 E. Bridge St.* ☎ *337/332–5406* 🌐 *www.chamber.breauxbridgelive.com.*

WHERE TO EAT AND STAY

For expanded hotel reviews, visit Fodors.com.

$ CAJUN ★ 🍴 **Café des Amis.** The culinary heart of downtown Breaux Bridge is in this historic, renovated storefront that's a block from Bayou Teche. Locals and visitors gather here to enjoy hospitality that is second only to the food. Soak in the ambience over cocktails or coffee at the bar, or take a table and try the extraordinary turtle soup or the crawfish corn bread. Breakfast here should be savored, from the java and fresh-squeezed orange juice to the *oreille de cochon* (pastry-wrapped boudin) and *couche-couche* (corn-bread-based cereal). Saturday mornings bring the extremely popular Zydeco Breakfast, featuring a band and dancing. [S] *Average main: $15* ✉ *140 E. Bridge St.* ☎ *337/332–5273* 🌐 *www.cafedesamis.com* ⏲ *Closed Mon. No dinner Sun. and Tues.*

$ CAJUN 🍴 **Poche's.** Order your authentic Cajun cooking at the counter of this butcher shop and lunch room, then eat in or take away. The daily specials will always stick to your ribs. Boudin, sausage, cracklings, and stuffed chicken are just a few of the items available for takeout. [S] *Average main: $8* ✉ *33015-A Main Hwy., 2 miles from center of Breaux Bridge* ☎ *337/332–2108* 🌐 *www.poches.com.*

$$ B&B/INN 🏨 **Bayou Cabins.** It's right on a main drag, but this collection of guest cabins still feels rustic and has personality galore. **Pros:** socializing with guests and locals in the café. **Cons:** though it looks rustic, you can hear the busy road nearby. **TripAdvisor:** "cute cabins," "authentic Southern charm," "real Cajun hospitality." [S] *Rooms from: $100* ✉ *100 W. Mills St., Breaux Bridge* ☎ *337/332–6158* 🌐 *www.bayoucabins.com* 🛏 *14 rooms* ⏲ *Restaurant closed Mon. and Tues.* 🍽 *Breakfast.*

$$ B&B/INN Fodor's Choice ★ 🏨 **Maison des Amis.** This 19th-century house on the bank of Bayou Teche has comfort and relaxation in mind. **Pros:** bayou views; steps from downtown Breaux Bridge. **Cons:** breakfast is outsourced to nearby restaurants, where you may have to wait. **TripAdvisor:** "fabulous location in a charming town," "unique architectural style," "beautiful accommodations." [S] *Rooms from: $110* ✉ *111 Washington St.* ☎ *337/507–3399* 🌐 *www.maisondesamis.com* 🛏 *4 rooms* 🍽 *Breakfast.*

NIGHTLIFE

La Poussière. This ancient Cajun honky-tonk has live music on Saturday and Sunday. ✉ *1301 Grand Point Ave.* ☎ *337/332–1721.*

ATCHAFALAYA BASIN

5 miles northeast of Breaux Bridge, 12 miles east of Lafayette.

The Atchafalaya Basin is an eerily beautiful 800,000-plus-acre swamp wilderness, the storybook version of mystical south Louisiana wetlands. Boating enthusiasts, bird-watchers, photographers, and nature lovers are drawn by vast expanses of still water, cypresses standing knee-deep in marsh and dripping with Spanish moss, and blue herons taking flight. The basin is best viewed from one of the tour boats on its waters, but it's possible to explore around its edges on the 7 miles of Henderson's

Alligators Up Close: Swamp Tours

12

The bayous, swamps, and rivers of south Louisiana's wetlands present a tantalizingly unfamiliar landscape to many visitors, and the best way to get better acquainted is by boat. Tour operators offer convenient departure times and hotel pickups in New Orleans. Most tour operators use pontoon boats, but—depending on the size of the group—a bass boat might be used. Anticipate from one to two hours on the water and 45 minutes to two hours' commute time to and from New Orleans. Prices are generally around $20 per person. Expect to see nutria, a member of the rodent family that resembles a beaver in appearance and size; egrets (a white, long-necked heron with flowing feathers); turtles; and the occasional snake. During the warmer months, alligator sightings are common. Many of the guides use either chicken or marshmallows to attract them. Plant life includes Spanish moss, cypress, water oaks, and water hyacinths (a member of the lily family). In the summer months, be prepared for the heat and humidity—and don't forget the insect repellent and a hat.

Cajun Country Swamp Tours. These tours are led by guide Walter "Butch" Guchereau, who was born, raised, and still lives on the banks of Bayou Teche in Breaux Bridge. An experienced outdoorsman with a degree in zoology and biology, Guchereau uses Cajun crawfish skiffs for his tours to make them environmentally unobtrusive. His son Shawn also leads tours. ⊠ *1209 Rookery Rd., Breaux Bridge* ☎ *337/319–0010* ⊕ *www.cajuncountryswamptours.com* ⊗ *Tours daily.*

McGee's Landing. Pontoon boats take passengers out daily for 1½-hour tours of the Atchafalaya Basin. McGee's is a 25-minute drive east of Lafayette. Tour times are contingent upon the presence of at least four passengers. The company also organizes canoe, kayak, and airboat trips. ⊠ *1337 Henderson Levee Rd., Henderson* ⊹ *From I–10, Exit 115 at Henderson; 1 block south of the highway turn left on Rte. 352 and follow it more than 2 miles east over Bayou Amy; turn right atop the levee onto Levee Rd.* ☎ *337/228–2384* ⊕ *www.mcgeeslanding.com* ⊠ *Tour $20* ⊗ *Tours daily 10, 1, and 3. Additional tour at 5 during daylight saving time.*

CLOSE UP

Evangeline

In all of Acadiana, St. Martinville is the spot where you can sense most vividly the tragic aspect of the Cajun story, whether in the tiny cemetery behind the main church, or at the bayou-side Evangeline Oak. Henry Wadsworth Longfellow's epic poem "Evangeline" (1847) is based on historic documents that chronicle a couple's tragic separation, a result of the British expelling Acadians from Nova Scotia in 1755. Evangeline Bellefontaine and Gabriel Lajeneusse were taken from each other on their wedding day. Once Evangeline arrives in Louisiana, she finds out Gabriel had been there, but left to live in the Ozarks. After years of searching for him, Evangeline finds Gabriel on his deathbed in Philadelphia.

Many believe the two represent real-life counterparts Emmeline Labiche and Louis Arceneaux, though those names themselves are based on another fictional version of the legend. According to the oft-told tale, the real-life lovers met for the last time under the **Evangeline Tree** at Evangeline Boulevard at Bayou Teche. Louis arrived in St. Martinville, a major debarkation port for the refugees, but it was many years before Emmeline came. Legend has it that the two saw each other by chance just as she stepped ashore. He turned deathly pale with shock and told her that, having despaired of ever seeing her again, he was betrothed to another. *The Romance of Evangeline* was filmed in St. Martinville in 1929. The movie was never distributed, but clips from it are incorporated in the film presentation at the Jean Lafitte National Historical Park Acadian Cultural Center in Lafayette. Its star, Dolores Del Rio, posed for the bronze statue of Evangeline that the cast and crew donated to St. Martinville; it's in the cemetery behind the church of St. Martin de Tours, near the final resting place of Emmeline Labiche.

Levee Road (also known as Route 5; off Interstate 10, Exit 115), which provides several opportunities to cross the levee and access swamp tours, bars, and restaurants on the other side.

WHERE TO EAT

$$
CAJUN
★

✕ **Pat's Fishermans Wharf Restaurant.** Adjacent to Bayou Amy, Pat's is the real deal, with heaping platters of seafood. On a cool night, get a table on the porch overlooking the bayou and go for the crawfish dinner, which presents the local favorite no fewer than eight different ways. The Atchafalaya Club, which is the area hot spot for Cajun dancing on Saturday nights, is next door. Accommodations are also available at Pat's Edgewater Inn, located on the same stretch. **$** *Average main: $20* ⊠ *1008 Henderson Levee Rd.* ☏ *337/228–7512.*

ST. MARTINVILLE

15 miles south of Breaux Bridge.

St. Martinville, along winding Bayou Teche, is the heart of Evangeline country. It was founded in 1761 and became a refuge for both Acadians kicked out of Nova Scotia as well as royalists who escaped the guillotine during the French Revolution. Known as Petit Paris, this little town was once the scene of lavish balls and operas, and you can still roam through the original old opera house on the central square. St. Martinville is tucked away from the state's major highways and misses much of the tourist traffic. It's a tranquil and historically interesting stop, although neighboring towns are better for dining and nightlife. The St. Martinville Tourist Information Center is across the street from the Acadian Memorial and African American Museum.

EXPLORING

Acadian Memorial. A video introduction, a wall of names of Acadian Louisiana refugees, and a huge mural relate the odyssey of the Acadians. Behind the small heritage center containing these memorials, an eternal flame and the coats of arms of Acadian families pay tribute to their cultural and physical stamina. ✉ *121 S. New Market St.* ☎ *337/394–2258* 🌐 *www.acadianmemorial.org* 🎟 *$3, includes admission to African American Musuem* 🕒 *Daily 10–4:30.*

African American Museum. This museum traces the African and African-American experience in southern Louisiana. Videos, artifacts, and text panels combine to create a vivid, disturbing, and inspiring portrait of a people. It is an ambitious and refreshing balance to the sometimes sidelined or romanticized references to slavery and its legacy. ✉ *121 New Market St.* ☎ *337/394–2273* 🎟 *$3, includes admission to Acadian Memorial* 🕒 *Daily 10–4:30.*

Longfellow-Evangeline State Historic Site. Shaded by giant live oaks draped with Spanish moss, this 157-acre park has picnic tables and pavilions and early Acadian structures. The on-site museum traces the history of the Acadians and their settlement along the Bayou Teche in the early 1800s. The modest house was built in 1815 of handmade bricks, and it contains Louisiana antiques. A one-hour tour includes many interesting details about life on the plantation. ✉ *1200 N. Main St. (Rte. 31), ½ mile north of St. Martinville* ☎ *337/394–3754 or 888/677–2900* 🌐 *www.crt.state.la.us/parks* 🎟 *$4* 🕒 *Tues.–Sat. 9–5.*

St. Martin de Tours. The mother church of the Acadians and one of the country's oldest Catholic churches, this 1836 building was erected on the site of an earlier church. Inside is a replica of the Lourdes grotto and a baptismal font said to have been a gift from Louis XVI. Emmeline Labiche, who may have inspired Henry Wadsworth Longellow's poem "Evangeline," is buried in the small cemetery behind the church. ✉ *123 S. Main St.* ☎ *337/394–6021.*

WHERE TO STAY

For expanded hotel reviews, visit Fodors.com.

$$$ B&B/INN 🏨 **Old Castillo Bed and Breakfast.** In the early 1800s this two-story red-brick building next to the Evangeline Oak and Bayou Teche was an inn for steamboat passengers and a gathering place for French royalists. **Pros:** there's no better place to stay in St. Martinville, as it's right by a number of attractions; friendly staff; delicious breakfast. **Cons:** if you have a downstairs room, you hear everything that happens downstairs; decor is a little dated. **TripAdvisor:** "an island of old-world charm," "quaint," "beautiful." [S] *Rooms from: $125*

✉ *220 Evangeline Blvd.* ☎ *337/394–4010 or 800/621–3017* ⊕ *www.oldcastillo.com* 🛏 *7 rooms* ❍ *Breakfast.*

NEW IBERIA

14 miles south of St. Martinville.

The town of New Iberia is the hub of lower Cajun Country, second only to Lafayette as an arts-and-culture draw. The grand homes of sugarcane planters dominate the residential section of Main Street, just off Bayou Teche, pointing to a glorious past at the center of a booming sugar industry. Park downtown or stay in one of the numerous B&Bs and you can easily walk to the bayou, restaurants, art galleries, and shops in the historic business district. Downtown stretches eight blocks east and west on Main Street (Route 182) from the intersection of Center Street (Route 14). The Shadows-on-the-Teche plantation home is at this intersection and is a good place to park.

EXPLORING

Bayou Teche Museum. The story of New Iberia's Spanish colonial roots and the role of Bayou Teche in helping nurture Cajun culture are on display in this small, well-produced museum, housed in a historic building that was once a grocery. Interactive exhibits cover the area's history, its colorful characters, and its culture. The museum's interior layout is based on the snakelike curves of Bayou Teche itself. ✉ *131 Main St., New Iberia* ☎ *337/606–5977* ⊕ *www.bayoutechemuseum.org* 💲 *$4* ❍ *Thurs.–Sat. 10–4.*

Conrad Rice Mill. The country's oldest rice mill that's still in operation, dating from 1912, produces distinctive wild pecan rice. Tours are conducted on the hour between 10 am and 3 pm. The adjacent **Konriko Company Store** sells Cajun crafts and foods. ✉ *307–309 Ann St.* ☎ *337/367–6163 or 800/551–3245* ⊕ *www.conradricemill.com* 💲 *Mill $4* ❍ *Mon.–Sat. 9–5.*

★ **Shadows-on-the-Teche.** One of the South's best-known plantation homes was built on the bank of the bayou for the wealthy sugar planter David Weeks in 1834. In 1917 his descendant William Weeks Hall conducted one of the first historically conscious restorations of a plantation home, also preserving truckloads of documents that helped explain day-to-day life here. The result is one of the most fascinating tours in Louisiana. Weeks Hall willed the property to the National Trust for Historic Preservation in 1958, and each year the trust selects a different historical topic to emphasize. Surrounded by 2 acres of lush gardens and moss-draped oaks, the two-story rose-hued house has white columns, exterior staircases sheltered in cabinet-like enclosures, and a pitched roof pierced by dormer windows. The furnishings are 85% original to the house. ✉ *317 E. Main St.* ☎ *337/369–6446 or 877/200–4924* ⊕ *www.shadowsontheteche.org* 💲 *$10* ❍ *Mon.–Sat. 9–4:30.*

WHERE TO EAT AND STAY

For expanded hotel reviews, visit Fodors.com.

$$ ✕ **Clementine.** Named for folk artist Clementine Hunter and employing
CAJUN   an insignia based on her signature, Clementine favors cuisine that might

be called nouveau Cajun: it's inspired by local ingredients and traditions, but subtly seasoned and artfully presented. For instance, the local grouper might be seared and served in a red curry sauce, and the the richness of roast duck might be complemented by the tang of a honey-and-raspberry glaze. Changing art exhibits by locals are introduced at bimonthly openings featuring wine and hors d'oeuvres. Clementine hosts live music on Friday and Saturday nights. [S] *Average main: $22* ✉ *113 E. Main St.* ☎ *337/560–1007* 🌐 *www.clementinedowntown.com* 🕒 *Closed Sun. and Mon. No lunch Sat.*

$$$ B&B/INN 🏨 **Bayou Teche Guest Cottage.** There could scarcely be a better way to appreciate the Queen City of the Teche than to spend a night in this simple, two-room, 18th-century cottage on the bank of the bayou, down the road from downtown attractions. **Pros:** pretty views; full kitchen with refrigerator; good location to explore New Iberia; if you want to be alone, this is the place. **Cons:** depending on what you expect from a bed-and-breakfast, you'll either find it charming or a bit worn around the edges. **TripAdvisor:** "the true essence of New Iberia," "great property and location," "romantic." [S] *Rooms from: $125* ✉ *100 Teche St.* ☎ *337/364–1933* 🌐 *www.bayoutechecottage.com* 🛏 *1 cottage* 💳 *No credit cards* 🍴 *Breakfast.*

$$$ B&B/INN 🏨 **Le Rosier.** A gracious reception awaits at this 19th-century house across from the Shadows-on-the-Teche plantation. **Pros:** easy walk into town; beautiful courtyard; good for groups. **Cons:** walls are thin; rooms on the small side. **TripAdvisor:** "friendly and comfortable," "lovely innkeepers," "charming." [S] *Rooms from: $130* ✉ *314 E. Main St.* ☎ *337/367–5306* 🌐 *www.lerosier.com* 🛏 *5 rooms* 🍴 *Breakfast.*

NIGHTLIFE AND THE ARTS

Sliman Theater for the Performing Arts. This intimate theater with a classic art deco facade is the site of the "Louisiana Crossroads" concert series, which features Louisiana musicians and others several times a month. ✉ *129 E. Main St.* ☎ *337/369–2337* 🌐 *www.acadianaartscouncil.org.*

AVERY ISLAND

9 miles southwest of New Iberia.

The Louisiana coastline is dotted with "hills" or "domes" that sit atop salt mines, and Avery Island is one of these. They are covered with lush vegetation, and because they rise above the surface of the flatlands, they are referred to as islands.

Avery Island is the birthplace of Tabasco sauce, which pleases the Cajun palate and flavors many a Bloody Mary

EXPLORING

👶 **Jungle Gardens.** This 170-acre garden has trails through stands of wisteria, palms, lilies, irises, and ferns and offers a lovely perspective on southern Louisiana wilderness. Birdlife includes ducks and geese, and there's also a 1,000-year-old statue of Buddha. These gardens belonged to Edward Avery McIlhenny, the son of the Tabasco company's founder, who brought back plants from his travels: lotus and papyrus from Egypt, bamboo from China. You can park your car at the beginning of

PARLEZ-VOUS CAJUN FRANÇAIS?

It's not uncommon while traveling through Cajun country to hear French—the Cajun version. Here are a few words that might help you enjoy and understand the lingo.

Allons: Let's go!

Bayou: A sluggish body of water, larger than a creek, but smaller than a river.

C'est la vie: Such is life.

Cher: Dear

Cochon de lait: A pig roast; literally, a suckling pig.

Étouffée: A stew mainly made with seafood, in which the "holy trinity" (celery, garlic, and bell pepper) is used.

Fais-do-do: A dance. French for "Go to sleep," which was what parents would whisper to their children so they could go dancing.

Lagniappe: A little something extra.

Laissez les bons temps rouler: Let the good times roll.

Roux: Flour browned in fat and used as a thickener in many Cajun dishes such as gumbo.

the trails and strike out on foot, or drive through the gardens and stop at will. ⊠ *Rte. 329* ☎ *337/369–6243* ⊕ *junglegardens.org* 🖃 *$8 Jungle Gardens and Bird City; $1 toll to enter Avery Island* ☉ *Daily 9–5.*

Bird City. The bird sanctuary on the southeast edge of Jungle Gardens is sometimes so thick with egrets that it appears to be blanketed with snow. The largest egret colony in the world (20,000) begins nesting here in February or March, and offspring remain until the following winter. Herons and other birds find refuge here as well. ⊠ *Rte. 329*

Tabasco Factory. Tabasco was invented by Edmund McIlhenny in the mid-1800s, and the factory is presided over by the fourth generation of the McIlhenny family. Tabasco is sold all over the world, but it is aged, distilled, and bottled only here, on Avery Island (these days the peppers themselves are mostly grown in Central and South America). You can take a factory tour, which lasts about 20 minutes and highlights the bottling process. The Jungle Gardens and Bird City are adjacent. ⊠ *Rte. 329* ☎ *337/365–8173 or 800/634–9599* ⊕ *www.tabasco.com* 🖃 *Tour free; $1 toll to enter Avery Island* ☉ *Daily 9–4.*

ABBEVILLE

15 miles south of Lafayette.

Abbeville has a number of historic buildings and two pretty village squares anchoring the center of downtown. It's a good stop for pleasant walks and for oysters on the half shell, a local obsession. The town sponsors the annual Giant Omelet Festival each November, when some 5,000 eggs go into the concoction. It's also the base for Steen's Cane Syrup.

Abbeville Tourist Office. You can pick up a self-guided walking-tour brochure at the Abbeville Tourist Office. Many buildings in the 20-block Main Street district are on the National Register of Historic Places. ⊠ *200 North Magdalen Sq.* ☎ *337/898–4114* ⊕ *www.abbevillemuseum.org.*

EXPLORING

St. Mary Magdalen Catholic Church. A fine Romanesque Revival building built in 1915, St. Mary Magdalen has stunning stained-glass windows. ✉ *N. Main and Père Megret Sts.* ☎ *337/893–0244* 🌐 *www.stmarymagdalenparish.org* 🕒 *Mon.–Sat. 8–5; Sun. mass 7, 9:30, and 11.*

WHERE TO EAT

$$ SEAFOOD 🍴 **Dupuy's Oyster Shop.** This small and simply furnished restaurant has been serving family-harvested oysters in the same location since 1869. Seafood platters feature seasonal specials. Steaks, pastas, and regional specialties like boudin balls and po'boys all round out the menu. [S] *Average main: $16* ✉ *108 S. Main St.* ☎ *337/893–2336* 🌐 *www.dupuysoystershop.com* 🕒 *Closed Sun. and Mon. No lunch Sat.*

$ CAJUN 🍴 **Richard's Seafood Patio.** You cross the Vermilion River on a vintage drawbridge and continue down a winding country road to find this classic Cajun "seafood patio," a no-frills dining room serving immense quantities of boiled crawfish, shrimp, and crabs. There's a full menu of fried and grilled items—and cold beer. Richard's opens at 5 pm and fills up almost immediately, so expect a wait. [S] *Average main: $15* ✉ *1516 S. Henry St., Abbeville* ☎ *337/893–1146* 🕒 *Closed Sun.*

MAURICE

10 miles north of Abbeville, almost 11 miles south of Lafayette.

Maurice is considered the gateway to Vermilion Parish, and lies between Lafayette and Abbeville. Many overlook this small town, but it's well worth the stop for Hebert's Specialty Meats' world-famous turducken and the Maurice Flea Market.

WHERE TO EAT

$ CAJUN 🍴 **Hebert's Specialty Meats.** A visit to Cajun country is not complete without stopping at Hebert's. This butcher shop is one of several contenders claiming to be the place that invented turducken—a turkey stuffed with a duck that's been stuffed with a chicken. You can grab a link of hot boudin to eat on the spot, or fill a cooler with andouille, deboned chicken, and other regional delicacies for later. [S] *Average main: $10* ✉ *8212 Maurice Ave.(aka Rte. 167)* ☎ *337/893–5062* 🌐 *www.hebertsmaurice.com.*

SHOPPING

Maurice Flea Market. From fine antiques to slightly rusted kitchen utensils, this is a treasure-hunter's paradise. Be prepared to spend more than an hour at this store. ✉ *9004 Maurice Ave.(Rte. 167)* ☎ *337/898–2282* 🕒 *Wed.–Sat. 10–5.*

Travel Smart
New Orleans

WORD OF MOUTH

"If you don't mind the heat and humidity, August is by far the cheapest month in New Orleans. If you can't stand heat and humidity and want cheap rates, December is your only option, as November is still high season. January after the Sugar Bowl is usually quiet, but it can get quite cold in January in New Orleans."

—bkluvsNola

GETTING HERE AND AROUND

New Orleans fills an 8-mile stretch between the Mississippi River and Lake Pontchartrain. Downtown includes the French Quarter, the Central Business District (CBD), Warehouse District, Tremé, and the Faubourg Marigny. Uptown includes the Garden District, Audubon Park, and Tulane and Loyola universities, as well as the Carrollton and Riverbend neighborhoods.

It's best to know your location relative to the following thoroughfares: Canal Street (runs from the river toward the lake), St. Charles Avenue (runs uptown from Canal), Interstate 10 (runs west to the airport, east to Slidell), and LA Highway 90 (takes you across the river to the West Bank). To get to the CBD from Interstate 10, exit at Poydras Street near the Louisiana Superdome. For the French Quarter, look for the Orleans Avenue/Vieux Carré exit.

Canal Street divides the city roughly into the uptown and downtown sections (though the CBD and Warehouse District, considered part of downtown, actually lie just upriver from Canal). Keeping a visual on the Superdome is the surest way to know where the CBD is; the French Quarter lies just to the northeast of it over Canal Street.

Streets that start in the French Quarter and cross over Canal Street change names as they go upriver. For example, Decatur Street becomes Magazine Street and Royal Street becomes St. Charles Avenue. Addresses begin at 100 on either side of Canal Street, and begin at 400 in the French Quarter at the river.

■ AIR TRAVEL

Flying time is 2½ hours from New York, 2¼ hours from Chicago, 1¼ hours from Dallas, and 4½ hours from Los Angeles. Book early for popular weekends such as Mardi Gras and Jazz Fest.

Airline Security Issues **Transportation Security Administration** ⊕ *www.tsa.gov*.

AIRPORTS

The major gateway to New Orleans is Louis Armstrong New Orleans International Airport (MSY), 15 miles west of the city in Kenner. There's an airport exit off Interstate 10. Plan for about 30–45 minutes of travel time from downtown New Orleans to the airport (more at rush hour). An alternative route is Airline Drive, which will take you directly to the airport from Tulane Avenue or the Earhart Expressway. Be prepared for stoplights and possible congestion.

Airport Information **Louis Armstrong New Orleans International Airport** ☎ *504/464–0831* ⊕ *www.flymsy.com*.

GROUND TRANSPORTATION
SHUTTLE BUSES

Shuttle-bus service to and from the airport and downtown hotels is available through Airport Shuttle New Orleans, the official ground transportation of Louis Armstrong International Airport. You can purchase shuttle tickets at the Airport Shuttle desk, located across from baggage claim areas 3, 6, and 12. To return to the airport, call 24 hours in advance of flight time. The cost one way is $20 per person, and the trip takes about 40 minutes.

Jefferson Transit also runs a bus between the airport, the CBD, and Mid-City, although it only goes to the CBD on weekdays. The trip costs $2 in exact change ($1.50 from Carrollton and Tulane avenues) and takes about 45 minutes. From the airport, you can catch the E-2 line on the second level near the Delta counter. Departures for the airport are every 10 to 15 minutes during peak hours and every 30 to 35 minutes in the middle of the day from Elks Place and Tulane Avenue across from the main branch of the New Orleans Public Library, and from the corner of Tulane and Carrollton avenues.

The last bus leaves at 6:52 from Tulane and Elks Place, 9:49 pm from Tulane and Carrollton.

Contacts Airport Shuttle New Orleans ☎ *504/522–3500 or 866/596-2699* ⊕ *www. airportshuttleneworleans.com.* **Jefferson Transit** ☎ *504/818–1077* ⊕ *www.jeffersontransit. org/busroutes.htm.*

TAXIS

A cab ride to or from the airport from uptown or downtown costs $33 for up to two passengers. For groups of three or more, the rate is $14 per person. Pickup is on the lower level, outside the baggage-claim area. There may be an additional charge for extra baggage. *See "Taxi Travel" for taxi companies and contact information.*

▌ BOAT TRAVEL

BY FERRY

The ferry ride across the river to Algiers is an experience in itself, offering great views of the river and the New Orleans skyline as well as the heady feeling of being on one of the largest and most powerful rivers in the world. Pedestrians enter near the Spanish Plaza and the Riverwalk shopping area and board the Canal Street Ferry from above. Bicycles and cars board from below on the left of the terminal. The trip takes about 10 minutes; ferries leave on the quarter and three-quarter hour from the east bank (New Orleans) and on the hour and half hour from the west bank (Algiers)—they run from 6 am to midnight. Hours at night may vary, so be sure to check with the attendants if you are crossing in the evening—it's no fun to be stranded on the other side. There are wheelchair-accessible restrooms on the ferry.

Information Canal Street Ferry ✉ *Foot of Canal at Convention Center Blvd.* ☎ *504/376–8180* ⊕ *www.friendsoftheferry.org* 🖭 *$1 cash round-trip per car only from Algiers to Canal Street, free for pedestrians.*

CRUISES

Large cruise lines like Carnival, Norwegian, and Royal Caribbean International depart from New Orleans.

For more information, visit the Port of New Orleans website at ⊕ *www.portno. com* or call ☎ *504/522-2551.*

Cruise Lines American Cruise Lines ☎ *800/460–4518* ⊕ *www. americancruiselines.com.* **Blount Small Ship Adventures** ☎ *866/730-5265* ⊕ *www. blountsmallshipadventures.com.* **Great American Steamboat Company** ☎ *888/749–5280* ⊕ *www.greatamericansteamboatcompany.com.* **Travel Dynamics International** ☎ *800/257–5767* ⊕ *www.traveldynamicsinternational.com.*

▌ BUS AND STREETCAR TRAVEL

GETTING AROUND BY BUS AND STREETCAR

Within New Orleans, the Regional Transit Authority (RTA) operates a public bus and streetcar (not "trolley") transportation system with interconnecting lines throughout the city. The buses are generally clean and on time. Buses run on a regular schedule from about 6 am to 6 pm. Smoking, eating, and drinking are not permitted on RTA vehicles. Buses are wheelchair accessible; streetcars are not.

ROUTES

The riverfront streetcar covers a 2-mile route along the Mississippi River, connecting major sights from the end of the French Quarter (Esplanade Avenue) to the New Orleans Convention Center (Julia Street). Nine stops en route include the French Market, Jackson Brewery, Canal Place, the World Trade Center, the Riverwalk, and the Hilton Hotel. This streetcar operates daily 7 am until 10:30 pm, passing each stop every 20 minutes.

The historic streetcars of St. Charles Avenue run from St. Charles Avenue at Common Street to the Riverbend at Carrollton Avenue roughly every 20 minutes. This line continues on along Carrollton

Avenue and stops at Claiborne Avenue in Mid-City. Streetcar service on St. Charles Avenue runs 24 hours a day, though wait times can be as long as 30 minutes between 11:30 pm and 3 am.

A third streetcar line runs along Canal Street from the river near Harrah's Casino to either City Park or the Cemeteries. Going from Harrah's Casino to the Cemeteries, it passes every 15 minutes. As it gets closer to City Park, it passes every 40 minutes. The Canal Street line operates from 5 am to about 3 am, with longer waits after midnight. A $135 million expansion of track, set to run past the CBD and the French Quarter, then eastward into residential Tremé, Faubourg Marigny, and Bywater is in the works for 2012–13.

COSTS

Bus and streetcar fare is $1.25 exact change plus 25¢ for transfers. Unlimited passes, valid on both buses and streetcars, cost $3 for one day, $9 for three days, and $55 for a month. The daily passes are available from streetcar and bus operators; three-day and monthly passes are available at many local hotels and at most Walgreens.

Bus and Streetcar Information RTA ☎ *504/248–3900* ⊕ *www.norta.com.*

TICKET/PASS	PRICE
Single Fare	$1.25
One-day VisiTour Pass	$3
Three-day VisiTour Pass	$9
One-month Unlimited Pass	$55

▌ CAR TRAVEL

CAR RENTALS

Renting a car in New Orleans is a good idea if you plan to travel beyond the French Quarter and the Garden District. However, if you plan to stick to the highly touristed areas, you may want to keep it simple and use taxis, streetcars, and an airport shuttle.

If you do decide to rent a car, rates in New Orleans begin at around $40 per day ($250 per week) for an economy car with air-conditioning, automatic transmission, and unlimited mileage. Prices do not include local tax on car rentals, which is 13.75%, or other surcharges, which can add another 10%–15% to your cost. All the major agencies, including Alamo, Avis, Budget, Hertz, and National Car Rental have outlets in New Orleans.

GASOLINE

Gas stations are not plentiful within the city of New Orleans. The downtown area is particularly short on stations. Head for Lee Circle if you need gas while in the downtown area. If you're in Uptown, there are stations along Carrollton Avenue.

PARKING

Meter maids are plentiful and tow trucks eager in the French Quarter. Avoid spaces at unmarked corners: less than 15 feet between your car and the corner will result in a ticket. Watch for temporary "no parking" signs, which pop up along parade routes and film shoots. The Central Parking website can help you find parking around town.

Garages Central Parking ⊕ *www. neworleans.centralparking.com.*

ROAD CONDITIONS

Surface roads in New Orleans are generally bumpy and potholes are common. Many were damaged in post-Katrina flooding. Along St. Charles Avenue, use caution when crossing over the neutral ground (median); drivers must yield to streetcars and pedestrians along this route. Afternoon rush hour affects New Orleans daily and backups on Interstate 10 can start as early as 3 pm. Ongoing construction on Interstate 10 may cause delays.

FROM NEW ORLEANS TO	ROUTE	DISTANCE
Atchafalaya Basin	I–10	124 miles
Avery Island	I–10, U.S. 90	168 miles
Baton Rouge	I–10	80 miles
Breaux Bridge	I–10, U.S. 31	130 miles
Lafayette	I–10	136 miles
St. Francisville	I–10, U.S. 61	105 miles
Oak Alley	U.S. 44	60 miles
Opelousas	I–10, U.S. 49	162 miles
San Francisco Plantation	U.S. 44	35 miles

▌ TAXI TRAVEL

Cabs are metered at $3.50 minimum for one passenger, plus $1 for each additional passenger, and $2 per mile. If you're trying to hail a cab in New Orleans, try Decatur Street, Canal Street, or outside major hotels in the Quarter or the CBD. Otherwise, call.

During Mardi Gras, it can be extremely difficult to get a cab; plan an alternate way home (or enjoy the party until public transportation starts up again in the morning).

Taxi Companies American ☎ *504/299–0386*. **United Cabs.** United Cabs ☎ *504/522–9771* ⊕ *www.unitedcabs.com.* **Veterans** ☎ *504/367–6767*.**White Fleet-Rollins Cab Co.** ☎ *504/822–3800.* **Yellow-Checker Cab** ☎ *504/525–3311.*

▌ TRAIN TRAVEL

Three major Amtrak lines run from New Orleans Union Passenger Terminal. The Crescent makes daily runs from New York to New Orleans by way of Washington, D.C. The City of New Orleans runs daily between New Orleans and Chicago. The Sunset Limited makes the two-day trip from Los Angeles to New Orleans en route to Orlando. It departs from New Orleans traveling westward on Monday, Wednesday, and Friday and leaves Los Angeles on Sunday, Wednesday, and Friday.

Information Amtrak ☎ *800/872-7245* ⊕ *www.amtrak.com.* **Union Passenger Terminal** ✉ *1001 Loyola Ave.* ☎ *504/299-1880.*

TRAIN ROUTE	SERVES	COSTS (APPROX.)
City of New Orleans	Chicago	$200
Crescent	New York	$300
Sunset Limited	Los Angeles	$130

ESSENTIALS

▌ CHILDREN IN NEW ORLEANS

Be sure to plan ahead and involve your youngsters as you outline your trip. When packing, include things to keep them busy en route. On sightseeing days try to schedule activities of special interest to your children. The *Times-Picayune* publishes a "Family Affairs" column in its Friday weekly arts and entertainment insert *Lagniappe* that lists upcoming events for families and kids. The Louisiana Children's Museum, the Audubon Zoo, and the Insectarium are excellent resources for activities that are both educational and fun.

Be sure to plan activities for kids in the French Quarter with an aim to avoiding Bourbon Street. Things are out in the open, whether you plan to see them or not. In the evening, Bourbon Street quickly becomes overloaded with large, noisy, and inebriated crowds. With kids in tow, it's best to steer clear.

If you're renting a car, don't forget to arrange for a car seat when you reserve.

Local Information New Orleans Convention & Visitors Bureau ⊠ *2020 St. Charles Ave., Garden District* ☎ *800/672–6124 or 504/566–5011* ⊕ *www.neworleanscvb.com.*

▌ DAY TOURS AND GUIDES

Given the variety of perspectives available in the city of New Orleans, a package tour can be a good option, especially for first-time visitors. Highlights will likely include the French Quarter and Riverwalk, with daytime visits to spots like Audubon Zoo, the Garden District, and possibly a plantation or swamp tour.

BUS TOURS

Several local tour companies give two-to four-hour city bus tours that include the French Quarter, the Garden District, Uptown New Orleans, and the lakefront.

Prices range from $30 to $70 per person. Both Gray Line and New Orleans Tours offer a longer tour that combines a two-hour city tour by bus with a two-hour steamboat ride on the Mississippi River.

New Orleans Tours leads city, swamp, and plantation tours and combination city–paddle wheeler outings. Tours by Isabelle (the oldest tour company in New Orleans, operating since 1979) runs city, swamp, plantation, and combination swamp-and-plantation tours.

Gray Line and Tours by Isabelle both offer tours of Hurricane Katrina damage and recovery. For those visitors interested in seeing the scope of the impact of the 2005 storm and keeping the local economy in motion, these tours offer perspective on the area's geography, ecology, and recovery. For the more personal experience, choose Tours by Isabelle.

PLANTATION TOURS

Full-day plantation tours by bus from New Orleans, which include guided tours through two antebellum plantation homes along the Mississippi River, are offered by Gray Line and New Orleans Tours.

Tours by Isabelle includes a stop for lunch (Note: The cost of lunch isn't included) in its full-day plantation package that traces the history of the Cajun people. Also available is the Grand Tour: a full-day minibus tour that includes a visit to one plantation, lunch in a Cajun restaurant, and a 1½-hour boat tour in the swamps with a Cajun trapper.

New Orleans Tours ☎ *504/592–1991* ⊕ *www.notours.com.*

RIVERBOAT CRUISES

The New Orleans Steamboat Company offers narrated riverboat cruises and evening jazz cruises up and down the Mississippi on the steamboat *Natchez*, an authentic paddle wheeler. Ticket sales and departures for the *Natchez* are at the

Toulouse Street Wharf behind Jackson Brewery.

New Orleans Paddle Wheel has a Mississippi River cruise aboard the *Creole Queen*, highlighting the port and French Quarter, departing twice daily from the Riverwalk. There is also an evening jazz dinner cruise from 8 to 10 (boarding at 7 pm, which is also when the band starts playing and the cash bar opens); tickets are available for the dinner and cruise, or just the cruise and live music. The company also offers a cruise to Chalmette Battlefield, the site of the Battle of New Orleans, that provides an opportunity to learn about the battle and tour the battle site. The ticket office is at the Poydras Street Wharf near the Riverwalk.

Cruise Operators New Orleans Paddle Wheel ☎ *800/445–4109 or 504/529–4567* ⊕ *www.creolequeen.com.* **New Orleans Steamboat Company** ☎ *800/365–2628 or 504/586–8777* ⊕ *www.steamboatnatchez.com.*

SPECIAL-INTEREST TOURS

For highlights of African American history and culture, contact Le'Ob's Tours. It runs prearranged group tours (20–30 people, with a minimum of 10–12 people) of the city, swamps, and plantations, as well as large-group jazz history tours, complete with club recommendations for the week of your visit. One of our favorites is the Louis Armstrong tour. Based in Houston since Hurricane Katrina, Le'Ob's runs specialty tours primarily during conventions and festivals. Call for reservations.

Macon Riddle's Let's Go Antiquing offers personalized shopping itineraries of the city's antiques stores, galleries, or boutiques based on your interests and preferences (not all tours are about antiques). The number for appointments is her residence; don't be afraid to leave a message.

The New Orleans School of Cooking, in the heart of the French Quarter, offers classes on Cajun and Creole cuisine. Visit the website for details about class schedules and rates.

Limousine services make arrangements for personal interests and private guides; rentals vary. Southern Seaplane will fly you over the city and its surrounding areas.

African American Tours Le'Ob's Tours ☎ *713/540–9399* ⊕ *www.leobstours.com.*

Cooking Classes New Orleans School of Cooking ☎ *800/237–4841 or 504/525–2665* ⊕ *www.neworleansschoolofcooking.com.*

Shopping Let's Go Antiquing ☎ *504/899– 3027* ⊕ *www.neworleansantiquing.com.*

SWAMP TOURS

Exploring an exotic Louisiana swamp and traveling into Cajun country is an adventure not to be missed. Dozens of swamp-tour companies are available. You can check at your hotel or the visitor center for a complete listing. *Many do not provide transportation from downtown hotels but those listed below do.* Full-day tours often include visiting a plantation home.

WALKING TOURS

Free one-hour walking tours along the Mississippi River levee, with a discussion of the interaction between the river and the city are given daily at 9:30 am by rangers of the Jean Lafitte National Historical Park and Preserve. Tickets are available at the Jean Lafitte Parks French Quarter Visitor Center starting at 9 am on the morning of the tour. Check the National Park Service website for details. Tickets are free, but tours are limited to 25 people. Two-hour general history tours, beginning at the 1850 House on Jackson Square, are given Tuesday through Sunday at 10 and 1:30 by Friends of the Cabildo.

Several specialized walking tours conducted by knowledgeable guides on specific aspects of the French Quarter are also available. Be sure to make advance reservations to confirm the tour is being offered. Heritage Tours leads a general literary tour as well as others focusing on either William Faulkner or Tennessee Williams.

The cemeteries of New Orleans fascinate many people because of their unique aboveground tombs. Save Our Cemeteries conducts guided walking tours of St. Louis No. 1 as well as Lafayette No. 1. Reservations are generally required.

Voodoo- and spiritual-themed tours are popular in New Orleans and several companies, including Haunted History Tours, Historic New Orleans Walking Tours, and New Orleans Spirit Tours have spooky options to choose from.

Contact Information Friends of the Cabildo ☎ 504/523–3939 ⊕ *www.friendsofthecabildo. org*. **Gray Line** ☎ 800/233–2628 or 504/569–1401 ⊕ *www.graylineneworleans.com*. **Haunted History Tours** ☎ 888/644–6787 or 504/861–2727 ⊕ *www.hauntedhistorytours. com*. **Historic New Orleans Walking Tours** ☎ 504/947–2120 ⊕ *www.tourneworleans.com*. **Honey Island Swamp Tours** ☎ 985/641–1769 ⊕ *www.honeyislandswamp.com*. **Jean Lafitte National Historical Park and Preserve: French Quarter Visitors Center** ✉ *419 Decatur St., French Quarter* ☎ 504/589–2636 ⊕ *www.nps.gov/jela/french-quarter-site.htm* ☉ *Daily 9–5*. **Jean Lafitte Swamp and Airboat Tours** ☎ 800/445–4109 or 504/587–1719 ⊕ *www.jeanlafitteswamptour. com*. **New Orleans Spirit Tours** ☎ 504/314–0806 ⊕ *www.neworleanstours.net*. **Save Our Cemeteries** ☎ 504/525–3377 ⊕ *www. saveourcemeteries.org*. **Tours by Isabelle** ☎ 877/665–8687 or 504/398–0365 ⊕ *www. toursbyisabelle.com*.

▌ GAY AND LESBIAN TRAVEL

New Orleans has a large gay and lesbian population spread throughout the metropolitan area. The most-gay-friendly neighborhood is the French Quarter, followed by the Faubourg Marigny, just outside the Quarter. Most bars for gay men are within these neighborhoods; lesbians may have to venture farther to nearby Metairie.

Throughout the year a number of festivals celebrate gay culture. The biggest festival of the year is the Decadence Festival. The city also has gay-friendly guesthouses and bed-and-breakfasts, particularly along Esplanade Avenue.

Faubourg Marigny Art and Books is the last independent gay-focused bookstore in New Orleans, and it's a good resource for LGBT information around town.

Ambush, a local biweekly newspaper, provides lists of current events in addition to news and reviews. You can find this publication at many gay bars and at Faubourg Marigny Art and Books.

Local Sources Faubourg Marigny Art and Books ✉ *600 Frenchmen St., Faubourg Marigny* ☎ 504/947–3700 ⊕ *www.fabonfrenchmen. com*.

▌ HEALTH

The intense heat and humidity of New Orleans in the height of summer can be a concern for anyone unused to a semitropical climate. Pace yourself to avoid problems such as dehydration. Pollen levels can be extremely high, especially in April and May. Know your own limits and select indoor activities in the middle of the day; you'll find the locals doing the same thing.

▌ MONEY

Prices throughout this guide are given for adults. Substantially reduced fees are almost always available for children, students, and senior citizens.

ATMs can easily be found on Decatur, Royal, and Chartres streets, close to Canal, at most gift shops, and in most bars in the French Quarter. These machines generally have high fees, but there are some that advertise fees as low as 99¢. As anywhere, use common sense when withdrawing cash and be aware of your surroundings. If getting cash at night, try to use machines in more populated areas.

ITEM	AVERAGE COST
Cup of Coffee	$2
Glass of Wine	$7–$10
Glass of Beer	$3–$6
Po' boy	$6–$10
One-Mile Taxi Ride	$3.50 plus $2 per mile
Museum Admission	$6–$18

▌PACKING

New Orleans is casual during the day and casual to slightly dressy at night. A few restaurants in the French Quarter require men to wear a jacket and tie. Take comfy walking shoes.

In winter you'll want a coat or warm jacket, especially for evenings, which can be downright cold. In summer pack for hot, sticky weather, but be prepared for air-conditioning bordering on glacial, and bring an umbrella in case of sudden thunderstorms. Leave the plastic raincoats behind (they're extremely uncomfortable in the high humidity). In addition, pack a sun hat and sunscreen lotion, even for strolls in the city, because the sun can be fierce.

Insect repellent will come in handy if you plan to be outdoors on a swamp cruise or in the city dining alfresco; mosquitoes come out in full force after sunset in warm weather.

▌SAFETY

New Orleans has long drawn unwelcome attention for its high crime rate. Tourists are seldom the target of major crimes but can, like other citizens, be the target of pickpockets and purse-snatchers. The New Orleans Police Department regularly patrols the French Quarter. Still, common sense is invaluable.

Know where you're going or ask the concierge at your hotel about the best route. In the French Quarter, particularly if you're on foot, stay on streets that are heavily populated. In other areas of the city it is often advisable to drive or take a taxi. High-end neighborhoods and derelict properties back up to one another throughout New Orleans, making aimless strolling a bad idea outside the Quarter. Try to stick to the recommended walks and areas in this book, and be aware of your surroundings.

Call a taxi late at night or when the distance is too great to walk; this is even more important if you've been drinking.

▌TAXES

A local sales tax of 9% applies to all goods and services purchased in Orleans Parish, including food. Taxes outside Orleans Parish vary and are slightly lower.

Louisiana is the only state that grants a sales-tax rebate to shoppers from other countries who are in the country for no more than 90 days. Look for shops, restaurants, and hotels that display the distinctive tax-free sign and ask for a voucher for the 9% sales tax tacked on to the price of many products and services. Present the vouchers with your plane ticket and passport at the tax rebate office at the Louis Armstrong New Orleans International Airport, near the American Airlines ticket counter, and receive up to $500 in cash back. If the amount redeemable is more than $500, a check for the difference will be mailed to your home address. Call the airport refund office for complete information.

Contact Airport Refund Office ☎ *504/467–0723* ⊕ *www.louisianataxfree.com.*

▌TIPPING

A standard restaurant tip is 15%; if you truly enjoyed your meal and had no complaints, 20% is more appropriate. If you use the services of the concierge, a tip of $5 to $10 is appropriate, with an additional gratuity for special services or favors. Always keep a few dollar bills on hand—they'll come in handy for tipping bellhops, doormen, and valet parking attendants, and for rewarding the many fine street musicians that entertain day and night. As always, use your discretion when tipping.

▌ VISITOR INFORMATION

For general information and brochures, contact the city and state tourism bureaus *below*. The New Orleans Convention & Visitors Bureau's website is a comprehensive source for trip planning, hotel and tour booking, and shopping in the city; you can also download brochures, coupons, walking tours, and event schedules, as well as find links to other helpful websites. The Louisiana Office of Tourism offers the same with a focus on the entire state.

Contacts Louisiana Office of Tourism ☎ 800/994-8626 ⊕ www.louisianatravel.com. **New Orleans Convention & Visitors Bureau** ☎ 800/672-6124 or 504/566-5011 ⊕ www.neworleanscvb.com.

ONLINE RESOURCES

The Louisiana Department of Culture, Recreation and Tourism's website gives a general overview of tourism in Louisiana, especially recovery efforts after Hurricanes Katrina and Rita.

New Orleans Online provides basic trip planning and travel tools. The New Orleans Multicultural Tourism Network produces a variety of multicultural heritage directories. The city's official site, ⊕ *www.nola.gov*, has updates on local issues and government affairs, as well as a neat "City Stories" section that profiles residents of note. Go to ⊕ *www. frenchquarter.com* for great links to event, accommodations, and parking information, as well as an interactive French Quarter map. And for that something extra, ⊕ *experienceneworleans.com* has links to a blog, podcast, and a fun video, in addition to the standard tourist sites.

For general information about events, hotels, and restaurants, check ⊕ *www. neworleans.com*. For Louisiana music coverage (plus other entertainment news), *OffBeat* magazine's website is a good bet, as is the radio station WWOZ.org with its Livewire Music Calendar. Everything you need to know about the New Orleans Jazz & Heritage Festival can be found at its website. Devoted entirely to Mardi Gras, ⊕ *www.mardigrasneworleans.com* includes histories, parade schedules, and other specific Mardi Gras information.

For arts happenings around town, ⊕ *www.artsneworleans.org*, a site of the Arts Council of New Orleans, has a calendar of art, music, dance, film, theater, literature, and culinary events in the city. The site also includes an artist directory and other resources.

Head to ⊕ *www.nola.com* for everything New Orleans; it includes links to the *Times-Picayune* newspaper, with news stories, nightlife, and more. The website of the *Gambit* weekly newspaper does a good job of representing varying perspectives on life in the city.

All About Louisiana The Louisiana Department of Culture, Recreation and Tourism ⊕ www.crt.state.la.us.

All About New Orleans City of New Orleans ⊕ www.nola.gov. **Experience New Orleans** ⊕ www.experienceneworleans.com. **Frenchquarter.com** ⊕ www.frenchquarter.com. **Neworleans.com** ⊕ www.neworleans.com. **New Orleans Multicultural Tourism Network** ⊕ www.soulofneworleans.com. **New Orleans Online** ⊕ www.neworleansonline.com.

Music, Festivals, and Events Arts New Orleans ⊕ www.artsneworleans. org. **Mardi Gras New Orleans** ⊕ www. mardigrasneworleans.com. **New Orleans Jazz & Heritage Festival** ☎ 504/558-6100 ⊕ www.nojazzfest.com. **OffBeat Magazine** ☎ 504/944-4300 ⊕ www.offbeat.com.

Periodicals The Times-Picayune ☎ 800/925-0000 ⊕ www.nola.com. **Gambit** ☎ 504/486-5900 ⊕ www.bestofneworleans.com.

INSPIRATION: BOOKS AND MOVIES

To prepare for your trip to New Orleans, rent *A Streetcar Named Desire*, starring Marlon Brando and Vivien Leigh. Seedy, steamy, and emotionally charged, this is the quintessential New Orleans film. Also check out Elvis in *King Creole,* a music-filled noir tale set in the French Quarter. Other New Orleans classics are *Jezebel, The Buccaneer*, and *Easy Rider.* You may also enjoy *Interview with the Vampire, Blaze, The Pelican Brief, Double Jeopardy* with Ashley Judd, *Runaway Jury* starring John Cusack, *Déjà Vu* with Denzel Washington, and *The Curious Case of Benjamin Button*, set in the Garden District. The HBO series *Treme* highlights New Orleans music and culture post-Katrina.

A necessary read for any New Orleans visitor is John Kennedy Toole's *A Confederacy of Dunces*. Ignatius J. Reilly, the book's bumbling protagonist, is as quirky as the city itself. Andrei Codrescu's *New Orleans, Mon Amour*, a collection of memoirs written over the last 20 years, is a humorous and touching read. For a look into life in old New Orleans, pick up anything by George Washington Cable. Since Hurricane Katrina, numerous books about the city have been published, notably *Nine Lives* by Dan Baum and *Zeitoun* by Dave Eggers. Visit any locally owned bookstore for the insider's perspective on the New Orleans literary scene.

INDEX

PHOTO CREDITS

tion/3410303485/ Attribution License. 75, Jack Miller. 77, Marigny Mardi Gras 05 by Team at Carnaval.com Studios http://www.flickr.com/photos/aforum/4256728324/ Attribution License. 78, orange home by Christian Paul http://www.flickr.com/photos/abundantc/3943278109/ Attribution License. 79, Molly Moker. 80, WWOZ 30th Birthday Parade Royal St Ann Treme by Information of New Orleans http://www.flickr.com/photos/infrogmation/5232168115/ Attribution License. Chapter 4: CBD and Warehouse District. 85, Mardi Gras World New Orleans Jimi Hendrix by http://www.flickr.com/photos/73577218@N00/4485533688/ Attribution License. 87, row by Payton Chung http://www.flickr.com/photos/paytonc/3269264529/ Attribution license. 88, Cheryl Gerber/Ogden Museum of Southern Art. 89, New Orleans RTA Streetcar No. 2021 by vxla http://www.flickr.com/photos/vxla/5097313121/ Attribution License. 90, SuperStock/age fotostock. Chapter 5: The Garden District. 97, Heeb Christian / age fotostock. 99, Ornate house in the Garden District of New Orleans by Frank Kovalchek http://www.flickr.com/photos/72213316@N00/5641789967/ Attribution License. 100, Lafayette Cemetery No. 1 by Kent Wang http://www.flickr.com/photos/kentwang/3196572112/ Attribution-ShareAlike License. 102, Kevin O'Hara / age fotostock. 104-05, Women's Opera Guild House by Chris Waits http://www.flickr.com/photos/chriswaits/5810694440/ Attribution License. 107, Christian Goupi / age fotostock. Chapter 6: Uptown and Carrollton-Riverbend. 109, Jeff Strout/Audubon Nature Institute New Orleans. 111, Richard Nowitz/New Orleans CVB. 112, Carl Purcell /New Orleans Convention and Visitors Bureau. 113 (bottom), St. Charle's street car by Chris Waits http://www.flickr.com/photos/chriswaits/5816630945/Attribution License. 113 (top), St. Charles Avenue Streetcar, New Orleans, Louisiana by Ken Lund http://www.flickr.com/photos/kenlund/3939109957/ Attribution-ShareAlike License. 115, Lindsay Glatz/Arts Council of New Orleans. 117, Audubon Nature Institute New Orleans. Chapter 7: Mid-City and Bayou St. John. 121, Front of the New Orleans Museum of Art by Frank Kovalchek http://www.flickr.com/photos/72213316@N00/5641841259/ Attribution License. 123, Chuck Wagner/Shutterstock 124, St_Louis_Cemetery_No.3 3 by Mr. Littlehand http://www.flickr.com/photos/73577218@N00/2408318619/ Attribution-ShareAlike License. 125 (bottom), St_Louis_Cemetery_No.3 by Mr. Littlehand http://www.flickr.com/photos/73577218@N00/2409151320/Attribution-ShareAlike License. 125 (top), Cypress Grove Kohn by Infrogmation of New Orleans http://www.flickr.com/photos/infrogmation/4101285391/Attribution License. 126, Bayou Pedal by Information of New Orleans http://www.flickr.com/photos/infrogmation/3557022567/ Attribution License. 128, City Park Bayou Bridge by Information of New Orleans http://www.flickr.com/photos/infrogmation/4766047720/Attribution License. Chapter 8: Where to Eat. 133, Chris Litwin. 134, Cochon Restaurant New Orleans. 138, George H. Long. 139 (bottom), Paul Rico. 139 (top), Tujague's Restaurant. 140, Ferbos Nickle A Dance Maison JP by Information of New Orleans http://www.flickr.com/photos/infrogmation/5155374013/ Attribution License. 141 (bottom), John Boutte by Robbie Mendelson http://www.flickr.com/photos/robbiesaurus/4587091504/ Attribution-ShareAlike License. 141 (top), Mimi's in the Marigny by Stephen Kennedy http://www.flickr.com/photos/shkizzle/5361131311/ Attribution License. 142, Besh Restaurant Group. 143 (bottom), Besh Restaurant Group. 143 (top), Drago's Seafood Restaurant. 144, Jonathan Bachman. 145 (bottom), Camellia Grill New Orleans by Mr. Littlehand http://www.flickr.com/photos/73577218@N00/4485527122/ Attribution License. 145 (top), Macaron by inoc http://www.flickr.com/photos/10918289@N07/3538698152/ Attribution License. 160, easyFotostock / age fotostock. 161, Café au lait and beignets by Leo http://www.flickr.com/photos/kaige/5319929111/ Attribution-ShareAlike License. 162 (left), Reika/Shutterstock. 162 (right), Cathy Yeulet/Hemera/Thinkstock. 163 (left), Jupiterimages/Comstock Images/Thinkstock. 163 (right), K Chelette/Shutterstock. 164 (top), Cochon Restaurant New Orleans. 164 (2nd from top), Emeril's Delmonico. 164 (3rd from top), Besh Restaurant Group. 164 (bottom), Emiliano De Laurentiis. 167, Cochon Restaurant New Orleans. 170, Emeril's Delmonico. Chapter 9: Where to Stay. 179, Loews Hotels. 180, Royal Sonesta Hotel. 188 (top), hotel monteleone by Christian Paul http://www.flickr.com/photos/abundantc/3943342033/ Attribution License. 188 (bottom), ritz carlton new orleans lobby by Britt Reints http://www.flickr.com/photos/emmandevin/5648064064/ Attribution License. 192 (top), royal sonesta hotel by Britt Reints http://www.flickr.com/photos/emmandevin/5648066874/ Attribution License. 192 (bottom), Harrah's New Orleans Media Department. 199 (top), Loews Hotels. 199 (bottom), Chimes Bed and Breakfast. Chapter 10: Nightlife. 205, Corbis Nomad / Alamy. 206, Brian Huff. 207 (top), The Museum of the American Cocktail. 207 (bottom), Jennifer Mitchell. 208, Brian Huff. 209, Hermes Bar at Antoine's by Gary J. Wood http://www.flickr.com/photos/garyjwood/4841565279/ Attribution-ShareAlike License. 217, www.nunstations.com by Michael Nyika http://www.flickr.com/photos/86931652@N00/3911239048/ Attribution-ShareAlike License. 220, Franz Marc Frei / age fotostock. 221 (top), Jim West / age fotostock. 221 (center left), jazz fest 2011 020 by djnaquin67 http://www.flickr.com/photos/11213280@N08/5692339536/ Attribution-ShareAlike License. 221 (middle center), Backstreet Cultural Museum in New Orleans by Ted Drake

NOTES

NOTES

NOTES

ABOUT OUR WRITERS

Food and travel writer **Beth D'Addono** lives part time in New Orleans and has been in love with the city for 18 years. She writes regularly for *Southern Living, AAA Traveler* magazine, *GO Magazine, Us Airways* magazine, *Wells Fargo Conversations,* the *Boston Globe, Inside Jersey* magazine, Orbitz, Taste, *gayot.com,* and others. She is also the author of *Must Sees New Orleans* (Michelin).

A New Orleans native, **Susan Langenhennig** has been chronicling the food, fashion, and culture of the Crescent City for 14 years as a writer for the *Times-Picayune* newspaper. She lives within walking distance to Magazine Street, which puts some of the city's best boutiques right near her doorstep.

Ian McNulty has been writing about Louisiana since moving to New Orleans in 1999. Today he is a regular contributor for publications including *Gambit Weekly* and the *New Orleans Magazine,* as well as the New Orleans NPR affiliate WWNO 89.9 FM. His book *Louisiana Rambles* was recognized as one of the top travel books for 2011 by the Society of American Travel Writers.

Robert D. Peyton is a native New Orleanian and a partner in the law firm of Christovich & Kearney, LLP. In addition to freelance writing for print and online publications, he writes the "Restaurant Insider" column for *New Orleans* magazine, the dining blog Haute Plates for *MyNewOrleans.com,* and maintains his own website, *www.appetites.us.* Robert updated the Nightlife chapter and wrote our food feature.

Todd A. Price has lived in a half-dozen cities throughout the U.S. and Europe, but now he calls New Orleans home. His column on drinks and nightlife appears each week in the *New Orleans Times-Picayune.* If it's Carnival time, he'll be the one shamelessly begging for beads. He updated the Where to Eat chapter and wrote our Mardi Gras (using his Ph.D. in parades) and cocktail features.

Troy Thibodeaux is a Louisiana native who moved to New Orleans a decade ago. He has written about the nightlife, sights, and people of his adopted home town for local and national publications. He lives with his wife and dog in the Faubourg Marigny section of New Orleans, where he takes every opportunity to savor the many dappled charms of this lovely old city.